Praise for
Debunking The 1619 Project

"Mary Grabar has done America a great service in her vitally important new book. She exposes the malicious fiction and nefarious
motives behind the *New York Times*' 1619 Project. In doing so, she
tells the unvarnished truth about a fundamentally decent country,
the United States of America."
    —**Dennis Prager,** nationally syndicated radio talk show host,
    founder of PragerU, and author of ten books, most recently
    The Rational Bible: Deuteronomy, the third volume of his
    commentary on the Bible

"Mary Grabar, who dissected the Howard Zinn charade, takes her
sharpened scalpel to The 1619 Project. This is a book that should be
read by every parent and every student concerned about the future
of our nation."
    —**Donald T. Critchlow,** Katzin Family Foundation Professor of
    History at Arizona State University

"The 1619 Project rightly is criticized for distorting history to suit
an ideological agenda. It claims that slavery—not freedom—defines
American history. By examining the history of slavery in America,
Mary Grabar illuminates the tragedy of slavery against the opposition it encountered from the principles and ideals that inspire the
nation. Americans both black and white have revered these principles from colonial times to now. *Debunking The 1619 Project* is a
fine and learned book and should be read by all."
    —**Larry Arnn,** president of Hillsdale College

"With The 1619 Project, the *New York Times* unleashed a feverous
malady of ingratitude and self-loathing upon the American body
politic. Mary Grabar's *Debunking The 1619 Project* is just the shot
of historical truth the doctor ordered. The 1619 Project's purpose is

to reframe American history, making slavery a uniquely American institution, denying that the American founding was hostile to slavery, insisting that historic American heroes such as Thomas Jefferson were hypocritical or deluded, and concluding that America itself has been morally corrupt from the beginning. Mary Grabar's *Debunking The 1619 Project* examines every significant contention of The 1619 Project and shows that they are all mistaken, egregiously mistaken. This is the book America needs now."

    —Kevin R. C. Gutzman, author of *Thomas Jefferson—Revolutionary* and *The Politically Incorrect Guide to the Constitution*

"Mary Grabar's *Debunking The 1619 Project* is a vital read in a nation where the pseudohistory of The 1619 Project is granted Pulitzers. True history requires coming to grips with ugly facts, but it also requires acknowledging America's unique greatness. Grabar's defense of true history is indispensable."

    —Ben Shapiro, host of *The Ben Shapiro Show* and founding editor of The Daily Wire

Debunking The 1619 Project

Debunking The 1619 Project

Exposing the Plan to Divide America

Mary Grabar

REGNERY
HISTORY
Washington, D.C.

Regnery History™ is a trademark of Salem Communications Holding Corporation
Regnery® is a registered trademark and its colophon is a trademark of Salem Communications Holding Corporation

Cataloging-in-Publication data on file with the Library of Congress

ISBN: 978-1-68451-177-8
eISBN: 978-1-68451-211-9
Library of Congress Control Number: 2021933880

Published in the United States by
Regnery History, an Imprint of
Regnery Publishing
A Division of Salem Media Group
Washington, D.C.
www.RegneryHistory.com

Manufactured in the United States of America

10 9 8 7 6 5 4 3 2 1

Books are available in quantity for promotional or premium use. For information on discounts and terms, please visit our website: www.RegneryHistory.com.

For Eugene D. Genovese (1930–2012),
in gratitude for all you left us

CONTENTS

CHAPTER 1
"The 1619 Riots"   1

CHAPTER 2
The Project Is Launched   11

CHAPTER 3
Canceling Thomas Jefferson—and 1776   41

CHAPTER 4
Declaring Independence "to Protect the Institution of
Slavery"?   65

CHAPTER 5
"Unlike Anything That Had Existed in the World Before"?   79

CHAPTER 6
A History Neither New nor True   105

CHAPTER 7
A Not So Simple Story   125

CHAPTER 8
The Wolf by the Ears   149

CHAPTER 9
Colonization and Freedom   181

CHAPTER 10
Taking Down Abraham Lincoln   193

CHAPTER 11
Choosing Resentment—or Freedom?   233

Acknowledgments   257
Notes   259
Index   317

CHAPTER 1

"The 1619 Riots"

By the summer of 2020, concerns about racism had reached a level of hysteria. While the vast majority of Americans believe in equal rights under the law and are opposed to racial discrimination, academics and activists often inappropriately obsess about race. In the summer of 2020, that obsession had gone far beyond the classroom or academic conference. It had entered Americans' everyday lives, and seemingly 24/7. No longer could Americans be assured that they would be able to enjoy a meal at a restaurant without a mob's screaming "Black Lives Matter!"—or even get there without encountering a roadblock of protesters. Americans bought books in an effort to learn *How to Be an Antiracist*, as the title of Ibram X. Kendi's book promised to teach. For those in denial that they needed to be taught not to be a racist, there was *White Fragility* by Robin DiAngelo. Both books' sales soared.[1] Self-flagellation was conducted not only on a psychological level but literally, as young white American men in chains and with whip marks on their backs were led by black men in a role-reversed "slave demonstration" in Charleston.[2] In Maryland, hundreds of white people obediently repeated after a black leader the vow not to "allow racism, anti-blackism or violence."[3]

America was terrible, and white Americans—all of them—were responsible. That was the prevailing new sentiment.[4] White Americans themselves were accepting it as creed that racism was in their "DNA," that all were guilty of the "original sin" of slavery, and that its effects were still all around, in everyday life, in the way innocent black men were hunted down by police in modern-day versions of slave patrols, in medical science that still used African Americans as guinea pigs, in polluted and unsafe minority neighborhoods, in African Americans' over-consumption of sugar, and so on.

These injustices went back to the nation's founding, it was charged. Furthermore, that very founding was a sham. America was not really founded in 1776, with our Declaration of Independence, but in 1619. That was "our nation's true founding,"[5] the date when America began—as a "slavocracy."[6]

The year 1619 had jumped into American consciousness the previous summer. Before then most Americans would not have been able to name, much less recognize, its significance.

That had changed in August 2019. From that point, vandals began adding "1619" to the graffiti being sprayed on statues.[7]

What had caused the shift? A special issue of the *New York Times Magazine* commemorating the four hundredth anniversary of what many take to be the beginning of slavery in the colonies and then the United States. But it was much more than a commemoration. Commemorations of the event appearing in other outlets attracted very little notice.

The special August 18, 2019, issue of the *New York Times Magazine* was called "The 1619 Project."[8] It was a "Project," indeed. It took a bold step beyond where even the most "woke" historians and educators had gone. It turned American history upside down and replaced America's origin date, and, with it, the American identity. As the original online version at the *New York Times* website said, the year 1619 was when a ship arrived at Point Comfort in the British [*sic*]⁹ colony of Virginia, bearing a cargo of 20 to 30 enslaved Africans. Their arrival inaugurated a barbaric system of chattel slavery that would last for the next 250 years. This is sometimes referred to as the country's original sin, but it is more than that: It is the country's very origin.

Out of slavery—and the anti-black racism it required—grew nearly everything that has truly made America exceptional.... The goal of The 1619 Project is to reframe American history by considering what it would mean to regard 1619 as our nation's true founding.¹⁰

It inspired a raging debate that continues to this day and shows no sign of abating—and that is dividing Americans more by the day.

The 1619 Project helped inspire the hatred that fueled the riots that would rage throughout 2020. Rioters, in a Taliban-like fury, tore down and defaced any and all traditional representations of American history. Indeed, Charles Kesler, a professor of government at Claremont McKenna College and the editor of the *Claremont Review of Books*, dubbed that mob violence "the 1619 riots."¹¹ And Nikole Hannah-Jones, the *New York Times Magazine* reporter "from whose mind the project sprang," agreed.¹² In a tweet, Hannah-Jones proudly embraced the "1619 riots" label as an "honor."¹³ In a public radio interview she explained, "I think [The 1619 Project] has allowed many Americans, particularly white Americans, to connect the dots they weren't connecting before," namely between "police violence and inequality."¹⁴ And, as she insisted in a CBSN interview, the destruction of property is not really violence. "Violence is when an agent of the state kneels on a man's neck until all of the life is leached out of his body," she said, referring to the death of George Floyd.¹⁵ Hannah-Jones had nothing to say about the twenty-five or more individuals, black and white, who had been killed in the riots.¹⁶

2020: The Summer of Woke

The presentation of distorted American history is bound to have an impact. The vilification of our country erupted into riots in the summer of 2020, ostensibly in reaction to the deaths of African Americans at the hands of white police.[17] The violence began, several weeks into an unprecedented lockdown due to a pandemic, after the May 25 death in Minneapolis of George Floyd, an African American man, agitated and under the influence of drugs, who was held down in a knee restraint by a white police officer. In Atlanta, on June 12, after an intoxicated Rayshard Brooks resisted arrest and shot at officers with a taser he took from one of them, he was shot dead. The Wendy's restaurant where he had fallen asleep in his car in the drive-thru lane, prompting the call for police, was subsequently burned down.[18] Footage of a naked, hand-cuffed Daniel Prude from a snowy night in March in Rochester, New York, released in early September,[19] led to rioting and rampages through restaurants by Black Lives Matter protesters.[20] The anger over the March 13 shooting of Breonna Taylor was revived. Over a three-month period from May 24 to August 22, 2020, almost 570 violent demonstrations took place in 220 locations across the country. The two weeks of rioting across twenty states following the death of George Floyd produced upwards of $2 billion in damages.[21] As we have seen, at least twenty-five Americans were killed.[22]

The 2020 protests differed from the BLM-instigated riots over the death of Michael Brown in Ferguson, Missouri, in 2014. In 2020, the destruction went beyond businesses to icons of American history, including Thomas Jefferson. The targets—unlike those of earlier years, notably in 2017 in Charlottesville—were not just Confederates, but slave owners and nineteenth- and twentieth-century figures deemed to be racists, including Abraham Lincoln, Union officers, and Ronald Reagan. In their rage, rioters even attacked monuments to black Union soldiers and abolitionists, as well as a saint, the Virgin Mary, a pioneer mother, and an elk.[23]

And the rioters were not just the usual troublemakers, purposeless young men of the "underprivileged" class. In fact, it sometimes seemed that the majority were from a multiracial group of college-educated young adults. Many were white "woke" millennials, part of a new left-wing cohort. They were the "only demographic group in America to display a pro-outgroup bias," that is, a preference for "other racial and ethnic communities above their own."[24] They seemed to be taking the new version of American history—the damning picture of our country as a "slavocracy"—to the streets. They took their anger out on monuments and statues—climbing atop them, hitting them with axes, blowtorching them, setting them on fire, beheading them, spray-painting them, pulling them down with ropes—in a frenzy of rage that led to the death of at least one young person when the statue-toppling went wrong.[25]

A statue of Thomas Jefferson outside a Portland, Oregon, high school was pulled down with bungee cords and stray wires. On the empty base were spray-painted the words "slave owner." It was one of "at least 150 statues and memorials that had been torn down or removed for safekeeping by local authorities in the aftermath of the May 25 death of George Floyd," the *Washington Post* reported on July 7. Hofstra University student Rosario Navalta, who back in 2018 had begun a campaign to remove a statue of Jefferson on her campus, expressed the prevailing view. She told a reporter that there was "no point" in keeping statues of slaveholding founding fathers. "All they do is remind everybody of the history of the United States and its role in perpetuating white supremacy and the institutionalization of anti-blackness." The statue was moved by the administration from its position in front of the student center to a less prominent place across the street.[26]

In Decatur, Georgia, a statue of Jefferson seated on a park bench in front of the old courthouse, pensively holding a pen above a portable writing table, was removed for safekeeping on June 19, 2020, by the private citizen who had donated it. A neighborhood news site featured a photograph of a young woman holding a sign that read,

"Thomas Jefferson: Child Rapist & Slaveholder / her name was Sally Hemings." The article claimed that Jefferson had "raped one of his slaves, Sally Hemings," and that she "gave birth to six of his children." It linked to the Monticello website, which authoritatively states that "Thomas Jefferson fathered at least six of Sally Hemings's children," but follows with a lengthy recount of the controversies that put the claim under serious question.[27]

In the summer of 2020, Washington, D.C., mayor Muriel Bowser had "Black Lives Matter" painted in huge letters on Sixteenth Street, which leads to the White House, and named a commission to look into renaming "dozens of structures in the nation's capital, including federal monuments and buildings in addition to local public schools." Denver public schools took up the issue, too. In December, the Falls Church, Virginia, school board unanimously decided to rename Thomas Jefferson Elementary School and George Mason High School. The reason given to reporters was that both men had owned slaves.[28] Among the forty-four schools slated to be renamed in San Francisco in January 2021 was Jefferson Elementary (and those named after George Washington and Abraham Lincoln).[29] Fortunately, after an outcry from parents the board rescinded its decision on April 6, 2021.[30] Still, a year after the riots, school districts around the nation are facing demands to change school names and in the process wipe away chunks of local and national history.[31]

A petition drive inspired by the 2020 riots is circulating to change the names of three high schools in Montgomery, Alabama, because of the namesakes' "ties" to the Confederacy: Jefferson Davis, Robert E. Lee, and Sidney Lanier[32]—the last a long-admired poet and composer who fought for the Confederacy. In Hampton, Virginia, a community college and elementary school named after the tenth president of the United States, John Tyler, are set to be renamed.[33] Would anyone give a hearing to the late, great scholar of slavery, Eugene Genovese, who told the American Society for Eighteenth-Century Studies in 1993, "The slaveholders, however great their crimes against black people, mounted the first and only serious native-born critique of the totalitarian tendencies that have run wild in our century"? The practice of dividing persons into demons and saints excludes the possibility of learning about the good our forebears did,[34] whether in leaving us songs or a government that has made America the freest and most prosperous nation in the world for the last two-plus centuries.

The mania extended to the corporate world. A new movement, unprecedented in scope, began in the summer of 2020. Companies succumbed to pressure of the slogan "White silence is violence." Employees were fired for the slightest infractions against the reigning idea that a national "conversation" needed to take place about race. Purges took place all around, even for anodyne social media posts or jokes. Even Mount Rushmore became a topic of speculation for the next teardown when it was learned that President Trump would deliver a speech there on the eve of the Fourth of July. His visit inspired condemnation of the "four presidents carved forever into the granite"—including, of course, Jefferson—as symbolic of the "fundamental brutality" of "Western [e]xpansion." The great-granddaughter of the sculptor objected to Jefferson for owning slaves and accused him of "genocide." She charged President Trump with "foment[ing] division" simply by virtue of giving the speech, which actually called on Americans to unite in honoring their heritage.[35] The National Guard was called in as protesters blocked the access road prior to Trump's arrival.[36]

"A Republic, If You Can Keep It"

In September of 2020, when President Donald Trump appointed a "1776 Commission" to create a patriotic and more accurate curriculum to serve as a corrective to the America-bashing 1619 Project, Nikole Hannah-Jones accused the commission of "conservative cynicism," called the retired Vanderbilt professor named as its vice chair "crazy," and retweeted an article by Ashton Pittman characterizing the initiative as "an effort to revive the widespread whitewashing of American history."[37] That article, on the Mississippi Free Press website, also criticized the appointment of outgoing Mississippi governor Phil Bryant to the committee[38]—less than two weeks after another article at the same site had put incoming Mississippi governor Tate Reeves's Patriotic Education Fund "in the playbook of totalitarian leaders," who want a resurgence of "white supremacy."[39]

Pittman's article panned the Constitution Day White House conference at which President Trump had announced his "patriotic education" agenda, in answer "specifically to the 1619 Project and also to the late historian Howard Zinn's 'A People's History of the United States,'" which, according to Pittman, "teaches history from a diverse, bottom-up perspective focused on workers, activists, grassroots organizers and everyday people—rather than from the vantage point of typically white, male leaders." Pittman was repeating Zinn's and the publisher's own promotional material.[40] The title of Pittman's article—"Trump Taps Ex-Gov. Bryant for '1776' Effort to Keep History Friendly to White 'Heroes'"—accurately describes his race-baiting attack on Trump: Pittman takes care to blame Trump for celebrating *white* heroes while studiously ignoring the fact that Trump had also mentioned many *black* heroes.[41]

In a January 2021 Martin Luther King Jr. Lecture at the Georgia Institute of Technology, Hannah-Jones was still denouncing the 1776 Commission (which, at that point, with Biden's inauguration less than a week away, was sure to be disbanded shortly) and claiming that The 1619 Project, a "story through the lens of slavery," was essential to understanding current events: "1776 will not explain what happened in the Capitol [on January 6, 2021]," she said, "but 1619 will."[42]

Denny McCabe, whose claim to fame is that he was one of Hannah-Jones's teachers in high school, also attacked President Trump's 1776 Commission and advocated the teaching of The 1619 Project. He also opposed the suggestion that Iowa schools forbid the use of Howard Zinn's *A People's History of the United States* and The 1619 Project. In an exchange with newspaper columnist Jacob Hall, McCabe described

America as "exceptionally fragile when it comes to learning an unvarnished history of ourselves": "We are exceptionally and blissfully ignorant when it comes to acknowledging the astonishing amount of white privilege we've accumulated. We are exceptionally resistant when alternate versions of our story such as The 1619 Project conflict with our cherished mythologies."[43]

But the real problem with The 1619 Project is not that it is in conflict with "our cherished mythologies." It's that, as this book will lay out in detail, The Project is in conflict with the historical facts and the actual truth about America—which, yes, we *do* cherish, if we have any gratitude for our lives of unexampled freedom and prosperity, and any hope to see those blessings continue into the future. Such concerns would seem to be far from the minds of The 1619 Project's creators and promoters, judging by their continuing willingness to foment shame and hatred for America, racial division and hostility, and even violence—as copious evidence, beginning with Nikole Hannah-Jones's unapologetic celebration of the "1619 riots," amply demonstrates. The 1619 Project is a mortal danger to the American experiment in self-government. If we want to keep the republic, then the task at hand—for those Americans who still share that hope, and that gratitude—is to face and defeat the threat. We must understand The 1619 Project: its divisive aims and its dishonest methods, its sweeping historical misjudgments and its blatant errors of fact. And we must drive its lies and its poisonous race-baiting out of our public institutions, beginning with the official curricula of our schools. It is in furtherance of that endeavor that this book is offered to the American public.

CHAPTER 2

The Project Is Launched

The cover of the August 18, 2019, issue of the *New York Times Magazine* was adorned with a photograph of a blackish, foreboding ocean captioned by these words: "In August of 1619, a ship appeared on this horizon, near Point Comfort, a coastal port in the British colony of Virginia. It carried more than 20 enslaved Africans, who were sold to the colonists. America was not yet America, but this was the moment it began. No aspect of the country that would be formed here has been untouched by the 250 years of slavery that followed. On the 400th anniversary of this fateful moment, it is finally time to tell our story truthfully."[1]

What greeted the reader once he turned past an advertisement for a new, highly revisionist Broadway production of *To Kill a Mockingbird* was a reiteration of the initial message, boldly announced in giant white type.[2] The number 1619 took up two-thirds of the vertical space against a black background. An introduction by *New York Times Magazine* editor Jake Silverstein appeared beneath the giant "1619" in the same white print, but much smaller: "It is not a year that most Americans know as a notable date in our country's history. Those who do are at most a tiny fraction of those who can tell you that 1776 is the year of our nation's birth."

A confusingly worded promise followed. Readers would be allowed in on a historical secret. The bombshell: "What if, however, we were to tell you that this fact, which is taught in our schools and unanimously celebrated every Fourth of July, is wrong, and that the country's true birth date, the moment that its defining contradictions first came into the world, was in late August of 1619?"[3] Not only was the birthdate of America changed. The founders' "self-evident" truths, "unalienable rights," and appeal to "the Supreme Judge of the world" were reduced to—in Marxist jargon—"defining contradictions."

The *Times* claimed that the exact date of this new birthing, unlike the traditional Independence Day, has "been lost to history," but has "come to be observed on Aug. 20." On—or at least around—that date "a ship arrived at Point Comfort in the British colony of Virginia, bearing a cargo of 20 to 30 enslaved Africans. Their arrival inaugurated a barbaric system of chattel slavery that would last for the next 250 years. This is sometimes referred to as the country's original sin, but it is more than that: It is the country's very origin."[4]

Instead of the "nation conceived in Liberty," in the words of the Gettysburg Address, the transformationalists at the *New York Times* now insisted that Lincoln's "last best hope of earth" was conceived in bondage, because "nearly everything that has truly made America exceptional" grew "[o]ut of slavery—and the anti-black racism it required."[5] Understanding American exceptionalism means recognizing not only such traditional markers as America's "economic might," "industrial power," "electoral system," and "the example it sets for the world as a land of freedom and equality," but also its "diet and popular music, the inequities of its public health and education, its astonishing penchant for violence, its income inequality . . . its slang, its legal system and the endemic racial fears and hatreds that continue to plague it to this day." The "seeds" for American exceptionalism were "planted" "long before our official birth date, in 1776, when the men known as our founders formally declared independence from Britain." According to The 1619 Project, what would become the United States in 1776 derived from an obscure event 150 years earlier, whose precise details remain shrouded to this day in uncertainty.

The announced "goal" of The 1619 Project goes beyond the standard claims of a historian who has unearthed new evidence to illumine darkened corners of the past. Indeed, The Project promised to do nothing less than "reframe American history" by "plac[ing] the consequences of slavery and the contributions of black Americans at the very center of the story we tell ourselves about who we are as a country." The country's identity—America's birthdate, exceptionalism, founders (demoted to "men known as our founders"), in fact, everything that defines "who we are"—is upended and made ready for jettisoning.

No doubt anticipating that the claims of The 1619 Project would likely be met with incredulity, the editor addressed the reader directly: "Perhaps you need some persuading."[6] Indeed.

Americans have been celebrating the Fourth of July for nearly 250 years—lately perhaps with less than unequivocal gusto, because of the fact that slavery has been playing a larger and larger role in school lessons and media. But to replace 1776 with 1619 would still be unthinkable for many. Just a month before the publication of The 1619 Project, Americans had celebrated the civic holiday as they had for centuries, with parades, picnics, and fireworks—the annual "recollections" Thomas Jefferson had hoped for in his dying days. Indeed, Fourth of July parades continue to be a distinguishing feature of Americana, with small towns like the one where I live, Clinton, New York, featuring a parade with tractors; tow trucks; high school bands; a children's bicycle contingent; local officials; "Hutch" the lawn service business owner tossing candy from his riding lawnmower to children decked out in red, white, and blue—and the pride of the village, volunteer fire department trucks in which some lucky little boy may get to ride.[7]

The participating children could have been read books checked out from the library in preparation for the exciting day. "It's America's birthday— / Happy Fourth of July! / On this star-spangled holiday / We'll wave our flags high!" begins one featuring a father eagle and eaglet.[8] Reprinted older books tell a simplified story about the founding and feature Thomas Jefferson writing the Declaration.[9] Publishers are careful to present a diverse cast of characters. In one 2019 Newbery Medal–winner, featuring a boy tagged by his dog as he excitedly participates in the parade, dancing in front of the gazebo, picnics, and the singing of the "Star-Spangled Banner" in front of the band shell in the town park when all stand and the "whole park is silent and still," the main character is white, but his best friend is black, as is his neighbor Sally, who surprises him with her singing at the talent show.[10]

It is not only conservatives who wear red, white, and blue on the Fourth. I've observed Democrats—candidates, officials, and members— marching in the parade and walked past their homes swathed in red, white, and blue bunting. In July 2019, who would have questioned a holiday that has been celebrated since 1777, through wars and depression, in the East and West, North and South?[11]

The proposed 1619 replacement founding date provides little reason for celebration. The Project's ten essays explore the many grim "aspects of contemporary American life, from mass incarceration to rush-hour traffic," that "have their roots," as editor Jake Silverstein's introduction states, "in slavery and its aftermath." The origins of these "familiar" phenomena, it is promised, will be revealed in the essays. Additionally, "17 literary works" will "bring to life key moments in African-American history." The introduction offers what has become known as a "trigger warning": "A word of warning: There is gruesome material in these pages, material that readers will find disturbing." Mind you, not "*may* finding disturbing"—as warnings tell us before we click on videos of murders and brutal attacks—but "*will* find disturbing." Will it be more disturbing than what most adults see in the news? The editors think so, and they think you should too: "That is, unfortunately, as it must be. American history cannot be told truthfully without a clear vision of how inhuman and immoral the treatment of black Americans has been. By acknowledging this shameful history, by trying hard to understand its powerful influence on the present, perhaps we can prepare ourselves for a more just future."

Sprawled across the next two pages is a table of contents (here called an "Index") above a "Literary Timeline" of the historical events prompting the creative works; "The 1619 Project Continues," describing related materials in "a special section" in the newspaper "on the history of slavery, made in partnership with the Smithsonian," an article in the Sports section, the launch of an audio series, and a "partnership" with the Pulitzer Center to bring The 1619 Project curriculum to students; and "Behind the Cover," explaining the cover photograph of "the water off the coast of Hampton, Va., at the site where the first enslaved Africans were recorded being brought to Britain's [*sic*] North American colonies"—to bring a sense of "grandeur" to the disembarkation of the Africans.

Turning the page, one sees a collection of photos of the contributors, almost all black[12] and purposely chosen by race, as the editor's introduction admits, describing the literary works as "all original compositions by contemporary black writers who were asked to choose events on a timeline of the past 400 years. The poetry and fiction they created is arranged chronologically throughout the issue, and each work is introduced by the history to which the author is responding."

The photographs show the contributors, all professionals with enviable positions in media and academia, looking aggrieved. No one smiles. The Howard University Law School students shown towards the end of the issue have similar expressions, reinforced by an upward camera angle. They were chosen for the fact that they can trace their ancestry to slaves.

Out of a total thirty-four contributors, only four are historians—Khalil Gibran Muhammad, Kevin M. Kruse, Anne C. Bailey, and Tiya Miles—and none of them is recognized as a leading expert in the history of slavery.[13] All four historians do advocacy scholarship, and the latter two, who devote *some* of their scholarship to slavery, wrote only short pieces for The 1619 Project. Indeed, Bailey, who teaches at Binghamton

University, contributed only an extended caption for a photograph. Miles's academic focus is in "conjoined Black and Native histories" and "nineteenth-century women's struggles." There is a scattering of academics in other fields, such as law, English, medical science, and Africana studies, but the overwhelming majority of the thirty-four contributors are not scholars; they are journalists (most associated with the *New York Times*) and creative types, poets, novelists, artists, and photographers.[14] Hannah-Jones, on staff of the *New York Times*, "covers racial injustice" for the magazine.[15]

The Project has a didactic feel. After all, as the introductory material proudly informs the reader, it was to be shipped to schools upon launch. The introduction is hardly inviting to the sophisticated reader. From the outset, it is insinuated that the skeptic who does not accept the history-shattering claims will fail the implied litmus test of compassion for slaves and their descendants. For a project that is intended to overturn over two hundred years of traditional history, it has little of the scaffolding of scholarship. The essays are not in the Montaignian tradition of assaying topics and inviting readers to consider a new perspective. The statement that the literary works will "bring to life key moments in African-American history" seems presumptuous to an adult reader, redolent of a textbook sales pitch or instructions within a textbook for the hapless student.

But the college student or recent graduate educated under the Common Core standards in place since the Obama administration is probably used to having songs and poetry infused into lessons about history, and to reading history or other "informational texts" in English class. With the breakdown of the disciplines under Common Core, the lines between fiction and nonfiction have been blurred. Similarly, under Common Core, interpretations matter more than facts, personal stories more than established history, and acceptance of diversity more than reason and logic.[16] To such readers, the inclusion of poems written to order in a document that purports to be making a serious case for correcting errors in our understanding of history may not seem too odd. Serious historians, though, did find The 1619 Project odd—and, as we shall see in chapters 3–8 below, very wrong, not just in its emphases, but in its facts.

A Very Different "Idea of America"

Prominent historians have objected to The 1619 Project's numerous mistakes and misrepresentations of fact, as we shall see in detail below, and also to the fundamental historical misjudgment on which the entire project is built: the misrepresentation of the United States as "inhuman and immoral," a regime indelibly stained by the "original sin" of slavery. This is the claim of Nikole Hannah-Jones in The 1619 Project's lead inaugural essay, which also proclaims that "[a]nti-black racism runs in the very DNA of this country." The title of that essay in the "Index" of the print magazine and in the list of links to the essays in the online version is "The Idea of America." But the first sentence of the longer callout on the first page of the essay itself makes clear just what Hannah-Jones's idea of America is: "Our founding ideals of liberty and equality were false when they were written." And so, she charges in the body of the essay, "black Americans, simply by existing, served as a problematic reminder of this nation's failings. White America dealt with this inconvenience by constructing a savagely enforced system of racial apartheid that excluded black people almost entirely from mainstream American life—a system so grotesque that Nazi Germany would later take inspiration from it for its own racist policies."[17] What a word bomb! Hannah Jones equates racial segregation (and only segregation in the United States) with Nazi genocide and concentration camps, with the jarring and anachronistic word "apartheid" thrown in.[18] There were no Nuremberg trials in the United States, and "white America" is afflicted with "endemic racism that we still cannot purge from this nation to this day." Alas, white Americans continue to believe that "black people" are "a slave race."[19]

Hannah-Jones's statements are treated as the pronouncements of a veritable genius—in the hushed words of the editor's introduction to

The 1619 Project—"from whose mind this project sprang."[20] Thus it is fitting that the opening of her essay is printed in huge letters (in the original print version) that proclaim, "Our founding ideals of liberty and equality were false when they were written. Black Americans fought to make them true. Without this struggle, America would have no democracy at all."

Hannah-Jones begins her essay with a personal story about her father, whom she recalls as a patriot who lovingly cared for the American flag and raised it on the appropriate occasions. Seeking a way to advance in a discriminatory society, he had joined the military in 1962, at age seventeen. But he was "passed over for opportunities" and "discharged under murky circumstances," left to eke out an existence with "service" jobs.[21] Thus the essay opens in a bitter tone, informed by the author's racial identity[22] and employing a common method of critical race theory: presenting history through "personal narratives."[23]

Hannah-Jones then recounts the history of her father's family, from what she inappropriately calls an "apartheid state"—a part of Mississippi that had the dubious distinction of having the most lynchings of blacks in the state—to Iowa, where her grandmother moved only to face Jim Crow again, though a de facto version of it. Generation after generation, her family had learned that hard work does not pay. So she could not understand why her father would fly the flag of a country that "refused to treat us as full citizens." It "felt like a marker of his degradation." But of late, she writes, she has come to understand what he knew: "that our people's contributions to building the richest and most powerful nation in the world were indelible, that the United States simply would not exist without us."

From that claim—that begins reasonably with the "indelible" "contributions" of black Americans but ends with the preposterous exaggeration that "the United States simply would not exist" without African Americans—Hannah-Jones segues into a re-creation of the 1619 arrival of the first cargo of Africans to what would become the United States. This landing preceded the arrival of the Pilgrims at Plymouth Rock by a year, she notes, and the decision by the English colonists "to form their own country" by 157 years. This timeline introduces the idea that the Africans were here first. The "Jamestown colonists bought 20 to 30 enslaved Africans from English pirates." These "pirates" [*sic*], she says, "had stolen them from a Portuguese slave ship that had forcibly taken them from what is now the country of Angola." They were "among the 12.5 million Africans who would be kidnapped" and brought in chains across the Atlantic Ocean, with 400,000 of them "sold into America," where they built the wealth of the nation—and taught Americans what democracy is.

These 400,000 Africans and their descendants "transformed the lands to which they'd been brought." The list of their accomplishments that follows is intended to convey the idea that all the prosperity of America from 1619 onwards was created by slaves. To wit:

> Through backbreaking labor, they cleared the land across the Southeast. They taught the colonists to grow rice. They grew and picked the cotton that at the height of slavery was the nation's most valuable commodity.... They built the plantations of George Washington, Thomas Jefferson and James Madison.... They laid the foundations of the White House and the Capitol, even placing with their unfree hands the Statue of Freedom atop the Capitol dome. They lugged the heavy wooden tracks of the railroads that crisscrossed the South and that helped take the cotton they picked to the Northern textile mills, fueling the Industrial Revolution. They built vast fortunes for white people North and South....[24]

The rhetorical device of anaphora—the repetition of "they" at the beginning of sentence after sentence—helps to create the impression that slaves are responsible for *everything* that made America prosperous. Other groups receive no credit, or even mention—except as the undeserving villains who profited from slave labor. There is at least one glaring error of fact here: the assertion that the hands that put the "Statue of Freedom atop the Capitol dome" were "unfree." One slave, Philip Reid, a skilled foundry worker, is known to have worked on the statue. But the installation of the statue took place in late 1863, with the final piece placed on top of the Capitol Dome on December 2, 1863. President Lincoln had signed the Compensated Emancipation Act on April 16, 1862, abolishing slavery in the District of Columbia, and by then Reid was a free man.[25]

The description of how white wealth was acquired from the "stolen labor" of slaves continues: "the second-richest man in the nation was a Rhode Island 'slave trader.'" America's war debts were paid off and "some of our most prestigious universities" were financed with the ill-gotten gains. Wall Street would not be "a thriving banking, insurance and trading sector" and New York City would not have become "the financial capital of the world" without the "relentless buying, selling, insuring and financing of [slaves'] bodies and the products of their labor."

Not only did the "bondage" of slaves make America wealthy, but "[b]lack Americans have also been, and continue to be, foundational to the idea of American freedom. More than any other group in this country's history, we have served, generation after generation, in an over-looked but vital role: It is we who have been the perfecters of this democracy."[26] Move aside, founders—or, rather, "the men known as our founders," to use editor Jake Silverstein's characterization.[27] "The United States is a nation founded on both an ideal and a lie," according to Hannah-Jones, because "the white men who drafted [the] words [in the Declaration of Independence] did not believe them to be true for the hundreds of thousands of black people in their midst." In contrast, "black Americans believed fervently in the American creed. Through centuries of black resistance and protest, we have helped the country live up to its founding ideals," thus acting as "perfecters." Then, confusing republican government and democracy, she writes, "Without the idealistic, strenu-ous and patriotic efforts of black Americans, our democracy today would most likely look very different—it might not be a democracy at all."

Returning to her strategy of listing "firsts," Hannah-Jones says that Crispus Attucks, "a fugitive from slavery" (whose actual identity remains murky), "gave his life for a new nation in which his own people would not enjoy the liberties laid out in the Declaration for another century." In fact, the Declaration would not even be written until years later: Attucks died in the Boston Massacre of 1770—more than six years before the decision to declare independence had been made. But fuzzy timelines, identities, and causal factors are employed to advance the idea that "the year 1619 is as important to the American story as 1776" and that "black Americans, as much as those men cast in alabaster in the nation's capital, are this nation's true 'founding fathers.'"[28]

Hannah-Jones heightens the contrast between the supposed "'true' founding fathers" she is celebrating and the previously recognized founding fathers she is damning by repeated references to Monticello as a "forced-labor camp," one of the many that imprisoned "one-fifth of the population within the 13 colonies." There the enslaved "struggled under a brutal system of slavery unlike anything that had existed in the world before"; slaves were not even "recognized as human beings" and had no legal rights.

She then proceeds to attack the character of Abraham Lincoln, presenting him as someone who heartlessly sought to banish black Americans through colonization. She lists the temporary successes of Reconstruction, with the election of blacks, and then the rise of Jim Crow in reaction. She highlights the horrible blinding of newly discharged World War II veteran Isaac Woodard, claiming that "[t]here was nothing unusual about Woodard's horrific maiming." Postwar, a "wave of systemic violence" included "hundreds of black veterans [who] were beaten, maimed, shot and lynched." Hannah-Jones blames racial disparities in income, health, and imprisonment on the continuing racism of white people. When it comes to the civil rights movement of the 1960s, Hannah-Jones credits blacks alone for showing the way to perfecting democracy through such measures as the 1965 Immigration Act. African Americans are presented as leading the way morally in spite of their status as the most persecuted:

"No one cherishes freedom more than those who have not had it. And to this day, black Americans, more than any other group, embrace the democratic ideals of a common good. We are the most likely to support programs like universal health care and a higher minimum wage, and to oppose programs that harm the most vulnerable.... [B]lack Americans suffer the most from violent crime, yet we are the most opposed to capital punishment. Our unemployment rate is nearly twice that of white Americans, yet we are still the most likely of all groups to say this nation should take in refugees."

She then flashes back to "the teal eternity of the Atlantic Ocean" and the Middle Passage. A romanticized and utterly false view of slaves' former lives in West Africa follows. "Just a few months earlier, they had families, and farms, and lives and dreams. They were free. They had names, of course, but their enslavers did not bother to record them." In America they learned that "black equaled 'slave.'" They were stripped of individuality and made into "property." To this day, the effects of slavery persist: in styles of dress with "the extra flair," created names, music that emerged from the sorrow songs—and poverty and crime. But it was "by virtue" of their "bondage" that blacks became the "most American of all."[29]

Hannah-Jones's essay introduces the themes of the other essays in The 1619 Project. These include one by Wesley Morris titled "American Popular Music": "For centuries, black music, forged in bondage, has been the sound of complete artistic freedom. No wonder everybody is always stealing it."[30] (Talk about casting a pall even on happy, positive things.) Another essay, by Matthew Desmond, attempts to quantify the contribution of slave labor to American economic growth.[31] The 1619 Project argues that the United States' economic might rests upon the labor of slaves whose descendants still suffer discrimination in a racist America.

And yet, The 1619 Project also contends, through their long-suffering from oppression and exploitation by whites, black Americans have been the nation's moral guides, advocating for "the common good" through signature programs of the Democratic Party such as universal health care. White Americans should listen and follow if they really believe in "democracy" (and racial equality). And black Americans need to be with the program.

"From Whose Mind This Project Sprang"

The Pulitzer Prize committee awarded Hannah-Jones its prize for commentary in 2020. And she has parlayed her authority and notoriety as the creator of The 1619 Project into further opportunities to push its racially divisive narrative of the American founding to its unfortunate logical conclusions. In the midst of rioting in July 2020, she told public radio station WBUR that The 1619 Project was helping "many Americans, particularly white Americans, to connect dots that they weren't connecting before," such as between "police violence and inequality." She cast The 1619 Project as a corrective to history books that embody a "nationalistic agenda." The "racial reckoning" that was emerging from the riots was helping to propel the movement for reparations,[32] a movement she had endorsed in another article for the *New York Times Magazine*, which featured elaborate, interactive graphics with the title "What Is Owed" in the same kind of giant yellow letters as on the street marking Black Lives Matter Plaza in Washington, D.C. In that article she reprised points from the *New York Times Magazine* issue introducing The 1619 Project, but she also added "a disproportionate number of deaths from both Covid-19 and law enforcement" to the litany of reasons for reparations[33]—a cause she continues to promote.

During her presentation commemorating Martin Luther King Jr. at the Georgia Institute of Technology, where she was fawned over by the college president for the "landmark" 1619 Project, she called President Trump a "white nationalist president" and claimed that "[w]hat kills [universal health care]" is "anti-blackness." In other words, white people oppose programs that benefit blacks out of racism, even when it goes against their own interests.

Her views are welcomed on cable news programs, especially MSNBC. On one segment she called for a "deprogramming" of Trump supporters, a "white labor force" that she claims is seeking to sustain its dominance.[34] On January 17, 2021, she appeared with Yale University historian David Blight and Ronald Chernow, author of several celebrated history books, including the one that inspired the Broadway hit *Hamilton*. Blight and Chernow essentially served as props for Hannah-Jones, taking the bait from host Jonathan Capehart to "link [the] pro-Trump Capitol riot and historical White supremacist mobs," as a Yahoo! headline reported.[35] Hannah-Jones's talking points on "white privilege" can be found in cartoons, as she herself acknowledged on the Oprah Winfrey Network, where she explained that those with "white privilege" can (analogically) swim faster because the current is with them.[36]

And Hannah-Jones is quite clearly profiting from the division she sows. She has soared to the top tier of "anti-racism" speakers. There she joins ranks with *White Fragility* author Robin DiAngelo, a white woman who was reported to have earned $12,750 for a talk at the University of Wisconsin in 2020. (That far exceeded her black co-panelist's fee; DiAngelo charges up to $30,000 for a sixty- to ninety- minute speech).[37] Hannah-Jones has become the go-to speaker at forums on diversity, at Martin Luther King Jr. holiday events, for Black History Month, and for annual symposia on civil rights history,[38] typically charging $25,000 per performance, a fee that has risen from around $10,000 in the past year, as a review of contracts from public universities reveals. Between September 16, 2019, and February 19, 2021, Hannah-Jones made thirty-three appearances on college campuses, many remotely after the pandemic hit. That approximately one-every-two-weeks figure does not include numerous other appearances in education, political, and social justice forums. Such lucrative honors show no signs of abating and include an appointment to a chaired professorship of "Race and Investigative Journalism" at the University of North Carolina at Chapel Hill,[39] honorary degrees,[40] election to the American Academy of Arts and Science,[41] and the publication by Penguin Random House of *The 1619 Project: A New Origin Story* and *The 1619 Project: Born on the Water*, a children's book, set for November 2021.[42] The University of North Carolina was denounced for giving her a five-year appointment rather than tenure.[43]

Meanwhile, The 1619 Project's creator refused to reply to multiple invitations to engage in debate with scholars, doxed a reporter from a conservative outlet who had asked about her possible role in ousting a longtime white reporter at the *Times* (who had innocently repeated the N-word for clarification in a discussion with a student), and smeared critics of The 1619 Project with charges of racism or craziness.[44]

On December 22, 2020, Hannah-Jones went on Twitter to disparage the selection of Carol Swain, an African American woman who is a former professor of law and political science at Vanderbilt, as vice chair of President Trump's 1776 Commission. The 1619 Project creator tweeted, "As Gov. Bryant joins Trump's effort to revise history, he's helping to revise the facts of current history as it unfolds in real time. Today he praised Carol Swain, the #1776 Black vice chair, as she called on God to help Trump stay in power. This, more than anything, speaks to the conservative cynicism of 1776 Project and the 1776 Commission. There ARE respected Black intellectuals and scholars who can make the conservative argument against 1619 without being crazy, and yet this is what they choose." Hannah-Jones did not specify why she thought the former Vanderbilt University professor was "crazy."[45]

Hannah-Jones's claim that "[t]here ARE respected Black intellectuals and scholars who can make the conservative argument against 1619" rings hollow given her behavior vis-à-vis Glenn Loury, the economics professor who teaches, among other classes, "Race and Inequality in the United States" at Brown University. Loury signed a petition prepared by the National Association of Scholars to have Hannah-Jones's Pulitzer Prize rescinded. An article about Hannah-Jones's talk on the Brown campus reported her as saying that she was "deeply hurt" by this action of Loury, someone she allegedly respected but implied was a traitor to his race. She "couldn't imagine signing on to a matter against another Black colleague...."

In spite of her pretensions of consideration for colleagues, Hannah-Jones had failed to acknowledge the three invitations sent to her by the National Association of Scholars to participate in its events.[46] Genuine academic collegiality requires the willingness both to engage in discussion using evidence and logic and to subject one's work to peer review. Hannah-Jones instead follows a pattern of behavior familiar to conservative professors on college campuses. She calls those with different views "crazy," ignores the critiques of experts in the field, and demands that her black critics remain silent. Instead of answering her critics in collegial discussions, Hannah-Jones chose to smear them in a very active Twitter campaign that featured links to race-baiting articles and her own pungent and tendentious comments (until she received criticism for posting the personal information of a reporter from the Washington Free Beacon, at which point she took a short hiatus).[47] For example, she tweeted out her criticism of the September 17, 2020, White House Conference on American History, which announced the formation of the 1776 Commission, of having a panel with "not a single Black historian on it," deeming this author, one of the panelists, racially suspect and ignoring the fact that the panel's moderator was Ben Carson, the African American secretary of housing and urban development.[48]

Hannah-Jones has assiduously cultivated her public persona as she slams critics and promotes herself and her products. In some photographs she prominently wears a "1619" gold pin. Until recently, her Twitter account header featured "1776" crossed out and replaced with "1619." Her Twitter bio identifies her as "Reporter @nytmag//Slanderous & nasty-minded mulattress//co-founder idabwellsociety.org//smart and thuggish//Creator #1619Project."[49] (Hannah-Jones has stated that she adopted the "mulattress" moniker from a contemporaneous description in the New York Times of Ida B. Wells, the famous journalist and anti-lynching activist.)[50] The Ida B. Wells Society for Investigative Reporting, founded by Hannah-Jones, describes itself as "a news trade organization with a mission of increasing the ranks, retention and profile of reporters and editors of color in the field of investigative reporting."[51] Most of the reporting focuses on racial issues, Hannah-Jones's career-long beat.

Hannah-Jones knows how to exploit the tensions between Americans outraged over having their tax dollars going to promote her material and the academics and activists on her side. When UNC–Chapel Hill changed the academic position from a tenured one to a five-year term for her, she posted on Twitter, "I've been staying off of here, but just know that I see you all and I am grateful."[52] The following day, during which protesters displayed their displeasure with the Board of Trustees at their meeting, she tweeted out, "I have been overwhelmed by all the support you have shown me." Their protests had "fortified" her "spirit" and "resolve." She reassured everyone she would be "OK," and said that "this fight is bigger than me, and I will try my best not to let you down."[53]

She knows how to parlay her identity into publicity. To reporters from friendly outlets, Hannah-Jones describes how she emphasizes her black identity. Sarah Ellison of the *Washington Post* noted, "Her hair is dyed firetruck red, her nails are long and acrylic, and she frequently wears a necklace that spells 'Black girl magic' in script." In describing her uncertainties about fitting in at the *New York Times* when she was hired in 2015 after stints at Pro Publica and newspapers in Raleigh and Portland, Oregon, Hannah-Jones said, "This has been my conscious choice my entire career. I was not going to try to adapt my sense of style to mainstream expectations."[54]

Hannah-Jones told *Glamour* magazine about getting ready to receive the Pulitzer Prize remotely, via Google Hangout, because of the pandemic. But she did not let the pandemic cramp her style. She explained, "I have my bright red hair. I put my lashes on. I got dressed, except I left on house slippers...." As beauty magazines point out, such rituals serve a larger purpose. Hannah-Jones told the reporter, "I said, 'This is for every black girl who's been told she has to shrink herself or her blackness in order to succeed.'" Hannah-Jones received the typical beauty magazine plaudits for her style: "Hannah-Jones has been serious about skin care and makeup" since working at Macy's selling cosmetics, "but her convictions about how products and fashion and even a solid eight hours of sleep each night might be used as tools of self-actualization are newer." These "tools of self-actualization" include Bath and Body Works Teak Mahogany candles, a Clinique three-step moisturizing set, and High West and Four Roses Small Batch bourbon. Links for these and multiple other products are highlighted in the text. Hannah-Jones also expressed her gratitude to Ta-Nehisi Coates, a journalist well known for writing polemics about race and reparations, for reminding her about the importance of "self-care" in the midst of such labors.[55] As she explained at the Georgia Institute of Technology event, the eight solid months writing The 1619 Project during her year's leave for book-writing was the "most emotionally taxing work" she had ever done.[56]

Hannah-Jones's Twitter name, Ida Bae Wells ("bae" is a current slang term for girlfriend or boyfriend),[57] is accompanied by a photo of her in a diva-like pose. In response to the formation of the group 1776 Unites, the self-described "Beyoncé of journalism" tweeted out a picture of herself pointing "at her bottom row of gold teeth with her pinky, a dismissive...hip-hop gesture."[58]

Teaching Hate

Despite Nikole Hannah-Jones's decidedly non-academic style, her refusal to address serious critics in a serious manner, and her lack of credentials with any relationship to education (her master's degree is in journalism, and she has never taught),[59] her work is being taken very seriously by our education establishment. In spite of its gross flaws, The 1619 Project has entered more than 4,500 schools, where it is being integrated into classrooms beginning at the elementary level.

The *Times* distributed materials—such as a "Reading Guide" to Hannah-Jones's inaugural 1619 Project essay that asks students to answer: "How has activism by black Americans throughout U.S. history led to policies that benefit all people living in the U.S.?"[60]—for the fall 2019 semester with the publication's educational partner, the Pulitzer

Center, a nonprofit funded by left-wing billionaire eBay founder Pierre Omidyar, whose Omidyar Network runs a program called "Reimagining Capitalism" and whose "team" includes Joelle Gamble, who has posted a photo of herself holding up a Black Lives Matter sign on Twitter. The elaborate coordination was no doubt helped by the fact that Sam Dolnick, assistant managing editor of the *New York Times*, sits on the board of directors of the Pulitzer Center (not affiliated with the Pulitzer Prize, which, as we have seen, Hannah-Jones won).[61] Omidyar has donated $213 million mostly to left-wing causes, such as George Soros's Open Society Foundations and the Tides Foundation, and with his wife has donated hundreds of thousands of dollars to Democratic candidates, including Hillary Clinton, and to the Democratic Congressional Campaign Committee. He has funded left-wing media sites, such as The Intercept.[62] He gave $100,000 to the NeverTrump PAC. Another funder is the Facebook Journalism Project.[63] These donations to the Pulitzer Center, a 501(c)(3) nonprofit organization, are tax deductible.[64] The *New York Times,* of course, is a *for*-profit company. But in a rare kind of business arrangement, the for-profit newspaper and its magazine enjoy the distribution and promotional services of the nonprofit Pulitzer Center. Taxpayers also support The 1619 Project by funding the Smithsonian National Museum of African American History and Culture. As the introductory material for The 1619 Project announced, the Smithsonian partnered with the magazine on producing a special section in the newspaper for the magazine. Inside this fifteen-page section was an explanation that its cover reproduced a "broadside, or public notice" advertising "a slave auction at the St. Louis Hotel in New Orleans on March 25, 1858." The section featured photographs, including of slave artifacts from the Smithsonian's National Museum of African American History and Culture; artwork; and a number of short articles about slavery.[65]

The justification for the entire 1619 Project came from another nonprofit, the corrupt Southern Poverty Law Center (SPLC), which claims to research and monitor hate groups. In 2017 it issued a survey purportedly revealing high levels of historical "illiteracy" about slavery. And on the *day* of the White House Conference on American History, September 17, 2020, it released a poll allegedly showing "overwhelming support for anti-racism education." Even the *New Yorker* has described the SPLC as a "highly profitable scam" that is itself plagued by racial discrimination and sexual harassment charges.[66] The SPLC selectively brands conservative groups as "hate" groups.[67]

The ink had barely dried on the magazine covers when the first two lesson plans, one dedicated to Hannah-Jones's essay, were distributed. They reached more than 3,500 schools at the beginning of the 2019–2020 school year. The package of instructional materials includes The 1619 Project's essays as well as lesson plans, exercises, "quizlet flashcards," and discussion questions. Indeed, the introductory matter of The Project with its directives suggests that a made-to-order curriculum had been put together well in advance of the publication of the special issue itself. Teachers are being enticed with grants of $5,000 to incorporate The 1619 Project into their teaching. Teachers fond of educational theory, ignorant of good historical scholarship, and challenged by students who are increasingly incapable of becoming "engaged" on an intellectual level welcome the ready-made lessons and bonus funds. A February 4, 2021, workshop for teachers titled "How to Get Involved in The 1619 Project Education Network" described how they could apply for the grants and explained that the poems were meant to "elevate emotions."[68] As Independent Women's Forum fellow Naomi Schaefer Riley learned in her investigation of The 1619 Education Project curriculum, "[s]traight lines" are drawn between recent events like Hurricane Katrina and slavery as students "look at the similarities in poems about the two." What the lessons teach is that slavery "is directly responsible for mass incarceration, for healthcare disparities and a variety of other social ills that have befallen African Americans...."[69]

This pedagogy has little to do with building a knowledge base about slavery, or any other aspect of history, and much to do with encouraging student activism. Riley reported that the 1619 label was used "on an article about 1960s student activism for civil rights and desegregation, linking that to 'the Climate March to demand action on global warming, and March for Our Lives to call for an end to gun violence.'"[70] These materials would seem to be tailor-made for the "action civics" being pushed under a civics education bill that emphasizes political protest and critical race theory.[71] In fact, they would seem to be particularly aimed at those students least able to resist such emotional manipulation. The 1619 Project curriculum is being adapted for after-school programs with a grant from the Charles Stewart Mott Foundation, which has as one of its primary missions the advancement of "learning" in less affluent communities.[72]

The 1619 Project has lined up an impressive number of well-heeled allies to aid in the distribution of its product. The 1619 imprint is being marketed in educational products made by the *New York Times*, such as *New York Times Upfront*, produced with the publisher Scholastic, a multinational publishing company that has a collaborative agreement to distribute *New York Times* materials. Newsela, a nonprofit that adapts news articles to grade-appropriate reading levels, provides quizzes and writing prompts (aligned with Common Core standards) to 6.1 million students, or 75 percent of American classrooms (its reach as of 2016). It is distributing The 1619 Project's essays, including one by Matthew Desmond whose headline reads, "In order to understand the brutality of American capitalism, you have to start on the plantation," for five grade levels, beginning in second grade.[73]

Hannah-Jones herself is actively involved in the promotion of her work at various levels of the educational system. On December 6, 2020, she was a keynote speaker at the annual meeting of the National Council for the Social Studies, the "largest professional association in the country devoted to social studies education."[74] Teachers who attend (on the public dime) earn continuing education credits. Panels on such matters as LGBTQ issues, statehood for the District of Columbia, "Interrogating White Supremacy in Social Studies," and "Black Panthers and Black Curriculum: A Black Male Teacher-Coaches Life-Inspired Revisionist History" promoted that year's theme: "Advancing Social Justice."[75] The council lobbies against legislative efforts to keep The 1619 Project out of schools. It has issued at least two statements, one rejecting "any effort by the federal [and state] government to silence social studies curriculum that explicitly addresses the centrality of slavery in the historical narrative of the United States" and another defending "the academic freedom of social studies educators."[76]

On February 25, 2021, Hannah-Jones discussed "Teaching Black History to Elementary and Middle School Students" as a panelist alongside Dr. LaGarrett King, director of the University of Missouri's Carter Center for K12 Black History Education. The event was part of the launch of the Pulitzer Center's The 1619 Project Education Network, which began with an initial cohort of forty teachers.[77] The Pulitzer Center, in collaboration with Howard University Law School and University of Miami School of Law, is even bringing The 1619 Project into law schools with the Law School Initiative series that kicked off on February 26, 2021, and featured six panelists.[78] The curriculum, produced by law school students and their professors, promises to "spark frank conversations about the legacy of slavery in legal education."[79] For this initiative, Hannah-Jones engaged in a March 10, 2021, webinar "conversation" about the "legacy of slavery in legal education."[80]

The 1619 Project arrived on college campuses at a propitious moment. As universities were seeking to meet demands for racial sensitivity training in riot-filled 2020, The Project appeared made-to-order. On June 2, 2020, at Hamilton College, for example, the vice president and dean of students called on the "Hamilton community" to honor "the black lives lost" and to participate in "actionable commitment by completing a racial equity commitment card" to be "shared via Hamilton's web and media platforms" along with students' photos. College deans offered students antiracism reading material to "aid in your thinking." Topping the list of recommended articles was "The 1619 Project."[81] At the University of Denver, the new "racial justice book club" was launched with The 1619 Project.[82] The 1619 Project was the assigned "common read" at the University of Oregon, Mount Holyoke College, and elsewhere.[83] Hannah-Jones was appointed to the advisory board of a new online newspaper titled The Emancipator, a project of Boston University's Center for Antiracist Research (directed by Ibram X. Kendi) and the *Boston Globe* "to reimagine *The Emancipator,* the first abolitionist publication in the United States, as a platform for 21st-century scholarship on systemic racism and the fight for racial justice"— prompted by the "year of mass protests" and police brutality and the need to "contextualize…systemic racism through historical analysis."[84] (A June 2020 poll in the midst of the rioting showed that 58 percent of young respondents with college degrees believed that the rioting was fully or partially justified.)[85]

The deal that the *Times* made with the Pulitzer Center ensured that *its* narrative surrounding the four hundredth anniversary of the Africans' arrival in Jamestown would dominate. No doubt other media outlets, such as *Time* magazine and *USA Today* (then boasting the largest circulation of any newspaper in the United States), which had prepared special features on the quadricentennial anniversary, looked on with envy. Perhaps *USA Today* had acted too soon, publishing for Black History Month in February 2019 an article by Morgan State University journalism professor E. R. Shipp titled "1619: 400 Years Ago, a Ship Arrived in Virginia, Bearing Human Cargo." Planned anniversary observations, such as those by the Association for the Study of African American Life and History (the "custodian of Black History Month"), the 400 Years of African-American History Commission established by Congress, the Hampton 2019 Commemorative Commission, and Virginia's 2019 commemoration, "American Evolution," barely registered a blip. Nor did anyone seem to notice Olivia Waxman's history feature in *Time,* which dutifully quoted various historians' recounting of the history.[86]

Nor could these and other news outlets boast of such promotional extras as the *New York Times*'s elaborate productions of podcasts, videos, and an ad campaign which premiered during the Oscars and featured singer Janelle Monáe in a long, flowing white dress on an ocean beach replicating the magazine cover. "In August 1619," she intoned, "a ship appeared...."[87] In some coming attractions, according to *Variety* magazine, Hannah-Jones is serving as "creative leader and producer in developing feature films, television series, documentaries, unscripted programming and other forms of entertainment with Black creative voices." The *Times* announced it had been searching for a producer.[88] In early April 2021, dozens of news stories excitedly announced that the streaming service Hulu would soon be carrying The 1619 Project documentary series, produced by Oprah Winfrey's Harpo Films, the *New York Times*, and Lionsgate Television.[89]

"Matters of Verifiable Fact"

While the *Times*, with the help of media allies, excelled in marketing and messaging The 1619 Project, The Project also drew immediate criticism. The most telling objections came not from conservatives but from respected historians on the left who were in sympathy with The 1619 Project's aims but concerned that the historical inaccuracies with which it was riddled would undermine its impact.

A letter to the *New York Times* by Princeton historian Sean Wilentz, signed also by four other prominent historians, "applaud[ed] all efforts to address the enduring centrality of slavery and racism to our history" and The 1619 Project's raising of "profound, unsettling questions about slavery and the nation's past and present." But in no uncertain terms, it asked that, because of the misrepresentation of "matters of verifiable fact" regarding "major events," the *Times*, in accordance with "its own high standards," "issue prominent corrections" in its publication and curriculum materials. It was not a matter of simple "framing" (alluding to the newspaper's own terminology). The historians charged that the distortions "suggest[ed] a displacement of historical understanding by ideology." Others putting their names to the letter were Victoria Bynum (Texas State University), James M. McPherson (Princeton), James Oakes (City University of New York), and Gordon S. Wood (Brown University).[90]

As *The Atlantic* acknowledged in the title of a December 23, 2019, article by Adam Serwer about the affair, "the fight over The 1619 Project is not about the facts."[91] The facts did not seem to matter to the historians whom Serwer interviewed when it came to political or racial solidarity. "I felt that if I signed on to that, I would be signing on to the white guy's attack of something that has given a lot of black journalists and writers a chance to speak up in a really big way. So I support the 1619 Project as kind of a cultural event," explained Nell Irvin Painter, a professor emerita at Princeton.[92]

But days before The 1619 Project was published, Painter had very extensively criticized President Trump for characterizing the Africans who arrived on the *White Lion* in exactly the same way The 1619 Project did—except that in his case it was a minor misuse of terminology in a twenty-minute speech, made in the course of an attempt to pay tribute to the ordeal of black American slaves, not an attempt to "reframe" all of American history as a race-based "slavocracy." On July 30, 2019, during a commemoration of the four hundredth anniversary of the creation of the Virginia House of Burgesses and, secondarily, the arrival of the slave ship the *White Lion*, Trump said, "As we mark the first representative legislature at Jamestown, our nation reflects upon an anniversary from that same summer, four centuries ago. In August 1619, the first enslaved Africans in the English colonies arrived in Virginia. It was a barbaric trade in human lives. Today, in honor, we remember every sacred soul who suffered the horrors of slavery and the anguish of bondage."[93]

Painter used the two-minute mention to take the president to the woodshed for "speaking within a post-eighteenth-century American ideology of race" and "essentialist" thinking—that is, seeing blacks as slaves in their essence—absurd charges, of course. She lectured the president of the United States in a way she would never lecture Hannah-Jones:

> People were not enslaved in Virginia in 1619, they were indentured. The 20 or so Africans were sold and bought as "servants"

for a term of years, and they joined a population consisting largely of European indentured servants, mainly poor people from the British Isles whom the Virginia Company of London had transported and sold into servitude.

Enslavement was a process that took place step by step, after the mid-17th century. This process of turning "servants" from Africa into racialized workers enslaved for life occurred in the 1660s to 1680s through a succession of Virginia laws that decreed that a child's status followed that of its mother and that baptism did not automatically confer emancipation. By the end of the seventeenth century, Africans had indeed been marked off by race in law as chattel to be bought, sold, traded, inherited and serve as collateral for business and debt services. This was not already the case in 1619.[94]

Insofar as this criticism is valid, it is much more pertinent to The 1619 Project than to President Trump's speech.[95]

And Manisha Sinha, University of Connecticut professor and author of *The Slave's Cause: A History of Abolition*, told Adam Serwer of *The Atlantic* that she did not agree with The 1619 Project's claim "that the American Revolution was just a slaveholders' rebellion." Nevertheless, she was unwilling to sign the letter, despite the existence of "legitimate critiques that one can engage in discussion with," because "[i]t was a worthy thing to actually shine a light on a subject that the average person on the street doesn't know much about."[96]

Perhaps even more damning were the charges of Leslie Harris, a Northwestern University professor who specializes in African American history and was actually a consultant on The 1619 Project. Prior to publication, Harris "vigorously disputed" Hannah-Jones's erroneous contention that protecting slavery was a "critical reason that the colonists declared their independence from Britain" and also supplied the editor at the *Times* with many historically accurate details about the conditions of enslavement in colonial times. The *Times* simply ignored her and published "inaccuracies" anyway, she revealed in an article she wrote for *Politico* titled "I Helped Fact-Check the 1619 Project. The Times Ignored Me."[97]

And yet the farrago of historical falsehoods and racially charged rhetoric that is The 1619 Project is headed straight toward history classrooms in schools across America. It is being taught in some schools already. It is no wonder that entire initiatives have been established to refute the error-riddled and dangerously divisive 1619 Project—by the National Association of Scholars, RealClearPolitics, the *New York Post*, and The Federalist, as well as 1776 Unites, a project of the Woodson Center, headed by longtime civil rights leader Robert Woodson. Others, including the Claremont Institute, the Heritage Foundation, the American Institute for Economic Research, and the Texas Public Policy Foundation have published numerous articles critical of The 1619 Project.

States are following the lead of Senator Tom Cotton's "Saving American History," a proposal to deny federal funding to schools that use The 1619 Project. Arkansas, Mississippi, Iowa, Missouri, and South Dakota have seen similar bills introduced.[98] The 2021 Arkansas bill, like a similar 2017 bill to remove Howard Zinn's *A People's History of the United States* from publicly funded Arkansas classrooms, failed. The Mississippi bill also died in committee. Legislation aimed at the related critical race theory has been passed or introduced in several states, although other states are taking action to *mandate* it.[99] In 2020 President Donald Trump appointed the 1776 Commission to provide a corrective alternative curriculum.

But when Joe Biden became president, things changed. Biden seemed to endorse The 1619 Project in his inaugural address, when he claimed, "A cry for racial justice some 400 years in the making moves us." He warned of "a rise in political extremism, white supremacy, domestic terrorism that we must confront." The battle against "racism, nativism, fear, and demonization," he insisted—much as The 1619 Project does—is "perennial." Incongruously, in the same speech, he also called for "unity" eight times—to fight "the forces that divide us."[100]

Biden disbanded the 1776 Commission on his very first day in the White House. Now partisan Democrats are pushing the Civics Learning Act of 2021; a similar, but disguised, bill, the Civics Secures Democracy Act, has the support of the same Republicans who supported Common Core. Both bills federalize civics education by allocating grants for "action civics" (classroom discussion of hot-button issues and student "action" in protests and internships)—the very kind of pedagogy The 1619 Project Curriculum promotes.[101] Vice President (then senator) Kamala Harris had praised The 1619 Project upon its launch as a "masterpiece," tweeting, "We must speak this truth: the very foundation of our country was built on the backs of enslaved people."[102] Neither Harris nor Biden seemed much concerned about the violent "action" that was already being fueled by the racially divisive 1619 narrative; on June 1, 2020, Harris had encouraged her followers to contribute to a bail fund for protesters who had been arrested for committing crimes in the Minneapolis protests.[103] Biden had blamed "right-wing militias" and "white supremacists" for precipitating the riots.[104]

Quite obviously—in spite of the laurels bestowed on it by progressive politicians, educrats, professors, cowering university presidents, woke readers of the *New York Times,* indoctrinated students, and Hollywood[105]—The 1619 Project is a polemic, steeped in ideology. The sins of commission and omission in The Project go deep and range wide. Its case for replacing 1776 with 1619 as the true founding of America is built up with half-truths and untruths. It manipulates language in ways both clever and obscene. It judges historical actors and events by inappropriate and impossible standards. As it spreads through our education system, The 1619 Project ranks with Howard Zinn's *A People's History of the United States* as a mortal threat to the health of the American republic. And, as Supreme Court justice Louis Brandeis suggested, sunlight is the best disinfectant. So it's essential to shine some light on The 1619 Project's dubious claims.

The most dubious of those claims, which are central to The 1619 Project, concern America's declaration of independence from Great

Britain. The case against Jefferson and the Declaration is the lynchpin of The 1619 Project. In order to replace the real 1776 founding of the United States with the supposed 1619 start of slavery and to demote America from a republic to a "slavocracy," they have to make the Declaration of Independence a gross act of hypocrisy imposed on the world by a criminally evil man. In today's parlance...they have to cancel Thomas Jefferson. And so we turn to 1776.

CHAPTER 3

Canceling Thomas Jefferson—and 1776

It was between June 11 and June 28, 1776, in rented quarters in a brick-layer's Philadelphia house, that the thirty-three-year-old delegate to the Second Continental Congress, Thomas Jefferson, drafted the Declaration of Independence, which would announce to the world the resolve of the colonies to break from King George and Mother England. He had reached Philadelphia four days late for the Congress, on May 14, 1776, after a rough winter in which his mother had died; he had been reluctant to leave his beloved Monticello and his wife of three years. He had wanted to be involved in creating a new government for Virginia.[1]

By the time Jefferson arrived in Philadelphia, the resolution calling on the colonies to adopt new governments where none "sufficient to the exigencies of their affairs had hitherto been established" had already been approved. On May 15, John Adams's radical preface to the resolution was adopted. Jefferson had to be satisfied with sending his third draft of the Virginia Constitution back home, containing just a few changes to the body of that document but also adding a preamble in which Jefferson charged George III with trying to establish "a detestable and insupportable Tyranny."

"Jefferson's first draft of that preamble," writes Pauline Maier, "became the first draft of Congress's Declaration of Independence," thus paving the way for republican government, rule by a sovereign people. It was an anxiety-inducing prospect, given that no such popular form of government was in operation at that time and that similar governments in history—in Athens, Rome, and England's Commonwealth of the 1650s—had ended.[2]

The Quintessential Founder

Thus Jefferson, as the author of the Declaration of Independence, the "nation's birthright,"[3] represents 1776 as no one else does. The Declaration makes him the quintessential founder of our nation as it was understood, loved, and celebrated through our history—until the new narrative about the American "slavocracy" began to replace it. The 1619 Project is the acme of that new narrative. It is the culmination of decades of leftist revisionism that have undermined Americans' understanding, appreciation, and love of our country. And if The Project's irresponsible creators and deep-pocketed donors succeed in their efforts to install this false history as the history that American children learn in school—as we have seen, efforts already well on the way to success—they will have cemented the hold of an utterly false and dangerously divisive narrative on the minds of future generations, rendering them incapable of continuing the great American experiment in self-government. Because Jefferson represents that experiment as no other founder does, it is no wonder that the ire of the mob that has been taught to hate America is directed at him in particular—at his statues and his face on Mount Rushmore, at the circumstances of his life, at his sins (both real and imaginary), at his supposed "hypocrisy."[4] Never mind that Jefferson's declaration that all men are created equal—however he might have fallen short of it—has resounded through history as the battle cry for the liberation of the oppressed.

At the time he was designated by the five members of the committee to draft the Declaration, Jefferson was still a young lawyer-politician. He was chosen because "his pen was known to be potent," as his biographer Dumas Malone put it, and because he came from Virginia, one of the colonies that, unlike New England, had been lukewarm about separation from England. What Jefferson stated in the Declaration was not original. His first draft of the preamble for the Virginia Constitution was based on the 1689 English Declaration of Rights and on ideas that had been in circulation for some time in the colonies. As he wrote to Henry Lee, his intent was not "originality" in "principles" or "arguments," but "to place before mankind the common sense of the subject, in terms so plain and firm as to command their assent."[5] The Declaration expressed Jefferson's belief in the human ability to advance more perfect justice. As he wrote in 1774, he believed "[t]he great principles of right and wrong are legible to every reader...." As historian Robert Paquette has pointed out, Jefferson's "certitudes about the formula that would unlock the secrets of the better angels of human nature made him susceptible to charges of naïveté or boyish credulousness from those who emphasized the darker side of human nature."[6] In his education, including at William and Mary, he had been particularly drawn to the ancient classics and mathematics. But throughout his life Jefferson was intellectually "omnivorous," appreciating the arts and probing scientific matters. A skeptic when it came to received wisdom, especially religious dogma, Jefferson was the champion of intellectual freedom, religious liberty, and free speech.[7]

The purpose of the Declaration was to justify the separation of the colonies from King George III. The opening combined a number of important ideas in what Malone describes as a "tone of dignity, solemnity, respectful firmness, and injured virtue which the circumstances required."[8] Its words were at one time memorized by schoolchildren: "When in the Course of human events, it becomes necessary for one people to dissolve the political bands, which have connected them with another, and to assume among the powers of the earth, the separate and equal station to which the Laws of Nature and of Nature's God entitle them, a decent respect to the opinions of mankind requires that they should declare the causes which impel them to the separation."[9]

The decision to declare independence was made on July 2, and from that date until July 4 the delegates debated changes to the Declaration. The committee made a few changes, some of which irked Jefferson. As Malone said in 1948 in *Jefferson the Virginian*, the first of the six volumes of his biography of Jefferson, *Jefferson and His Time*, these and other changes—"the history of the evolving text of the Declaration"— have "been studied by scholars with great care." Some minor changes are credited to John Adams and Benjamin Franklin. But "We hold these truths to be sacred and undeniable" was changed by an unknown hand to "We hold these truths to be self-evident," and it may be that "inalienable" was changed to "unalienable" through a printer's error.[10]

Mostly there were deletions. The final paragraph was shortened and made more direct, with Lee's resolution taking the place of Jefferson's assertion of independence. Into the last sentence was inserted the phrase "with a firm reliance on the protection of divine providence." Jefferson's final words were kept but with capitalization added: "we mutually pledge to each other our lives, our Fortunes, and our sacred Honor."[11]

It is for the words of the Declaration of Independence that Jefferson is most remembered in our nation's history—even with all that followed in his career as Virginia state legislator, governor, member of Congress, minister to France, secretary of state under George Washington, vice president, president, planter, and founder of the University of Virginia, the nation's first secular and publicly funded university. Jefferson's influence was so great on Americans of various philosophical and political persuasions who claimed his words, ideas, and actions that a major book by newly minted history professor Merrill D. Peterson, titled *The Jefferson Image in the American Mind*, was published by Oxford University Press in 1960 and won the prestigious Bancroft Prize the next year.

Peterson called Jefferson "a baffling set of contradictions: philosopher and politician, aristocrat and democrat, cosmopolitan and American. He authored the nation's birthright, but he also wrote the Kentucky Resolutions," which put forth the idea of state nullification of federal law. "He was the friend of Washington, but the enemy of his administration." He was remembered for his presidential achievements, including the Louisiana Purchase and "the disaster of the Embargo." His mind was "bewildering in its range and complexity."[12]

As Dumas Malone pointed out in his review of Peterson's book, Jefferson—in contrast to the "stationary" George Washington—"has varied from generation to generation, almost from decade to decade." Jefferson has been embraced by "diverse groups," including "advocates of states' rights and crusaders against slavery, Jacksonian Democrats and Lincoln Republicans, imperialists and pacifists, Liberty Leaguers and New Dealers."[13] The Democratic Party has held annual Jefferson Day dinners, but the father of modern small-state conservatism, Albert Jay Nock, wrote a short biography of Jefferson that applauded his vision of a nation of independent yeomen farmers and tradesmen.

"Everyman was his own Jeffersonian," Peterson wrote in his 1960 book, and as Malone noted in his review, they sought to "square their own purposes with his ideals, perceiving that these were basic in the American experiment in freedom and democracy." When he died at the age of eighty-three, he was lauded in "the encomium of 1826" as "the Apostle of Liberty." This was how Nicholas Biddle eulogized Jefferson— for "a perpetual devotion, not to his own purposes, but to the pure and noble cause of public freedom"—before the American Philosophical Society, "where the president's chair Jefferson had once occupied was draped in black." Already those praising Jefferson in eulogies focused on what they saw as the "apex" of his devotion to liberty: the Declaration of Independence.[14]

Peterson opens his book with the touching and once famous story about the deaths of Jefferson and John Adams, Jefferson's "friend, sometimes foe, of fifty years." Both men died on the fiftieth anniversary of the reading of the Declaration of Independence. "Is it the Fourth?'" Jefferson had asked his doctor the evening before. When assured it soon would be, he drifted off to sleep and remained unconscious until, as his doctor wrote, "about one o'clock [the morning of July 4] he ceased to exist." On a chain around his neck was discovered a locket with a lock of hair from his wife Martha, who had died only six years after the reading of the Declaration. Five hours later, John Adams uttered his "last words, 'Thomas Jefferson still survives.'" Jefferson left the nation the Declaration of Independence and a holiday that, in Peterson's opinion, "belonged to him."¹⁵

And although he was too weak in 1826 to commit to attending the Independence Day Jubilee ceremonies in Washington, D.C., Jefferson did write a letter that became his "last testament to the American people." It was printed in newspapers and "engraved as a souvenir." Jefferson wrote, "May the Jubilee be to the world... the signal of arousing men to burst the chains" that were oppressing them "and to assume the blessings and security of self-government." He left the hope that this "palpable truth" was being seen: "that the mass of mankind has not been born with saddles on their backs, nor a favored few booted and spurred ready to ride them.... For ourselves, let the annual return of this day, forever refresh our recollections of these rights, and an undiminished devotion to them." As Peterson pointed out, "The charmed death of Jefferson and of his venerable friend made the Jubilee a solemn monument in American memory...."¹⁶

Yet, several months before his death, Jefferson had been so deeply in debt that he had "obtained permission from the state... to dispose of much of his property by lottery"—and he was saved from doing so only by "friends and admirers" who raised the funds after hearing about his plight.¹⁷ Per his directions, Jefferson's funeral was conducted "without pomp and ceremony," with "[b]lack-craped students, followed by the local citizenry, trudg[ing] through a downpour up the mountain's slope" at Monticello. His tombstone identified those achievements he most treasured: "Author of the Declaration of Independence / of the Statute of Virginia for religious freedom / & Father of the University of Virginia." But Jefferson's life was celebrated nationwide with honors at military stations, commemorative exercises, and days of public homage—in Richmond, with nearly the entire "populace" taking part in a mock funeral procession and listening to Governor John Tyler's eulogy; in Baltimore, where thirty thousand attended the services featuring as guest Charles Carroll, the last surviving signer of the Declaration; and in Boston, where Daniel Webster gave a ninety-minute oration in Faneuil Hall.[18]

Falling off His Pedestal

In the new introduction to the 1998 reissue of *The Jefferson Image in the American Mind*, Peterson stated that much more could have been written about Jefferson's image in the intervening years since 1960, when the book first appeared. Jefferson's character was so elusive that popular depictions failed to capture it. But in the days following World War II, when "totalitarianism threatened to engulf the world" and Dumas Malone was writing his first volume of the Jefferson biography, Jefferson was viewed as an avatar of freedom.[19]

But World War II "and the exposure of Nazi atrocities," as well as the "changing post-war climate of opinion," inspired research into slavery, and specifically investigations into slave rebellions and the capacity of slaves to resist their bondage, according to Robert Paquette.[20] The field of historical research on American slavery exploded in subsequent years. And young historians often brought a new attitude and energy to the study of the institution.

The shift was indicated by, for example, thirty-three-year-old David Brion Davis's accusation at an inaugural lecture at the University of Oxford in 1970 that Jefferson "had only a theoretical interest in promoting the cause of abolition," and that "[w]hen still in France [1784–1786], and incidentally while helping one J. D. Derieux buy land and slaves in America, [Jefferson] received inquiries from both the French and British abolition societies." (Little is known about Derieux, and Davis failed to provide a source that would establish his claim either in the lecture or in his 1975 book *The Problem of Slavery in the Age of Revolution 1770–1823*.) Davis did acknowledge that "it would have been imprudent if not improper for the American Minister to have joined a French reform society" and that Jefferson, who represented both Virginia and South Carolina and was tasked with finding "new markets for American produce," was aware of the importance of slave labor. But Davis charged that the "purity he preserved in France did not equip him to speak out later against the spread of slavery into Kentucky, Tennessee, Mississippi Territory, or Louisiana."[21]

Davis is considered to be one of the giants in the history of slavery, and deservedly so, but this speech marks a change in tone in the writings on Jefferson, as if the historians had come to a monument to chisel away at its features. Even the title, "Was Thomas Jefferson an Authentic Enemy of Slavery?," seems to put Jefferson in the dock. That kind of question, centering on what historical figures *should* have done, increasingly became the focus of scholars assuming positions of tenure in the halls of academe. Many had gone to graduate school instead of Vietnam, extending the length of the higher education that had become widely accessible to the post–World War II generation. "The decade of the 1960s produced 5,884 doctorates [in history], as compared with 7,695 for the whole period 1873–1960," reported Harvard historian Oscar Handlin as he ruefully recounted the changes in his profession. A larger share of these sixties-era doctorates were completed at universities outside the Ivy League.[22] The New Left that emerged after the early years of the 1960s was an undisciplined lot in many ways, including in their scholarship. Even their borrowed Marxist ideas were not applied with any coherence. Standards deteriorated.[23]

The fervor of the civil rights and anti–Vietnam War protests infused the profession, which began to focus on narrow topics, rejecting as subjects the traditional giants, the leaders who had bequeathed a government, literature, and philosophy. These greats of history were now seen through the judgmental lens of the present. Scholars "bent their arguments" to the needs of the present—equal rights for blacks, women, and other groups outside of the ruling white patriarchy.[24] Victim groups became the subjects of the new scholarship.

"Few scholars remained detached enough from their subjects to hold back from the persistent quest for villains and heroes," Handlin remarked. A reversal of stereotypes took place. "If the immigrants were no longer sinister undermen, or the Negroes childlike savages, or the Indians barbarians, then they were saintly victims, whose difficulties stemmed from the evil intentions of individual or group antagonists." As a result, "[m]ost of the vast published outpouring on blacks and slavery after 1965" was "faulty in research, poor in expression, and, for interpretation decked out in the fashionable rags of the moment." Three hundred and fifty years were telescoped, the seventeenth and eighteenth centuries neglected, and slavery seen only through the lens of the antebellum South. Categories such as "race and bondage" were conflated; inter-group differences and conflicts and distinctions between freedmen and slaves were ignored.[25]

The focus on micro-histories—the details of the lives of individuals or small communities—led to a loss of the big picture and historical context. The injustices suffered by individuals could be blamed on oppressors without any investigation of the larger forces at work at that point in time. Lost in the focus on victims was an understanding of the momentous changes that would lead to the condemnation and remediation of the very injustices against which the historians were purportedly taking a stand. In the process, entire categories of people, by virtue of their race, ethnicity, and sex, were cast as representative of a system rotten with racism and sexism. Those claiming membership in the designated victim groups (women, African Americans, and so forth) were granted authority by virtue of their identity; their accusations against the giants of the past carried added weight.

Heaping such blame on traditional American heroes exacerbated racial conflict, something that had been the goal of the Soviet Communists from the time they established a beachhead with a New York City office in 1919. In 1920, Vladimir Lenin stated in "The Negroes in America"—the fourteenth point of the sixteen theses submitted to the delegates of the Comintern's Second Congress—that "Negroes" were to be "a strategically important element in Communist activity." The following year, the Communists stated that the "sufferings" of "Negroes" were to be fixed on the "bourgeoisie and the Capitalist-Imperialist System!"[26]

Six decades later, in 1980, Howard Zinn, communist professor at Boston University, took advantage of the trends that the New Left had ushered in to write *A People's History of the United States*, which remains a bestseller and is widely used in classrooms to this day. The same attribution of the "sufferings" of "Negroes" to the "bourgeoisie and the Capitalist-Imperialist System" runs throughout Zinn's book. He claims that capitalist America nurtured a slave system that "developed quickly into a regular institution, into the normal relations of blacks to whites in the New World," which instituted racism that "accompanied the inferior position of blacks in America for the next 350 years."[27]

Zinn placed the responsibility at the feet of the founders—all of whom he deemed hypocrites. The Declaration of Independence, "the great manifesto of freedom," did not apply to slaves, Zinn snarked. Jefferson owned "hundreds" of slaves "until the day he died." Southern slaveholders and northern merchants created a new government whose aim was "to maintain their [own] privileges, while giving just enough rights and liberties to enough of the people to ensure popular support." Within this context, the Declaration's words rang hollow. Only white men—many of them slaveholding white men—had signed it and formed the new government that it had ushered in, which was irredeemable and had to be overthrown. In line with the new political trends, but under the claim that he was uncovering the real history long hidden by old-school racist historians, Zinn purported to be writing a "bottom-up" history of slaves, workers, women, Indians, and other marginalized groups—although these heroes often turned out to be well-known radical activists or anonymous mouthpieces for communist dogma.[28]

The old-school historians, in contrast, believed that the American system *could* be reformed. Merrill Peterson, the Jefferson scholar, was known on the campus at the University of Virginia "for his liberal views" and for being "[o]utspoken on the subject of integration," wrote an obituary writer on October 2, 2009. After civil rights marchers were attacked by police in Selma, Alabama, in 1965, Peterson famously gave a "fervent and eloquent speech at the campus rotunda" and called Selma "a vital link in the heritage of American liberty."[29]

Yet in 1998, in the new introduction to the republication of his book, Peterson had bemoaned the idea that because it was "asserted, often vociferously of late, that [Jefferson] lived and died a slaveholder...he must have been a demon, a hypocrite, or an enigma." Peterson believed that the book that had made the most lasting impact on Jefferson's reputation in the last quarter of the twentieth century was Fawn M. Brodie's 1974 bestseller *Thomas Jefferson: An Intimate History*, which, according to an Associated Press story announcing Brodie's death in 1981, "focused on an affair that Jefferson allegedly had with a slave woman" named Sally Hemings. Brodie, in line with the new trend in history, focused on the victim in the story. Brodie claimed that Jefferson had fathered all of Hemings's children, taking as "the single most important" piece of evidence for that claim the "Reminiscences of Madison Hemings," allegedly recounted by Sally Hemings's son Madison to Samuel Wetmore, who published it in the *Pike County Republican* in 1873. The allegations in these "Reminiscences" revived rumors that had been spread in 1802 by Jefferson's political foe James T. Callender, who took revenge for Jefferson's refusal to appoint him to the position of postmaster of Richmond by writing a series of articles alleging that in the late 1780s Jefferson had taken a slave girl with him to France as a concubine. This alleged episode would be "tantalizingly" portrayed in the 1995 film *Jefferson in Paris*.[30] Peterson had addressed the topic in his book in 1960.[31]

In an attempt to convince skeptics, Brodie had published an article in *American Heritage*, before her book came out, laying out her sources. Brodie suggested that the racial "taboo" of miscegenation had kept the information buried. She countered the conclusions of Malone and Peterson with those of "certain black historians...including Lerone Bennett," who in 1954 had published an article in *Ebony* magazine titled "Thomas Jefferson's Negro Grandchildren."[32] Bennett, however, was not a historian, but a magazine journalist with an agenda. He coined the term "Black Power."[33]

Annette Gordon-Reed, a law professor who had served as counsel to the New York City Board of Corrections, revived the Brodie thesis in her 1997 book *Thomas Jefferson and Sally Hemings: An American Controversy*. The timing of her book, the year before DNA testing was conducted in 1998, aroused suspicion.[34]

Gordon-Reed took off from Brodie's racial angle, with the added authority of her identity as a black woman. She insisted, by way of drawn-out legalistic explanations, that she was presenting history based on the most exacting standards of evidence. At the same time, she questioned evidence that came from a different (non-black) source and suggested that it was being used for racist purposes. In fact, she opens the first chapter: "It has become a cliché to refer to the 'invisibility' of black people in the United States as a way of suggesting that blacks are neither really seen nor heard by their countrymen. The term, which conveys the sense of powerlessness that many blacks feel, is a useful but not totally accurate metaphor. It would be more correct to say that most white Americans do see and hear blacks but only when and how they want to see and hear them."[35] This charge was leveled particularly at historians who doubted the word of a former slave, Madison Hemings. In matter of fact, though, they more doubted the person recording the former slave's words—that is, the person writing Madison Hemings's story as "memoirs" in "a Republican newspaper in Ohio in 1873."[36]

In January of 2000, DNA testing revealed that any one of over two dozen Jefferson men could have been the father of one of Sally's children, Eston. In the same month, Gordon-Reed's article in the *William and Mary Quarterly* repeated claims that the "suppression of the Hemings story" was "another example of white supremacy at work."[37] Her author's note for the 2000 edition of *Thomas Jefferson and Sally Hemings* began with similar accusations about the motivations of the "Old Guard" historians who "continued to ignore what was really at stake: proper regard for the humanity and integrity of blacks who were enslaved at Monticello."[38]

In her 2008 book *The Hemingses of Monticello*, Gordon-Reed continued to make charges of racism and sexism. The chapter "Sarah Hemings: The Fatherless Girl in a Patriarchal Society" announces her approach on the first page: "When we think of the young Sally Hemings in Paris dealing with Thomas Jefferson, we must acknowledge that she was born into a cohort—eighteenth century enslaved black women— whose humanity and femininity were constantly assaulted by slavery and white supremacy." And lest anyone see any redeeming qualities in Jefferson, who had a reputation for showing concern about his slaves, she writes that Jefferson's "worldview took in 'women, children, and slaves' as individuals whose similar attributes required that they be put under the protection (read control) of white men."[39]

Gordon-Reed's scholarship continues in the same vein, as is evidenced by titles she has edited: *Racism in America* (2002) and *Race on Trial* (2002). Gordon-Reed's two books on the Hemingses appear in college syllabi across the country, most often in history courses, but also in literature, law, anthropology, and women's studies. Most recently, in a 2021 volume edited by Ibram X. Kendi and Keisha N. Blain, she contributed an essay recounting the alleged relationship between Jefferson and Sally Hemings.[40] Her 2016 book *"Most Blessed of the Patriarchs": Thomas Jefferson and the Empire of the Imagination* was co-written with Peter Onuf.[41]

Prompted by the fact that unproven evidence was being presented as established historical fact, a newly organized Thomas Jefferson Heritage Society appointed the Scholars Commission on the Jefferson-Hemings Issue. In 2011 it published a book-length report titled *The Jefferson-Hemings Controversy: Report of the Scholars Commission*; it expanded on the report that had been published in 2001.[42] Drawing on the historical evidence, including the "Memoirs of a Monticello Slave," the thirteen scholars (with one mild dissent) concluded that Jefferson's younger brother Randolph had most likely fathered Sally Hemings's son Eston.

Writing in the *Wall Street Journal*, University of Virginia professor and *Report* editor Robert F. Turner corrected the initial rumor from Callender alleging that a young slave girl was Jefferson's "concubine." In actuality, Sally Hemings "attended to Jefferson's young daughters, who lived in a Catholic boarding school across town in Paris that had servants' quarters." Turner suggested that historians promoting Callender's version were motivated by the desire to diminish Jefferson's "iconic status" as author of the Declaration of Independence.[43]

Gordon-Reed was clearly aware of the expanded 2011 report that had applied scholarly analysis to the popular but unproven belief that Jefferson had fathered several of Sally Hemings's children, because on September 7, 2014, she tweeted a story about DNA tests' "proving" Jack the Ripper's identity and asked, sarcastically, "Are we sure it was not Randolph Jefferson?" At a public forum, Gordon-Reed, along with historians on the staff of the Thomas Jefferson Foundation, likened anyone opposing her view to a member of the "Flat Earth Society."[44]

The adversarial approach to history has come to prevail. Those historians who don't pursue identity politics are now fighting a rearguard action from the margins to which they have been relegated by the leftists now holding power. The historian who attempts to recreate the past with understanding—that is, to get beyond her present view, rather than to see the past through "woke" moral standards—is maligned as "Old Guard," or worse. Historical figures are no longer understood—they are either valorized or demonized. Peterson's point that Jefferson was being portrayed as a "demon, a hypocrite, or an enigma" turned out not to be hyperbole, as a November 30, 2012, *New York Times* op-ed by professor of legal history Paul Finkelman demonstrated. The title of the article was "The Monster of Monticello."[45]

The battles over race and gender obscured Jefferson's achievements and historical significance, as Professor Kevin Gutzman, author of *Thomas Jefferson—Revolutionary*, pointed out in 2017: "Where formerly Jefferson scholars and the interested public mentioned the [Hemings] matter in passing, if at all, they now commonly foreground it." The *Publishers Weekly* review of *Jefferson: Architect of American Liberty* by John Boles, he noted, had mentioned "the Virginian's relationship with Sally Hemings," but not the Declaration of Independence, the Virginia Statute for Religious Freedom, the Louisiana Purchase, or the University of Virginia. Gutzman wondered "why so many historians feel bound to editorialize on [Jefferson's] life as a slaveowner."[46]

Sadly, the same thing is true of textbooks, which tend to "follow professional historiography."[47] Little allowance seems to be made either for students' differing levels of maturity or for historical significance—a departure from what seems to have been the case back in 1966, when the California distributor of the *Land of the Free*, a then-controversial eighth-grade textbook co-written by John Hope Franklin, refused to change the adopted text to reflect W. E. B. Du Bois's membership in the Communist Party, stating that it would amount to "character assassination" and that, similarly, they did not "mention Washington's towering rages, Jefferson's slaveholding, Clay's rakish life...."[48]

But such facts would soon be seen as important and appropriate for schoolchildren to learn. A 1995 book, *Molding the Good Citizen,* reviewed the changes in the portrayal of Jefferson, among other founders, in history textbooks and found that "[t]oday's books measure Jefferson's words against contemporary standards of equality—for women, blacks, and native Americans, as well as for white men." They discovered that shifts had occurred since 1943: First George Washington's role had been diminished, and because of "our increasing love of equality, primary emphasis" had been placed on the Declaration of Independence. While a 1949 textbook by Eugene Barker and Henry Steele Commager had praised the Declaration and noted its foundational purpose in the government of the United States, a 1967 book by Henry Bragdon and Samuel McCutchen went further, describing how the Declaration had "operated toward ending Negro slavery, giving women the right to vote, enlarging job opportunities and extending the chances for education."[49]

But in the 1980s the Declaration, which had acquired "a place of honor" as "a symbol of liberty and freedom," became subject to "marginal nitpicking." Textbooks still treated the expansion of federal powers, evidenced by Jefferson's Louisiana Purchase, positively, as they had since the 1940s, and celebrated the flexibility of the Constitution. But in the books of the 1980s, some authors criticized the Louisiana Purchase for its impact on Indians and scrutinized Jefferson's view of Native Americans. Most significant was the changed treatment of Jefferson and slavery—from silence in the 1940s, to nuanced attention in the 1960s and early 1970s that included his concern for slaves and his overall objections to the institution, to the 1980s, when "the textbooks openly criticize[d] Jefferson for his views and actions regarding slavery." One 1982 textbook by Lewis Todd and Merle Curti charged Jefferson with being "well aware that slavery contradicted the ideals set forth in the Declaration of Independence." Jefferson was presented as a racist: "Jefferson did not want the full **abolition**, or ending, of slavery. He feared that white people and black people could not live peacefully side by side, especially in the southern states.... Jefferson also accepted the false, but common, thinking of his time that black people lacked the capacity for self-government. . ." [emphasis in the original].[50]

Textbooks have diverted attention from the ideals of the Declaration to the person of Jefferson, who is cast in the way Gordon-Reed presents him, as a white male supremacist. The alleged Jefferson–Hemings relationship takes center stage in major textbooks. The 2020 edition of *The American Pageant* presents it as established fact: "Liberal-thinking Jefferson, with aristocratic head set on a farmer's frame, was a bundle of inconsistencies. By one set of tests, he should have been a Federalist, for he was a Virginia aristocrat who lived in an imposing hilltop mansion at Monticello. This eloquent champion of liberty, who called the slave system a 'hideous blot' on the republic, owned six hundred other human beings, including Sally Hemings, with whom Jefferson had a decades-long relationship that produced several children."[51]

The student is then directed to "See Examining the Evidence: The Thomas Jefferson–Sally Hemings Controversy, Section 10-3, p. 213."[52] Such "evidence" sections have become popular in student lessons. They suggest to the high school student that he is as capable of examining primary documents as a historian with a Ph.D. and encourage him to come to his own judgment on controversial historical topics on the basis of very selective evidence. This practice serves to give students a wildly inflated sense of their own expertise and knowledge—which, in reality, has diminished each year, as surveys of student knowledge demonstrate. The "Examining the Evidence: The Thomas Jefferson–Sally Hemings Controversy" section in *The American Pageant* gives no "evidence" besides a political cartoon. It describes the story's genesis in the polemics of James Callender, a "firebrand journalist and *provocateur*," in the aftermath of the 1800 election and its dissemination by Federalist newspapers. The reproduced cartoon, "A Philosophic Cock," is explained as an attack on Jefferson, "depicting him as a rooster and Hemings as a hen." The rooster, a "symbol of Revolutionary France," was chosen as an attack on Jefferson's radical sympathies. The authors admit that Jefferson "resolutely denied" the affair but claim that new sources shed "light" on what had seemed to be a politically motivated rumor. Perhaps alluding to journalist and Black Power advocate Lerone Bennett's *Ebony* article, they say that new evidence was revealed in the 1950s, but that "Dumas Malone's calculation that Jefferson had been present at Monticello nine months before the birth of each of Hemings's children" is "most convincing." In fact, Malone went to great lengths to put the rumor to rest, dedicating an appendix to the issue in the first volume of his Jefferson biography, and Herman Belz pointed out in "The Legend of Sally Hemings," published in *Academic Questions* in 2012, that it cannot be verified that *Sally* was at Monticello nine months before the birth of each child.[53] Finally, in a misrepresentation of the results of the DNA testing, the textbook writers assert that the "DNA testing of the remains of Jefferson's white and possible black descendants...helped establish the high probability that Jefferson had fathered Hemings's youngest son and the likelihood that he was the father of all of her children."[54]

The 2019 edition of the Advanced Placement textbook *By the People* also presents Jefferson's paternity of Hemings's children as "highly likely" according to DNA testing and calls it "the consensus of most historians who have studied Jefferson's life." The discussion occurs within the context of Jefferson's "personal life" of luxuries at Monticello—in contrast to the publicly visible "simplified social scene at the White House." Even as he defended "republican equality in social relations," Jefferson's "aristocratic" lifestyle, with the lavish entertainment of guests, offering the "finest food and wine," was possible because "[s]laves did all of the hard work and took care of the president's every need."[55]

A section titled "Thinking Historically" in this AP textbook by James W. Fraser, who teaches history and education at New York University but holds a Ph.D. in the history of American education,[56] gives a one-paragraph background summary of the alleged Jefferson–Hemings relationship and refers to "historian" Annette Gordon-Reeds's *The Hemingses of Monticello*, claiming that it "traces not only the story of Sally Hemings but also the story of the intertwined generations of the Jefferson and Hemings families." Why is the "story" important? Because it "raises many questions for historians, including questions about the relevance of Jefferson's personal relationship with Sally Hemings in terms of judgments about his political career and as president." Two questions then appear under the category "Thinking Critically." The first is labeled "Argument Development" and asks, "Was it possible for a slave woman and a powerful older free man who claimed ownership of her to form a truly consensual relationship in the early 1800s? How would you frame an argument either way?" The second question, labeled "Analyzing Secondary Sources," asks, "What bearings might Jefferson's relationship with Sally Hemings have on his complex attitudes about the institution of slavery? What does an understanding of the Jefferson-Hemings family tell us about the nature of American slavery and society in the early 1800s?"[57]

Thomas Jefferson is presented as one of the founders whose private lives and hypocritical stances all need to be scrutinized, a task justified in the statement claiming:

The revolutionary leaders—Washington, Adams, Jefferson—
have become cardboard characters. Their words have been
invoked too often, their deeds too sanitized. But if today's
citizens are to make sense of the Revolution and the creation
of a new nation, they need to see those leaders as real. In
addition, people today need to realize that many other actors
were also asserting their place in—or, in the case of enslaved
Africans, American Indians, and Loyalists, on the margins
of—the new nation. Those known as the "founding fathers"
were far from the only actors.[58]

Among those neglected figures, Fraser tells students, were women
who after the Revolution were "far less willing to leave political or domestic decisions to men" and "[p]oor farmers" who felt "that their grievances
had not been addressed."[59] *The American Pageant* similarly explains, "If
social and political egalitarianism confounded Revolutionary-era
colonists, both radicals and conservatives could agree that whatever form
the new nation took, white males would do the shaping. American leaders
expected women to remain confined to home and hearth, African Americans to cotton- and cane-field, and Indians to the unsettled West." The
Revolution, however, did start "a conversation" about being more
inclusive.[60]

The greatest flaw in the founders' republic, however, was slavery, as
By the People pounds into the heads of AP students. That book points
out that among "the most important changes" to the Declaration was the
removal of "Jefferson's passionate attack on the slave trade, which was
hypocritical in light of the fact that Jefferson owned many slaves and made
no move to free them." And other members of Congress were motivated
by their "investments" in the slave trade. "However, no one suggested
removing Jefferson's assertion that the king 'has endeavored to bring on
the inhabitants of our frontiers, the merciless Indian savages,' even when
they all knew that it was whites on the frontiers who were invading Indian
territory...."[61] The "whites" were the bad guys: "Violence between white

Americans and Indians continued long after the Indian Wars in the East had ended. Individual Indians were easy marks for white attack. Similarly, slaves could do little to protect themselves against the violence that was always a part of the slave system. The beating, rape, and killing of slaves was seldom considered a matter of concern for anyone but those on the plantation."[62]

No wonder members of the millennial and Generation Z cohorts look upon our nation's history and government with a jaundiced eye. Surveys reveal an alarming loss of patriotism, and even of faith in our republican form of government and in the free enterprise system.[63] It should not be surprising that "white privilege" and "systemic racism" have become accepted as gospel truth. And this is the kind of history that America's young people were learning even before The 1619 Project. Now new curricula are being pumped into school systems across the country based on a project that irresponsibly asserts in an even more extreme and didactic manner that the American Revolution was "empowered" by slavery and claims that Jefferson and the other founders "believed that independence was required in order to ensure that slavery would continue."[64]

Already the "1619 riots" in the woke summer of 2020 saw the author of the Declaration of 1776 become a particular target of the mob. We have seen in detail above how they expressed their fury. Jefferson's statues were vandalized and toppled or had to be removed to save them from being destroyed.[65] "Thomas Jefferson" was slated to be scrubbed from public schools that had been named in his honor.[66] And his image on Mount Rushmore became a flashpoint for the protesters, with the great-granddaughter of the sculptor accusing Jefferson of "genocide."[67]

Nikole Hannah-Jones makes Jefferson a particular target of her attack on the founders. In her 2021 Martin Luther King Jr. Lecture denouncing the 1776 Commission, she argued that we cannot "ignore that Jefferson was an enslaver" and claimed that he kept a careful ledger to see how productivity on his farms could be improved through the "torture" of slaves.[68] Her inaugural essay for The 1619 Project indicts

Jefferson as an "enslaver" and analogizes his plantation to a Nazi concentration camp by referring to it as "the forced-labor camp he called Monticello"—one of the many such camps that imprisoned "one-fifth of the population within the 13 colonies," where the enslaved "struggled under a brutal system of slavery unlike anything that had existed in the world before."[69]

And the desire for American independence from Britain was motivated by the desire to protect such a brutal form of slavery—a lie by which The 1619 Project's creators aim to bring down the Declaration and 1776 and substitute 1619 as "our true founding."[70]

Tactical Retreats

As we saw above, the jaw-dropping allegation that the Revolution was fought in defense of slavery has been widely criticized by some of the most prominent historians in this field—including by left-leaning scholars, and even by one expert who served as a consultant on The 1619 Project and whose pre-publication warnings against printing the false claim were ignored. As a result, the *Times* has had to backpedal—to a certain extent. Hannah-Jones and her editor "adjusted" their original claim by adding two words. Thus the online version of Hannah-Jones's inaugural essay now makes the scaled-back allegation that "one of the primary reasons *some of* the colonists decided to declare their independence from Britain was because they wanted to protect the institution of slavery [emphasis added]."[71]

At least the *Times* has acknowledged that correction—although without being willing to frankly call it a correction, saying instead that "the passage has been adjusted."[72] Other significant alterations to the The 1619 Project as originally published have been made without the acknowledgment that "journalistic ethical standards would require."[73]

Perhaps most significantly, the *Times* deleted the reference to 1619 as "our true founding"—without acknowledging the correction. Phillip Magness, a senior fellow at the American Institute for Economic

Research, documented that silent correction of the original online version of the editors' "Introduction," which originally asserted, "The 1619 project is a major initiative from The New York Times observing the 400th anniversary of the beginning of American slavery. It aims to reframe the country's history, *understanding 1619 as our true founding, and* placing the consequences of slavery and the contributions of black Americans at the very center of our national narrative [emphasis added to highlight the words that were subsequently deleted]." The *Times* silently corrected that claim approximately four months after publication. Thus the same passage, in the current electronic version of that "Introduction," which has been retitled "Why We Published The 1619 Project" and redated December 20, 2019, now says, "The 1619 Project is an ongoing initiative from The New York Times Magazine that began in August 2019, the 400th anniversary of the beginning of American slavery. It aims to reframe the country's history by placing the consequences of slavery and the contributions of black Americans at the very center of our national narrative."[74]

Another similar claim, this one in the original print version of Silverstein's "Introduction," has also been changed. In the printed magazine, he said, "1619. It is not a year that most Americans know as a notable date in our country's history. Those who do are at most a tiny fraction of those who can tell you that 1776 is the year of our nation's birth. What if, however, we were to tell you that *this fact, which is taught in our schools and unanimously celebrated every Fourth of July, is wrong, and that the country's true birth date,* the moment that its defining contradictions first came into the world, was in late August of 1619?" [Emphasis added to highlight the words that were scrubbed in the unacknowledged correction.] In the current version at the *Times* website, the passage now reads, "1619 is not a year that most Americans know as a notable date in our country's history. Those who do are at most a tiny fraction of those who can tell you that 1776 is the year of our nation's birth. What if, however, we were to tell you that the moment that the country's defining contradictions first came into the world was in late August of 1619?"[75]

Even the introductory paragraph originally printed on the cover of the *New York Times Magazine* has been silently altered. A crucial sentence printed there is missing from the current online version: "America was not yet America, but this was the moment it began." The "moment" that the sentence referred to was the arrival and sale of the Africans in Virginia. A reference to the "250 years" of slavery following that moment has also been scrubbed. What all these midnight alterations—including changing the "British colony" to an "English" one in one online version but not in another[76]—suggest is a staff out of its depth even when it comes to lying about history and scrambling to cover it up.

Fortunately, a pdf of the printed magazine makes it impossible to permanently hide the disingenuous edits to the print edition, and diligent investigators such as historian Phillip Magness, Jordan Davidson of The Federalist, and Becket Adams of the *Washington Examiner* have preserved altered passages from the original online edition (as well as some of the computer code altering them) for posterity.[77]

But these retreats from The 1619 Project's most indefensible claims were only tactical. Under pressure, Hannah-Jones backpedaled vigorously and disingenuously, claiming that The Project "does not argue that 1619 is our true founding" and dismissing the original online edition at the *Times* website, which contained the "true founding" language, as "some ancillary digital promotion copy, which you know is not journalism and changing promotional copy does not require an editor's note." Her own Twitter account—which featured the statement "I argue that 1619 is our true founding" and a header with the date July 4, 1776, struck through and replaced with August 20, 1619—gave the lie to her pretense.[78] In any case, as *New York Times Magazine* editor Silverstein told Bret Stephens, the *New York Times* opinion writer who drew attention to the deletion of the material, it was "wrong" to think that "1776 is the year of our nation's birth" and to posit 1619 as America's "true birth date." For the editor, the edit was "immaterial." Most important was "the project's stated aim," which "remained": "to put 1619 and its consequences as the true starting point of the American story."[79] And, in fact, the current version of Jake Silverstein's introductory essay on the *Times* website still claims that "[t]he goal of The 1619 Project is to reframe American history by considering what it would mean to regard 1619 as our nation's birth year" and argues that chattel slavery is not only America's "original sin" but "the country's very origin."[80]

One wonders what other technological sleights of hand, "adjustments," clarifications, and accusations of reader ignorance and stupidity will come. It is obvious that the creators of The 1619 Project are used to covering up their lies about our country's birth narrative. So let's get beyond the insults, accusations, and demonization. The picture is a bit more complicated than the morality tale of "enslavers" and "perfecters of this democracy" told in The 1619 Project.[81]

CHAPTER 4

Declaring Independence "to Protect the Institution of Slavery"?

Charging the American revolutionaries with "duplicity" for claiming to be slaves of Britain, Hannah-Jones asserts, "Conveniently left out of our founding mythology is the fact that one of the primary reasons the colonists decided to declare their independence from Britain was because they wanted to protect the institution of slavery." As we have seen, this claim proved impossible for even the *New York Times* to defend, so it was "adjusted" and scaled back to the assertion that protecting slavery was a primary reason for "some of" the colonists to declare independence.[1] But even the vaguer claim still implies that protecting slavery was a significant motivation for the American Revolution, especially in light of the additional claims, which were not "adjusted":

> By 1776, Britain had grown deeply conflicted over its role in the barbaric institution that had reshaped the Western Hemisphere.
>
> In London, there were growing calls to abolish the slave trade. This would have upended the economy of the colonies, in both the North and the South.

The wealth and prominence that allowed Jefferson, at just 33, and the other founding fathers to believe they could successfully break off from one of the mightiest empires in the world came from the dizzying profits generated by chattel slavery. In other words, we may never have revolted against Britain if the founders had not understood that slavery empowered them to do so; nor if they had not believed that independence was required in order to ensure that slavery would continue. It is not incidental that 10 of this nation's first 12 presidents were enslavers, and some might argue that this nation was founded not as a democracy but as a slavocracy.

The claim that defending slavery was a "primary" reason colonists decided to declare independence garnered perhaps the largest number of responses from historians, including non-conservatives such as Sean Wilentz and Leslie Harris. As we saw in chapter 2, Harris, who specializes in African American history, teaches at Northwestern University, and had been used by the *Times* as a consultant, revealed that she had "vigorously argued against" this passage with the newspaper's fact-checker. But it was left in, and Hannah-Jones then repeated the claim, saying on Georgia public radio "that the patriots fought the American Revolution in large part to preserve slavery in North America."[2]

And that wasn't Harris's only problem with the supposed facts with which The 1619 Project purported to be correcting the historical record. As the historian explained, besides ignoring her advice and publishing "the incorrect statement about the American Revolution anyway.... In addition, the paper's characterizations of slavery in early America reflected laws and practices more common in the antebellum era than in Colonial times, and did not accurately illustrate the varied experiences of the first generation of enslaved people that arrived in Virginia in 1619." Were the authors simply ignorant of the true facts? If so, it wasn't for lack of telling. As Harris pointed out, before publication she had answered "several questions probing the nature of slavery in the Colonial era" from a *Times* editor asking "whether enslaved people were allowed to read, could legally marry, could congregate in groups of more than four, and could own, will or inherit property." Harris said that she had explained "these histories as best I could—with references to specific examples" because the answers "vary widely depending upon the era and the colony." These important historical distinctions also never made it into The 1619 Project.[3]

Thomas Jefferson is the prize exhibit in Hannah-Jones's dubious case that protecting slavery was a main reason for colonists to declare independence. And what, exactly, is her evidence that independence, Jefferson, the Declaration, and the Revolution were pro-slavery? Bizarrely, the fact that Jefferson fulminated *against* slavery in his original draft of the Declaration:

> Jefferson and the other founders were keenly aware of this hypocrisy. And so in Jefferson's original draft of the Declaration of Independence, he tried to argue that it wasn't the colonists' fault. Instead, he blamed the king of England for forcing the institution of slavery on the unwilling colonists and called the trafficking in human beings a crime. Yet neither Jefferson nor most of the founders intended to abolish slavery, and in the end, they struck the passage. There is no mention of slavery in the final Declaration of Independence. Similarly, 11 years later, when it came time to draft the Constitution, the framers carefully constructed a document that preserved and protected slavery without ever using the word.

Cornell University professor Edward Baptist, whose deeply flawed 2014 book *The Half Has Never Been Told: Slavery and the Making of American Capitalism* is foundational to The 1619 Project's economic arguments, also takes a swing at Jefferson, who he claims "tried to blame King George III for using the Atlantic trade to impose slavery on the colonies," and thus set a precedent for white "scapegoaters."[4] Baptist was exposed in 2016 for having "inflated statistics, invented facts, and altered quotes."[5] That didn't stop Hannah-Jones from repeating these themes in her essay, or The 1619 Project from publishing Matthew Desmond's "Capitalism," which relies on Baptist.[6] David Waldstreicher, another of Hannah-Jones's sources, psychoanalyzes Jefferson, claiming that the deleted passage possibly functioned "as a kind of therapy, an insurance policy against Jefferson's own bad conscience." The author of the Declaration had "the need to spin the spiraling politics of slavery"—to confirm "British guilt and American innocence" "without advancing the cause of abolition."[7]

Twisting a Well-Known History Out of Shape

In spite of The 1619 Project's claims to revealing new historical information, the deletion of Jefferson's passage attacking slavery, like other changes in the Declaration, is not news. It was treated at length back in 1948, when Dumas Malone, continuing a long-running scholarly discussion, called the "charge against the King about the slave trade" the "most important single" deletion from the Declaration and ascribed the change largely to opposition by South Carolinians and Georgians.[8] It even made its way into popular culture: the removal of Jefferson's indictment of slavery from the Declaration at the South Carolinian delegates' insistence was dramatized—with literary license—as a key plot point in the popular musical *1776*, the 1969 Broadway hit and Tony-winning "Best Musical" that was made into a 1972 film, which reached an even wider audience in decades of television reruns.[9] The Broadway show was revived in 1997, the same year that historian Pauline Maier published her popular history *American Scripture: Making the Declaration of Independence*, which also treated the issue at length. In his 1984 *The Radical Politics of Thomas Jefferson: A Revisionist View*, Richard K. Matthews, too, assigned significance to the paragraph in which Jefferson had addressed "the immoral conduct of the king in aiding the perpetuation of the slave trade."[10] Most historians do.

Jefferson was irked about the deletion, complaining in his notes that his section "reprobating the enslaving the inhabitants of Africa, was struck out in complaisance to South Carolina & Georgia, who had never attempted to restrain the importation of slaves.... Our Northern brethren also I believe felt a little tender under those censures; for tho' their people have very few slaves themselves yet they had been pretty considerable carriers of them to others."[11] And he made sure it was not deleted from the historical record, circulating several handwritten copies and reproducing it in his *Autobiography*.[12] The deleted passage, which expands on Jefferson's preamble to the Virginia Constitution, begins, "He [King George] has waged cruel war against human nature, violating it's most sacred rights of life and liberty in the persons of a distant people who never offended him, captivating & carrying them into slavery in another hemisphere or to incur miserable death in their transportation thither. This piratical warfare, the opprobrium of INFIDEL powers, is the warfare of the CHRISTIAN king of Great Britain, determined to keep open a market where MEN should be bought & sold, he has prostituted his negative for suppressing every legislative attempt to prohibit or to restrain this execrable commerce."[13]

The omitted material goes on to charge King George with instigating revolts by these slaves: "And that this assemblage of horrors might want no fact of distinguished die, he is now exciting those very people to rise in arms among us, and to purchase that liberty of which he has deprived them, by murdering the people on whom he also obtruded them: thus paying off *former* crimes committed against the LIBERTIES of one people, with crimes which he urges them to commit against the LIVES of another."[14]

This paragraph was ultimately shortened and changed to say, "He has excited domestic insurrection against us, & has endeavored to bring on the inhabitants of our frontiers the merciless Indian savages, whose known rule of warfare is an undistinguished destruction of all ages, sexes, & conditions."

Jefferson was repeating charges from his 1774 *A Summary View of the Rights of British America*, prepared for the First Continental Congress:

"The abolition of domestic slavery is the great object of desire in those colonies, where it was unhappily introduced in their infant state. But previous to the enfranchisement of the slave we have, it is necessary to exclude all further importations from Africa; yet our repeated attempts to effect this by prohibitions, and by imposing duties which might amount to a prohibition, have been hitherto defeated by his majesty's negative."[15]

The control of the slave trade was an important part of Jefferson's planned pathway toward both sovereignty and the gradual abolition of slavery. The 1619 Project twists the evidence. British government officials appointed by King George had often thwarted American antislavery initiatives.

In 1921, African American historian Benjamin Brawley offered a survey of the colonists' efforts to end or curb the slave trade.[16] The American colonies, for a variety of reasons, *had* passed laws against the slave trade, only to have them nullified by the British government. These attempts took place in the context of the hardening of slavery in the North American colonies, as the status of black laborers had evolved from that of the African captives purchased from Africans, captured from a Portuguese slave ship, brought to Virginia on the *White Lion*, and sold—as best we can tell—into some form of indentured servitude. The condition of race-based and life-long chattel slavery passed down from mother to child developed in a historical process of which The 1619 Project creators seem to be ignorant—even willfully ignorant, given their omission of the facts that historical consultant Leslie Harris gave the *Times* about the development of slavery from the colonial to the antebellum period.

This history is not little-known or newly discovered. Nearly a hundred years before The 1619 Project, Brawley recounted the thirteen different ways that slavery evolved in the mainland colonies[17] after a beginning so happenstance that "[a]bout the last of August" 1619—that is, the latter part of August 1619—is the closest we have to a date for it, as Captain John Smith recounted the unexpected arrival of "twenty Negars" in "a dutch man of warre" in his *Generall History of Virginia*.[18]

Brawley also detailed the many attempts on the part of the North American colonists to limit or end the slave trade during this period.[19] Even as slavery in what would become the United States was becoming more established in law, and harsher, some Americans were moving to oppose it by at least stopping the continual supply of new victims from Africa.

In Massachusetts, "Negroes were first imported" from Barbados around 1636 or 1637. Slavery was first sanctioned in 1641 for "captives, taken in just wars" (Indians) and for "such strangers...sold to us" ("Negroes"). Although Massachusetts was the first to "definitely legalize slavery, in course of time she became also the foremost representative of sentiment against the system." Early on, in 1771, a bill to end slave importations was passed by the Massachusetts asssembly. But it failed to win the royal governor's "assent."[20]

As Brawley recounted, slavery in New York began under Dutch rule and continued after English rule was established in 1664, with the enactment of a slave law in 1665 similar to Massachusetts's. "New Hampshire, profiting by the experience of the neighboring colony of Massachusetts, deemed it best from the beginning to discourage slavery," and though the number of "Negroes" there was negligible, an act was passed in 1714 "to regulate the conduct of slaves, and another four years later to regulate that of masters." A year after the grant was given for what are now Maryland and Delaware in 1632, the first enactment on slavery was passed by the legislature. In Delaware and New Jersey slavery was introduced by the Dutch but was not regulated by statute until 1702.

In Pennsylvania, although references to "Negroes" appear as early as 1639, strong objections were made to their importation. "[William] Penn in his charter to the Free Society of Traders in 1682 enjoined upon the members of this company that if they held black slaves they should be free at the end of fourteen years." In 1688 four citizens of Germantown signed and presented to the Quakers a document protesting "against Negro slavery...'the first formal action ever taken against the barter in human flesh within the boundaries of the United States.'" About eight years later, the Quakers themselves began to actively oppose slavery, although in 1700 Pennsylvania, which until then had had equal laws for black and white servants, began to "more definitely fix the status of the slave." In 1705, measures were taken against the importation of slaves, in part because of competition with white labor. Efforts to impose duties on imported slaves were disallowed by England in 1712 and in 1715, until 1729, when they were whittled down to two pounds. Slavery was officially recognized in Connecticut in 1650. Rhode Island in 1652 enacted a law "that all slaves brought into the colony should be set free after ten years of service." But by 1708 "the slave-trade was indirectly legalized by being taxed," and Rhode Island merchants became the leading slave traders to the colonies.

In North Carolina, slavery, long controlled by custom, was not recognized by law until 1715. The colony of Georgia, chartered in 1732, initially forbade slavery, on the basis of the need to defend the other English colonies from the Spaniards to the south. But pressure came from planters inspired by South Carolina, and slavery was legalized in Georgia in 1749.[21]

And Virginia, the first of the colonies to receive slaves, did not institute a fully elaborated slave code until nearly a century later, in 1705.[22] Yet, as Brawley notes, "Before 1772 Virginia passed not less than thirty-three acts looking toward the prohibition of the importation of slaves," only to see each one "annulled by England."[23]

As England became the eighteenth-century leader in the slave trade, importations to profitable plantations in the southern mainland colonies grew. England encouraged the importation of slaves, Brawley maintained. And unlike the pushers of The 1619 Project's counter-narrative, he has copious evidence to support his position. Brawley cited a British Committee on Foreign Plantations declaration from around 1663 that called black slaves "the most useful appurtenances of a plantation," and a Lords Commissioners of Trade statement twenty years later that "'the colonists could not possibly subsist' without an adequate supply of slaves." In fact, royal governors "were warned that the colonists would not be permitted to 'discourage a traffic so beneficial to the nation.'"[24]

While proposed laws against slave importation may sometimes have been inspired by selfish reasons—to prevent the need to direct resources to guard against insurrection or to assert sovereignty—they were also fueled by "new equalitarian ideals."[25] That was the case in Massachusetts, where only the veto—which Jefferson would call the "negative for suppressing every legislative attempt to prohibit or to restrain this execrable commerce"—of the King George–appointed governor prevented the anti-slavery activists' bill to end the import of slaves from becoming law, in an example that does seem to bear out Jefferson's charge that "the CHRISTIAN king of Great Britain" was "determined to keep open a market where MEN should be bought & sold." Anti-slavery sentiment was also on the march in Rhode Island, which led "the way" in July 1774 with a "law providing that all slaves imported thereafter should be freed," as Edmund S. Morgan notes in *The Birth of the Republic 1763–89.*

"Under this same impulse the Continental Congress in 1774 agreed to discontinue the slave trade and to boycott those who engaged in it. Connecticut, Delaware, Virginia, Maryland, South Carolina, and North Carolina passed laws in the 1770's and 1780's either forbidding or discouraging the importation of slaves,"[26] and the northern states soon followed by acting to end slavery itself, either by legislation or by judicial interpretation of language in state constitutions.[27] Contrary to Hannah-Jones's contention that a primary reason for America's deciding for independence was to protect slavery from a Britain that was "deeply conflicted" over the slave trade, the truth is the opposite: anti-slavery opinion and efforts by the American colonists in the 1760s and 1770s contributed significantly to the formation of the movement to end the slave trade in London—a movement that did not formally begin there until 1787.[28]

In fact, as David Brion Davis, one of the foremost authorities on the history of slavery, notes, Britain entered "the nineteenth century as the leading 'Slave Power' in the New World. By 1805, with the victory at Trafalgar, Britannia literally ruled the waves. As a result of its strategic conquests and virtual monopoly of the African slave trade, Britain enjoyed unprecedented control over the labor supply of Caribbean and Latin American slave plantation societies."[29]

Jefferson's anti-slavery argument in the passage deleted from the Declaration, like its earlier iteration in his *Summary View of the Rights of British America* for the 1774 Continental Congress, was part of his mission, carried out successfully later as president, to end the Atlantic slave trade, which he called an "abomination."[30] The *Summary* was published as a pamphlet by friends in Williamsburg and then reprinted in Philadelphia and twice in London. "Consequently," as John P. Kaminski points out in *A Necessary Evil? Slavery and the Debate over the Constitution*, "when Jefferson arrived in Philadelphia as a delegate to the Second Continental Congress, he had already established a reputation as a radical opponent of British policy...."[31]

Thomas Jefferson, "Enslaver"

Robert Paquette points out that Jefferson saw the end of the slave trade as "a necessary first step" to abolition.[32] Jefferson would consistently maintain that "total emancipation" of the slaves should be the ultimate goal—but he hoped that the end of slavery would be accomplished gradually, without black massacres of whites—"with the consent of the masters, rather than by their extirpation."[33] But according to Nikole Hannah-Jones, Jefferson was simply a hypocrite—an "enslaver" who wrote about emancipation, human rights, and equality while profiting from slavery and "torture."[34]

Thomas Jefferson was born in 1743, when slavery was fully entrenched in the southern colonies; he was surrounded by slaves from infancy. His first "recollection," from when he was two or three years old, was of "being carried on a pillow by a mounted slave" on a journey through the countryside from one estate to another, as Dumas Malone relates.[35] Unlike Abraham Lincoln, who was "born to physical hardship," and Benjamin Franklin, who knew "town life," Jefferson "grew up in the generous society which had been created in a new country and a warm climate by a group of planters, cultivating tobacco and relying on slave labor. From his earliest memories his financial position was assured, and the best educational opportunities which the Colony afforded were...available to him," thanks to his father Peter Jefferson, an enterprising and adventurous land speculator and planter.[36]

Jefferson's upbringing was not like Benjamin Franklin's hardscrabble boyhood as a printer's apprentice or the backwoods poverty experienced by Lincoln, who was hired out as a laborer by his father. Jefferson's place as a member of Virginia's gentry smoothed the way to his position in the Continental Congress, as it likely had his first election to the Virginia House of Burgesses at the age of twenty-five. But for him, service in the Continental Congress was "more of an obligation than a privilege"—one that took him away from his intellectual loves.[37]

When his father Peter Jefferson died in 1857, Thomas Jefferson was only fourteen years old. Upon reaching the age of twenty-one, he entered into his inheritance: slightly more than half his father's land, of his choice (the remainder going to his younger brother), "along with a proper share of the livestock, half of the slaves not otherwise disposed of, and the residue of the estate," as well as Peter's "books, mathematical instruments, cherry-tree desk and bookcase; and his designated servant, the 'mulatto fellow Sawney,'" who was "the most valuable slave."[38]

Thomas Jefferson's total inheritance was five thousand acres, but until his mother's death he was responsible for taking care of her portion, renting her slaves from her and farming it. At the age of twenty-two, the year before he began practicing law, Jefferson owned at least twenty slaves of his own.[39] But Jefferson the Enlightenment man of ideas did not inherit his father's talent for wealth-building. Even before his marriage on January 1, 1772, Jefferson's "land transactions" were "on the negative side," probably because he needed cash.[40]

On January 14, 1774, according to an entry in his Farm Book, Jefferson owned forty-one slaves and rented eleven from his mother. "Of these, twenty were laborers in the ground and four were discharged from labor because of age or infirmity."[41] When Jefferson went to Philadelphia in 1776 he was accompanied by a slave, "his servant Bob."[42] Malone is using Jefferson's term here; Jefferson disliked slavery so much that he spoke of those who were legally his slaves "as servants or as his people."[43] Bob was Robert Hemings.

Hannah-Jones describes how the young Robert Hemings "waited nearby to serve at his master's beck and call" even as Jefferson "drafted the text making the case for a new democratic republic." She asserts that Hemings, who was the half brother of Jefferson's own wife, "would enjoy none of those rights and liberties" that Jefferson put into the Declaration.[44]

No. Robert Hemings was the first slave that Jefferson freed. The deed of manumission, dated December 24, 1794, when Hemings was thirty-two years old, is accessible online.[45] It is the third item that comes up on a Google search for "Robert Hemings."[46]

Jefferson was sincere in his belief in the natural rights of all men and his hopes for the eventual abolition of slavery, as his life and work testify.

Was Jefferson an "immediatist abolitionist"? Did he call for abolition immediately, regardless of consequences?

No. And, as we shall see, his reasons included concern for the welfare of the slaves—given the inescapable realities of the time.

In many ways, Jefferson was a radical for his time. But he was also a pragmatist and understood that consequences of extreme actions by men in positions of leadership could have devastating effects.

That may not satisfy the creator of The 1619 Project. But she and the other contributors have strayed far from historical scholarship done by historians of the past, including pathbreaking black historians. They well understood the suffering of their forebears. But they also understood the realities of the time, the context in which this nation was formed—and America's unique promise. No doubt, they would have been stunned to hear the statement that slavery in America was "unlike anything that had existed in the world before."

Quite to the contrary, as they would correct her, and as we shall see in chapter 5.

CHAPTER 5

"Unlike Anything That Had Existed in the World Before"?

Nikole Hannah-Jones claims that "Jefferson's fellow white colonists... created a network of laws and customs, astounding for both their precision and cruelty, that ensured that enslaved people would never be treated as [human beings]"—and guaranteed that black people's status as "a subhuman race" would persist long after legal slavery ended. There were, she explains, "about 130 enslaved people that worked on the forced-labor camp [Jefferson] called Monticello," where they "struggled under a brutal system of slavery unlike anything that had existed in the world before."[1]

The condition of these "chattel" slaves was "heritable and permanent," meaning that the "enslaved status" would be passed "onto their children." An enslaved person was "not recognized as [a] human being but as property that could be mortgaged, traded, bought, sold, used as collateral, given as a gift and disposed of violently." Slaves "could not legally marry" and were "barred from learning to read," meeting "privately in groups," and owning property. "They had no claim to their own children, who could be bought, sold and traded away from them on auction blocks alongside furniture and cattle.... Enslavers and the courts did not honor kinship ties to mothers, siblings, cousins.... Enslavers could rape or murder their property without legal consequence...."[2]

This description of chattel slavery is not at all groundbreaking. In fact, it reads very much like the generic, or universal, description David Brion Davis gave in an essay published more than half a century ago, in 1968. According to Davis, the "slave was legally defined as a thing," "as at once a person and a piece of movable property," with the owner having the right to the "offspring of his female slaves" and the "right to move, sell, trade, bequeath, or give away his chattel property." Furthermore, "[t]he definition of the slave as chattel property implied a condition of rightlessness on the part of the slave." Slaves could not testify against free persons, and they were "denied legal marriage" and "legal claim to their wives and children." They "were prohibited from carrying arms, traveling at night or without permission, and acting with disrespect toward a freeman." "The penalties for such crimes as theft and assault were...more severe for slaves than for others." The "murder of a slave was thought to merit only a modest fine."[3]

But though the characteristics of slavery that Hannah-Jones lists are the same as those Davis lists, her description is glaringly wrong in one critical particular. When she claims that the slaves at Monticello "struggled under a brutal system of slavery unlike anything that had existed in the world before," she is making an error of such magnitude that only a profound ignorance of history can excuse it. "[U]nlike anything that had existed in the world before"? In reality, chattel slavery has existed across the world and throughout history, at one end of a continuum of a wide variety of extreme forms of servitude, some of them—as we shall see in detail later in this chapter—more oppressive and brutal than slavery in North America, and far beyond what the slaves at Monticello experienced. Hannah-Jones's claim flies in the face of abundant evidence from thousands of years of human history. Her contention that chattel slavery in America was unique in the history of the world is simply, demonstrably false.

Different Circles of Hell

Slavery, by its very definition, is a vulnerable and tenuous existence. Orlando Patterson, an authority on global slavery, describes the condition of the slave as "socially dead." First, he is "violently uprooted from his milieu" and "desocialized and depersonalized." Then he is introduced "into the community of his master," but as a "nonbeing." The state of enslavement consists of powerlessness and alienation from one's own blood relations and ancestors, with threat of separation from close family—spouses and children—ever present.[4] These characteristics apply across space and time.

As Davis points out, "[T]he slave was legally defined as a thing not only in the Southern United States but in ancient Egypt, Babylonia, Greece, and Rome." Richard Hellie, in a similar summary, adds tribes in the American Northwest and the "Dahomeans of West Africa"; these too "viewed slaves as things, with no rights or privileges." Davis continues: "[T]he Roman conception of the slave as at once a person and a piece of movable property prevailed in medieval France, Italy, and Spain; it was extended to Latin America and was incorporated into the 1685 Code Noir for the French colonies; and it reappeared in the laws and judicial decisions of British North America. A Virginia court merely affirmed the ancient Latin concept of chattel slavery when it ruled that 'Slaves are not only property, but they are rational beings, and entitled to the humanity of the Court, when it can be exercised without invading the rights of property.'" The American master's assertion of the right to "the offspring of his slaves" and the right to "move, sell, trade, bequest, or give away his chattel property" was an extension of the "legal notion of slavery that had persisted in Europe for more than two thousand years." The prohibition against slaves' carrying firearms or traveling without permission was common throughout the Western Hemisphere. The right to kill a slave with "impunity" was common to the "ancient Near East, the Roman Republic, Saxon England, and under certain circumstances in the Iberian Peninsula and Latin America."[5]

Though it is hard for us to imagine a worse fate than slavery as it existed in North America, slaves in other societies sometimes faced even worse prospects, such as the possibility of being used as human sacrifices, often in slow, torturous ways. Despite the editorial "word of warning" to readers of The 1619 Project that "[t]here is gruesome material in these pages, material that readers will find disturbing," there is no mention by Hannah-Jones or the other contributors of these atrocities.

Slave societies in pre-Columbian America, Western Africa, and Asia used slaves for ritual sacrifice—a practice dropped in monotheistic and capitalist cultures. According to the *Macmillan Encyclopedia of World Slavery*, "Examples [of human sacrifice of slaves] range from ancient Egyptian internment of servants with deceased royalty, through ritualized Roman confrontations of slave gladiators against savage lions and the regular immolation of large numbers of war captives in the 'annual customs' in the nineteenth-century West African kingdom of Dahomey, to the formal slaughter of single slaves by small communities of Native American hunters and gatherers."[6] In pre-Columbian America, the Tlingit and Nootka of northwestern North America (present-day British Columbia, Washington, and Oregon) "sacrificed slaves at potlatches, funerals, and other ceremonies. The Tlingit would throw bound slaves on funeral pyres of deceased relatives.... The Aleuts in Alaska often killed slaves in mourning ceremonies and in other tribal or family celebrations." The Aztecs of Mexico were famous for sacrificing as many as twenty thousand people (mainly slaves) a year, then eating parts of their bodies. The Tupinamba of present-day Brazil "turned captured enemies, including women and children, into slaves, whom they later sacrificed and sometimes ate." Others engaging in such practices include the Toradjas (in an area of present-day Indonesia), the Maori of New Zealand, and Hawaii's native people.[7]

Thanks to Muslim records, we know "that the practice of human sacrifice was widespread in West Africa in early times." In the tenth century, Ibn Hawqal referred "to the sacrifice of female slaves at the funerals of wealthy men" in the kingdom of Ghana. In the eleventh century, al-Bakri gave a "detailed account of royal funerals in Ghana, which involved the burial (apparently alive) of personal servants of the king in the royal grave. In the fourteenth century, Ibn Battuta refers to human sacrifice at the funeral of the king in Gobir, in Hausaland, involving the burial alive of friends and servants of the king and of children contributed by the leading families of Gobir." In Gobir in the 1490s, Egyptian scholar al-Suyuti recorded "the practice of substitutionary sacrifice, the killing of slaves by sick people in order to save themselves from death."[8]

Europeans also kept records of such practices: one of the earliest to do so was Valentim Fernandes, who in the early sixteenth century noted the burial of wives and attendants in the graves of kings in two African societies; slightly later, in 1539, Christian missionaries complained to the king of Benin about "his persistence in 'human sacrifices, idolatries and diabolical incantations night and day.'" They "feared that they themselves might be sacrificed 'should his fetish tell him to do so.'" In 1540 Olfert Dapper referred "to the killing of slaves at funerals of noblemen" in what is modern-day Sierra Leone, and in Benin at funerals of private citizens, including eighty slaves sacrificed at the funeral of one wealthy woman. Slaves were sacrificed at festivals, such as the Yoruba's Ogun festival. On the Ivory Coast, offerings of human sacrifices were made to gods. Twenty or twenty-three victims died for the festival in honor of deceased kings in Benin in 1786.[9]

Dahomey, the "highly autocratic and military kingdom" that dominated the area known as the "Slave Coast," saw "funeral ceremonies for King Kpengla, who died in 1789," involving the killing of some 1,500 persons, many of them war captives, over a period of two years. It is estimated that over 100 victims were sacrificed for kings at annual celebrations known as the "Watering of the Graves." King Gezo, who ascended to the throne in 1823, increased the number of victims slaughtered during these commemorations to between 249 and 300, believing that his predecessor had been overthrown for neglecting the practice of human sacrifice—which continued until the French conquest of

Dahomey in the 1890s. In the West African state of Old Calabar, "human sacrifices were occasionally offered to deities," but most were at the funerals of important men. Funeral sacrifices were abolished in 1850 "largely as a result of European influence."[10]

Most of those killed for funeral sacrifices in West Africa were wives and slaves of the deceased, and they were "at least loosely correlated with the numbers of wives and slaves that the kings and chiefs concerned possessed." The purchase of slaves for sacrifice also attested to the deceased's wealth and status. Such sacrifice in West Africa "served above all to advertise wealth and to reinforce royal authority."[11]

In Yorubaland (today Nigeria, Togo, and Benin), human sacrifice among the Ondo was not effectively ended until the British put a stop to it by force.[12] The end of the slave trade brought a quick succession of four kings between about 1845 and 1872, along with warfare, instability, and the intensification of such practices as offering sacrifices during festivals in Orisa worship. On the last day of the festival, writes Olatunji Ojo, "the ritual victim...in chains, was paraded through the streets, where many people took the opportunity to perform...supplication...and thereby transfer their sins to the victim." Then, "the victim was taken to Ora's grove and beheaded." The most valuable slaves, those in their prime, were sacrificed at the funerals of wealthy and powerful men. In 1880, the funeral of Lisa Edun, "the richest and most powerful Ondo citizen," was "accompanied by the killing of seventeen slaves, two of whom were reportedly buried alive." Old slaves who were considered worthless to their owners were sold for sacrifice. Slave wives, along with "females categorized as 'special' women," were also often reserved for sacrifice.[13]

What ended the practice were protests from potential victims and Christian missionaries (some of whom were former slaves), and "interventionist colonial regimes." "Starting in the 1860s, Britain began to treat the Yoruba hinterland as an extension of its Lagos colony...." When the anti-sacrifice agreements between 1869 and 1880 were violated, Consul Edward Hewett was sent to remind the Ondo chiefs and get a new treaty signed on December 9, 1880. Human sacrifice became clandestine, and potential victims organized and sought protection from British officials and missionaries. After two slaves were killed in a funeral in 1893, Governor George Denton sent out a warning, then had disobedient Yoruba chiefs arrested and exiled. As a result, no more cases of human sacrifice were reported after 1893.[14]

Slavery and Punishment

While Hannah-Jones calls slavery as it existed at Jefferson's Monticello "a brutal system of slavery unlike anything that had existed in the world before," in fact the discipline and punishment of slaves throughout history has "stretched the boundaries of the perverse mind," as Robert Paquette explains in a wide-ranging encyclopedia article on the topic:

> During the Roman Republic, the *paterfamilias* enjoyed virtually absolute power over his slaves, although during the Empire the state narrowed the ground on which masters could kill their slaves and reserved to itself punishment for insurrection and other major crimes by slaves. Slaves could be tortured and executed for failing to prevent a master's suicide. If a master died by violence in his own house, domestic slaves "within earshot" of the crime could be tortured and executed. Whipping was a slave punishment appropriate for wrongdoing and small crimes. Mutilation and branded foreheads identified runaway slaves. Many Roman estates had a place of detention... for unruly slaves. More serious troublemakers suffered death by burning, by being thrown to wild beasts, or more frequently, by having the head and neck immobilized with a wooden fork.... Until Constantine abolished crucifixion, it ranked as the most common form of slave execution. To inspire a salutary terror, more than six thousand crucified

followers of Spartacus were lined along the Appian Way from Capua (where the slave revolt began) to the gates of Rome.

Such practices were also common among the Greeks, Muslims, and Africans. "To some extent, every Western European country looked to the Roman past for guidance and broadly wrote slave law for its American colonies." While punishment of slave conspirators and insurrectionaries in the Americas originally "entailed a horrifying process of torture, mutilation, prolonged execution, and desecration of the corpse," slave discipline in what would become the United States became less torturous over time. By the time of Nat Turner's revolt in 1831, hanging had widely replaced the more excruciating forms of execution. Slaveholders referred to agricultural manuals that guided them on meting "punishment proportional to the crime," with "minimum force necessary for correction."[15]

Every region used its own natural products for one common form of punishment: whipping—with "*kargo*-tree switches in the Sokoto Caliphate, rhinoceros-hide lashes in South Africa, hippopotamus-hide lashes in East Africa, manatee-skin whips in Cuba...cowskin scourges in Barbados." Various limits were set: "The Spanish slave code of 1789 set a whipping limit of twenty-five lashes; the British Caribbean and states of the antebellum South tended to heed the biblical injunction (Deuteronomy 25:3) and limit stripes to thirty-nine." Still, in spite of legal limits, "slaves in every slave society died from receiving well beyond a hundred stripes."[16]

Confinement and branding were also used, though branding's popularity declined in the late eighteenth century because of pressure from humanitarians, except in South Carolina where it lasted until 1833. In East and West Africa, masters "fastened slaves with an iron collar to which a log or beam was attached by a chain—the infamous *kongo*, as it was called in Zanzibar." While laboring in the fields in the Caribbean "disobedient slaves wore collars and chains, the worst ones with bells, spikes, hooks, wood blocks, and other aggravating features."[17]

In North America, masters often used alternatives to corporal punishment, such as threats of a return to field work for urban and domestic slaves, sale to a Caribbean plantation—a viable threat precisely because conditions for slaves there were so much worse than conditions in the North American colonies—cut rations, reduced privileges and leisure time, canceled holiday celebrations, more rigorous tasks, and, in the case of men, dress in women's clothing. Rewards included "choice tasks, better food, housing, and clothing; more leisure time; permission to travel off the estate; and land for the cultivation of garden crops; and cash payments."[18]

This at least marginal softening of the conditions of enslavement in North America prevailed not just in typical rewards and punishments, but in other areas as well. Slaves in North America were sometimes "allowed to testify in certain civil cases or give evidence against a master accused of treason" and "to plead benefit of clergy and to give evidence in capital cases involving other slaves." Slave marriages were not legally recognized in Protestant America, but in practice, unlike Latin American masters, "North American masters often recognized such marriages and tried to keep families intact." By the early nineteenth century, "the killing or maiming of a Negro bondsman" was put on "the same level of criminality as the killing or maiming of a white man," and courts in southern states sometimes "held that slaves were protected by common law against such crimes as manslaughter or unprovoked battery. Georgia and North Carolina both held that slaves had a right to trial by jury, and North Carolina went so far as to recognize a slave's right to resist unprovoked attack." Such laws were often not enforced, and slaves generally were prohibited from testifying against white men. Still, as David Brion Davis concedes, "[O]ne can plausibly argue that in terms of legal protections and physical welfare American slaves by the 1850's were as favorably treated as any bondsman in history."[19]

Even Hannah-Jones's (unoriginal) claim that black slaves were seen as "subhuman" is not accurate.[20] "It is misleading," Davis points out, "to say that Anglo-American law never recognized the Negro slave as a human personality whose rights to life, food, and shelter were protected by law.

There was ample precedent for the 1846 ruling of a Kentucky judge that 'A slave is not in the condition of a horse.... He is made after the image of the Creator. He has mental capacities, and an immortal principle in his nature.... The law...cannot extinguish his high born nature, nor deprive him of many rights which are inherent in man.'"[21] Masters, Jefferson among them, did not deny that their slaves were human beings with desires and wills of their own. Even in the infamous passage in his 1785 *Notes on the State of Virginia* that is regularly quoted as evidence of Jefferson's racist belief in the natural inferiority of blacks, he hesitates to draw conclusions that "would degrade a whole race of men from the rank in the scale of beings which their Creator may perhaps have given them."[22]

To be sure, some slaves in North America were treated with unspeakable cruelty. But even the worst of those sufferings were by no means unprecedented in world history, which is rife with slavery, torture, human sacrifice, and other forms of oppression. Our horror at slavery is part of our inheritance from the Western tradition that goes far back to church fathers such as Saint Basil the Great, who lived in the fourth century. In contrast to Roman law, he said family relations of the enslaved should be honored.[23] Church laws against abuse of slaves eventually evolved into a movement to abolish slavery itself among Quakers, Evangelicals, and Enlightenment thinkers in the eighteenth century.[24] The *abolition* of slavery was truly a radical idea in human history. Today, we rightly recognize slavery itself as a crime against humanity, deserving of our absolute condemnation in all its forms. But that understanding should not blind us to the undeniable fact that slavery was accompanied by more gruesome conditions in some places and times than in others—and that the conditions in the American South in general, and at Jefferson's Monticello in particular, were far from the most "brutal" in history. Hannah-Jones attempts no balanced, fair-minded judgment on this issue. And her eagerness to define America by "a brutal system of slavery unlike anything that had existed in the world before" leads her into innumerable historical misjudgments and errors of fact.

Consider her assertion that Jefferson's slaves "were legally tortured, including by those working for Jefferson himself. They could be worked to death, and often were, in order to produce the highest profits for the white people who owned them." Visitors to Monticello, such as the French nobleman Duc de La Rochefoucauld, did not see such things. He observed that Jefferson's slaves were treated "as well as white servants." Jefferson "animated" them "by rewards and distinctions," as well as by punishment.[25] While being a slave is no enviable position, the evidence shows that Jefferson was better than most slave owners. Perhaps the best authority on the issue is the senior historian at the Thomas Jefferson Foundation at Monticello, Lucia Stanton. In an article titled "Those Who Labor for My Happiness: Thomas Jefferson and His Slaves," Stanton does not shirk from admitting that slaves were punished, but she demonstrates that the punishments were less than at most other places. Jefferson liked to motivate his slaves with "rewards" and did not like to punish. Overall, the slaves at Monticello enjoyed a greater amount of freedom than most slaves in Virginia, and a number of them were literate.[26] Hannah-Jones's claim is wildly overblown. Even from a strictly economic perspective, it made no sense to work slaves "to death." In fact, as prices for slaves rose, masters in the American South kept slaves from doing the most dangerous jobs if cheap labor from Irish or German immigrants could be found to replace them. Thus, in the antebellum South, Irish immigrants were employed in jobs "considered too hazardous even for slaves," such as coal-mining and building canals and railroads.[27]

The extreme and stereotyped view of slaves solely as "victims" with a "destroyed culture" was one shared by abolitionists, "subsequent historians," and "proslavery advocates and latter-day racists," according to Robert William Fogel and Stanley L. Engerman, but that view began to change as scholars after World War II examined plantation documents and records and the testimony of the former slaves themselves as recorded in the Works Project Administration oral histories.

By the 1960s the view had shifted "from regarding slaves mainly as victims to seeing slaves as actors able to forge, under constraints, their own lives and culture." At the forefront of this recognition of slaves' agency was Eugene Genovese.[28] In *Roll, Jordan, Roll*, which is now considered a classic history of slavery, Genovese distinguished between the relations of slaves and masters in the Caribbean, where slaves lived on plantations in single-sex barrack-like conditions with little interaction with masters (who were often absentee owners), and in the United States, where resident masters interacted with—and intruded on—their slaves. Such living arrangements reflected the maturation of slavery, a paternalistic approach that did not deny control and punishment, but one that required recognition of "mutual obligations—duties, responsibilities, and ultimately even rights."[29]

The fact that slaves were subject to punishment under the law was an implicit recognition of their human capabilities, their independent wills—a point that the escaped slave and abolitionist leader Frederick Douglass would make in arguing for abolition. Like many other slaves, Douglass did learn to read as a boy—by exchanging food pilfered from his master for lessons from sympathetic poor white boys. About half the slave states made it illegal to teach slaves to read, with stricter laws emerging after Nat Turner's rebellion in 1831. But local ordinances and the whims of slave owners made such laws difficult, if not impossible, to enforce. Frederick Law Olmsted, in his travels through the South in 1854, found that "higher law notions seem[ed] to prevail" among some and that it was "not uncommon to find that some of the domestic servants of a family have been taught to read by their mistresses or white playfellows." He guessed that "one in five of all household servants" and one in a hundred of "field-hands" "might be able to read haltingly."[30] Slaves in the antebellum South actually had a higher literacy rate than Russian serfs or Eastern European peasants at the same time.[31] A recent estimate puts the literacy rate of slaves at 10 percent. Mission schools taught some slaves owned by Cherokee Indians to read.[32]

Other Forms of Servitude

In the eighteenth century there were large numbers of slaves or persons in comparable categories of extreme dependency living in every continent except Antarctica. As Adam Smith wrote in 1776, the only place on the planet where one did not see slavery throughout most of the land was Western Europe. As the renowned economist Thomas Sowell points out, Smith was writing when "slavery still existed in Russia, Poland, Hungary, and in parts of Germany," when, in fact, "Western Europe was the only region of the world where slavery had been 'abolished altogether.'"[33] Of course, this did not include the colonies of Western Europe. English and British ships carried more than three million slaves to the Americas, less than four hundred thousand of whom ultimately came to North America. The British Caribbean imported more than two million and the French Caribbean more than one million (most to Saint-Domingue). Brazil imported almost five million.[34]

While it is true that chattel slavery was not a status legally applicable to whites in the North American colonies, most of the world's population, including whites across the globe, were living in some form of servitude in the eighteenth century. In Europe, millions lived under the system of serfdom that had arisen at the end of the Roman Empire, beginning "as a contractual relationship in which land and security had been exchanged for labor and fealty." As Shane O'Rourke explains in *The Cambridge World History of Slavery,*

> Serfdom, like slavery, was a protean institution...embedded in a wider system of privileges and responsibilities in which the lord or seigneur, as well as compelling labor service from the peasant, exercised an array of judicial, social, and physical power over the peasant. The original exchange of labor had expanded into obligations to supply produce to the lord, to use his mill, to buy beer at his tavern, to ask for permission for his children to marry...to pay to transfer his tenancy to

the next generation, and so on.... The serf was subject to the jurisdiction of his lord's court and he could be fined, beaten, or imprisoned by the order of the court.[35]

Serfdom (villeinage) had largely passed away in England and Wales by the sixteenth century, but in Eastern Europe "a second serfdom" arose at around the "same time that slavery was developing in the New World." As the international grain market expanded, the "free peasantry in Prussia, parts of the Austrian Empire, and the Polish-Lithuanian Commonwealth" became serfs. The situation got worse as you went east: "In Prussia and the Austrian Empire, the serfs still had the protection of the law," but in the Polish-Lithuanian Commonwealth and in Russia, the peasants, "like slaves, existed outside the protection of the law.... Peasants could be bought, transferred from place to place, and their families broken on the whim of the lord."[36]

According to the historian Peter Kolchin, serfs in eighteenth-century Russia had become "personal property" and were "indistinguishable from slaves." Although the legislative code of 1649 had prohibited the movement of serfs, noblemen acted as if the serfs who lived and worked on their land were their own personal property. By the end of Peter I's reign (1682–1725) and continuing through that of Catherine II (1762–1796)—she actually applied the Russian word for slave to serfs—"any idea that serfdom meant simply prohibition of movement or that serfs were tied to the land was gone. Serfs could be bought and sold, traded, won and lost at cards."[37] It was not until Western ideas about equality and freedom challenged the system, beginning in Western Europe and spreading east, that serfdom was abolished. The major emancipations of serfs in continental Europe began in Savoy, Italy, in 1771, but it was not until the period of the American Civil War that Russia and Romania freed their serfs, in 1861 and 1864, respectively.[38]

And then there was the enslavement of white Europeans and Americans by Muslims in North Africa, a topic which garners disbelief these days, as Bruce Bawer related in an August 1, 2020, article, written shortly after a statue of Miguel de Cervantes, the great Spanish writer who was enslaved for five years in Algiers, was defaced in San Francisco. Bawer's post on Facebook about the fact that over one million whites had been sold into slavery in Africa from the 1400s to the 1800s was met with incredulity or dismissal. These slaves were abandoned by the European powers until the eighteenth century, when they began making payments to North African powers to protect their citizens. But after declaring independence the United States refused to pay such tribute, and ultimately Thomas Jefferson as president sent the Marines to North Africa, where "under the command of William Eaton, U.S. Consul in Tripoli, they blockaded ports, attacked fleets, and won the decisive 1805 Battle of Derna" in the First Barbary War. The Second Barbary War, with the assistance of British and French naval actions, "radically diminished the Islamic trade in white slaves." With the French colonization of North Africa and advancements in Western ships and armaments, it came to a complete end.[39]

Even whites who were not literally enslaved worked in servitude in abysmal conditions. Some, like the Irish peasants, faced starvation. Thomas Sowell points out that in the 1830s "[s]laves in America had a longer life expectancy than peasants in Ireland, ate better, and lived in cabins" that were better built and more spacious than the "huts" of Irish peasants. Though legally free, the Irish "lived as a conquered people in their own land." The British had confiscated most Irish land and become landlords to Irish tenant farmers, and they ruled absolutely, including in asserting sexual access to wives and daughters[40]—in the manner of some slave owners.

And some Irish were forcibly sent to the colonies, including to North America. Most were "taken up as vagrants by virtue of Elizabethan statute," an authority that was abused by merchants and ship captains.[41] A May 1653 proclamation declaring "that all laws in force in England…be enforced in Ireland" led to overseers falsely charging the Irish with vagrancy, idleness, and begging in order to sell them.[42]

Later, in the nineteenth century, the Irish, like most other immigrants to America, came in the hold of cargo ships, where men and women slept on shelves three feet wide and six feet long, "stacked up with just over two feet of space between them," with "no toilet facilities" and brackish river water to drink. Epidemics of typhus, cholera, and other fatal diseases erupted. In the worst year, 1847, about forty thousand, or 20 percent, of the Irish famine immigrants died on the way to America or upon landing. "By comparison," Thomas Sowell has pointed out, "the loss of life among slaves transported from Africa in British vessels in the nineteenth century was about 9 percent."[43]

The British forced many other whites into servitude through impressment—forced service in the navy. About half of the five hundred thousand men mobilized to fight the wars against France and Spain between 1688 and 1815 were impressed. Sailors were "second only to enslaved Africans as the largest group of forced laborers in the eighteenth-century British Empire," though "a very distant second to slaves, both in total numbers and in the condition of their bondage" (seamen went free at the ends of wars and received wages and other material benefits).[44] Quakers and members of other religious groups subject to the Conventicle Act of 1664, which forbade attendance at unlawful religious meetings, were exiled for their third offense, and those who could not pay their transportation were indentured.[45]

Indentured Servitude

This brings us to those who were already living and working in Jamestown in 1619 when the privateering vessel carrying Africans arrived. The indentured servants working in the tobacco fields that day were not employed in free or wage labor. They made up 70 to 85 percent of the European immigrants in the Chesapeake region for most of the seventeenth century. They "played a central role in the development of British America" as the earliest of roughly 250,000 indentured migrants to reach the colonies in the seventeenth century.[46] Throughout the seventeenth century, indentured servants made up 80 percent of Europeans arriving in Virginia and Maryland; between 1700 and 1775, they made up 90 percent.[47] Thus we can say that in the seventeenth century white indentured servants were the major labor force. Even as late as 1649, blacks, numbering three hundred, made up only 2 percent of Virginia's population of fifteen thousand.[48]

Jefferson's second draft of the Virginia Constitution (1776) opposed forms of servitude including indenture.[49] Indentured servants agreed to contracts of servitude because it seemed like a preferable option given the harsh conditions of the time. In seventeenth-century England, as a result of the shift from an agricultural to a mercantile economy, large numbers of the poor were "turned away from their manorial occupations and set adrift.... [They] swarmed to the cities, idle, masterless, unwanted persons." They turned to crime, as Abbot Smith recounts in *Colonists in Bondage: White Servitude and Convict Labor in America, 1607–1776*, and the punishments were draconian—with three hundred crimes categorized as felonies. Stealing "anything of value greater than a shilling, was thus made punishable by death." As a result, thousands "were condemned to the gallows." Such punishment, however, was "profoundly mitigated by two practices, the pleading of clergy and the granting of royal pardons." Under the "ancient theory that all who could read were in holy orders," anyone who could read was spared death and only branded on the thumb. Royal pardons were also granted to ordinary offenders; at least half of felons sentenced to death received them. And before 1718, those pardoned could be transported to the colonies. Although it was illegal to "inflict a penalty of exile or transportation," it was "not illegal to pardon a felon upon the condition that he transport himself out of the country." Like exiled religious dissenters, criminals who had been pardoned on condition of self-exile but could not pay for their own transportation indentured themselves as servants in exchange for their passage. Sheriffs and merchants stood at the ready to arrange the transportation of the destitute and to profit from the arrangements.[50]

Some indentured servants were mere children. Poor children wandering the streets of London posed a problem, so around 1617 authorities consulted with the Virginia Company about indenturing them. A collection authorized by the lord mayor was taken up, and a hundred children were sent to Virginia in 1618. Several hundred arrived during the 1620s. In 1619, the company sent young women to the colony to be sold to the planters as wives.[51] Some of the indentured were children sent by their parents to learn a trade, to establish a foothold in the New World for their families, or both. The word "kidnap" is derived from the young and naïve victims of agents who "filled ships with human cargoes by using deceit, drink, and violence on their unwary marks."[52]

German "redemptioners," who were sold upon arrival to pay for their transportation, fell victim to unscrupulous emigrant agents who stole their meager possessions from their baggage. Sailors often picked off what the agents missed. Unable to speak English, redemptioners became "easy victims to unscrupulous merchants and captains, signing agreements they could not understand." Once in Pennsylvania, families were sometimes split apart and "sold into remote parts of the province," with children between ages five and ten bound out to serve until they reached the age of twenty-one, while those under five were given away for free and required to serve until age twenty-one in exchange for "their bringing up."[53] Once they had fulfilled their indentures, the Germans could expect a modest payment or land. But the land was often in the frontier territory of the Mohawk Valley or western Pennsylvania, where many were killed by the Indians or enslaved by them.[54]

And that was the fate of those who survived the crossing of the Atlantic, a journey that typically took eight to ten weeks during the seventeenth and eighteenth centuries.[55] Seasickness and poor nutrition weakened passengers and led to the spread of fatal diseases in the tightly packed quarters. On slave ships, even the white crewmen died in staggering numbers from disease and poor nutrition. In fact, although slaves died in greater numbers during the Middle Passage, the crewmen died in greater numbers if the three legs of the voyage—to Africa, to the Caribbean or the American South to sell the slaves, then home to New England or Europe—are taken into account. The Germans and Irish who took the place of English indentured servants in the eighteenth and nineteenth centuries suffered high mortality on the terrible sea voyages. As we have already seen, the mortality rate at sea for Irish immigrants in one year of the potato famine was higher than the average rate for slaves in the Middle Passage. In 1749, two thousand Germans died on voyages to Philadelphia alone.[56]

Once on shore, the indentured servants, especially the later arrivals, who did not have prearranged contracts, would be advertised in the newspapers and then inspected on board by prospective buyers who "walked them up and down, felt of their muscles, judged their states of health and morality, [and] conversed with them to discover their degrees of intelligence and docility." Some servants compared themselves "to horses displayed for sale." Sometimes merchants came aboard and bought them by the lot, then drove "them through the country 'like a parcel of Sheep,' and selling them here and there." Such degrading behavior, Smith tells us, was "the accustomed thing."[57]

While indenture offered opportunities for many who otherwise had none, the path was not easy. In British North America contracts were usually longer and indentured servants faced a likelier chance of being resold than in the French colonies or in England.[58] Because of the longer terms and "the colonial legislation that came to define the institution," indentured servitude in North America was "more clearly a genuine system of white servitude than its English counterpart."[59] Once indentured servants began their terms, they were considered "property" or "chattel of the master."[60] They did enjoy "such rights as the ability to sue in court and to give testimony, rights typically denied to black slaves," but they were "universally subject to strict requirement of specific performance of their contractual obligations by colonial courts, and were subject to harsh punishment for attempts to avoid them," according to David Galenson.[61] Or they could just be sold by the master.[62] Indentured servants were dependent on their masters for food, shelter, and clothing, and they could not travel more than ten miles from their premises without a written pass.[63] They could not marry without their master's consent.[64]

Punishment of indentured servants, like that of slaves, commonly involved whipping. In fact, whipping was a punishment still common in England and in the colonies well into the nineteenth century for wide swathes of the population. Masters whipped their servants and husbands whipped their wives "to a reasonable degree without criticism," as Abbot Smith remarks.[65] Children, particularly male children, were frequently whipped in homes and schools. Soldiers, too, were routinely punished by whipping.[66] For disobedience, the indentured servant could be punished with up to ten lashes[67] or with an extension of his or term.[68] More severe whippings were sometimes given. In 1673, for "scandalous and abusive language against his master," a servant was meted thirty-nine lashes and required to make an apology on his knees in the General Court of Middlesex County, Virginia.[69] Indentured servants were also whipped for running away, and for fornication—twenty-one lashes administered to both the man and woman.[70]

In Jamestown in 1619, the "first legislative body in America" drew up laws governing indentures. After affirming the laws of England, recognizing contracts made there and upholding the authority of the British officials, they outlined colonial conditions, prohibiting trade with Indians and women servants' marrying "without the consent of their masters." For the crimes of swearing and Sabbath-breaking (for which freemen paid fines), servants were to be whipped. "Finally," as Smith recounts, "sitting rather as a high court than as a legislative body, they heard a petition of Captain William Powell against one of his servants for various misdoings, and sentenced the culprit to stand four days with his ears nailed to the pillory."[71]

Indenture often offered opportunities to learn a trade or acquire a plot of land. But according to Smith, "ambitious and intelligent" servants were in the minority.[72] He estimated that "about one in ten was a sound and solid individual, who would if fortunate survive his 'seasoning' work" and eventually become "decently prosperous." Another one in ten might "become an artisan, following his trade in some town, or perhaps a hired overseer on a plantation, and thus live a useful and comfortable life without owning any land."

What about the rest? "The other eight died during their servitude, returned to England after it was over, or became 'poor whites,' and occupied no substantial position in the colonies either as workers or proprietors.... Doubtless they were not the vicious wretches observers claimed them to be, but certainly they were shiftless, hopeless, ruined individuals, raked up from the lower reaches of English society by emigrant agents, kidnappers, and officers of the law."[73]

Among the minority who made good in expanding their land holdings, sometimes by marriage, seven served as burgesses in the Virginia Assembly in 1629 and fifteen in the Maryland Assembly of 1637–1638. A few acquired fame: Charles Thomson, "for many years secretary of the Continental Congress, Matthew Thornton, a signer of the Declaration of Independence, Matthew Lyon, the belligerent congressman...Daniel Dulany, a distinguished lawyer of the early eighteenth century in Maryland," and Benjamin Franklin's maternal grandmother.[74]

Regardless of Smith's low opinion of them, indentured servants ensured the survival of colonies south of New England. "Without such immigration," historian Aaron Fogelman remarks, "they would have collapsed. Nearly 150,000 English immigrants arrived before 1700, providing labor, markets, and settlers...."[75]

Peculiar, but Not Uncommon

While the treatment of indentured servants may strike modern sensibilities as degrading and cruel, and though there were cases where they died from overwork or ill treatment, they did have rights under the law denied to slaves. And, providing they behaved, indentured servants could look forward to release from bondage. Masters sometimes manumitted slaves, but increasing legal restrictions were put on the practice throughout the antebellum South.

In North America chattel slavery on the basis of race evolved from what was likely a form of indentured servitude—as Nell Irvin Painter pointed out, though not in relation to The 1619 Project, where her correction was more needed. Yes, the "20 or so Africans" arriving on the *White Lion* were sold. They joined "a population consisting largely of European indentured servants, mainly poor people from the British Isles...."[76] Indeed, during those early years, they would likely have been working side by side in the tobacco fields with the white indentured servants.

But by the time of the American Revolution, four hundred thousand slaves, the largest group in the thirteen colonies, made up about 17 percent of the total population. In contrast, Germans and Scots-Irish (from Northern Ireland) were each about 10 percent.[77] Slaves made up much larger shares of the population in the southern states: 41 percent in Virginia, 34 percent in North Carolina, 37 percent in Georgia, and 53 percent in South Carolina.[78] Their large numbers were due to natural increase. This excess of slave births over slave deaths was a result of conditions much better than those endured by slaves in the Caribbean and Brazil,[79] where slaves were often housed in single-sex barracks[80] and slave owners replenished their supply of slave labor not by natural increase but by buying new slaves. Economist Thomas Sowell explains the grim calculus: "In a country much closer to Africa, such as Brazil, where slave prices were accordingly cheap, slaves might be worked to death and then replaced by new arrivals, but this was too costly to be done in the United States...."[81]

Hannah-Jones's description of Monticello as a "forced-labor camp" is meant to recall the twentieth-century camps of the Nazi and Communist regimes, where millions deemed genetically inferior or ideologically suspect were either outright murdered or worked to death.[82]

To the contrary, slavery in the United States was part of a commonly accepted practice of the time. It evolved within a complex transnational and global network of trade and cross-cultural exchanges. In *The Cambridge World History of Slavery*, Sue Peabody comments on the "remarkable continuity in the ways that European, African, and American societies legitimated the process of enslavement." Likewise, David Eltis remarks, "The similarity of the mechanisms for depriving people of their liberty on all four continents is striking."[83]

Thomas Sowell sums up the historical continuities:

> In ancient Rome, individual Romans might be reduced to slavery as punishment for transgressions, but ordinarily slaves were non-Romans captured in battle or acquired in trade. Similarly, in a later era, it was common for the Ottoman Empire to enslave Europeans or Africans...or for people in Asia to enslave both non-Asians and Asians belonging to a different race or class.... [E]xcept for debt-bondage or bondage as punishment, the process of enslavement has generally been one of enslaving outsiders of one sort or another, whether by race, religion, nationality, or other characteristics. For centuries in Europe, it was considered legitimate for the Christians of Western Europe to enslave "pagans" from the Balkans or Eastern Europe....[84]

Definitions of "outsider" varied among Muslims, Christians, and non-Muslim West Africans. Religious difference that translated into ethnocentric prejudice justified mass enslavements the world over long before Columbus ventured from the Spanish port of Palos in 1492. In 1786, John Adams and Thomas Jefferson, meeting in London with the ambassador from Tripoli, learned that the Koran specified that "all nations who should not have acknowledged their authority were sinners," so that it was the Muslims' duty "to make slaves of all they could take as Prisoners." In West Africa, according to Peabody, "[e]thnic or political ties were the crucial distinction." Enslavement was passed down through the generations. A man's "lineage, down to the fourth generation," could be sold if he had been condemned as a witch, according to the sixteenth-century Portuguese traveler Alvares d'Almada.

Those found guilty of murder or adultery, or unable to pay fines, were sometimes enslaved.[85]

"Human nature produced war, and war produced slaves," explains Robert Paquette in his article on methods of enslavement in the *Macmillan Encyclopedia of World Slavery*. In fact, "respected ancient and modern thinkers defended enslavement as a leap forward in human progress, for while the alleged barbarians of the world had put prisoners of war to the sword, civilized people had put them to work. War supplied millions of such enslaved outsiders to the Roman Empire, the Muslim world, and the plantation economies of the Americas."[86]

Other methods of enslavement were described by the French philosopher Jean Bodin in 1576. These included brigandage, kidnapping, piracy, and self-enslavement to avoid starvation, debt, and crime. Many people were born into slavery, including in West Africa, ancient Rome, China, and the Near East. The ancient Greeks acquired child slaves through abandonment or sale by their parents. In China, a person—or his relatives—could be enslaved for committing a crime, and "unknown numbers" were driven to enslave themselves and to sell their children into slavery by poverty and famine. "A true slave society" that relied on insiders "emerged in medieval Korea during the Koryo dynasty (AD 918–1392)."[87]

Was slavery in America really "unlike anything that had existed in the world before"? What about the Middle Ages, when "Muslims obtained large numbers of Christians and pagan slaves from Danish Vikings, who raided and subjugated the Anglo-Saxons; and from Swedish Vikings, who penetrated into Russia and reduced many Slavs to slavery"; when "Jewish merchants acquired slaves for Muslim consumers throughout the Mediterranean and beyond, and in Verdun (northern France) apparently set up a notorious house of castration to produce valuable eunuchs"; when Ottoman Turkish slave traders "purchased captive Caucasian women and children from Caucasians. . ."?[88]

How about Anglo-Saxon England before the Norman Conquest of 1066? At that time, slaves made up "about 10 percent of the total population, and 20 percent in some counties," the numbers fluctuating "with the intensity of violence: invasions, warfare, raiding, and kidnapping. Anglo-Saxon invaders enslaved Celts; Viking invaders enslaved Anglo-Saxons, warring Anglo-Saxon kingdoms enslaved Anglo-Saxons." And self-enslavement "became as familiar as the dislocation, poverty, and debt generated by the chronic warfare and raiding."

There are also the Byzantine Empire, the Ottoman Empire, Russia, the Muslim empire, the native tribes of North, Central, and South America, the shifting nations of Africa, and more.[89] Because of the wider geographical reach of European civilization, "outsiders" came from farther distances. By the fifteenth century, slavery in Europe, where it still existed, "was confined to non-Christians or natives of Africa and their immediate descendants. A similar pattern was established in the Islamic world," writes Eltis.[90]

What *was* new, different, and unusual in Thomas Jefferson's day was freedom, including free labor for wages. Thomas Paine's "polemical response" to Edmund's Burke's *Reflections on the Revolution in France*— Paine claimed "that it was an unspeakable violation of the natural rights of man that one person should be owned as the property of another"— was a novel and revolutionary idea at the time, as Robert Paquette pointed out at a Constitution Day event in 2020. He stressed, "*In no way*, from a global perspective, did the Old South's peculiar institution look peculiar in the sense of being uncommon." In fact, "the far more recent, far more peculiar, institution is free or wage labor, where labor is left to contract and consent." Thus Jefferson should be given credit for moving "expeditiously to end the Atlantic slave trade with the help of friends in Congress at the soonest possible date."[91]

Ironically, it was not slavery in North America that was "unlike anything that had existed in the world before." Far from it. As copious evidence demonstrates, forms of slavery just as brutal had been tragically, deplorably common through all of world history; and even crueler forms of enslavement—involving large-scale human sacrifice and the routine use of torture to death—are also well known to history.

But there was something else in eighteenth-century America that really was "unlike anything that had existed in the world before." It was a sea change in thinking. It began in the West, evolved through the centuries, spread to the colonies, and was daringly implemented in a new form of popular government. It was kicked off with a Declaration of Independence and fought for in a Revolutionary War. Recognition of the "unalienable Rights" of "Life, Liberty, and the pursuit of Happiness" which the founders had staked their lives and sacred honor on spread. Within this context, the belief that slavery or servitude was the preordained lot of some human beings was rejected unequivocally.

That the American experiment offered unprecedented opportunities and blessings was a fact recognized even by those who had no or only partial access to them. These, of course, are African Americans, who were either enslaved or faced discrimination. But they appreciated far more—and knew far more—than the participants in The 1619 Project. And that included the meaning of the year 1619.

CHAPTER 6

A History Neither
New nor True

Nikole Hannah-Jones and the editors of the *New York Times* would have readers believe that their Project is a revelation about a long-lost history. But in fact, the events of August 20 (or thereabout), 1619—when the *White Lion,* an English privateering vessel operating under a Dutch letter of marque, arrived at Jamestown carrying twenty or so Africans taken from a Portuguese slave ship—have long been well known by historians, and also long commemorated by African Americans. The introductory paragraph printed on the cover of the *New York Times Magazine* issue that inaugurated The Project ends, "On the 400th anniversary of this fateful moment, it is finally time to tell our story truthfully."[1] Ironically, that statement itself is anything but truthful.

A Century of Commemorating 1619

Hannah-Jones did not discover the significance of the year 1619. Going back more than a hundred years before The 1619 Project, a long list of black Americans have remembered the 1619 landing as a watershed event, a kind of inglorious Plymouth Rock landing for African Americans. In 1913, for example, the prominent lawyer, writer, and civil rights activist James Weldon Johnson, to commemorate the Emancipation Proclamation, composed the poem "Fifty Years 1863–1913," which asked readers to

> Look farther back! Three centuries!
> To where a naked, shivering score,
> Snatched from their haunts across the seas,
> Stood, wild-eyed, on Virginia's shore.[2]

In 1883, a book considered to be the "earliest attempt at a comprehensive and scholarly history of African Americans" was published by abolitionist George Washington Williams, the first black graduate of Andover-Newton Seminary.[3] Its title is *History of the Negro Race from 1619 to 1880*. Williams called Virginia "the mother of slavery as well as 'the mother of Presidents.' Unfortunate for her, and unfortunate for the other colonies, and thrice unfortunate for the poor Coloured people, who from 1619 to 1863 yielded their liberty, their toil,—unrequited,—their bodies and their intellects to an institution that ground them to powder. No event in the history of North America has carried with it to its last analysis such terrible forces."[4]

In his 1897 *Past and Future of the Negro Race in America*, William Decker Johnson, a minister of the African Methodist Episcopal Church and founder of an industrial college in Georgia, marked 1619 as a "fatal, or eventful, year" when "the slave trade traveled from Africa to America" and "fourteen Negroes were carried by a Dutch man-of-war to Virginia" to be sold to the English colonists.[5] Decorated black Civil War veteran Joseph T. Wilson also noted the year 1619 in his popular history *The Black Phalanx: A History of the Negro Soldiers of the United States in the Wars of 1775–1812, 1861–'65*, published in 1887.[6] He refers to 1619 as the year beginning a period of "resignation to fate" and "bondage" in America, without "hope of liberty"—until 1770.[7]

In his 1922 classic *The Negro in Our History*, Carter G. Woodson, founder of the groundbreaking *Journal of Negro History*,[8] described the appearance of the "Dutch manne-of-war" that sold the people of Jamestown "twenty negars." He commented that this event "introduce[d] in the United States the curse of slavery from which this country has not yet been thoroughly redeemed."[9] "The Ship" was also featured in poet and fiction writer Arna Bontemps's 1948 juvenile history, *Story of the Negro*, as the title for his first chapter. It opens, "The story begins with a mystery—a ship without a name. It flew under the Dutch flag and had the appearance of an armed trader...." It was "the ship that brought the stolen Africans to the young colony at Jamestown."[10]

In 1950, J. Saunders Redding opened *They Came in Chains* with this description:

> Sails furled, flag drooping at her rounded stern, she rode the tide in from the sea. She was a strange ship; indeed, by all accounts, a frightening ship, a ship of mystery. Whether she was trader, privateer, or man-of-war no one knows. Through her bulwarks black-mouthed cannon yawned. The flag she flew was Dutch; her crew a motley. Her master, a Captain Tope. Her true registry? Unknown. Her port of call, an English settlement, Jamestown, in the colony of Virginia. She came, she traded, and shortly afterwards was gone. Probably no ship in modern history has carried a more portentous freight. Her cargo? Twenty slaves.[11]

Though this paragraph suggests an ominous beginning, Redding also notes that near Jamestown "Negro slaves had lived almost a hundred years before. But they rebelled, and the Spanish settlement they helped to found was soon abandoned."[12] In a 2017 article in *Smithsonian* magazine, historian Michael Guasco points out that enslaved Africans, "part of a Spanish expedition to establish an outpost" in 1526 in what is present-day South Carolina, had rebelled, thus ending the

Spaniards' plans. And there are suggestions that scores of Africans who had been plundered from the Spanish accompanied Sir Francis Drake when he arrived at Roanoke Island in 1586. Guasco complains of the "overstated significance of 1619—still a common fixture in American history curricul[a]."[13]

To be sure, the year 1619 makes a stark contrast with 1620. The Pilgrims were religious dissenters who came to North America on the *Mayflower* of their own free will. Historical and popular accounts have depicted that event with varying degrees of accuracy. But insofar as the Pilgrims' story is about overcoming obstacles to build a new community in a strange land, the similar achievement of African Americans, who in 1619 had to travel a much longer distance in a state of servitude, deserves a gloried remembrance. The November 16, 1893, issue of the *Christian Recorder*, a black newspaper, asked the question, "What has the Negro done to develop America?," and ranged over a "territory of investigation" of that question from "the present moment as far back in 1619, when our unfortunate forefathers were first preceded to this country as base, ignoble slaves." In 1898, that same newspaper said that 1619 was "the beginning," and 1863 "the ending of the most iniquitous system of wrong robbery and oppression that ever prevailed in the world's history."[14]

Whether the anniversary of the Emancipation Proclamation or 1619 should mark the "phenomenal progress" of African Americans was a topic of debate in the pages of *The Freeman* in 1909.[15] In July 1919, W. E. B. Du Bois, the editor of the NAACP monthly organ *The Crisis*, appealed to readers to send announcements about tercentenary celebrations. The following month he reported on a "celebration of the 300th anniversary of the landing of Negros in America" that drew over "1,000 colored persons" to Charleston, South Carolina. Conducted under the "auspices of the United Colored Churches," the event "set forth Negro American progress and achievement in pageant, pictures, music and speech." Tercentenary celebrations in Richmond and Kansas City also emphasized the progress made.[16]

Errors of Fact and Law

Hannah-Jones and the other creators of The 1619 Project fail to acknowledge this long history of commemorating 1619. Instead they pose as groundbreakers who are revealing hitherto unknown history—now that "it is finally time to tell our story truthfully." As we have seen, that "finally" is not accurate—and neither is the "truthfully." There are profound historical errors at the heart of The 1619 Project—for a thorough examination of the claims that slavery in the North American colonies was "unlike anything that had existed in the world before" and an unusually "brutal system," see chapter 5 above; for the claim that the colonists declared independence "to protect the institution of slavery," see chapter 4. It is clear that the history recounted by The 1619 Project is riddled with mistakes of fact, small and large.

Consider Nikole Hannah-Jones's account of the 1619 events on which The Project is based. According to her inaugural essay, the "Jamestown colonists bought 20 to 30 enslaved Africans from English pirates" who "had stolen them from a Portuguese slave ship that had forcibly taken them from what is now the country of Angola." They were "among the 12.5 million Africans who would be kidnapped" and brought in chains across the Atlantic Ocean, with 400,000 of those "sold into America," where they built the wealth of the nation and taught Americans what democracy is, thus becoming the true founders.[17]

It's unclear where Hannah-Jones got her figure of "20 to 30 enslaved Africans." The historical sources—John Rolfe's 1620 letter to Sir Edwin Sandys and Captain John Smith's 1624 *Generall History of Virginia*—mention, respectively, "20. and Odd Negroes" and "twenty Negars."[18] Linda M. Heywood and John K. Thornton's account of the 1619 arrival, published in the *Virginia Magazine of History & Biography* for the quadricentennial of the event, explains that the "'20. and odd Negroes' who came to Point Comfort in 1619 were captured on the high seas from a Portuguese vessel making its way from Luanda, Angola, to Vera Cruz, Mexico." The men who extracted the slaves from the Portuguese vessel were privateers rather than the "pirates" of Hannah-Jones's description.

"A privateer was an armed vessel, or the commander and crew of a vessel, that was licensed to attack and seize the vessels of a hostile nation." After a designated amount of the goods was given to the sovereign, the rest was divided among the ship owners, captain, and crew. A "pirate" was legally defined in English law from the time of Henry VII as someone who robs and plunders on the sea, and piracy was subject to punishment under the law. But during the Thirty Years' War (1618–1648) the practice of seizing "shipping of any sort from the Spanish and Portuguese" was "unofficially renewed" by the English and Dutch. In 1619, two English privateers received letters of marque (licenses to capture enemy shipping)—John Jope, captain of the *White Lion*, from Prince William of Orange; and Daniel Elfrith, captain of the *Treasurer*, from the Duke of Savoy. The Portuguese ship they attacked, the *São João Batista*, originally carried 350 slaves, but each English privateer was able to take only about 30 slaves apiece.[19]

But that distinction is a minor point compared with the historical sleight of hand that follows. How did these Africans come to be on the Portuguese ship in the first place? Hannah-Jones refers to "the Portuguese slave ship that had forcibly taken them from what is now the country of Angola." Here, as elsewhere in The Project, she couples distortion of American history with romanticization of West African history. Honest black intellectuals such as Thomas Sowell, without ignoring the suffering of slaves in America, acknowledged that West Africa was a great slave-trading region "before, during, and after the white man arrived" and that "[i]t was the Africans who enslaved their fellow Africans...."[20]

And much earlier, abolitionist Frederick Douglass, who minced no words in his condemnation of white slaveholders, also disparaged "the savage chiefs of the western coasts of Africa, who for ages have been accustomed to selling their captives into bondage and pocketing the ready cash for them."[21] Black Civil War veteran Joseph Wilson wrote that the slave had been "[r]educed from his natural state of freedom by his misfortune in tribal war, to that of a slave, and then transported by the consent of his captors and enemies to these shores...."[22] *Journal of Negro History* founder Carter Woodson admitted, "That the Negro should be enslaved was in the halcyon days of the institution no exception to the rule. Slavery was once the normal condition of the majority of the inhabitants of the world." The Muslim slave trade, which "extended to the very interior of the continent and became the most cruel traffic in human flesh theretofore known to the world," had "only of late...been decidedly checked...."[23]

J. Saunders Redding, who was the first black American to teach at an Ivy League college, pointed out in 1950 that slavery was "an old, old story" and "in existence since the first man who, by luck or the dim recognition of his superior endowment, discovered that he held an edge over a rival.... Slavery became entrenched in human customs before man had got well used to walking upright." Redding was no conservative, but his description of slavery as "one of the oldest and most widespread institutions on Earth" is very much like Thomas Sowell's. Before Columbus's first voyage, Africa probably had more slaves than any other continent. "There was slavery in Africa," Redding wrote, "long before the coming of the white man." It was especially prevalent along the west coast of Africa, "an area that teemed with barbaric life," where "millions of people" were "divided into hundreds of small, independent tribes. Proximity led to quarrels on the faintest pretext; quarrels led to war. Strong, victorious tribes, when they did not kill, took captives and made them slaves."[24]

Facts about the operation of the slave trade in West Africa, though well known by scholars both black and white during the nineteenth century, have often been glossed over for ideological purposes. W. E. B. Du Bois fell for this temptation, tending to ignore or explain away such unpleasantness as the continued slavery in Liberia in the 1920s and 1930s and the exploitation of African laborers by Africans with blanket pronouncements about European and American imperialism. Africana studies departments have followed suit. Popular accounts of slavery, though detailed in their descriptions of the voyage and the travails of slaves on

American plantations, strongly imply that white slave traders kidnapped Africans as they were enjoying being "free" with "families, and farms, and lives and dreams," as Hannah-Jones puts it.[25] Rather than admitting the truth about a trade in which African peoples were deeply involved, she speaks generally of "people stolen from western and central Africa" and "kidnapped from their homes" and claims, of the 1619 arrivals in particular, that the Portuguese slave ship "had forcibly taken them from what is now the country of Angola."[26] While it is literally true that the Portuguese slave ship had "forcibly taken" them from Africa—in the sense that they were being transported against their will—it is not true, as Hannah-Jones cleverly insinuates, that they were "taken" by the Portuguese sailors in the sense of being "kidnapped from their homes" and reduced to slavery by those European men. This fudging of the facts allows Hannah-Jones to sidestep the issue of African agency in the human trafficking.

The vast majority of slaves brought to the Americas derived from exchanges with West African traders. The story of the Africans who were brought ashore to Jamestown is a slightly different story from most, but they were certainly not kidnapped by the crew of the slave ship. Those who landed in Jamestown in 1619 came from the Kingdom of Ndongo in the Kongo-Angola region of precolonial West Africa. Under a charter given to Paulo Dias de Nováis, the kingdom had become a Portuguese colony in 1575 and was ruled by war-faring kings who "demanded about a dozen slaves each year from its several hundred local political leaders, called sobas," as historians Linda M. Heywood and John Thornton explain. Portugal waged war alongside African allies in Angola. Congolese who had converted to Catholicism supported Nováis as soldiers and porters. "Using his naval capacity, and by making strategic alliances with Ndongo's opponents or local provincial rulers," Nováis made an "inland push" by way of the Kwanza River, capturing "thousands of slaves," which he exported to Brazil or the Spanish Indies. Dias de Nováis died before he could finalize the initial conquest, and in 1590, a year after his death, the Ndongo inflicted a crushing defeat on a Portuguese army sent against them.

Chastened by this defeat, the Portuguese crown encouraged the simple purchase of slaves, although some governors still sought to maximize profits by capture. One of these, Luis Mendes de Vasconcellos, augmented his forces with the Imbangala, a fierce marauding itinerant band of warriors, and with "dissident Ndongo nobles." With these allies, Vasconcellos was able to overwhelm the Ndongo army and, as a result, was able to export fifty thousand slaves over a three-year period. The war captives were marched to Luanda, sold to Portuguese traders, and then placed on board the *Sâo Joâo Batista*. The *White Lion* and the *Treasurer* intercepted the ship on its way to the Spanish colonial port of Vera Cruz.[27]

Until the late nineteenth century, Western European slave traders remained largely confined to the West African littoral because of epidemic disease and resistance by Africans to European intrusions farther inland. Interior campaigns had little hope of success without the support of African allies. "Portuguese soldiers could not win unsupported by Africans and were regularly massacred when they tried to do so," as the attempt "to conquer the Bissagos Islands" in 1535 had demonstrated.[28] The coastline of Africa, severely lacking in natural harbors, made it almost impossible for Europeans to make "seaborne attack on the mainland." In 1456, the Portuguese crown had sent Diogo Gomes "to negotiate treaties of peace and commerce with the African rulers on the coast," and such trade—on the Africans' terms—became the "rule."[29] Europeans were happy to take advantage of the "large-scale trading and possession of slaves," already long in place and integral to Africa's domestic economy.[30] According to the Slave Voyages database, about 390,000 slaves were imported into the North American colonies and states. The total number for Great Britain's colonies was nearly 3 million. In contrast, Brazil imported almost 5 million slaves.[31]

Within West Africa, war and lesser acts of violence predominated as the means of enslavement. While the presence of Western European traders in West Africa certainly stimulated the trade in slaves within certain parts of the region, mass enslavements also occurred for reasons internal to Africa. Even "government-sponsored assistance programs," in which Portugal provided military aid and advanced European weaponry to Kongo at several times in the late fifteenth and the sixteenth centuries, were not decisive in outcomes.[32]

John Thornton, a leading authority on the Kingdom of Kongo, addressed another common claim of "many scholars in recent years": that Europeans forced Africans "through commercial weakness, into accepting trade that ultimately placed Africa in its current situation of dependency and underdevelopment."[33] In the eighteenth century, the heyday of the slave trade, the terms of trade (moving relative average of the value of imports versus the value of exports) were in favor of West Africa. In other words, West Africans were demanding more from Europeans for slaves and getting it. Nor were all the items sold by Europeans "essential commodities," for "Africa had well-developed industries" producing iron and other commodities. In West Africa, the source of most of the slaves sold to the New World, gold and iron mining "flourished at least as early as the fourteenth century." It first attracted the Arabs and, in the fifteenth century, the Portuguese. Conspicuous consumption by African people was a major motivator for Africa's trade with Europe. There was prestige in owning European cloth.[34] Textiles were far and away the most valuable item used by Europeans in their trade for African slaves.

"The peoples of Ghana and Nigeria used iron hoes and other agricultural implements, and the Yoruba of southern Nigeria enjoyed a reputation for fine work in copper and tin," wrote Eugene Genovese in an early work. The Dahomey, famous as slave traders, and the Ashanti, Yoruba, and other groups had civilizations marked by division of labor, a carefully regulated system of trade, craft guilds, and an emerging class structure. Agriculture, employing crop rotation and agricultural diversification, was done on plantations with slave labor. The Dahomey especially had a reputation for "industriousness." They

> had large crown-owned plantations worked by slave gangs
> under the direction of overseers whose business was to

maximize output. Debt peonage was a well-established institution. Among the Nupe, slaves did a great deal of agricultural labor and reportedly numbered in the thousands by the time of the British conquest. The more primitive tribes of northern Nigeria had been conquered and enslaved by the Nupe before the beginning of the nineteenth century. The Ashanti had an elaborate system of family land ownership and imposed a light *corvée* on those of low status. The tribes of the Ashanti hinterland practiced slavery, debt peonage, and systematic agriculture. The Ashanti defeated one of these tribes, the Dagomba, at the end of the seventeenth century and obligated it to produce two thousand slaves annually. The Ibo of southeastern Nigeria, slave traders as well as a source of slaves, produced several important crops with servile labor. During the eighteenth and early nineteenth centuries the great West African peoples—the Yoruba, Dahomey, and Fulani—fought continually for control of southwestern Nigeria, and each in turn enslaved thousands during the wars.[35]

Land was not usually privatized in West Africa, so privatization of labor became an especially important way of using the land. It is virtually impossible to disentangle political and economic motives in African enslaving. Although an African slave might be lucky enough to be adopted into a family, he also might suffer the worst luck to live as a "pariah who could be shifted from one household to another by sale," or even to be ritually executed.[36]

For much of the history of the Atlantic slave trade, both Europeans and Africans conducted trade under state control. In Europe, private profit was viewed as an incentive, but was not essential in making determinations; state revenues were. "In the case of the northern Europeans after 1600," explains Thornton, "the state's role was vested in the hands of parastatal chartered companies, such as the Dutch West

India Company, the English Royal Africa Company, or the French Senegal Company, which made their own arrangements with private traders." Thus, the notions that the "profit orientation" of Europeans was greater than that of Africans, or that Europeans "possessed superior commercial organization, or were able to restrict imports to Africa in such a way as to exercise a partial monopoly," are not true.[37]

The scholarship on slavery is vast, but Hannah-Jones has not mastered it. In shaping The 1619 Project, she drew instead on the work of the polemicist Lerone Bennett, to which she was introduced in high school.[38] On December 22, 2020, she tweeted, "I first came across the date 1619 in a one-semester high school Black studies class. That teacher, Mr. Ray Dial, sent me my class project from nearly 30 years ago and it blew my mind in so many ways." She also posted a copy of her one-page paper, written in 1992, and a scan of an article by Lerone Bennett in *Ebony* magazine that Dial had also sent her.[39]

She added, "Mr. Dial always referred to his students as Dr. I can still hear his voice in my head when he called me in class: Dr. Hannah. He was the only Black male I ever had and one of a handful of Black teachers in my high school and his presence meant everything to me."

She continued to gush on Twitter: "This is the man who gave me Cheikh Anta Diop's *African Origins of Civilization* to read as a 10th grader! Learning Black history saved my life and transformed my future."[40] (Diop's claims that the achievements of classical Greek civilization were derived from Egypt and that the Greek heroes were really black Africans were exposed as false by classicist Mary Lefkowitz in *Not Out of Africa* in 1996, decades before this tweetstorm.)[41]

When, at her speech at Georgia Tech, she was asked where she got her "vision" for The 1619 Project, Hannah-Jones said that she realized she had been "working toward the moment" since she was given Bennett's *Before the Mayflower*, first published in 1961. At that moment in tenth grade, she had become "incorrigible." She refused to say the Pledge of Allegiance or stand for the National Anthem.[42]

Bennett does acknowledge the existence of slavery in Africa (as Hannah-Jones does not), but that concession is soon overwhelmed by his description of the arrival of the *White Lion* in 1619—with a "momentous cargo" of assorted Africans. The slave trade it launched was "people living, lying, stealing, murdering and dying... a black man who stepped out of his hut for a breath of fresh air and ended up, ten months later, in Georgia with bruises on his back and a brand on his chest." With a series of dramatic lines beginning "The slave trade was," Bennett lays out a litany of horrors: "a black mother suffocating her newborn baby because she didn't want him to grow up a slave," "a kind captain forcing his suicide-minded passengers to eat by breaking their teeth," "a bishop sitting on an ivory chair on a wharf in the Congo and extending his fat hand in wholesale baptism of slaves who were rowed beneath him, going in chains to the slave ships," and so on.[43]

One can imagine the impact of these and similar descriptions on a sixteen-year-old girl. In her class paper the teenaged Hannah-Jones simply repeated bromides about the importance of black history. As a biracial child, she seems to have experienced some issues regarding her identity. In an interview, she revealed how her maternal white grandparents had at first disowned her mother for marrying a black man, until her older sister was born. She said they were "prejudiced against Black people not related to them."[44] It's very understandable if she was going through some emotional turmoil and latched onto her teacher, and onto this writer who had coined the term "Black Power" and would be eulogized in his February 16, 2018, *New York Times* obituary as "a leading scholarly voice during the racial ferment of the 1960s."[45]

Hannah-Jones is not the only one to have been taken in by Lerone Bennett's "history." Morgan State journalism professor E. R. Shipp referred to Bennett's *Before the Mayflower* in her article on the 1619 quadricentennial for *USA Today*: "'Few ships, before or since, have unloaded a more momentous cargo,' historian and journalist Lerone

Bennett wrote." The landing provided "an origin story" for black readers, who had been "accustomed to being told in myriad ways that blacks
had no history." Indeed, "the notion that their ancestors' presence in
America predated the 1620 arrival of the Pilgrims story was a mind-
boggling revelation."[46]

Surprising Jamestown

When the first English settlers arrived on the North American mainland, they came from a country whose laws frowned on slavery and
whose people gloried in their liberties. The *White Lion*, with its cargo
of black captives, may well have taken the English colonists by surprise.
As historian Lorena Walsh explains, "Before the late 1630s or early
1640s, there is no evidence that Chesapeake settlers envisioned African
slaves as a possible solution to the scarcity of laborers," even though
"Englishmen who attempted to seat colonies in more southerly areas
almost universally incorporated enslaved Africans" and "more educated
settlers" would have read about "African slavery in the Spanish colonies
in travel literature," with some maybe even getting "firsthand accounts
from Virginia company leaders with long experience in the West
Indies...." As Walsh also recounts, another "dozen or so" "negroes"
arrived a few days later on the *Treasurer*, the other ship that had taken
slaves from the Portuguese slaver, and by March 1620 "there were a total
of thirty-two unnamed 'negroes'...listed in that year's muster." By the
1624–25 census there were twenty-three blacks, most "survivors from
the *São João Bautista*," in Jamestown.[47]

Generally, at the time, "negroes" were "considered a special
category of labor explicitly set apart from 'Christian' servants,"—
categories borrowed from Iberian precedents. The word *negro* had
been used as a generic term for Africans and as a synonym for *slave*
by the Portuguese and other Europeans since the early sixteenth
century.[48] This was a shift from the view of the ancient Greeks, who
looked down on the "barbarians," and the Western Europeans of the

Middle Ages, who looked down on the Slavs, from which our word "slave" is derived.[49]

But in the third millennium BC, black captives appeared in Egyptian iconography and then were "portrayed with increasing frequency and realism from the fifteenth century BC through Hellenistic and Roman times," David Brion Davis points out. The Arabs and other Muslims, who "were the first people to develop a specialized, long-distance slave trade from sub-Saharan Africa," were also "the first people to view blacks as suited by nature for the lowest and most degrading forms of bondage."[50] As the sources of supply changed within the Muslim world, Muslim intellectuals anticipated Europeans in adopting the biblical Curse of Ham to excuse the mass enslavement of sub-Saharan Africans.[51]

That the first Africans landed in colonial Virginia suffered servitude seems clear. Whether they were slaves for life remains unclear. In colonial Bermuda, also settled by the Virginia Company, the first Africans were treated as indentured servants, but with a lifetime tenure of servitude. In Virginia, white indentured servants predominated in the labor force for much of the seventeenth century, and on the plantations, blacks and whites "worked side by side in the fields," though they lived apart. They both cleared the land, felling and removing trees, clearing brush, and turning virgin soil "without benefit of good plows and sometimes even without draft animals."[52] Both blacks and whites were treated with "impunity" by masters.[53]

A case in point is Anthony Johnson. It seems that most historians believe he arrived in 1619, was known as "Antonio," and later anglicized his name. James Horn, the author of *1619: Jamestown and the Forging of American Democracy*, believes he came to Virginia on either the *White Lion* or the *Treasurer*, the privateering ships that had taken slaves from the Portuguese ship. In 1625, he was listed on a plantation owned by Edward Bennett and had married "'Mary a Negro Woman' who had lived on the same plantation from 1623." Horn claims that they were "still enslaved" fifteen or twenty years later, but moved with their children to another plantation in Northampton County.[54] So if they were sold as indentured servants, their terms were longer than the typical seven-year terms for whites.

According to noted historian Ira Berlin, the Bennetts had "allowed Antonio to farm independently while still a slave, marry, and baptize his children." When he and his family gained their freedom, Antonio anglicized his name. Johnson then took his family to join the Bennetts, who had become his patrons, across the Chesapeake Bay to the Eastern Shore of Virginia, where they farmed. In 1651, Anthony Johnson earned a headright, or a land grant, of 250 acres for sponsoring servants into the colony (typically 50 acres were awarded for each settler). Johnson and his sons did well for themselves, acquiring land and slaves.[55]

Whether Johnson had been a slave or an indentured servant has not been established definitively. But by 1654, at which point he was a free man, he was engaged in a dispute with John Casar, an African who claimed that he had fulfilled his seven-year indenture to Johnson and took refuge with neighboring white planters, Robert and George Parker. Johnson claimed that Casar (also spelled Casor or Cassaugh) was his slave and went to court. The court ruled against Robert Parker for "unrightly" keeping "Casor from his r[igh]t mayster Anth. Johnson." Political science professor John H. Russell, the lead author of an article published in the *Journal of Negro History*, explained that the court had given "judicial sanction to the right of Negroes to own slaves of their own race." That Johnson was granted damages from the Parkers further demonstrated that the law was "impartial" toward black masters.[56]

While slavery was solidifying in Virginia, Anthony Johnson was doing his part to affirm his right to own slaves. Ironically, this was the first court ruling in Virginia on slave ownership. Russell noted that, to his knowledge, "no earlier record...of judicial support given to slavery in Virginia" had been found—"except as punishment for crime."[57]

By 1670 a statute of Virginia stated, "No negro or Indian though baptized and enjoyed their ffreedome shall be capable of any purchase of Christians *but yet not debarred from buying any of their owne nation* [emphasis added].".." Russell explains that "Christians" meant "persons of the white race." Given that "[i]ndentured servitude was the condition and status of no small part of the white population of Virginia when this law was enacted," one can infer "from this prohibition upon the property rights of the free Negroes...that colored freemen had at least attempted to acquire white or 'Christian' servants."[58]

Russell, anticipating the objection that "the case of the slave John Casor" was "exceptional and peculiar to an earlier period in the growth of slavery before custom had fully crystallized into law," argued that the "paucity of examples" of similar cases actually reveals that "slave-owning by free Negroes was so common in the period of the Commonwealth as to pass unnoticed and without criticism by those who consciously recorded events of the times." The evidence lies in "[d]eeds of sale and transfer of slaves to free Negroes, wills of free Negroes providing for a future disposition of slaves, and records of suits for freedom against free Negroes." He adduced numerous examples: A 1795 court record from Henrico County, Virginia, shows that George Radford had bought a "negro slave" woman from James Radford. Judith Angus, "a well-to-do free woman of color of Petersburg" who died in 1832, had stipulated in her will that her "two slave girls should continue in the service of the family until they earned enough money to enable them to leave the State and thus secure their freedom according to law." In the Hustings Court of Richmond, Sarah, a slave, filed a suit of freedom against Mary Quickly, a free black woman. Russell also records the observations of older blacks who recalled that black masters often had so much difficulty in controlling their slaves that they sold them; these stories were recorded in tax books and court records, as well.[59]

"Free Blacks in Seventeenth-Century Maryland" by Ross M. Kimmel follows Anthony Johnson and family to Somerset County, Maryland, in the early or mid-1660s.[60] According to J. Douglas Deal, author of *Race and Class in Colonial Virginia: Indians, Englishmen, and Africans on the Eastern Shore*, the move to Maryland was prompted by John Johnson's refusal to give up "illicit sexual liaisons" with a white servant of another household in Virginia.[61] In Maryland, the Johnsons quickly regained the status they had held in Virginia, with Anthony leasing a three-hundred-acre plot. Anthony died shortly thereafter, and in 1670 John and his son, also named John, "recorded their livestock in the county records, and in 1677 the younger John bought a forty-four acre lot which he named 'Angola,'" in tribute to the family's origins. The elder John seems to have "attained the status of any freeman possessed of substantial estate," and was even identified as a "planter." When he appeared in court for having fathered a child with a woman not his wife and then for having, along with two white men, stolen corn from an Indian, his treatment was the same as that given to white men. These facts, plus those from several other court cases—of Robert Butchery in 1690 for "fathering the bastard child of a white servant girl," of a "Grinedge" in 1699 for cohabiting with a white woman, of John Covey considered an outlaw in a 1694 case, and of two slaves who gained their freedom through petitions to the court— led Kimmel to conclude that all these black men, "having rid themselves of the taint of slavery," seem "to have been treated with the same judicial deference due white English freemen."[62]

Douglas Deal, on the other hand, has objected to the use of the Johnson family as an example of the idea that—to quote Ira Berlin— "black men could join whites in the mad scramble for land, servants and status in early Virginia." Deal notes the attention that Anthony Johnson received, including in a New Deal–era WPA-sponsored book, *The Negro in Virginia*, which maintained that he had "defended his right to retain another black man as his slave before any statutes defined slavery in the colony" and that "[a]s men of property, standing, and long residence in Virginia," the Johnsons were among "perhaps a dozen native Africans in what was the first Negro community in America." Deal charges Russell, Kimmel, and others with "hyperbole" inspired by a desire to gloss over racism: "What better counterpoint to the seemingly inexorable growth of plantation slavery and racism than the example of free blacks who accumulated property, imported white servants, and held black slaves themselves?"[63]

Public records, Deal argues, "suggest the economic and social decline of th[e] third generation of the Johnson family." Johnson's grandsons were "neither landowners for long nor artisans of any standing in the community." Some ended up as sharecroppers. Their run-ins with the law continued, and while in some cases they had their day in court, in others they seem to have been cheated. Deal interprets the records to mean that the Johnsons were discriminated against. Ultimately, he concludes, the "Johnson family history contains much evidence of the Sisyphean struggle of freed slaves and their descendants to acquire land and become part of the predominantly white society of early Virginia."[64]

The Johnsons lived through the gradual development and ossification of the elaborate system of race-justified slavery that is familiar to us from the founding era and the antebellum South. But, as both Nell Irvin Painter and Manish Sinha have made clear, that system did not suddenly spring into place in 1619.[65] It was developed slowly over the subsequent decades—including by means of court rulings such as the one in which Anthony Johnson established his legal ownership of John Casor. Anthony Johnson's life, in particular, provides counterevidence to the claim that American slavery was simply a white endeavor motivated by racism from its beginning.

That the Johnsons did suffer in subsequent generations because of racism and an increasingly codified system of slavery justified on the basis of race, no one doubts. Yet their complicated lives reflect the complicated nature of race relations in seventeenth-century America and later, as we shall see. So, no, America did not begin as a white "slavocracy," as *The 1619 Project* claims. In fact, Anthony Johnson and family were simply among the first of many—white and black alike—who, when they could, advanced themselves by enslaving others.

CHAPTER 7

A Not So Simple Story

There is a great deal of evidence, both anecdotal and official, that a significant number of African Americans acquired slaves when given the opportunity to do so. In recent years scholarly research on this issue has confirmed anecdotal evidence from stories, legends, and interviews. Presbyterian minister and writer Calvin Dill Wilson, who in 1905 and 1912 attempted to gather such information for the *North American Review* and *Popular Science Monthly*, would no doubt have been glad to know that scholars would be going to county courthouses and reviewing records. One senses his frustration in the article he published in 1905 reporting that he had "asked dozens of Southern people, of advanced years, about negroes owning slaves," only to have been told "that they 'never heard of such a thing.'" Wilson acknowledged the difficulty of even asking such questions: "Psychologically, after all we have read and heard of the pathos and tragedy of negro slavery, it is of strange interest and unaccountable inconsistency that the negroes themselves should at times have had no apparent compunction in regard to buying their fellows at the block...." The one book to which he was directed by the

Library of Congress "barely glance[d] at the subject." Booker T. Washington told Wilson that he had no "personal recollections" of such slave owners. Historians and attorneys in Louisiana, where the French and Spanish traditions of interracial marriage prevailed, could offer only recollections and no documentation. But in Maryland, he learned that "pure blacks, who had themselves been slaves and had been manumitted were frequently slave-owners." One county court record he found revealed that "Draper Thompson, free negro…in 1824 bought and sold a negro man at public auction out of an estate for three hundred dollars." And an "aged man, William W. Davis, eighty-eight years of age," told Wilson that "he knew Thompson well in his own boyhood, that at one time he lived on a large farm, the Cremona Tract; he did not allow his slaves to associate with his own family, but made them eat and sleep in a separate house," and when entering his home each of his slaves had "to doff his hat and carry it under his arm while doing so."[1]

Wilson also related other stories, including from a "Philip Roberts, a respectable colored man of Glendale, Ohio, who was a slave in Kentucky" and who told him "that he knew 'Old Free Isaac,' in Trimble County, Kentucky, who owned several negroes." He said that "this same negro sold his own son and daughter South, one for $1,000, the other for $1,200." And, Wilson reported, "Mr. Stevenson Archer, of Mississippi, states that he knew a pure-blooded negro, born free, by name Nori…who had before the Civil War, a large plantation in Mississippi, and owned about a hundred negroes. He was exacting, but not cruel, and he took excellent care of his slaves." Wilson also recounted cases where slaves were purchased by family members to protect them.[2]

Wilson continued his research after the publication of his original article. In 1907, he wrote to W. E. B. Du Bois, who was then teaching at Atlanta University, but Du Bois answered that he did not know where he would be able to "find much authentic data." Most black slave owners, he guessed, were probably "mulattoes of the extreme Southern gulf states." Du Bois suggested Wilson contact local historians there, as well as Colyer Merriweather of the Southern History Association and "a Mr.

A. H. Stone," both of Washington. Du Bois asked that Wilson share whatever information he found, for he was "curious...to know how much fact is behind the general statement."[3]

"Practically a Lost Chapter"

In a 1912 article, Wilson bemoaned the fact that the issue had "become for our generation practically a lost chapter," with the full data never having been and probably never to be collected, given that much of the pertinent material had probably "perished through the burning of court houses, state houses and similar depositories of documents." But at the Connecticut Historical Society, Wilson had found "a bill of sale from Samuel Stanton...dated October 6, 1783, to Prince, a free negro, of a slave woman named Binar." And in the deed books of St. Augustine, Florida, he had found a record naming "Joseph Sanchez, a colored carpenter, who sold to Francisco P. Sachez a negro slave for three hundred dollars." Also, "[i]n 1724, a servant named Margaret was sold to Scipio, 'free negro man and laborer of Boston.'" And the "early records of Mobile, Ala." showed that "Juan Batista Lusser, in 1797, was one of these negro slave-holders, as were also Julia Vilard, Simon Andry and the house of Forbes." Wilson lists accounts of free blacks owning family members, including one in which a son sold his father after an argument. "Mr. George W. Brooks, of Atlanta," recalled a colony "of free negroes, many of them named Epps," in Person County, North Carolina, thought "to be descendants of the slaves set free by Mr. Epps, the brother-in-law of Thomas Jefferson." Brooks recalled hearing a "free negro named Billy Mitchell" telling about his courtship of his future wife, whose father owned slaves, one of whom was so light-skinned as to appear white. Billy Mitchell then became a slave owner himself.[4]

More examples included John Carruthers Stanly, born in Craven County, North Carolina, in 1722 of a white father and a mother from Africa. He married a black woman, became a successful barber, and owned sixty-four slaves and two large plantations. A "colored brick mason in New Bern," a "dark mulatto" named Doncan Montford, owned slaves, one of whom, Isaac Rue, also a mason, he sold to a lawyer named George S. Altmore. Rue married a free black woman. Their children were free under North Carolina law. "One of their grandsons, Edward Richardson, was at one time postmaster of New Bern, appointed to the office by a Republican president." There was the case of Dilsey Pope in Columbus, Georgia, who sold her husband to a white man in anger, and then to her regret could not get him back. Wilson reported that a 1790 census listed 48 free "negro slaveholders" owning 143 slaves. "The 'List of the Taxpayers of the City of Charleston, S.C., 1860,' names one hundred and thirty-two colored people who paid taxes on three hundred and ninety slaves in Charleston." From among the "large number of individual instances of slaveholders in Kentucky, Tennessee, Virginia, Maryland, both the Carolinas, Missouri, Georgia, Alabama, Florida, the District of Columbia, Delaware, Mississippi, and Louisiana," Wilson named a few, including "Thomas Blackwell, who lived in Vance County, N.C.," and "owned a favorite negro name Tom...a fine blacksmith," who "around 1820" was allowed to "buy his freedom at a price far below his worth.... Tom prospered and bought two or three slaves"; William Chavers, "a well-educated negro who bought a good deal of land in Vance County, from 1750 to 1780" and "owned a good many slaves"; and Chavers's descendants, who "for several generations were slaveholders." Quoting observations by Frederick Law Olmsted in "The Cotton Kingdom" and "A Journey in the Seaboard Slave States," Wilson concluded his 1912 article by noting how little additional information he had been able to acquire since 1905 in spite of inquiries to "state librarians, public librarians, historians, historical societies and a host of individuals." There was "no treatise specifically on the theme" of his research, not even an encyclopedia article, but "only scattered references...in a few books and in files of newspapers. The bulk of the facts is still buried in unpublished documents in court houses, historical societies and libraries. There are probably a few hundreds of people still living who have recollections of this phase of slavery. So we are justified in calling this subject, in its completeness, a lost chapter."[5]

Though many of these records, like other records of African Americans, have been lost, many have been found since Calvin Wilson wrote his article. But the issue has been discussed very little—as Wilson guessed, for "psychological" reasons. And also for political reasons. Attention on black slave owners would complicate the kind of narrative that The 1619 Project advances, which presents blacks and whites as monolithic groups of victims and exploiters, respectively. One rarely, if ever, finds mention of black slave owners in textbooks and curricula. A teacher who even knows about this aspect of slavery will be instructed to "downplay" it in the classroom—something I observed firsthand during the question-and-answer session of a panel discussion at the 2014 meeting of the Organization of American Historians. The panel, "Boundaries of Freedom: Teaching the Construction of Race and Slavery in the AP U.S. History Course," was put on by the College Board, which writes the Advanced Placement exams and guidelines, and included a presentation by UC Irvine professor Jessica Millward on using playacting in class, such as of a slave owner whipping a six-months-pregnant slave while she lies facedown, her belly in a hole to protect the future "property."[6]

The dramatization of the history of blacks who owned slaves, in contrast, seems to cause discomfort, as is evidenced by Janet Maslin's review of Edward P. Jones's Pulitzer Prize–winning historical novel *The Known World* for the *New York Times*.[7] The book is historically accurate,[8] but Maslin downplays "the unusual setting" of "the unsettling, contradiction-prone world of a Virginia slaveholder who happens to be black." And while she admits "[s]uch situations did exist," she also takes care to say that "Mr. Jones teases his reader by occasionally citing some nonexistent scholarly treatise on the subject."[9]

The fact is that scholarly treatises on this subject do exist. Carter Woodson's 1922 *The Negro in Our History* examined the class distinctions among "free Negroes," with "social lines" as "strongly drawn as between the whites and the blacks." Many of the "well-to-do free

Negroes...owned slaves, who cultivated their large estates. Of 360 persons of color in Charleston, 130 of them were, in 1860, assessed with taxes on 390 slaves. In some of these cases, as in that of Marie Louise Bitard, a free woman of color in New Orleans, in 1832, these slaves were purchased for personal reasons or benevolent purposes.... They were sometimes sold by sympathetic white persons to Negroes for a nominal sum on the condition that they be kindly treated." Wealthy free blacks able to own plantations with slaves were exceptions among the "well-to-do" persons of color, who were usually in the artisan class in southern cities. Woodson did find several striking examples, though: "Thomy Lafon of New Orleans," who owned half a million dollars in real estate; in 1833 Solomon Humphries, owner of a successful grocery store in Macon, Georgia, "accumulated about twenty thousand dollars worth of property, including a number of slaves"; "Cyprian Ricard bought an estate in Iberville Parish, with ninety-one slaves, for about $225,000"; in Natchitoches Parish, Marie Metoyer "possessed fifty slaves and an estate of more than 2,000 acres," and Charles Rogues "left in 1848 forty-seven slaves"; Martin Donato of St. Landry, who upon his death in 1848 left "a Negro wife and children possessed of 4,500 arpents of land, eighty-nine slaves and personal property worth $46,000."[10]

Woodson expanded on this research in *Free Negro Owners of Slaves in the United States in 1830*, published in 1924.[11] John Hope Franklin devoted part of a 1943 monograph to the subject.[12] And in the twenty-first century, Paul Heinegg, an engineer by training, published his research about his wife's ancestors from North Carolina, who had "descended from a community of African Americans who had been in Virginia since the colonial period," as a biographical note states. He extended his research to that of other families in Virginia, North Carolina, South Carolina, Maryland, and Delaware, and found white acceptance of blacks and ownership of black slaves by black free persons to be more widespread than one would think.[13]

Changing Laws and Conditions

Although a 1670 act in the Virginia House of Burgesses stipulated that "all servants not being Christian imported into this colony by shipping shall be slaves for their lives," and another Virginia law, in 1682, denied freedom to imported "Negroes, Moors, Mullatos or Indians,"[14] the line "between freedom and slavery was extraordinarily permeable," as the historian Ira Berlin remarks in the foreword to Paul Heinegg's genealogical study, and "[v]arious peoples of European, African, and Native American descent crossed it freely and often. In such socially ill-defined circumstances, white men and women held black and Indian slaves and white servants, and black men and women did like. Peoples of European, African and Native American descent—both free and unfree—worked, played, and even married openly in a manner that would later be condemned by custom and prohibited by law.... Everywhere whites, blacks, and Indians united in both long-term and casual sexual relations, some coerced and some freely entered."[15] Such racial intermingling had long been known in the black community and had been discussed frequently by African American journalist George S. Schuyler (1895–1977) in the *Pittsburgh Courier*.[16]

The very existence of the laws against "miscegenation" serves as proof of the frequency of sexual relationships that crossed the race barrier. Schuyler, who was married to a white woman, routinely attacked the hypocrisy of such laws and commented on the famous Rhinelander case in the 1920s, when Leonard Rhinelander sued (unsuccessfully) for an annulment of his marriage to Alice Jones Rhinelander because she had not disclosed her mixed racial heritage.[17] But Schuyler did not have the luxury of investigating genealogical records. Heinegg, who did, found that "most free people of color had their beginnings in relations between white women (servant and free) and black men (slave, servant, and free). The mixed-race children of servant and slave women and white men of property made up a scant 1 percent of the free children of color" in the colonial period. The relationships in the other 99 percent often represented "long-term and loving commitments."[18]

Heinegg documents the "legal proscriptions on sexual relations between white and black, particularly between white women and black men" that became harsher over time. Mixed-race children became illegitimate by definition. They could be bound out to servitude for upwards of thirty years, and their mothers, if servants, received additional terms of servitude. The legal rights of free blacks became increasingly circumscribed, as "they were barred from voting, sitting on juries, serving in the militia, carrying guns, owning dogs, or testifying against whites."[19] These gradually tightening restraints on African Americans contradict the "slavocracy" origin thesis of The 1619 Project.

And yet, there were exceptions, in contrast to the black-white picture painted in The 1619 Project. Despite their increasing legal disabilities, by the mid-eighteenth century "a small cadre" of prosperous, "property-owning free people of color had emerged in the Southern colonies. Even as slaveholders tightened the noose of proscription and exclusion, these landed, prosperous free men and women made their presence felt," appearing in court to protect "themselves and their property" and seeking "out churches to register their marriages and baptize their children." Sometimes they assisted "their less fortunate brethren, helping to protect them from unscrupulous men and women who sought to transform free people of color into slaves, either through legal chicanery, illegal subterfuge, or outright force."[20]

Heinegg says, "Many free African American families that were free in colonial North Carolina and Virginia were landowners who were generally accepted by their white neighbors"; most of these families had originated in Virginia, where they became free in the seventeenth and eighteenth centuries. Especially welcomed by whites were blacks moving to frontier areas in North Carolina. They were not seen as a threat because the overall percentage of slaves was low, and because "several of these African American families owned slaves of their own." The fact that they owned land also made them more acceptable. Mulattoes had a special status. In the Caribbean they enjoyed a higher status than those of pure African descent. In mid-eighteenth-century North Carolina, mixed-race families were counted in some years by state tax assessors as "mulatto" and in other years as white.²¹

Slavery was being codified on the basis of race, with laws making it more difficult for blacks to purchase slaves for commercial purposes, as Russell explained in the *Journal of Negro History*,²² but Heinegg found exceptions:

- "On 9 November 1762 many of the leading residents of Halifax County petitioned the Assembly to repeal the discriminatory tax against free African Americans, and in May 1763 fifty-four of the leading citizens of Granville, Northampton, and Edgecombe Counties made a similar petition. They described their 'Free Negro & Mulatto; neighbors as persons of Probity & good Demeanor [who] chearfully contribute towards the Discharge of every public Duty injoined them by Law.'"
- "In March 1782 a Continental officer observed a scene in a local tavern at Williamsboro, North Carolina: 'The first thing I saw on my Entrance was a Free Malatto and a White man seated on the Hearth, foot to foot, Playing all fours by firelight: a Dollar a Game.'"
- "By 1790 free African Americans represented 1.7% of the free population of North Carolina, concentrated in the counties of Northampton, Halifax, Bertie, Craven, Granville, Robeson, and Hertford where they were about 5% of the free population.... In these counties most African American families were landowners, and several did exceptionally well."
- "The Bunch, Chavis and Gibson families owned slaves and acquired over 1,000 acres of land on both sides of the Roanoke River in present-day Northampton and Halifax counties, and the Gowen family acquired over 1,000 acres in Granville County."

- "William Chavis, a 'Negro' listed in the 8 October 1754 muster roll of Colonel William Eaton's Granville County Regiment, owned over 1,000 acres of land, a lodging house frequented by whites, and 8 taxable slaves. His son Philip Chavis also owned over 1,000 acres of land, traveled between Granville, Northampton, and Robeson counties, and lived for a while in Craven County, South Carolina."
- "John Gibson, Gideon Gibson and Gibeon Chavis all married the daughters of prosperous white planters. Some members of the Gibson, Chavis, Bunch and Gowen families became resolutely white after several generations."
- "Some members of the Gibson family moved to South Carolina in 1731 where a member of the Commons House of Assembly complained that 'several free colored men with their white wives had immigrated from Virginia.' Governor Robert Johnson…summoned Gideon Gibson and his family to explain their presence there and after meeting him and his family reported, 'I have had them before me in Council and upon Examination find that they are not Negroes nor Slaves but Free people, That the Father of them here is named Gideon Gibson and his Father was also free, I have been informed by a person who has lived in Virginia that this Gibson has lived there Several Years in good Repute and by his papers that he has produced before me that his transactions there have been very regular, That he has for several years paid Taxes for two tracts of Land and had several Negroes of his own, That he is a Carpenter by Trade and is come hither for the support of his Family.'"[23]

"Many of the free African Americans who were counted in the census for South Carolina from 1790 to 1810 originated in Virginia or North Carolina" and, according to the surviving court records, included "at least three families [who] were the descendants of white slave owners who left slaves and plantations to their mixed-race children: Collins, Holman, and Pendarvis. James Pendarvis expanded his father's holdings more than fourfold to 4,710 acres and 151 slaves. John Holman, Jr., established a plantation with 57 slaves on the Santee River in Georgetown District and then returned to his homeland in Rio Pongo, West Africa to resume the slave trading he learned from his English father," thus becoming "probably the first and only African-born entrepreneur who resided in Africa as an absentee planter in the New World."[24]

In "Black Masters: The Misunderstood Slaveowners," published in the *Southern Quarterly* in 2006, historian Larry Koger gives, among other examples, William Raper, born in the mid-1700s, "either freeborn or an emancipated slave," who became "a bricklayer of Charleston City" and "provided the economic tools which helped establish one of the largest slaveowning families in St. Paul's Parish in Colleton County." By 1787, he owned ten slaves who had been "acquired as laborers"; he trained three as bricklayers. Raper's will "requested that his daughter Ruth Gardiner should have the slave, John (the son of his slave, Tamer) after the death of his wife. He also provided his granddaughter Susan Elizabeth Gardiner with Tom, a skilled bricklayer, Tamer, and Bella." According to the 1790 census, another bricklayer, George Gardiner, who had once been a "commercial slave," was listed at the time of his death in 1797 as the owner of seven slaves; he left them to his daughter. Koger explains, "During the late 1790s, many, if not the majority of free black slaveholding families held slaves to exploit their labor." He concluded, "The southern experience of slavery was a diverse system not exclusively exploited by white Americans. Afro-American slaveowners also played a minor role in the saga of American Slavery."[25]

In the nineteenth century, as Heinegg recounts, "Many free African American families sold their land" and "headed west or remained in North Carolina as poor farm laborers," "probably the consequence of a combination of deteriorating economic conditions and the restrictive 'Free Negro Code,'" which was largely a reaction to Nat Turner's 1831 slave rebellion in nearby Southampton County, Virginia. John Hope Franklin described a series of restrictive laws passed from 1826 through the 1850s, wherein "[f]ree African Americans lost the right to vote and were required to obtain a license to carry a gun."[26]

The number of free blacks in the United States was 60,000 in 1790, nearly doubled in 1800, and then tripled in 1810 after the Louisiana Purchase. By 1830, there were 300,000 free blacks in the United States.[27] Louisiana, specifically New Orleans, was one of the places with the best opportunities for free blacks, who "invested heavily in real estate and slaves." As John W. Blassingame noted in his 1973 study *Black New Orleans, 1860–1880*, "Negroes" owned $2,214,020 worth of New Orleans real estate in 1850, much of it in the center of the city. Many "were successful as money lenders, real estate brokers, grocers, tailors, and general merchandising agents.... One of the best-known businesses was the import house operated by Cécée Macarthy, who inherited $12,000, which she increased to $155,000 by the time of her death in 1845. A free Negro undertaker, Pierre Casanave, relying on his predominantly white clientele, built a business valued at $100,000 in 1814." In 1830, "735 Negro masters owned 5 or more slaves; and 23 Negro masters owned from 10 to 20 slaves." A significant number held only "one or two slaves, usually members of their own families whom they often manumitted; such masters entered 501 of the 1,353 manumission petitions in the emancipation court between 1827 and 1851."[28]

Complex Relations

Race relations were complex in New Orleans. Free black men were required to serve as city guardsmen and to go "on slave patrols in the parishes to keep the peace." In 1811, free persons of color were recognized for the significant role they had played in suppressing what amounted to the largest slave insurrection in United States history. New Orleans had the largest proportion of free persons of color of any city in the antebellum United States. Whatever the prejudices in New Orleans, a significant number of those persons surmounted barriers to become wealthy and successful. As a result, during Reconstruction, New Orleans blacks overall fared better than blacks in other places. Blassingame writes, "The role of blacks in [the] New Orleans economy...while restricted, still enabled them to compete successfully against whites in many areas after the war. Much of the black success...during Reconstruction was a direct result of the large number of highly skilled free Negro men in antebellum New Orleans." Their wealth allowed them to form benevolent associations and found private schools.[29]

In his first book, *The Free Negro in North Carolina: 1790–1860*, published in 1943, noted African American historian John Hope Franklin charted the status of the "Negro" in terms of population, legal rights, and economic and social life in a state that was "reportedly more liberal than most southern states."[30] Overwhelmingly, Franklin found, blacks fared poorly and were victims of discrimination, especially those who were enslaved.[31]

Franklin claimed that "[t]he possession of slaves by free Negroes was the only type of personal property that was ever questioned during the ante-bellum period." For a black man to acquire slaves and thus "improve his economic status" was seen by some "as a dangerous trend." There was the question: "If the free Negro was not a full citizen, could he enjoy the same privileges of ownership and the protection of certain types of property that other citizens enjoyed? Around this question revolved a great deal of discussion at the beginning of the militant period of the anti slavery movement."[32]

The 1833 North Carolina Supreme Court case *State v. Edmund* gave the answer in the affirmative: free blacks under North Carolina law *were* considered to be citizens with property rights that included the right to hold slaves. The decision, by Supreme Court judge Joseph Daniel, went for the black slave owner and against the black slave. The case involved a runaway slave named Edmund who had concealed his status and was working as a steward on a ship, where he hid another slave owned by a black man named Green. Edmund was imprisoned and was appealing his case. As Franklin explained, "[I]t was contended…that the prisoner, a slave, was not a person or mariner within the meaning of the act [of 1825] and that Green, the owner of the concealed slave, was a mulatto and hence not a citizen of the State and could not own slaves." Judge Daniel, however, ruled, "By the laws of this State, a free man of color may own land and hold lands and personal property including slaves." As Franklin commented, Judge Daniel was "well satisfied from the words of the act of the General Assembly that the Legislature meant to protect the slave property of every person who by the laws of the state are entitled to hold such property."[33] Daniel also wrote in his ruling, "The prisoner, although a slave, is a 'person' in the natural acceptation of that term; a slave is a person capable of committing crimes, and subject to punishment."[34]

"The decision of Judge Daniel remained the accepted view," wrote Franklin—until "the hostility between the sections" developed "into open conflict" and "the free Negro in the South witnessed an almost complete abrogation of his rights." This abrogation involved a law "passed during the momentous session of 1860–1861," stating that "no free Negro, or free person of color shall be permitted or allowed to buy, purchase, or hire for any length of time any slave or slaves…." Admittedly, the number of slaves owned by blacks had been declining, as it had been among white slave owners. The law, however, "provided that free Negroes already possessing slave property would not be affected…."[35]

Franklin found that black slave owners usually held only one to three slaves. "[T]he petitions of free Negroes to manumit relatives suggest that a sizable number of slaves had been acquired" for that purpose.[36] And most of "the free Negroes who owned property" possessed only "small estates."[37]

Yet there were "notable exceptions"—such as "the eleven slaves held by Samuel Johnston of Bertie County in 1790; the 44 slaves each owned by Gooden Bowen of Bladen County and John Walker of New Hanover County in 1830; and the 24 slaves owned by John Crichlon of Martin County in 1830." Franklin names "several" free blacks who "amassed a considerable amount of property during their lifetime." One, Louis

Sheridan, a slave owner, started "with a small store in Bladen County in the early years of the nineteenth century" and developed it into "a business that was among the largest in his section of the State." His race seemed to have been no obstacle in making extensive "business connections with leading New York merchants" and, through former North Carolina governor John Owen, meeting "other influential men, including Arthur Tappan" (a white businessman, philanthropist, and abolitionist). Sensing a coming clampdown on blacks, especially free blacks, after the "circulation of a 'seditious' pamphlet, *Walker's Appeal*, by David Walker, a free black native of nearby Wilmington, and the outbreak of Nat Turner's Slave Rebellion in Virginia in 1831, coupled with the rising tide of abolitionism in the North," Sheridan looked to Liberia for opportunities for "full freedom and prosperity." So he freed his slaves, "presumably on the condition they accompany him to Liberia," sold his "enormous estate," and emigrated to Liberia in 1837, where he set up business.[38]

However, Sheridan was not happy in Liberia and wrote to Tappan back in America, complaining about the "peculiar barbarousness of this country and its yet more barbarous natives." After Tappan released Sheridan's letter, resistance to colonization arose. But Sheridan decided to stay in Liberia in order to fulfill his commitments to investors. He served on the Colonial Council and continued to serve after 1839, when "the American Colonization Society proclaimed the Commonwealth of Liberia...and appointed [Thomas] Buchanan, an old acquaintance of Sheridan's, as governor." After Buchanan's death in 1841, Sheridan opposed the new governor, a "mulatto." Sheridan died of an illness in 1844, having inspired "more hostility than admiration among his fellow Americo-Liberians," whom he called "crazy," and who, in turn, did not want to accept his exacting ways.[39]

"Successful and Respectable"

In 1990, University of North Carolina–Greensboro history professor Loren Schweninger followed up on John Carruthers Stanly, the successful barber and son of an African mother and white father who had been featured in Calvin Dill Wilson's 1912 article "Negroes Who Owned Slaves" (where his name was spelled "Stanley"). Schweninger published his story in a book, *Black Property Owners in the South, 1790–1915*, and in an article in the *North Carolina Historical Review* titled "John Carruthers Stanly and the Anomaly of Black Slaveholding."[40] As the title of Schweninger's article indicates, black slaveholders were an "anomaly," but they did exist. Stanly got his start when, as a slave, he was "hired out as an apprentice barber." He learned the trade quickly, establishing his own barbershop in New Bern while still a bondsman. Stanly's owners, convinced that he could support himself, freed him in 1798. By then he had expanded his business and was bringing on slave apprentices. He amassed a large number of slaves to work on his various properties as well as in his shop, and he was well respected and accepted by the white community. His family even had a pew in the white church.[41] Stanly was referenced in an article written about the North Carolina Constitutional Convention of 1835, which argued against a proposal to deny free blacks the right to vote, on the grounds that it "would be highly unfair to the most successful and respectable members of this class, men like John C. Stanly of New Bern."[42]

Stanly built his wealth on slave labor. "Like his white neighbors, he became a regular bidder at slave auctions.... By 1820, Stanly had thirty-two slaves listed in his household in New Bern, including several who worked in his barbershop and as house servants." Fifteen were children under the age of fourteen. "On his plantations he controlled another ninety-five blacks.... In all, Stanly controlled 127 blacks who were listed in the population census as residing in his household in New Bern or on one of his plantations." At least one of the slaves he purchased was only two years old. He bought field hands usually as teenagers, but some were as young as nine. Even as restrictions were placed on "free Negroes" after "the abortive slave insurrection in neighboring South Carolina, led by the freed black Denmark Vesey, in 1822, and rumors of a similar plot in North Carolina," Stanly maintained his position, buying more slaves to work under his three white overseers. By the late 1820s he had become "the largest slave owner in Craven County, and one of the largest in North Carolina." Schweninger explains, "In his treatment of his bondspeople, Stanly differed little from his white neighbors. One New Bern resident, Colonel John D. Whitford, recalled that Stanly was a 'hard task-master' who demanded long hours in the fields and 'fed and clothed indifferently.'" The record suggests "that Stanly would have few pangs of conscience about selling a slave away from his parents." By 1860 his net worth far exceeded the average for white Southerners, which was less than $4,000. Schweninger explains, "Stanly's $21,200 worth of real property would have placed him in the top one half of one percent among white men in the nation at midcentury; and his 1820s total estate was seventeen times the average for southern whites...on the eve of the Civil War." Ironically, his fortunes took a temporary downturn when he backed a loan for his white half brother.[43]

Schweninger notes a surprising fact: in 1838 Stanly "wrote the American Colonization Society in behalf of Lott Holton, an elderly man" who wanted to emancipate seventeen young slaves and send them to Africa. "Whatever happened to the seventeen slaves was not revealed in the record, but the paradox of a free Negro slaveholder who continued to hold his own slaves seeking to assist a white slaveholder in 'returning' his slaves to Africa symbolized the ambiguous nature of blacks holding their brethren in bondage."[44]

Black plantation owner Andrew Durnford regularly communicated with a white man, John McDonogh, who acted as his agent in buying slaves. In an article in *Louisiana History*, David O. Whitten reproduces Durnford's correspondence regarding transactions in the 1830s. Slaves were notated only by first name and age, along with the amount paid and shipping costs. Whitten comments, "The letters presented here transmit the tone of a neglected aspect of the domestic slave trade, the attitudes of a black man on the enslavement of his race, and general obstacles encountered in transporting coffles [groups of slaves chained together] from the old to the new slave states." McDonogh became a vice president of the American Colonization Society and "shipped eighty-five freed slaves to Liberia in the 1840s." In his will, he "left a large bequest to the society" and "provided for the emancipation of most of his remaining slaves for shipment to Liberia." McDonogh's correspondence with Durnford, Whitten notes, exposes "the apparent paradox of a black slave owner on a slave buying expedition being entertained by a white abolitionist."[45]

Other free blacks in North Carolina prospered. In the 1860 census, John Hope Franklin found "fifty-three free Negroes who possessed more than $2,500 worth of property," including Jesse Freeman of Richmond County ($20,300), James D. Sampson of New Hanover County (over $36,000), Hardy Bell of Robeson County ($14,000), and Lydia Mangum of Wake County ($20,816).[46] Sampson was one of the free Negroes who "experienced little difficulty in securing employment in North Carolina in the building trades" during the antebellum boom times, despite pro-testations by white workers. He became a "respected and wealthy citizen of Wilmington" through "his own industry as a carpenter" and shrewd investment in real estate. Franklin counted Sampson as among those in antebellum North Carolina "who were not only satisfied with their own position but with the general structure of North Carolina society as well." He quoted an editorial in the Fayetteville *Observer* lauding the conduct of the "slaves and other colored population," and a letter by "a prominent New Bern citizen in 1854" that praised "the displays made by" the "elegantly" dressed "Negro Elite" on Sundays at the Episcopal church. That letter noted that "a large number of [the] young men and several of our merchants" had "negro wives or 'misses' and [kept] them openly, raising up families of mullatoes."[47]

The situation was similar in South Carolina, as Larry Koger and Carter Woodson before him observed. The "artisan class" of urban "free Negroes" faced less discrimination than they did in the North. That was especially true in Charleston, where they comprised "[a] large portion of the leading mechanics, fashionable tailors, shoe manufacturers, and mantua-makers," wrote Woodson in 1922. As we have seen, some launched themselves into the class of the wealthy. Class distinctions had been established by 1820, and elite slaveholding blacks like Jehu Jones were certainly tolerated—even well liked, if not fully accepted—by white society. "Many within the white aristocracy," Koger states, "viewed the elite community of Afro-Americans as a safe class of people who understood the virtue of slavery and protected the southern system of labor."[48] For example, an editorial in the December 9, 1835, *Charleston Courier* praised the conduct of the local free blacks as "for the most part so correct, evincing so much civility, subordination, industry and propriety, that unless their conduct should change for the worse, or some stern necessity demand it, we are unwilling to see them deprived of those immunities which they have enjoyed for centuries without the slightest detriment to the commonwealth."[49]

Racial boundaries were also weak when it came to the impoverished. Poor and orphaned children of both races were "bound out until the age of twenty-one by the county courts." In New York City, both white and black people of means set up philanthropic organizations and orphanages for such black children.

Free blacks often sought to distinguish themselves from slaves and former slaves. They resisted forced integration with the formerly enslaved in schools during Reconstruction. Heinegg recounts that "Hamilton McMillan, a Democrat from Robeson County, took advantage of the fact that the African Americans who had been free since colonial times resented the loss of status they experienced when they had to attend the 'Colored' schools with the former slaves. In order to secure their votes for the Democrats, he helped pass a law which allowed them to have their own separate schools."[50]

The class division evident in such places as New York City, where an established and wealthy group of free blacks lived in the eighteenth and nineteenth centuries, carried through into the twentieth century.[51] Harlem became a thriving black mecca largely through the efforts of enterprising black real estate investors who saw an opportunity in the overbuilding by whites. They sold and rented to blacks, driving out whites, and then charged high rents to blacks. In his autobiography, George Schuyler described how long-established black Yankee families shunned black migrants coming north to Syracuse, New York, where he grew up at the turn of the twentieth century. A Dr. Dumas of Louisiana (a "distinguished" "mulatto"), who had inherited his wealth from plantation-owning forebears who had built their wealth with slave labor, helped Schuyler on his reporting forays through the South in the 1920s and 1930s.[52]

Anecdotes of black slave ownership abound, but since at least 1922, when Carter G. Woodson scoured census records for his groundbreaking *Free Negro Owners of Slaves in the United States in 1830*, scholars have also tried to quantify levels of ownership. According to two Canadian researchers, Woodson misinterpreted those records in part and, as a result, overestimated the number of slaves owned by blacks for benevolent purposes. David L. Lightner and Alexander M. Ragan reexamined the evidence and published their findings in the *Journal of Southern History* in 2005. "Woodson's claim," they wrote, "appears plausible, for there were indeed many impediments to manumission in the South— and thus many reasons for blacks to own relatives and loved ones rather than buy them and then simply set them free." By the antebellum period, free blacks were also burdened with annual registrations and fees, as well as higher poll taxes and fines, under the threat of temporary bondage for nonpayment. In order to practice in their limited number of trades they had to purchase expensive badges and licenses.[53] And, Lightner and Ragan concede, though the biographies of four black slave owners—John Stanly (covered in "John Carruthers Stanly and the Anomaly of Black Slaveholding" and *Black Property Owners in the South, 1790–1915*, both by Loren Schweninger),[54] Andrew Durnford (David O. Whitten, *Andrew Durnford: A Black Sugar Planter in the Antebellum South* and "Slave Buying in 1835 Virginia as Revealed by Letters of a Louisiana Negro Sugar Planter"),[55] William Ellison (the subject of Michael P. Johnson and James L. Roark's *Black Masters: A Free Family of Color in the Old South*, 1984),[56] and William Johnson

(*The Barber of Natchez* by Edwin Adams Davis and William Ransom Hogan, 1954),[57]—are "arresting," they "provide no indication of what proportion of black slaveholders were similarly exploitative."[58]

The "most powerful challenge" to Woodson's high estimate of the proportion of slaves who were owned by free blacks for benevolent reasons, Lightner and Ragan assert, comes from Larry Koger's 1985 *Black Slaveowners: Free Black Slave Masters in South Carolina, 1790–1860*. The research of Koger, whose account of the free black bricklayer William Raper we discussed above, included "exhaustive research in census returns, tax lists, legal documents, business directories, newspaper accounts, and other sources." Lightner and Ragan reexamined the raw census data used by Woodson in his 1924 book and corrected the errors pointed out by Koger. They found that correct comparisons between white slaveholders and black slaveholders showed that "slave owning was fairly widespread among the free black population." The 3,699 black slave owners constituted "almost exactly 2 percent of 182,070, the total of free black population of the South." Admitting that the number may appear small, they point out that it is actually a significant proportion, given "the small percentage of the total white population who were slaveholders," 223,898 out of a total population of 3,660,758—or "almost exactly 6 percent." In fact, going by the census data, "a southern white was just three times more likely to own slaves than was a southern free black"—a finding "more striking" in light of the fact that there was a "substantial *undercount* of black slave owners." And on a national level, "a white American was not even *twice* as likely as a free black American to be a slaveholder in 1830," given the fact that the majority of whites lived in the North.[59]

Lightner and Ragan's estimates are conservative. They worked from the assumption that all the black slave owners who owned only a small number of slaves were benevolent, whereas in reality there must have been some who owned one or two slaves for exploitative purposes. They conclude that "Woodson was correct when he said that the *majority* of black slaveholders were motivated by benevolence," though the number of exploitative slave owners was "more substantial and their slaveholdings far more significant than Woodson implied."[60]

As Koger and others have pointed out, just as some slaves were treated harshly and even viciously by some white slave owners, the same was true of some black slave owners.[61] The race of the owner did not determine how slaves were treated.

Created Equal

Alas, slaves, by virtue of their status, were at the mercy of their owners. A Frenchman traveling through the sugar country of Louisiana in 1803 observed that among the Creole planters the "fine feelings of humanity are quiescent or dead as far as the slaves are concerned" and that slaves worked "the land, like a mule, like an ox." An "organized service of overseers, leaders, watchmen...with whips in their hands" were ready to punish—but with only "a few lashes or days in the dungeon," so as not to lose valuable workers.[62]

But attitudes changed. In 1776, Americans declared that "all men are created equal." And then they fought a Revolution in pursuit of that idea. This new notion spread across the globe, including to a tobacco plantation in Maryland, where in 1803 an overseer decided to quit his lucrative position because of the new difficulties of his job. James Eagle wrote to his boss, "I am now drawing towards 50 years of age I have spent 21 of that time on this place the first part of it much more agreeable than the latter." In Lorena Walsh's article "Slave Life, Slave Society, and Tobacco Production in the Tidewater Chesapeake, 1620–1820," she explains, "The slaves he supervised had decided they, too, had an inalienable right to freedom. Eagle found 'they Get much more Dissatisfied Every year & troublesome for they say that they all ought all to be at there liberty & they think that I am the Cause that they are not.'" Their behavior had changed: they gave him so much "trouble" that half the time the overseer was in "hot blood" and unable to "[c]onduct my business as I ought to do."[63]

Thomas Jefferson may not have freed his slaves in the manner and time frame his critics demand centuries later, but his words helped set in motion a new philosophy that had worldwide repercussions. As Ira Berlin has noted, "Prior to the American Revolution and its idea of universal equality, there were few [abolitionist] movements to contemplate, let alone to join." When blacks filed suits for freedom—as they did, for example, in Connecticut in 1779—they used the language of the Declaration of Independence.[64]

CHAPTER 8

The Wolf by the Ears

Thomas Jefferson appears never to have acknowledged an encounter with a black slave owner. But given that there were almost a thousand black slave owners in Virginia, he could very well have met one.

At the time of Jefferson's death in 1826, there were more than one hundred black slave owners in the District of Columbia. In Richmond and Petersburg in 1830, about one in four black households included slaves. Those blacks who owned and worked slaves likely did not have the education or the leisure to engage in the debates leading up to the American Revolution—to read and discuss the ideas from Montesquieu, Rousseau, and Adam Smith that were circulating at the time. Nor were they in positions of authority where they could weigh in on the issues of the day. The black slave owner was busy, as John Hope Franklin explained, trying "to improve his economic status."[1]

Accusations against Jefferson for having "only a theoretical interest in promoting the cause of abolition"[2] are common. Sophomoric witticisms and judgmental comments—like Sean Wilentz's quip that though Jefferson wrote in his *Notes on the State of Virginia*, "I tremble for my country," he "would never tremble enough to free more than a handful of his own slaves"—sadly mar otherwise solid histories. More seriously, Wilentz complains, "Neither [Jefferson] nor most other first-rank southern political leaders took up the anti-slavery cause too publicly or too vociferously."[3]

"What an Incomprehensible Machine Is Man!"

In 1786, when he was serving as the American minister to France, Jefferson wrote these moving words to the editor of the *Encyclopédie Méthodique*, deploring how so many of his liberty-loving countrymen were blind to the evils of slavery:

> What a stupendous, what an incomprehensible machine is man! who can endure toil, famine, stripes, imprisonment, & death itself in vindication of his own liberty, and the next moment be deaf to all those motives whose power supported him thro his trial, and inflict on his fellow men a bondage, one hour of which is fraught with more misery than ages of that which he rose in rebellion to oppose. But we must await with patience the workings of an overruling providence, & hope that that is preparing the deliverance of these, our suffering brethren. When the measure of their tears shall be full, when their groans shall have involved heaven itself in darkness, doubtless a god of justice will awaken to their distress, and by diffusing light & liberality among their oppressors, or at length by his exterminating thunder, manifest his attention to the things of this world, and that they are not left to the guidance of a blind fatality.[4]

As Dumas Malone correctly noted, after Jefferson returned to America in 1789 he did not again publicly articulate the "moral indignation" about slavery that he had expressed so eloquently in that letter. The overriding question, as Malone acknowledged, is why.[5]

Edward P. Jones titled his pre–Civil War historical novel *The Known World* to highlight the limitations of someone who was not allowed to go beyond the "known" plantation. In an earlier time, the phrase was a reference to what lay beyond the uncrossed ocean. All individuals act within their own "known world"—while trying to glimpse one beyond. What would a world without slavery look like? That was a question that bedeviled Jefferson. He had read enough history to know that actions of statesmen with the best of intentions could bring on calamitous consequences.

As a statesman, he had also learned the limitations of what one member of a governing body could accomplish. David Brion Davis pointed out that Jefferson, from the time of his "election to the Virginia House of Burgesses to his departure for France as American Minister," had experienced only "a series of rebuffs" for his efforts to eliminate or reform slavery. "Soon after his election to the House of Burgesses, at the age of twenty-six... [Jefferson] succeeded in persuading Richard Bland to move 'for certain moderate extensions of the protection of the laws' to slaves." As a result, Jefferson recalled, Bland was "denounced as an enemy of his country."[6] The bill, which had proposed opening up manumission, illegal in Virginia in 1768, was written and seconded by Jefferson, but never even put to a vote.[7]

Jefferson introduced a clause prohibiting the "future importation of slaves" in his draft of a constitution for Virginia in 1776, but again "met defeat." Then, in 1783, in another draft, "he provided for the freedom of all children born of slaves after the year 1800."[8] But that clause was not adopted either because, as Jefferson wrote to Jean Nicolas Demeunier, the editor of the French *Encyclopédie Méthodique*, "the moment of doing it with success was not yet arrived, and... an unsuccessful effort, as too often happens, would only rivet still closer the chains of bondage, and retard the moment of delivery to this oppressed description of men."[9] In 1784, Jefferson's committee submitted to Congress a measure that would have excluded slaves "from the western territories, again after the year 1800."[10] But once again, Jefferson's proposal failed. Davis believed these efforts to be genuine. But he called them "the high-water mark of [Jefferson's] reform zeal" and indicted Jefferson for not maintaining such "zeal" into middle and old age. And he judged Jefferson's explanation of the failure of his 1783 proposal—that the "disposition of the legislature" of Virginia was not "ripe" for such a measure—to be "strained."[11]

However, as Winthrop Jordan points out, "It was neither timidity nor concern for reputation which restrained him; in fact he had good reason to think that antislavery pronouncements might *solidify* the institution" [emphasis added]. South Carolinian Francis Kinloch warned Jefferson about the "general alarm" that the "passage in your Notes occasioned amongst us.... [T]he word 'emancipation' operates like an apparition upon a South Carolina planter."[12]

In 1788, Jefferson declined an invitation to become a member of the abolitionist Société des Amis des Nois, explaining to Jean Pierre Brissot de Warville that though he "ardently" wished to "see an abolition not only of the trade but of the condition of slavery," he was in France "as a public servant; and those whom I serve having never yet been able to give their voice against this practice, it is decent for me to avoid too public a demonstration of my wishes to see it abolished. Without serving the cause here, it might render me less able to serve it beyond the water...."[13]

Robert Paquette puts Jefferson's dilemma into perspective, writing, "Jefferson learned early on...that the process could not be hastened when the economic interest of slaveholders did not coincide with their professed virtue."[14] (And as we saw in chapters 6 and 7 above, such self-interest was not limited to white planters in the American South. Black slave owners, like white slave owners, defended their property rights in slaves.) Jefferson understood competing interests: property rights, states' rights, the moral responsibility to abolish an immoral institution while preserving the union. In order to balance them, Paquette explains, Jefferson sought a "plan of gradual emancipation" that would proceed "under tightly controlled conditions with options for removing those liberated from the sites of their enslavement. Only with the decline of the slave's value and importance, state by state, would the virtue of emancipating slaves by popular majorities gain strength in the South."[15]

Jefferson described his proposed revision of laws in his *Notes on the State of Virginia*, which was written for "a sympathetic audience of French elites," responding to questions "put to him a few years before by Count François de Barbé-Marbois."[16] The manuscript, which Jefferson brought with him to Paris in 1784, was given to a printer to print two hundred copies anonymously in order to keep it from public eyes, "primarily because he feared an unfavorable reaction to his remarks on the subject of slavery and his criticisms of the 1776 Constitution of Virginia." Some "unfavorable" comments did come, when *Notes* was reprinted without his permission—in the form of a broadside during the campaign of 1796 by "A Southern Planter," who, quoting the "wild project" of emancipation, wrote that should Jefferson become president and "*three hundred thousand* slaves [be] set free in Virginia, farewell to the safety, prosperity, the importance, perhaps the very existence of the Southern States" [emphasis in the original]. During the election of 1800, a new edition was published, including an "Argumentative Dissertation, on Mr. Jefferson's Religious Principles." *Notes on the State of Virginia* followed Jefferson long after his death—but to opposite effect. Davis recounts that Martin Duberman in his 1964 play *In White America* transformed "the father of democracy into the father of racism" by having an actor simply "recite selected passages from *Notes on Virginia*, often in a supercilious tone."[17]

The plan for the emancipation of slaves that Jefferson laid out in *Notes on the State of Virginia* called for keeping children "with their parents to a certain age, then to be brought up, at the public expense, to tillage, arts, or sciences, according to their geniuses," to age eighteen for females, twenty-one for males, "when they should be colonized to such place as the circumstances of the time should render most proper, sending them out with arms, implements of household and of the handicraft arts, seeds, pairs of the useful domestic animals, &c., to declare them a free and independent people, and extend to them our alliance and protection, till they have acquired strength; and to send vessels at the same time to other parts of the world for an equal number of white inhabitants; to induce them to migrate hither...."[18]

Jefferson then asked the question, "Why not retain and incorporate the blacks into the State?" Here is where the easy cherry-picking is, in Jefferson's answer: "Deep-rooted prejudices entertained by the whites; ten thousand recollections, by the blacks, of the injuries they have sustained; new provocations; the real distinctions which nature has made; and many other circumstances, which will probably never end but in the extermination of the one or the other race." Certainly, slavery as it became institutionalized and spread exacerbated prejudice. But this was also a time when prejudice against many groups was openly displayed, as is evidenced by characterization of the group that taunted the British soldiers during the Boston Massacre of 1770 as a "motley rabble of saucy boys, negroes and mulattoes, Irish Jeazues, and outlandish Jack tars" by the anti-slavery Yankee John Adams.[19]

Jefferson then proceeds to speculate—deploying his knowledge of the cutting-edge "science" of his day—on observable physical racial characteristics. Primary among them is "color," and Jefferson, employing what is racism to modern ears, wonders if "the black of the negro resides in the reticular membrane between the skin and scarf-skin, or the scarf-skin itself," or "proceeds from the color of the blood, the color of the bile." Other physical differences include "less hair on the face and body" and more tolerance for heat, which he speculates is because they "secrete less by the kidneys, and more by the glands of the skin...."

Jefferson, not surprisingly, reported behaviors (as he saw them) that did not accord with the dominant cultural values—for example, the alleged lack of concern for the future that was evidenced by slaves' staying up to the late hours "induced by amusements" after a day's "hard labor." While conceding that Africans and African Americans "are at least as brave, and more adventuresome," than whites, he thought these characteristics might "proceed from a want of forethought, which prevents their seeing a danger till it be present." Jefferson also found blacks wanting in intellect, romantic fidelity, and the arts. Comparing the accomplishments of black slaves unfavorably with the slaves of the Roman Empire, who were much worse treated, and asserting that improvement "in body and mind" comes from "their mixture with whites," Jefferson offered "that their inferiority is not the effect merely of their condition of life." But this was "a suspicion only."[20]

Jefferson, open to being proven wrong, offered another "conjecture" open to verification by "further observation"—that though "nature has been less bountiful to them in the endowments of the head...[in] those of the heart she will be found to have done them justice." He allowed for the fact that the "disposition to theft with which they have been branded, must be ascribed to their situation, and not to any depravity of the moral sense," for "without reciprocation of right," such laws become "mere arbitrary rules of conduct, founded in force." That "a change in the relations" would change one's "ideas of moral right or wrong" goes back to Homer; it is not "peculiar to the color of the blacks." Jefferson hypothesized "that in time, cultivated in a friendly society," and with education, "blacks can become fully equal to the other Americans."

In words that would be picked up and repeated by abolitionists, Jefferson wrote that slavery was harmful to both parties. "The whole commerce between master and slave," he wrote, "is a perpetual exercise of the most boisterous passions, the most unremitting despotism on the one part, and degrading submissions on the other." It had devastating effects on children, who witnessed and imitated such "tyranny." One half of the citizens "trample on the rights of the other."

Slavery destroys not only "the morals of the people," but also "their industry"—here Jefferson is echoing Adam Smith—for "no man will labor for himself who can make another labor for him."[21] Ultimately, for Jefferson and many other slaveholders, the institution of slavery was incompatible with the founders' great experiment in republican government. Jefferson asked, "[C]an the liberties of a nation be thought secure when we have removed their only firm basis, a conviction in the minds of the people that these liberties are a gift of God? That they are not to be violated but with his wrath? Indeed I tremble for my country when I reflect that God is just; that his justice cannot sleep forever; that considering numbers, nature and natural means only, a revolution of the wheel of fortune, and exchange of situation is among possible events...."[22]

"A Change Already Perceptible"

Jefferson hoped that his fellow citizens would see the light. "We must be contented to hope," he wrote in that same passage, that the "considerations of policy, of morals, of history natural and civil...will force their way into everyone's mind." In fact, he thought he was seeing a "change already perceptible, since the origin of the present revolution. The spirit of the master is abating, that of the slave rising from the dust, his condition mollifying, the way I hope preparing, under the auspices of heaven, for a total emancipation, and that this is disposed, in the order of events, to be with the consent of the masters, rather than by their extirpation."[23]

In this hope and belief, Jefferson was not self-deceived. The change he thought he could see beginning in 1781 was precisely the transformation that, two decades later, would drive Maryland overseer James Eagle to quit a job being made impossible by increasingly "troublesome" slaves claiming "that they all ought to be at there [sic] liberty."[24]

Contrast Jefferson the rationalist, who proceeded cautiously, with a fellow member of the Virginia gentry, Robert Carter. Carter was a slaveholder who, inspired by a mystical religious or political vision, threw caution to the wind. He did free his 400-plus slaves, but he did it after an intense religious conversion, which was not the experience of the deist Thomas Jefferson. Carter not only lost his wealth, he was ostracized and targeted by mobs and fled to Baltimore. Carter's action was noble, but it was of little or no consequence to the hundreds of thousands of blacks who remained enslaved. He may have laid treasure up for himself in heaven, but he is the "forgotten" founding father, who had no more impact in this world than that offered by his personal example.[25]

Carter's action is applauded by his biographer Andrew Levy, who uses his example to rebuke the other founders. But, as we shall see, Jefferson did take quiet actions that had a cumulative effect. That is not to mention that his advocacy on issues outside the domain of slavery, such as for the Bill of Rights and particularly the right to free speech, would prove to be absolutely essential to achieving abolition and civil rights.[26] Indeed, the very structure of the republican government that Jefferson helped bring into being made such reforms possible.

Hannah-Jones's claim that "neither Jefferson nor most of the founders intended to abolish slavery" is simply not true.[27] Her statement that "when it came time to draft the Constitution, the framers carefully constructed a document that preserved and protected slavery without ever using the word" ignores the fact that such ambiguity indicates the *discomfort* with slavery among many of the founders.[28] Benjamin Franklin and Alexander Hamilton became members of anti-slavery societies.

As Robert Paquette points out, Jefferson, living in Paris as minister to France, followed the framing of the Constitution from afar. He "queried George Mason about how the delay in the abolition of the Atlantic slave trade written into Article 1, section 9, could have happened: Georgia and South Carolina, Mason told Jefferson in 1792, 'struck up a bargain with the three New England States.'"[29]

In "The Rights of British America" (1774), Jefferson had insisted that as the first step, "previous to the enfranchisement of the slave...it is necessary to exclude all further importations from Africa."[30] But Jefferson also consistently maintained the ultimate goal he set forth in his *Notes on the State of Virginia*: "total emancipation."[31]

As Paquette says, "[T]he thirty-nine signatories to the Constitution had every right to glory in their great experiment in republican government. As self-governing freemen, they stood in stark contrast to the majority of humanity, which lived at the time in abject servitude of one kind or another.... The framers...tended to regard slavery, at least in the abstract, as an evil." Jefferson was in line with the thinking of most of them in believing that "gradual extinction of the institution…would be brought about under controlled conditions by the future action of sovereign states."[32]

In his message to Congress on December 2, 1806, in the run-up to 1808, the earliest date that the Constitution allowed the end of the slave trade, President Jefferson urged the legislature "to withdraw the citizens of the United States from all further participation in those violations of human rights which have so long continued on the unoffending inhabitants of Africa and which the morality, the reputation, and the best interests of our country have long been eager to proscribe." In terms of enforcement, some senators favored the death penalty, seeing the slave trade as a kind of piracy. The congressmen from Rhode Island, a state long active in slave trading, were unwilling to go beyond "forfeiture, fines, and imprisonment." But even the stipulation that slaves being transported along the Atlantic coast had to be certified as not imported was viewed by John Randolph as a "pretext of universal emancipation." As the sectional fissure grew, Jefferson abstained from the debates out of "political prudence" and a "desire to unify his party and the country."[33]

Gradual emancipation, however, was not coming fast enough to satisfy a burgeoning anti-slavery crusade. And slave insurrections and threats of slave insurrections by a population growing prolifically by natural reproduction alarmed Jefferson and other southerners. In 1790, slaves made up about a third of the population in the southern states.[34]

As the slave population was growing in the United States, developments in the French colony of Saint-Domingue, on the western third of the island of Hispaniola—which would be known as Haiti after its independence in 1804—caused alarm. In the eighteenth century, this French colony was the richest in the Americas, with a population of fifty thousand free people, half of them persons of color, some of whom were plantation owners, and nearly five hundred thousand slaves, producing an estimated 40 percent of France's total trade. The French Revolution disturbed these relations. By inspiring various groups to appeal to their assemblies for greater freedoms, the Revolution instigated competition and division among groups of free persons—between poor whites and the wealthy planter class, and between white and colored planters. Slaves, many of them young men with military experience in their native African lands, saw the opportunity to rebel.[35]

In the last week of August 1791, they rose up under the lead of privileged slaves and burned hundreds of plantations. In 1794, the very year that revolutionary France decreed a general emancipation throughout the empire, freed black slave owner Toussaint Louverture rose to prominence as commander of the revolutionary forces in the colony's North Province. Years later, after Louverture had become Saint-Domingue's supreme leader, he declared himself governor for life. In 1802 Napoleon sent a massive expeditionary force to recapture the colony. Louverture was captured in 1802 and sent to prison in France, where he died a year later. Jean-Jacques Dessalines, a former slave who had already engaged in battles of reprisal against "free colored opponents of Louverture's forces" in the South Province, took over the struggle, retaliating against the French and "killing or driving out almost all the remaining whites." An estimated one hundred thousand Haitians were killed in the war, and the island's population "fell between 30 and 50 percent between 1789 and 1804." Independence was declared on January 1, 1804, but Dessalines was assassinated in 1806.[36] Haiti fell into authoritarian rule—something that both Jefferson and Alexander Hamilton had predicted.[37]

Internationally, the revolution provided unprecedented inspiration for the enslaved and struck fear in slaveholders. Stewart R. King writes that it "moved slaveholders in the southern United States to rethink their initial applause for the French Revolution. The 'horrors' of St. Domingo appear over and over again in the slaveholder discourses until the end of the Civil War."[38]

The bloody slave uprising in Saint-Domingue also inspired a literate slave named Gabriel in Richmond, Virginia, to plan a revolt in 1800. Jefferson and others feared that these events portended violence in the American South.[39]

Without question, the slave revolution inspired displays of militancy among blacks in the United States, as historian Sara Fanning recounts. In 1797 in Boston, a former slave named Prince Hall gave a speech entitled "A Charge to African Masons," which "linked the struggle for racial uplift to the freedom struggles of Haitians." On July 4, 1804, the year Haiti declared independence under Jean-Jacques Dessalines, "a few hundred black Philadelphians...formed military units...and marched through the city's streets," reportedly knocking down a young man, robbing him, and "threatening death to several others."[40] American whites were alarmed, as Winthrop Jordan documented in *White Over Black: American Attitudes Toward the Negro, 1550–1812*. Congressman David Bard of Pennsylvania, in arguing for a tax on imported slaves, warned of a possible re-creation of Saint-Domingue, where blacks "have become masters of the island." He pointed to the possibility that the "European Powers" would arm them in the same way they had "armed the Indians against us." In the Ninth Congress, John Clay described the new Haitian republic as "black despotism and usurpation."[41]

Refugees from Saint-Domingue had been arriving in the American South in large numbers since 1793. They brought slaves with them. "They write from Charleston that the NEGROES have become very insolent, in so much that the citizens are alarmed, and the militia keep a constant guard. It is said that the St. Domingo negroes have sown those seeds of revolt...." reported the *New-York Journal and Patriotic Register* in October 1793. According to Jordan, "Two months later Secretary of State Thomas Jefferson wrote to warn the governor of South Carolina of two mulattoes coming from St. Domingo to incite insurrection." In 1799, when Congress passed a bill opening trade with the Haitian revolutionary leader Toussaint Louverture, Jefferson warned Madison, "We may expect therefore black crews, and supercargoes and missionaries thence into the southern states...." In 1802, John Cowper of Norfolk wrote Governor Monroe that he and his neighbors were concerned about "the presence of French Negroes 'whose dispositions, I apprehend, will be influenced by the accounts which are daily arriving and published concerning the horrid scenes of St. Domingo.'"[42] The November 10, 1802, Richmond *Recorder* accused American editors of "fomenting restlessness among Virginia's slaves by reprinting the St. Domingo constitution."[43]

The southern states enacted protective measures. Between 1793 and 1795, South Carolina and North Carolina restricted or banned entry of slaves or persons of color from the West Indies. In Baltimore, disorderly slaves, if not removed from the state by their owners, "were to be sold to the West Indies," according to legislation passed in 1797.[44] In 1803 a federal bill was passed that prohibited the entrance of "any negro, mulatto, or other person of color, not being a native, a citizen, or registered seaman of the United States, or seamen, natives of countries beyond the Cape of Good Hope" into any state that prohibited it.[45]

Gabriel's abortive insurrection gave new impetus to the idea of colonization. After meeting in secret session, the Virginia government sent President Jefferson a request to purchase land to which the conspirators could be sent.[46] Jefferson, who disliked capital punishment and understood that the slaves were fighting for their natural rights, went so far as to ask the American ambassador in London, Rufus King, to inquire about such an option in Sierra Leone, a British refuge for Africans rescued from the illegal slave trade. Nothing came of the scheme at the time.[47] On November 24, 1801, in his letter to Virginia governor James Monroe, Jefferson referred to the "tragedy" of 1800 and posed possibilities for colonization in the western territory, settlement in the north in Indian land (an idea he abandoned because of the "rigorous" climate), or transport to Spanish holdings to the south. He settled on the West Indies, which were "[i]nhabited already by a people of their own race & color," with "climates congenial with their natural constitution," and where they would be insulated "from other descriptions of men." The "most promising portion," Jefferson thought, was "the island of St. Domingo, where the blacks are established into a sovereignty *de facto*, & have organized themselves under regular laws & government." Africa would offer a last resort "if all others more desirable should fail us."[48]

The fear of slave revolts would continue to mount, but it would be several years before action was taken on colonization.

"A Fire-Bell in the Night"

By the time of the 1819 debate on admitting Missouri to the Union, Jefferson had reversed himself on his earlier 1784 plan to forbid the expansion of slavery into the new states. He now advocated "diffusionism." Jefferson's shift in thinking occurred during the Saint-Domingue revolution. It began in 1796 during the debate about the extension of slavery into the Mississippi territory. Two of Jefferson's congressional allies advocated the expansion of slavery as a way to weaken it by breaking up dangerous concentrations of slaves in Virginia and other South Atlantic states. The goal was the peaceful end of slavery.

The "Missouri question," Jefferson wrote to Congressman John Holmes, presented a "momentous question, like a fire-bell in the night." It filled him with "terror." "[W]e have a wolf by the ears, and we can neither hold him, nor safely let him go. Justice is in one scale, and self-preservation in the other." Warning that the sacrifices of "the generation of 1776" could be "thrown away by the unwise and unworthy passions of their sons," Jefferson expressed hope that they would "dispassionately weigh the blessings…against an abstract principle" and "pause before they would perpetrate this act of suicide on themselves." In any case, he urged that the "abstract principle" of justice requiring emancipation was "more likely to be effected by union" than by the "scission" that he foresaw as the inevitable ultimate result of drawing "a geographical line, coinciding with a marked principle, moral and political," between southern slave states and northern free states. Though in 1784 he had opposed the spread of slavery to the western territories, he now argued for its "diffusion over a greater surface," which he said "would not make a slave of a single human being," but rather "would make [the slaves] individually happier, and proportionally facilitate the accomplishment of their emancipation, by dividing the burden on a greater number of coadjutors."[49]

As Peter Onuf explains in *The Mind of Thomas Jefferson*, Jefferson anticipated that the refusal "to allow the 'diffusion' of the slave population in new states...would increase the danger of servile insurrection and therefore strengthen the institution of slavery."[50] Admitting Missouri as a free state, Jefferson told Holmes, would violate states' rights by imposing the will of Congress and would be "the death knell of the Union."[51]

By 1824—in the wake of the Missouri Compromise, which had admitted Missouri to the Union as a slave state but had drawn the very "geographical line" that Jefferson had warned against between future slave and future free states at the 36th parallel, with sectional divisions growing as he had anticipated they would—Jefferson was again urging the colonization solution. As Onuf remarks, Jefferson's demand for "a national commitment to compensated emancipation and colonization," deviated "remarkably" from his position as a "proponent of limited government." The "Missouri controversy" had "radically transformed the political and constitutional context of colonization." Jefferson "implicitly warned northerners that this next great national discussion on the future of slavery must proceed from different premises. Only by talking about what the nation must do for slave owners, not for slaves, would it be possible to devise a colonization scheme that would not insult the honor or jeopardize the vital interests of southern states."[52] Northern abolitionists—many of them utopian radicals who ignored political realities—would operate from very different premises.

"Complimentary Epistles"

Jefferson wrestled with the problem of slavery his entire life, shifting his thinking as sectional tensions grew. When he was only weeks away from death, he wrote privately to James Heaton, "A good cause is often injured more by ill-timed efforts of its friends than by the arguments of its enemies. Persuasion, perseverance, and patience are the best advocates on questions depending on the will of others." The "cause" of ending slavery required a "revolution in public opinion." Jefferson's "sentiments" had been "forty years before the public," and, he wrote, had he "repeated them forty times, they would only have become more stale and threadbare." He knew he would not live to see his wishes "consummated," but they would be, "living or dying," in his "most fervent prayer."[53]

To the end of his life, Jefferson, though stubborn, retained a willingness to change his opinions in light of "scientific" evidence. In France in the 1780s, he had translated and taken careful notes on the views of slavery[54] expressed by the *philosophe* Marie Jean Antoine Nicolas Caritat, Marquis de Condorcet, who was a "descendant of an ancient aristocratic family" and a "noted mathematician, philosopher, statesman, and more recently a revolutionary," and who in 1777 "became perpetual secretary of the Académie Royal des Sciences, and in 1782 elected a member of the French Academy."[55] In 1791, when he was back in the United States and serving as secretary of state, Jefferson received a letter and manuscript copy of an almanac from a sixty-year-old free black man named Benjamin Banneker, which he wrote about to Condorcet.

Banneker had been born in Maryland to a free black couple who owned a tobacco farm. He was a precocious and intellectually curious child. Banneker, who never married, continued to live on and work the family farm with his mother until she died. He was befriended by George Ellicott, the fourth son of Andrew Ellicott, who came from a large Quaker family and was one of the founding brothers of a new grist mill and store enterprise in the remote area between the Patapsco River and Blue Ridge Mountains. George took up surveying at age sixteen and applied this skill in the construction of the Baltimore-Frederick Turnpike. George lent Banneker his prized books on astronomy, as well as a telescope, instruments, and a table by which Banneker taught himself astronomical forecasting. Banneker became the assistant of Major Andrew Ellicott (a surveyor and George's cousin), and they, along with Major Pierre Charles L'Enfant, made up the three-man team assigned to survey the site for the new federal capital along the banks of the Potomac. Banneker's arrival in March 1791 was announced in the Georgetown *Weekly Ledger*, which heralded him as "an Ethiopian whose abilities as surveyor and astronomer already prove that Mr. Jefferson's concluding that that race of men were void of mental endowment was without foundation."[56] In fact, it was Jefferson who had agreed to Banneker's appointment to the team, upon the suggestion of Major Andrew Ellicott.

As a boy, Benjamin Banneker had attended a rural one-room school where he was taught with "several white children and two or three black children," including future life-long friend Jacob Hall. Hall's "father had been a slave belonging to Walter Hall, a wealthy planter in Anne Arundel County," and "had been given his freedom and a bonus of thirteen acres of land in Baltimore County for his faithful service." Banneker's schooling, like that of most farm boys, was limited to the short session in winter,[57] but like Jefferson he was an intense observer of the natural world, a reader, and a tinkerer. In his early twenties he became "famous in his community and in literature" for constructing a wooden clock modeled on a watch.[58]

Another timepiece—an elaborate eight-foot-tall clock that was constructed by Joseph Ellicott and his son Andrew IV and displayed in Ellicott Mills—intrigued Banneker and led to his friendship with George. Banneker was about fifty-eight years old when George Ellicott lent him the materials necessary to undertake a study of astronomy.[59] Banneker had sent his calculations to George, who, suitably impressed, agreed to support him in his plans to publish an almanac.

Banneker entered scientific circles and was accepted as a fellow scientist. By all accounts his interest was purely in science. But this brotherhood of science also advanced the cause of abolitionism and expanded on similar post-Revolutionary efforts by such men as Charles Crawford, Moses Brown, and Benjamin Franklin. Benjamin Rush, a signer of the Declaration of Independence, civic leader, and a physician and chemistry professor by profession, became involved in the abolitionist cause in 1773 and advanced black freedom and equality by composing a testimonial to the talents of a black physician named James Derham practicing in New Orleans. As historian Winthrop Jordan wrote, "Dr. Rush was happy to call Dr. Derham a brother in science and commended him to the Pennsylvania Abolition Society as an example of Negro achievement." Rush was also responsible for making the public aware of Thomas Fuller from Maryland, who had been brought from Africa at the age of fourteen and become known as the "African calculator." Though illiterate, Fuller was a mathematical genius able to calculate enormous sums in his head. The *Columbian Centinel*, one of the outlets that advertised the abilities of the "*untutored Scholar*," speculated that had the "opportunities of improvement been equal to those of thousands of his fellow-men, neither the Royal Society of London, the Academy of sciences at Paris, nor even Newton himself, need have been ashamed to acknowledge him a Brother of Science" [emphasis in the original].[60]

Banneker was widely heralded for his almanac. The first two editions, published in 1791, included a letter by Dr. James McHenry—a former medical student of Benjamin Rush who served as a surgeon in the Revolutionary War, in the Maryland Senate for two terms, as a member of the Constitutional Convention in Philadelphia in 1786, and as secretary of war under George Washington and John Adams. McHenry vouched that the calculations had been done by Banneker himself. McHenry pointed out that Banneker's abilities offered a refutation to "Mr. *Hume*'s doctrine, 'that the Negroes are naturally inferior to the whites, and unsusceptible of attainments in arts and sciences'"— evidence that "the Rays of Science" "alike illumine the Minds of Men of every Clime" [emphasis in the original]. The almanac had been approved by David Rittenhouse, who at the time was "America's greatest luminary in the field of astronomy," in Jordan's description.[61] Banneker's almanac was also endorsed by another popular figure in scientific circles, William Waring, a mathematics teacher at the Friends' public school in Philadelphia and author of papers and books on astronomy, who was soon (in 1793) to be elected to the American Philosophical Society.[62]

Banneker, who "had little if any experience of oppression and cruelty to Negroes," was initially "put out" by Ellicott's and other Quaker abolitionists' focus on his race, according to his biographer Silvio Bedini. In Banneker's opinion, "the proposed almanac was of interest and value because of the competence of his astronomical calculations." Bedini, who was deputy director of the National Museum of History and Technology of the Smithsonian Institution, corrects the record regarding Banneker's motivation in writing to Jefferson: "Banneker's letter to Jefferson has been generally construed as evidence that he realized how he could be cited as an example of the Negro's mental capacity in refutation of Jefferson's statements to the contrary. There is serious doubt that such was indeed the case."[63]

Bedini argued that Banneker, who lived a "life of modesty, prudence, and dignity," would not have "conceived, without the guidance and encouragement of others, a letter so deliberately planned to evoke a statement of position from the statesman who had avoided a public commitment on the subject [of slavery] whenever possible." Bedini surmises that the letter was "suggested" to Banneker by the Ellicotts or their associates in the abolitionist movement.[64]

Writing to Jefferson, Banneker was aware of the possibility that "a letter from an unknown amateur almanac maker could…be offensive to the statesman," Bedini explained. But, on "careful thought," Banneker identified himself with "Jefferson's interests in relation to the survey of the Federal Territory."[65] He respectfully appealed to Jefferson, imploring him to remember "that time in which the arms and tyranny of the British crown were exerted with every powerful effort in order to reduce you to a state of servitude."[66] Banneker, Bedini stresses, "gave no indication that he was otherwise informed of Jefferson's expressed opinions or writings on the subject of the Negro, and he did not refer to his *Notes on the State of Virginia*. Instead, he likened the slavery of the Negroes to the enslavement of the colonies by the British Crown and the justification for the correction of one state of oppression on the basis of the other."[67]

Jefferson received the letter and almanac on August 26, 1791, in Philadelphia. His reply on August 30 was, as Bedini characterized it, "straightforward and written very much in the manner in which he responded to the many others who submitted their proposals or evidence of achievement in the field of science."[68] On the issue of race and ability,

Jefferson wrote, "No body wishes more than I do to see such proofs as you exhibit, that nature has given to our black brethren, talents equal to those of the other colors of men, and that the appearance of a want of them is owing merely to the degraded condition of their existence, both in Africa & America.... [N]o body wishes more ardently to see a good system commenced for raising the condition both of their body & mind to what it ought to be...."

Jefferson then informed Banneker that he had "taken the liberty of sending your Almanac to Monsieur de Condorcet, Secretary of the Academy of Sciences at Paris, and member of the Philanthropic society, because I considered it as a document to which your whole colour had a right for their justification against the doubts which have been entertained by them."[69]

When Jefferson forwarded the materials to Condorcet, he wrote that he was "happy to be able to inform you that we have now in the United States a negro...who is a very respectable mathematician." Jefferson revealed that he had also "procured him to be employed under one of our chief directors in laying out the new federal city on the Potowmac, & in the intervals of his leisure, while on that work, he made an Almanac for next year...which I inclos to you."[70]

Further vouching for Banneker, Jefferson wrote, "Add to this that he is a very worthy & respectable member of society. He is a free man. I shall be delighted to see these instances of moral eminence so multiplied as to prove that the want of talents observed in them is merely the effect of their degraded condition, and not proceeding from any difference in the structure of the parts on which intellect depends."[71]

Bedini interpreted this action as demonstrating Jefferson's "intention to provide Banneker with the best possible exposure if his work deserved it. In writing to Condorcet he was paying Banneker a great honor. Not only was the Académie the foremost body of scientific learning in France," but Condorcet was "one of the country's foremost scholars." Around the time he would have received the letter, in September of 1791, Condorcet became secretary of the Legislative Assembly, where he was "among the first to support a proposal for a republic" and "drew up the memorandum that led to the suspension of the king and summoned the national convention." He was captured and imprisoned on March 27, 1794, and on the next morning was found dead.[72]

Not surprisingly, because of the increasingly difficult political situation in France, no reply to Jefferson's letter from Condorcet has been found; Jefferson's hopes that Banneker's work would be reviewed positively by one of the Académie's committees and therefore "shed honor on the scientific work of the New World" were dashed.[73]

Banneker was nonetheless proud to have had his almanac treated with such respect. He filled out his remaining days on the farm pursuing his scientific interests, as well as publishing his almanac annually until 1797. In 1809, two years after Banneker's death, Jefferson received a short volume from Abbé Henri Grégoire titled *Literature of Negroes*, containing "biographical sketches of fifteen Negroes of note, including Banneker." It included Jefferson's letter replying to Banneker (with some factual errors). Jefferson answered Grégoire, writing that he would have been happy "to see a complete refutation of the doubts I have myself entertained.... My doubts were the result of personal observation on the limited sphere of my own State, where the opportunities for the development of their genius were not favorable, and those of exercising it less so." He said that he had expressed those thoughts about blacks in *Notes on the State of Virginia* with "great hesitation." And in any case, he pointed out, "talent" was not a "measure" of "rights": "Because Sir Isaac Newton was superior to others in understanding, he was not therefore lord of the person or property of others." And he was optimistic: "[T]hey are gaining daily in the opinions of nations, and hopeful advances are making towards their re-establishment on an equal footing with the other colors of the human family."[74]

Bedini suggested that "Jefferson's politeness to Grégoire was not completely sincere," adducing the evidence of a letter Jefferson wrote to his friend Joel Barlow which shortly afterward described Grégoire's book in uncomplimentary terms: "His credulity had made him gather up every story he could find of men of color (without distinguishing whether black, or of what degree of mixture), however slight the mention, or light the authority on which they are quoted." Jefferson also expressed his suspicions that Banneker had been assisted by Ellicott, who "never missed an opportunity of puffing him." The "long letter" from Banneker—which, as we have seen, was greatly influenced, if not composed, by Banneker's abolitionist friends—showed "him to have had a mind of very common stature indeed." Jefferson insisted, somewhat defensively, "It was impossible for doubt to have been more tenderly or hesitatingly expressed" than it was in his *Notes on the State of Virginia*, and that "nothing" was "further from my intentions, than to enlist myself as a champion of a fixed opinion, where I have only expressed a doubt. St. Domingo will, in time, throw light on the question."[75]

As Bedini notes, "Jefferson's comments about Banneker come as somewhat of a surprise" after his letter to Banneker and the steps he took to forward on the materials from Banneker to Condorcet. Jefferson's defensiveness may be explained by an assumption on Jefferson's part that Banneker's letter had been prompted by his reading *Notes on the State of Virginia*. But according to Bedini, "there is considerable question" whether Banneker was even aware of this work.[76]

The irritation about Banneker that Jefferson expressed in his letter to Barlow may be partly explained by a scandal back in the 1790s, when Banneker's correspondence with Jefferson had been published and distributed widely.[77] Writing to Barlow, Jefferson might have been remembering how he had fallen into a trap when the two letters were published, initially in a 1791 pamphlet, but then in Banneker's almanac of 1793—and given particular prominence in a Philadelphia edition, an issue "particularly directed to the interests of the antislavery movement." Late in 1792, the correspondence had also been widely circulated as a fifteen-page pamphlet, which was reprinted the following year due to demand.[78] Jefferson's political enemies leapt on this evidence of his sympathies. In *The Pretensions of Thomas Jefferson to the Presidency Examined* (1796), South Carolina's arch-Federalist William Loughton Smith asked accusingly, "What shall we think of a *secretary of state* thus fraternizing with negroes, writing them complimentary epistles, stiling them *his black brethren,* congratulating them on the evidence of their *genius,* and assuring them of his good wishes for their speedy emancipation?" [Emphasis in the original.][79]

Back to 1619

"In the controversy that ensued over Jefferson's candidacy for the presidency a few years later," Bedini comments, "he was attacked simultaneously from both sides, by those who foresaw in the liberation of Negro slaves a danger to the entire property system in the Southern states, and by those who supported the abolition of slavery." Banneker, as a result of the actions of his well-intentioned friends, became "the symbol of the oppressed Negro."[80]

Little could Jefferson, Banneker, Banneker's abolitionist friends—or anyone before 2019—have imagined, however, the use to which this event would be put in The 1619 Project.

The spot reserved for Banneker is in a "broadsheet," a special section in the August 18, 2019, issue of the *New York Times*, co-produced with the Smithsonian Museum of African American History (ironic, given Banneker's biographer's affiliation with the once venerable Smithsonian). This section, marked off by a cover featuring a "broadside" announcement for a slave auction, also features photographs of slave artifacts.

There is a column titled "A Powerful Letter" in this broadsheet, about 250 words long and illustrated with a crude Edvard Munch–style drawing of a seemingly beleaguered Banneker in the foreground, with a smaller Jefferson hovering behind his shoulder. The tribute is to Banneker, but it is hardly flattering to Banneker, and certainly not to Jefferson. About half of the short column is dedicated to repeating the case against Jefferson as a "lifelong enslaver," presenting his condemnation of King George for the slave trade as the clever ruse of a hypocrite, stating, "This language was excised from the final document" along with "all references to slavery" in a "stunning contrast to the document's opening statement about the equality of men." The equality clause is not, in fact, "the document's opening statement"; it is in the second paragraph of the Declaration. But historical accuracy gets swept aside in the rush to point out that "Jefferson was a lifelong enslaver. He inherited enslaved black people; he fathered enslaved black children; and he relied on enslaved black people for his livelihood and comfort." And Jefferson "openly speculated that black people were inferior to white people and continually advocated for their removal from the country."[81]

Banneker is described as "a free black mathematician, scientist, astronomer and surveyor" who wrote Jefferson arguing against this "mind-set," "urging him to correct his 'narrow prejudices' and to 'eradicate that train of absurd and false ideas and opinions, which so generally prevails with respect to us.'" And it continues: "Banneker also condemned Jefferson's slaveholding in his letter and included a manuscript of his almanac.... Jefferson was unconvinced of the intelligence of African-Americans, and in his swift reply only noted that he welcomed 'such proofs as you exhibit' of black people with 'talents equal to those of the other colors of men.'"[82]

This completely falsifies both sides of the exchange. Banneker's actual letter, which runs to fourteen paragraphs, says *nothing* about "Jefferson's slaveholding"—in fact it contains no personal criticism at all of the author of the Declaration. The 1619 Project misrepresents Banneker as an embittered man lashing out at Jefferson—the very opposite of the respectful tone of his letter.

Far from angrily attacking Jefferson, the letter by Banneker (and his Quaker friends) presents a general and polite abolitionist argument that avoids personal criticism of Jefferson's slaveholding. The Pulitzer Center's 1619 Project "Reading Guide" for students advertises the "broadsheet" as "a collection of artifacts and documents from the collection of the Smithsonian's National Museum of African American History and Culture." The broadsheet is promised to provide "a primary source-driven history of slavery in three time periods," but there is not even an excerpt from the correspondence between Banneker and Jefferson, much less a full "primary source" to read for oneself. While full-page photographs of slave bondage and other implements take up four pages and count as "artifacts,"[83] there is not even a link to Banneker's and Jefferson's letters—the "documents" with obvious relevance to this story—which are readily available online.[84]

Here are the points Banneker makes in his letter to Jefferson, paragraph by paragraph: First, he respectfully appeals to the "distinguished and dignified station in which you stand," in contrast to "the almost general prejudice and prepossession which is so previlent in the world against those of my complexion." Second, he summarizes that prevalent opinion: "[W]e are a race of Beings who have long laboured under the abuse and censureship of the world" and have been seen as "brutish" and "[s]carcely capable of mental endowment." In the third paragraph, Banneker implies that Jefferson is *better* than those who hold such opinions: "...report that has reached me, that you are a man *far less inflexible* in Sentiments of this nature, than many others; that *you are measurably friendly and well disposed towards us...ready to Lend your aid*"; the fourth paragraph expresses Banneker's wish to "eradicate that train of absurd and false opinions which so *generally* prevail with respect to us" and refers to "[y]*our sentiments concurrent with mine*"; in paragraph five Banneker appeals to the "duty of those who maintain for themselves the rights of human nature and who profess the obligation of Christianity"; in paragraph six he says, "[Y]ou could not but be Solicitous that every Individual...might with you equally enjoy the blessings" of "those esteemable laws which preserve to you the rights of human nature"; in seven, he explains, "I am of the African race," but not under "tyrannical thralldom" (in other words, he is a free black); in eight, he likens the state of slavery to British tyranny; in nine, he repeats the famous words from the Declaration of Independence, "We hold these truths to be Self evident, that all men are created equal, and that they are endowed by their creator with certain unalienable rights, that among these are life, liberty, and the pursuit of happiness"; in ten, he says, "[H]ow pitiable it is to reflect...that you should at the Same time be found guilty of that most criminal act, which you professedly detested in others, with respect to *yourselves* [plural, clearly referring to white Americans in general]"; in eleven, he refers to the Book of Job and does not "presume to prescribe methods...otherwise than by recommending to you, and all others, to wean *yourselves* from those narrow prejudices which you have imbibed...and as Job proposed to his friends 'Put your *Souls* in their Souls' stead'"; in paragraph twelve, he gets to his original purpose, directing Jefferson to the almanac (having "unexpectedly and unavoidably" been led to implore on behalf of the enslaved); in paragraph thirteen, he tells Jefferson that the almanac is a culmination of "my own assiduous application to Astronomical Study"; in the final paragraph, he explains how he completed the almanac despite the time devoted to his duties mapping out the federal territory, and that he wants Jefferson to have a copy in his own handwriting. He signs off, "Your most Obedient humble Servant" [emphasis added].[85]

The Project also paints a false picture of Jefferson brusquely dismissing Banneker. As we saw above, The 1619 Project's short description of Jefferson's answering letter presents him as giving Banneker a quick brush-off. In fact, as Bedini noted, Jefferson granted Banneker the same courtesy he extended to white men of science.[86] And The 1619 Project omits *any* mention of Jefferson's considerable efforts on Banneker's behalf[87]—his role in Banneker's appointment to the three-man team surveying the new District of Columbia and his forwarding Banneker's letter and almanac to a noted mathematician and member of the French Academy, specifically as evidence of blacks' mathematical aptitude. Jefferson explained to Banneker that he was sending the almanac to Condorcet "because I considered it as a document to which your whole colour had a right for their justification against the doubts which have been entertained of them." His letter ends with the customary courtesy, "I am with great esteem, Sir Your most obed' humble serv." The great honor of the U.S. secretary of state's introducing his work to the prominent French man of science is ignored. Of course, The Project, which excises white people from history—other than those it casts as "enslavers"—ignores the existence of the interracial, though largely white, brotherhood of science that was working to end slavery and accepted Banneker as an equal.

Incidentally, those doing the physical labor on the streets that Banneker helped lay out were German indentured servants brought in by the American government to help construct the city of Washington.[88]

Halting Steps toward Freedom

As Dumas Malone pointed out, Jefferson's options were limited. Among slave owners, Jefferson was better than most. He tried to see that his slaves were well treated. He "noted the years of his slaves' birth, grouped them in families," often designating their "particular occupations." He kept "careful and detailed lists showing the distribution of blankets, food, and clothing in successive years," in contrast to many like Andrew Durnford, who kept lists only by first name and age, and saw these individuals only as commodities to be bought and sold. Jefferson's were the ledgers of a "systematic" man "who, in the absence of a wife, was trying to take care of...dependents."[89]

Though Jefferson tried to make his plantations more productive, experimenting and buying new machinery, he was not the ruthless master that The 1619 Project makes him out to be. In fact, he found the "governance of others distasteful." But he liked being at Monticello. The future president wrote to Angelina Church in 1793 that he eagerly anticipated being "liberated from the hated occupations of politics" and returning to his farm. La Rochefoucauld found Jefferson in the fields directing the harvest and described him as displaying "a mild, easy and obliging temper, though he is somewhat cold and reserved. His conversation is of the most agreeable kind, and he possesses a stock of information not inferior to that of any other man. In Europe he would hold a distinguished rank among men of letters...."[90] Both white visitors and his own slaves recalled him singing minuets while walking, and playing the violin in the parlor.[91]

Jefferson was troubled when he was forced to sell slaves, as happened in the 1780s when he had to sell about fifty of the total two hundred (along with land) to pay off debts from his father-in-law. He made stipulations when he sold slaves, such as in the sale of eleven in 1792, when he ordered that a "family of four was to be kept intact, and an old couple were to go with their two sons if they wished—no charge being made for them." The old couple "chose not to go" though, "preferring to remain at Poplar Forest in honorable retirement."[92]

When Jefferson manumitted slaves, he wanted to ensure that each one "was prepared for freedom in his opinion, and had a good place to go to." In the 1790s he emancipated two members of the Hemings family.

The first, as we saw in chapter 4 above, was Robert Hemings. He had been Jefferson's personal servant until Jefferson sailed for France in 1784, and during Jefferson's years as secretary of state (1790–1793) he had received training as a barber at Jefferson's expense and been allowed to hire himself out. Robert Hemings married Dolly, a slave owned by Dr. Frederick Stras, had a child with her, and moved with her and her master to Richmond. Dr. Stras agreed to pay Jefferson the low price of sixty pounds to free Robert Hemings, who would pay him back.

James Hemings, who had accompanied Jefferson to Paris and Philadelphia and been taught "'the art of cookery' at great expense," was freed at his request after he returned to Monticello and trained the new cook, according to an agreement Jefferson had made with him. "In due course, when James reached the age of thirty, Jefferson freed him and gave him $30 to bear his expenses to Philadelphia...."[93]

In 1814, the seventy-one-year-old Jefferson, by then retired to Monticello, received a letter from fellow Virginian Edward Coles, the twenty-seven-year-old secretary to President Madison (and younger brother of Isaac Coles, who had been Jefferson's secretary). The "deferential letter" from Coles asked Jefferson "to devise and promote a plan for the general emancipation of the slaves in their state" and urged that "the author of the Declaration of Independence could do more than anybody else to bring the 'hallowed principles' of this document into full effect."[94]

Jefferson responded, recounting the abuse that Richard Bland had received forty years earlier for introducing Jefferson's measure allowing manumission in the Virginia legislature, and describing his own hopes in "the younger generation...after the flame of liberty had been kindled in every breast, & had become...the vital spirit of every American." Jefferson reiterated his desire for a "gradual extinction" of slavery and promised all his "prayers," "the only weapons of an old man." The "enterprise," he wrote, required "the young...those who can follow it up." So he urged Coles to "come forward in the public councils, become the missionary of this doctrine." As for those still enslaved, he said, "My opinion has ever been that, until more can be done for them, we should endeavor, with those whom fortune has thrown on our hands, to feed and clothe them well, protect them from all ill usage, require such reasonable labor only as is performed voluntarily by freemen, & be led by no repugnancies to abdicate them, and our duties to them; and to commute them for other property is to commit them to those whose usage of them we cannot control."[95]

Coles, however, chose to leave rather than become a "missionary" in Virginia. But it took him five years. In the spring of 1819, Coles was finally able to move to Illinois, in what was then the western territory. He went there knowing that a position as registrar of the United States land office at Edwardsville awaited him. Before he left, Coles had to arrange his affairs carefully, ensuring he left enough to take care of the needs of two old slave women staying in Virginia. He emancipated ten others en route to Illinois, giving each of the three families 160 acres of land in Illinois. For "his remaining slaves, a woman and her five small children, he purchased the woman's husband from a Virginia neighbor." They settled in St. Louis, Missouri, where they were made legally free in 1825.[96]

As the Coles case illustrates, in the early nineteenth century it was no simple thing to free slaves. Poor laws restricted what the slave owner could do. In order to prevent a number of freed blacks from becoming wards, various stipulations were put in place. Many states required that the master obtain a "certificate" for a healthy slave under a specified age, ranging from twenty-eight to forty-five, asserting that he or she was capable of self-support. Eleven states allowed for manumission if the master posted bond. Some states used the bond as security that the freed slave would leave the state, as ten states, including Virginia, required. Even some states that did not have a bond requirement held the former master responsible for those he had freed if they came in need. In 1815 the Virginia law was changed to allow for exceptions for good behavior, as determined by the court.[97] Also in Virginia, if the slaveholder failed to provide transportation out of state, the person could be re-enslaved by any Virginian. Of course, anyone of good conscience would go beyond manumitted slaves' transportation costs.[98]

And even with the safeguards Coles provided—such as land for freed slave families, for which James Madison "commended" him—there was no assurance, as Madison also pointed out, that they would enjoy "all the rights of white Americans." Though slavery was officially illegal in Illinois, a de facto form of it existed in the state, where "blacks were held as indentured servants for extremely long terms" and then, as they neared completion of their terms, "were often kidnapped and sold into slavery in the South."[99] In 1829 Illinois passed a law requiring incoming blacks to post a bond of $1,000, more than most Americans earned in a year.[100]

Madison's concerns were justified. Coles found himself fighting lawsuits that attempted to void the freedmen's emancipation and question the title to their land. "Seeing the difficulties his freed slaves often faced," Coles "urged them to seek resettlement in Liberia and offered to provide financial support," but they chose to stay. Coles decided to return east— as Ralph Ketcham speculates, because he became "weary of the hostility and harassment." There he "met and married Sally Logan Roberts, a wealthy Philadelphian, whose dowry provided a comfortable living there for the rest of their lives." Ketcham describes Coles's subsequent efforts, such as urging the aged James Madison to free his slaves and supporting the work of the American Colonization Society. His eldest son died on the battlefield in the Civil War—fighting for the Confederates.[101]

Jefferson, in his twilight years, could not do what Coles did as a young man. As Malone writes, Jefferson's "unavoidable problem at this stage of drought and depression was not how to free his slaves, but how to feed them."[102]

Four weeks before Jefferson's eighty-third birthday, on March 16, 1826, the author of the Declaration drafted and signed his will. The next day he added a codicil for "specific purposes," as Dumas Malone details: a walking staff to James Madison, watches to all the grandchildren, his books to the university, freedom to certain slaves. The slaves were tradesmen: "Burwell...a glazier, John Hemings, the carpenter; Joe Fosset, the blacksmith; and Madison and Eston Hemings, apprentices of John, who were to be freed on attaining maturity." Additionally, Burwell was left $300 "with which to buy tools or use in some other way." John Hemings and Joe Fosset "were to keep their tools" and also to "be provided with houses that were located at a convenient distance from the probable scene of their future labors...." Jefferson successfully appealed to the legislature to grant them permission to remain in the state. As Malone remarks, "These freedmen could take care of themselves. The same could not have been said of the large body of his slaves. To have turned them loose...would have been no kindness to them, and, in view of [Jefferson's] indebtedness may have been illegal as well as impracticable."[103]

Jefferson freed only a few of his slaves. But Coles was able to employ Jefferson's words to forward the fight for abolition. He published part of Jefferson's letter during his campaign for governor of Illinois.[104] Coles was elected governor in 1822, three years after his arrival in Illinois. "Two years later, he led the antislavery forces in opposing the call of a state constitutional convention that would have legalized slavery."[105] Six years after that, in 1830, a young man named Abraham Lincoln moved into the free state of Illinois.

CHAPTER 9

Colonization and Freedom

Jefferson had long believed that colonization was necessary for bringing about a peaceful end to slavery. As Peter Onuf explains, Jefferson saw the slave population as a "captive nation" that threatened the American republic. Thus, the enslaved should be emancipated, expatriated, and colonized. "Then, having 'declare[d] them a free and independent people,' the United States could recognize and help secure the equal rights of Africans as a people in the family of nations. Jefferson believed that national self-determination was for enslaved Africans—as it was for revolutionary Americans—the threshold for the actual exercise of an individual's natural rights."[1]

After the onset of the Saint-Domingue revolution, Southerners became concerned about its fallout in the United States, and they were not "placed more at ease by Denmark Vesey's attempted insurrection in 1822," as Benjamin Brawley put it. With blacks outnumbering whites in South Carolina—the black-to-white ratio had gone from "43.73 to 66.28 in 1790" to "52.77 to 47.23" in 1820—white South Carolinians began to "regard our Negroes as the *Jacobins* of the country, against whom we should always be upon our guard," in the words of Edwin Holland, a

South Carolina newspaper editor quoted in Brawley's *Social History of the American Negro.*[2]

But colonization had been discussed years before the black population growth in the Deep South, before the slave revolt in Saint-Domingue, before even the American Revolution. As Carter Woodson detailed in 1922 in *The Negro in Our History*, a scheme for "restoring the Africans to their native land" had been "developed by the Quakers under the inspiration of George Keith as early as 1713," and it was subsequently entertained as an option by those who desired "to ameliorate their condition by emancipation, but who were unable to think of incorporating them into their own society to live with the whites on an equal plane of equality." A closer home for freed blacks was proposed by abolitionist and teacher Anthony Benezet, who suggested they be settled in the American West. That idea garnered the support of Thomas Jefferson, among others. But the liberation of slaves who had participated in the Revolution, the expectation that more slaves would be emancipated, and the freed slaves' integration into American society made colonization less appealing—until slaveholders began seeing free blacks as a threat.[3]

Support from Whites and Blacks and across the Political Spectrum

As Brawley and Woodson both note, colonization was embraced by some blacks. Africa represented opportunities to advance—and to spread the gospel. In 1808 Samuel J. Mills, a white theology student, formed a missionary society with fellow students of Andover and Princeton, and then "a school for Negroes" in Parsippany, New Jersey. Those initiatives interested Robert Finley, a Presbyterian minister who called the first meeting "to consider the project of sending Negro colonists to Africa." In a February 14, 1815, letter to John P. Mumford, Finley recommended the plan as beneficial both to Africa and to "our blacks." Also in 1815, Paul Cuffe, the son of a father "who was once a slave from Africa and of an Indian mother," having acquired some wealth, traveled to England,

Africa, the West Indies, and the South and brought to Sierra Leone "a total of nine families and thirty-eight persons." Brawley reports that these settlers were "well received," but that Cuffe died two years later.[4]

Paul Cuffe's action resulted in growing support for colonization. Finley had communicated with Cuffe; Samuel J. Mills; Hezekiah Niles, editor of the *Niles Register*; Elijah J. Mills, "a Congressman of Massachusetts"; and "Elisha B. Caldwell, clerk of the United States Supreme Court." The first meeting of the American Colonization Society in 1816 was attended by several prominent individuals, including "Henry Clay, the compromiser, Francis Scott Key, the author of the Star-Spangled Banner, John Randolph, a United States Senator from Virginia, Judge Bushrod Washington, [a nephew] of George Washington, and Charles March, Congressman from Vermont."[5] Officers were elected on New Year's Day 1817 in Washington, D.C. The previous month, Charles F. Mercer, in order to obtain "a resolution calling on the federal government to secure territory outside the United States as a refuge," had produced in the House of Delegates of Virginia the unpublished correspondence of 1801–1802 "between President Jefferson and Governor Monroe regarding the possible establishment of a settlement for deported blacks."[6] Under the Monroe administration, land was purchased in Liberia. Lott Cary, a black Baptist preacher who served as governor of one of the provinces of Liberia, would be among the first black political leaders there.[7] Although it seems that Jefferson never officially endorsed the organization, his January 21, 1811, letter to John Lynch, published in the April 11, 1817, *Richmond Enquirer,* had opined that colonization would allow "the seeds of civilization" to be brought to Africa, "the country of [the slaves'] origin."[8]

The prospect of colonization was greeted optimistically, according to Woodson:

> The problem then was to develop in this country a number of
> intelligent Negroes who might constitute a nucleus around
> which a government could be established. Here we see that

the blacks were encouraged to develop the power to work out their own salvation. It gave an impetus to the movement for more thorough education of the Negroes at the very time when the South was trying to restrict them in such opportunities. Those Negroes to be sent out were to be trained in the manual arts, science, and literature, and in the higher professions. John B. Russwurm, an alumnus of Bowdoin, the first Negro to be graduated by a college in the United States, went as an educator to Liberia....[9]

Liberia continued to represent hope for both blacks and white emancipators. As we have seen, Louis Sheridan freed his slaves, presumably on the condition that they accompany him to Liberia, in 1837. Around the same time, John Carruthers Stanly was helping Lott Holton in his quest to free his slaves and send them to Liberia. White slave owner John McDonogh, who had helped Andrew Durnford, a black man, buy slaves, became a vice president of the American Colonization Society and freed and sent eighty-five of his slaves to Liberia in the 1840s. In his will, McDonogh "left a large bequest to the society" and "provided for the emancipation of most of his remaining slaves" and their transportation to Liberia. Later black enthusiasts for colonization included Martin Delany, a doctor and journalist, and Alexander Crummell, an Episcopal priest.

In the mid-1820s, colonization was supported by the Manumission Society and was viewed as a preventative for the moral degradation that it was thought would emerge as a result of an increasingly discriminatory society. According to historian Leslie Harris, some believed that colonization would provide opportunities for blacks to "prove their equality with whites by Christianizing native Africans and building up the economic infrastructure in Africa. Once blacks in Africa demonstrated their true abilities, whites in America would realize that slavery and racism were wrong and would welcome blacks in America. Other supporters of colonization argued that the possibility of sending freed blacks to Africa

would increase voluntary emancipation in the southern states and ultimately end slavery." At the 1826 meeting of the American Convention
of Abolition Societies, delegates from the New York Manumission Society put forth resolutions for recommending to Congress "the gradual,
but certain, extinguishment of slavery, and the transportation of the
whole coloured population, now held in bondage, to the coast of Africa,
or the island of St. Domingo."[10]

Colonization was also embraced by the radical young Scottish heir-
ess, abolitionist, and feminist—and presumed mistress of the Marquis
de Lafayette—Frances (Fanny) Wright. She had previously visited the
United States and published a positive traveler's account. She and her
younger sister joined Lafayette as he made a "triumphal tour" of the
United States at the invitation of President James Monroe, lasting from
August 15, 1824, to September 3, 1825. The tour included two grand
visits to Monticello and the University of Virginia. Jefferson, then eighty-
one years old, managed to recover from a digestive ailment in time for
the extravagant celebrations. After dinners and speeches marked by
tearful tributes to the days of the American Revolution, Jefferson and
Lafayette visited privately, reminiscing "about the American and French
revolutions" and discussing "the low state of political liberty in Europe
and the problem of slavery in the United States." After the ten-day stay
of the main party, Lafayette left to visit James Madison. Fanny Wright
and her sister remained at Monticello a bit longer because "one of them
was ill."[11] She and Jefferson continued to discuss the problem of slavery,
and he expressed approval of a plan she had to purchase government
land in the American South as a commune for fifty to a hundred slaves,
where they would spend five years preparing to become colonizers and
working to pay off their costs. Jefferson confided to her that the fate of
slaves had been "thro' life that of my greatest anxieties."[12]

Wright is a prominent figure in the pantheon of radical heroes that
University of Massachusetts English professor Holly Jackson celebrates
in *American Radicals: How Nineteenth-Century Protest Shaped the
Nation.* Wright is noted for her rejection of feminine conventions—by

speaking in public, dressing in men's clothes, being sexually promiscuous, and, after involvement with other utopian communities, founding the Nashoba utopian community in Tennessee, per the plan she had described to Jefferson. In 1826 Wright acquired eighteen slaves, promising the man who had inherited and was anxious to sell them that they would be well treated and emancipated and colonized in fifteen years, "or sooner if they had paid back by their labor what Wright had spent on them plus the cost of resettlement abroad." But in spite of Wright's expressed egalitarian ideals, the project was not run on egalitarian principles: it commenced in March 1826, and by June one slave had already been punished with solitary confinement and a diet of bread and water. Separated from the whites, restricted, and punished, these people were treated worse than many slaves.[13]

Wright had to leave Nashoba for a time because of illness, and the men in charge in her absence flogged and sexually assaulted the slaves.[14] She returned in January 1828, only to leave shortly afterwards for "adventures" of "touring American cities and scandalizing audiences, writing lectures on intellectual and social freedom, fighting against officials who challenged her right to speak, founding the Hall of Science and addressing crowds of workingmen and freethinkers there," while around thirty people "remained in bondage at her Nashoba estate" under the supervision of an overseer. She did plan to free them through colonization (making the decision for them) by sailing with them to Haiti from New Orleans at the end of a lecture tour.

An estimated thirteen thousand African Americans had moved to Haiti in 1824 and 1825, during the height of a publicity push for the Haitian emigration movement, which was supported by black abolitionist James Forten. Many of them had returned disappointed by the black-ruled nation's denial of citizenship rights and economic opportunity.[15] But this did not stop Wright. She had met Jean-Pierre Boyer, the president of Haiti, during a stop in Philadelphia on the tour with Lafayette. "In January 1830, Wright had her slaves transported from Nashoba down the Mississippi to New Orleans," from whence they departed for a month-long journey on a chartered brig. President Boyer greeted Wright and her party "profusely" and defrayed her expenses. He settled her slaves on his own land, promising that he would eventually set them up on their own farms. Wright and William S. Phiquepal d'Arusmont—a lover of hers, from the utopian community of New Harmony, whom she had brought along on the trip—"ended up staying longer than she had expected, enjoying dinners and garden parties with the mixed-race Haitian aristocracy...." But by the end of March she was feeling the effects of an unplanned pregnancy, which interrupted her plans to "quickly return to her lecture career" and implement a grand design for American public schools. Jackson writes that "the trip effectively ruined her life." On July 1, 1830, after delivering a final lecture to three thousand at the Bowery Theatre, and no longer able to hide her pregnancy, "she sailed for France, not only disappearing mysteriously from her public work, but cutting contact even with close friends." She did marry Phiquepal about six months after their daughter was born. But Fanny Wright faded into obscurity.[16]

In Haiti

What happened to the thirty black slaves Wright brought to Haiti? Jackson does not say. But she does comment on Wright's feminist legacy. Fanny Wright's picture was featured on the frontispiece of the first in a six-volume set titled *History of Woman Suffrage*, a project undertaken by Elizabeth Cady Stanton and colleagues and published from 1881 to 1922. Ironically, Wright's daughter Silva described her mother's radical work as "infidel trash" and testified against women's suffrage in 1874.[17]

Wright did not leave any record of the slaves she owned, but from what we know about the fates of most others transported to Haiti, they likely did not fare well—in spite of Boyer's assurances. By 1830, after more than a dozen years of civil war between various factions, and after many American immigrants had left in disgust because of false promises from Boyer, the conditions no doubt were not good for them.

The creation of Haiti in 1804 as the result of the Saint-Domingue revolution failed to end the country's domestic violence and racial tensions. In *Caribbean Crossing: African Americans and the Haitian Emigration Movement*, historian Sara Fanning sums up the challenges arising from the fact that a slave state "governed by a tiny elite" had "bequeathed few institutions or foundations to the new nation." After the death of revolutionary leader Toussaint Louverture, Haiti was governed by a succession of authoritarian rulers: Jean-Jacques Dessalines, Alexandre Pétion, Henri Christophe, and Jean-Pierre Boyer. Major issues concerned "land, labor, and diplomatic recognition," but there were also problems of racism and corruption.[18] Dessalines's massacres had effectively reduced Haiti's white population to marginalization. The remaining mulattoes and blacks, many of whom were African born, fought each other in regional and national struggles for power. Mulattoes often exhibited racial prejudice against blacks.[19]

Beginning with Toussaint Louverture, Haitian rulers tried to attract blacks from the United States and other countries to repopulate the land after bloody fighting.[20] Dessalines continued with this strategy, trying to fill a labor shortage. It is not known whether he was aware of Jefferson's idea of exporting blacks after Gabriel's Rebellion. He wrote Jefferson a friendly letter in the hope of restoring trade between Haiti and the United States. But Jefferson appears not to have answered. Under Jefferson's presidency, American policy shifted. John Adams's anti-French administration had permitted the selling of military supplies and food to the island's revolutionary army. But Jefferson, as president, supported an embargo on the Haitian trade.[21] After economic conditions deteriorated and Dessalines proposed the expropriation of land, he was assassinated by, as Fanning puts it, "a cabal of [newly established] landowners and military personnel."[22] The island was carved in two, one part ruled by Christophe, a former slave who had commanded the northern army, and the other ruled by Pétion, "the military hero from the south of Haiti" with a mulatto following. Both leaders reinstituted the forced-labor laws of Louverture. In the North they were enforced by "more than four thousand military police stationed at individual plantations"; on the plantations in the South, which had been given to Christophe's political "cronies," work habits were similarly regulated.[23] Christophe, bed-bound from a stroke, committed suicide as an avenging mob threatened him.[24]

In 1819, Boyer used military force to begin to unite the "dominions in the fractured nation." In 1822, he took "advantage of the chaos produced by the Spanish American wars of independence" and captured the whole of Saint-Domingue without bloodshed.[25] But that year the Denmark Vesey conspiracy impeded Boyer's effort to get diplomatic recognition from the United States through an American emigration scheme. According to Fanning, "During the trial, accusers outlined an elaborate and detailed plot that even featured Boyer as an active agent who had planned to provide ships and give refuge to the rebels in Haiti."[26] Yet Boyer persisted in presenting Haiti as friendly both to American businesses and to anti-slavery advocates, promoting emigration as, in Robert Paquette's description, "a way to shrink the tumor of slavery."[27] In 1824, Haiti became the (unnamed) cornerstone of the plan of Ohio and eight other northern states for emancipation.[28] "Boyer's offer to finance emigration to his nation won him some powerful U.S. media supporters who had become disillusioned with the African colonization project," says Fanning.[29] Haiti was also viewed hopefully by abolitionists in the "free produce movement" to boycott produce from slave labor.

The campaign was too successful. Rather than the expected one thousand immigrants, a total of four thousand came. There was not enough government land set aside for them all, except in far-flung regions where most of the immigrants did not want to go. Many chose to take up the offer of sharecropping near Port-au-Prince to learn how to farm.[30] When a drought drove many of the settlers to the city, they were exposed to an outbreak of smallpox. By March 1825, "two hundred emigrants had returned to the United States."[31] And Boyer had not fulfilled his promise to develop the shipyard in Samana, to which 460 immigrants had been lured by offers of land and business setup opportunities.[32] Failing to get recognition from the United States, Boyer looked to ally with France. In the treaty, Haiti agreed to pay 150 million francs as indemnity for the land and slaves lost by French plantation owners in the revolution. To finance the indemnity, the patent tax, "a form of business license, had to be increased."[33] Things got worse. "In a drastic attempt to jump-start productivity," on May 1, 1826, Boyer enacted the Code Rural—forced labor on plantations.[34]

"The Americans who remained in Haiti may have found the debates over Haiti's independence, coupled with the Code Rural's ruthless enforcement, difficult to reconcile with their expectations of Haiti as a black land of the free," explains Fanning. "Worse, Boyer agreed to a British provision that a runaway slave 'from the British colonies' who made his or her way to Haiti would be restored to the British colonial authorities."[35] Artisans and skilled laborers who had been lured by the advertisements found no need for their services.[36] And the emigrants who had faced new voting restrictions in America found themselves denied the right to vote that had been promised to all men over the age of twenty-one after one year of residency in Haiti. When a group living in Port-au-Prince prepared to vote and "put up a fellow settler, a Methodist minister, as a candidate," the Americans "entered in at one door" of the polling place and were ushered out the opposite one—past the voting booth. Settlers were also denied the right to serve on juries, which had also been denied them in New York through discriminatory measures.[37] The economic situation became so bad it is estimated that more than two-thirds of the settlers scrambled to make it back to the United States.

But, as Fanning says, "Haiti's history of throwing off the double yoke of colonialism and slavery remained a powerful symbol of what the descendants of Africa could accomplish. Haiti, abandoned by its American supporters, continued its struggle to gain political and diplomatic acceptance against a hostile world and fought this battle virtually alone throughout the nineteenth century and into the twentieth. This did not have to be."[38]

True enough. But the international neglect conjoins with other factors in explaining the failure: reports of the suffering and deaths of black emigrants, the interracial warfare, the false advertising about business opportunities, the failure to follow through on the developments of the promised shipyard, forced labor, the denial of citizenship rights. In the end, Boyer had no one to "blame but himself."[39]

So it should not be surprising that the number of supporters declined and few responded to the call for colonization by the abolitionist Benjamin Lundy in his newspaper *Genius of Universal Emancipation* in the 1830s.[40] Once it was learned what conditions were like in Haiti, a considerable number of black migrants to Haiti thought a return to America provided more hope after all.

CHAPTER 10

Taking Down
Abraham Lincoln

Within the context of the events taking place during his lifetime, Thomas Jefferson comes off as the prudent voice of reason and statesmanship. Given the situation as it was, Monticello could have been a worse place. Certainly the slaves "rescued" by Fanny Wright did not benefit from her radical idealism. Even the free blacks who emigrated to black-run Haiti found themselves denied political rights and facing hunger and forced labor on plantations.

Jefferson had predicted what would happen in Haiti, and he had good reason to fear the same happening in his own country. The founder understood that governing was a balancing act. He cannot be reduced to an "enslaver"—the label with which The 1619 Project has smeared him. His "lived experience" (to use a term popular among his detractors) was that of a member of the gentry in the founding generation. Born and raised on a Virginia plantation, his first memory was of being carried in the arms of a black man—a slave, true, but one trusted with a three-year-old boy on horseback, hardly the picture one gets from The 1619 Project.

Jefferson deserves to retain the title "Apostle of Liberty."

And Abraham Lincoln deserves to retain the title "Great Emancipator."

Abraham Lincoln's story is very different from Jefferson's. His hard-scrabble upbringing caused him to reject the "spirit that says, '*You work* and toil and earn bread, and I'll *eat* it.'" He took a very public stand against slavery—particularly in the Lincoln-Douglas debates of 1858, when he ran for the Senate. Lincoln argued against the pro-slavery sena-tor Stephen Douglas: "He contends that whatever community wants slaves has a right to have them. So they have, if it is not a wrong. But if it is a wrong, he cannot say people have a right to do wrong."[1] Lincoln's principles were so well known that seven Southern states seceded from the Union out of fear that his election as the first Republican president was a mortal threat to the institution of slavery.

It is a measure of Nikole Hannah-Jones's utter lack of historical perspective that in her telling both Jefferson and Lincoln are simply evil white men representing a racist America. Her "Idea of America" essay goes from discrediting the Apostle of Liberty to discrediting the Great Emancipator.

In The 1619 Project, the broad brushstrokes used to paint a picture of Jefferson and "most of the founders" as racists are applied to "white Americans" generally, as history merges with dubious psychological theorizing. With independence, supposedly, America could no longer transfer guilt to Britain and thus was forced to claim the "sin" of slavery as her own: "The shameful paradox of continuing chattel slavery in a nation founded on individual freedom, scholars today assert, led to a hardening of the racial caste system." The cultural belief that "black people were subhuman...allowed white Americans to live with their betrayal."[2] Hannah-Jones bolsters the diagnosis of a national white guilt complex by citing Leland B. Ware, Robert J. Cottroll, and Ray-mond T. Diamond, who claim in their book *Brown v. Board of Educa-tion* that "white Americans, whether they engaged in slavery or not, 'had a considerable psychological as well as economic investment in the doctrine of black inferiority.'[3]

This leads to Hannah-Jones's discussion of the 1857 *Dred Scott* decision, which declared any attempt to prohibit the spread of slavery unconstitutional. Hannah-Jones quotes Chief Justice Roger Taney's words, from the majority opinion in the case, that blacks "were so far inferior, that they had no rights which the white man was bound to respect; and that [all blacks] might justly and lawfully be reduced to slavery." Taney, however, was not expressing his own opinion in this statement. As Charles Warren explains in his multivolume history of the U.S. Supreme Court, Taney was "recit[ing] it historically as the view held by men in general, in the eighteenth century." Taney, who sympathized with the plight of blacks, was nonetheless a states-rightist and Constitutionalist. To be sure, Taney's words have been misrepresented for over 160 years, including by abolitionists.[4] But Hannah-Jones goes further, claiming on the basis of this well-known quotation that this Supreme Court decision "enshrined" the thinking that "black people" were a "slave race"—a "caste" not entitled to the rights of "We the People." "This belief, that black people were not merely enslaved but were a slave race," she declares, "became the root of the endemic racism we still cannot purge from this nation to this day."

Actually, no. Far from enshrining racism in America, the *Dred Scott* decision solidified and energized *opposition* to slavery—so much so that we had a civil war and ended it.

Frederick Douglass, the famous abolitionist who had escaped from slavery, was actually "thrilled" with the *Dred Scott* decision because it won people over to the abolitionist cause. It also inspired Illinois Senate candidate Abraham Lincoln to change his outlook: he went from regarding the Supreme Court as "the nation's supreme authority" to putting his "faith in natural law" as expressed in the Declaration of Independence. *Dred Scott* came on the heels of the 1854 Kansas-Nebraska Act, which had made Lincoln lose hope in the demise of slavery by natural extinction. Lincoln's "House Divided" speech "appealed to the court of public opinion" and was a "smashing success," launching Lincoln onto the national stage.[5] It also won enthusiastic praise from Frederick Douglass, who had adopted the same position in 1851.[6] Lincoln's speech inspired the abolitionist zealot John Brown.

There is no mention in The 1619 Project of the "House Divided" speech. In fact, Hannah-Jones chooses to skip over not only the "House Divided" speech but such other significant events as the Lincoln-Douglas debates, Lincoln's election as the first Republican president, the secession of the Southern states, and the outbreak of Civil War, and to focus instead on another, much later and relatively insignificant event. She leaps over all those, going straight from her commentary on the 1857 *Dred Scott* decision to August 14, 1862, "a mere five years after the nation's highest courts declared that no black person could be an American citizen." And what is the significance of that momentous date? On August 14, 1862, "President Abraham Lincoln called a group of five esteemed free black men to the White House for a meeting. It was one of the few times that black people had ever been invited to the White House as guests. The Civil War had been raging for more than a year, and black abolitionists, who had been increasingly pressuring Lincoln to end slavery, must have felt a sense of great anticipation and pride."

Indeed, this event "was the first time a group of blacks met with a president on a 'matter of public interest.'" The meeting had been arranged by Reverend James Mitchell, the Lincoln-appointed commissioner of emigration, who had been active in Midwestern colonization societies along with Lincoln. Hannah-Jones's wording implies that the men invited were prominent leaders well known in the black community. However, according to John Stauffer, the author of *Giants: The Parallel Lives of Frederick Douglass and Abraham Lincoln*, "four of the five men were recently freed slaves and probably illiterate."[7]

Hannah-Jones says, "The president was weighing a proclamation that threatened to emancipate all enslaved people in the states that had seceded from the Union if the states did not end the rebellion. The proclamation would also allow the formerly enslaved to join the Union army and fight against their former 'masters.' But Lincoln was worried about what the consequences of this radical step would be. Like many white Americans, he opposed slavery as a cruel system at odds with American ideals, but he also opposed black equality."

Then she quotes two sentences by Lincoln—without identifying the source: "Free them, and make them politically and socially our equals? My own feelings will not admit of this; and if mine would, we well know that those of the great mass of white people will not." Abraham Lincoln did say those words. But when did he say them, and in what context? Not at the 1862 meeting at the White House. In fact, not as President Lincoln at all. The quotation is plucked out of Lincoln's first debate with Stephen Douglas, on August 21, 1858, when Lincoln criticized Douglas for his unwillingness to challenge court decisions such as *Dred Scott*—the one Hannah-Jones claims "enshrined" the "doctrine of black inferiority."

The year before, in Springfield, Illinois, in his speech about the decision, Lincoln had already called it "erroneous." He had charged that while Douglas and Taney both "argue that the authors of [the Declaration of Independence] did not intend to include negroes, by the fact that they did not at once, actually place them on an equality with the whites," the founders also did not "place all white people on an equality with one or another.... [T]he authors of that notable instrument intended to include *all* men, but they did not intend to declare all equal *in all respects*." The statement that "all men are created equal" being "of no practical use in effecting our separation from Great Britain," it was placed there "for future use," as "a stumbling block to those who in after times might seek to turn a free people back into the hateful paths of despotism."[8] In that same speech Lincoln had delineated the difference between the Republican and Democratic parties: "The Republicans inculcate...that the negro is a man; that his bondage is cruelly wrong, and that the field of his oppression ought not to be enlarged. The Democrats deny his manhood; deny, or dwarf to insignificance, the wrong of his bondage; so far as possible, crush all sympathy for him, and cultivate and excite hatred and disgust against him."⁹

In the first of the Lincoln-Douglas debates, Lincoln had said that anybody who, like Douglas, agreed with "the Dred Scott decision" was essentially endorsing "in advance" a "second Dred Scott decision" which would nationalize slavery: "It is merely for the Supreme Court to decide that no *State* under the Constitution can exclude it...."¹⁰ Lincoln had said the same thing even earlier, in his "House Divided" speech in Springfield, in which he had argued, "Either the *opponents* of slavery, will arrest the further spread of it, and place it where the public mind shall rest in the belief that it is in course of ultimate extinction; or its *advocates* will push it forward, till it shall become alike lawful in *all* the States, *old* as well as *new—North* as well as *South*."¹¹

Lincoln took his stand firmly on the opposing side. He made politic concessions to the racial prejudice of his day. But he refused to budge an inch on the fundamental rights of blacks: "[T]here is no reason...why the negro is not entitled to all the natural rights enumerated in the Declaration of Independence, the right to life, liberty and the pursuit of happiness. I agree with Judge Douglas he is not my equal in many respects—certainly not in color, perhaps not in moral or intellectual endowment. But in the right to eat the bread, without leave of anybody else, which his own hand earns, *he is my equal and the equal of Judge Douglas, and the equal of every living man*" [emphasis in the original].¹²

Hannah-Jones dishonestly highlights one statement from the Lincoln-Douglas debates while ignoring the sum total of other speeches that clearly spell out Lincoln's belief that the Declaration includes blacks, his goal of the "ultimate extinction" of slavery, and his assertion of black personhood. And she follows up this distorted picture of President Lincoln's stance on black Americans with a distorted picture of the White House meeting: "That August day, as the men arrived at the White House, they were greeted by the towering Lincoln and a man named James Mitchell, who eight days before had been given the title of a newly created position called the commissioner of emigration.... After exchanging a few niceties, Lincoln got right to it. He informed his guests that he had gotten Congress to appropriate funds to ship black people, once freed, to another country."

And he told them the reason why: that both races "suffer" by living together.

Lincoln's height—six feet, four inches—is given an ominous spin: he is described as "towering," as if standing over the black men in an intimidating manner. This is a very different picture of the meeting from that in even left-leaning histories whose authors do not shy from criticizing Lincoln—neither John Stauffer's *Giants* nor David Blight's *Frederick Douglass: Prophet of Freedom*, for example, imply that Lincoln's posture was menacing in any way.[13] And Hannah-Jones infuses more dark drama: "You can imagine the heavy silence in that room, as the weight of what the president said momentarily stole the breath of these five black men." She inserts yet another reminder about 1619: "It was 243 years to the month since the first of their ancestors had arrived on these shores, before Lincoln's family, long before most of the white people insisting that this was not their country."[14]

Actually, it is doubtful that any of the men meeting with Lincoln that day were descendants of the twenty or so Africans from the *White Lion*. Hannah-Jones's statement implies that all four and a half million blacks (four million slaves and half a million free) living in the United States in 1862 had as their "ancestors" the people who came aboard the *White Lion*. This would be like claiming that the *Mayflower* Pilgrims are the "ancestors" of all white Americans. Recall that even in 1649, thirty years after the arrival of the *White Lion*, blacks made up only 2 percent of Virginia's population.

But Hannah-Jones continues her narrative of good in the face of oppression, recounting American history literally in black-and-white terms. She claims that in spite of such treatment and the fact that the "Union had not entered the war to end slavery but to keep the South from splitting off," "black men had signed up to fight" and "[e]nslaved people were fleeing their forced-labor camps…trying to join the effort, serving as spies, sabotaging confederates, taking up arms for his cause as well as their own. And now Lincoln was blaming them for the war." He even said that "without the institution of slavery and the colored race as a basis, the war could not have an existence…." Edward Thomas, the chairman of the delegation, "informed the president, perhaps curtly, that they would consult on his proposition. 'Take your full time,' Lincoln said. 'No hurry at all.'"

Hannah-Jones then jumps ahead again, to Lee's surrender at Appomattox three years later. "Contrary to Lincoln's view," she informs us, "most [black Americans] were not inclined to leave, agreeing with the sentiment of a resolution against black colonization put forward at a convention of black leaders some decades before: 'This is our home, and this our country. Beneath its sod lie the bones of our fathers…. Here we were born, and here we will die.'"

Some Details Left Out

It is true that the Union had entered the war to keep the South from splitting off, but Hannah-Jones does not explain why. Because Lincoln did not go to war over slavery does not mean he did not care whether or not slavery continued, as she implies. Credible historians of an earlier time recognized the constitutional and practical limits Lincoln faced. As John Hope Franklin wrote decades ago, unity was the "only legitimate basis for prosecuting the war," and to have any hope of winning Lincoln had to have the support of the Northern and border states.[15] "Lincoln had to move cautiously…for constitutional, political, and military reasons." Furthermore, his "views on emancipation" were known.[16] "As a young man he told a New Orleans group in 1831, 'If I ever get a chance to hit that thing, I'll hit it hard.'" In 1842, while still a member of the Illinois House, he told a Cincinnati audience that "[s]lavery and oppression must cease, or American liberty must perish."[17]

As early as 1849 Lincoln had introduced a bill in Congress for the gradual emancipation of slaves in the District of Columbia, and in the 1850s he repeatedly restated his position.[18] Lincoln bristled at suggestions that he was "'soft' on the question of slavery," Franklin points out, quoting a letter Lincoln wrote to a friend in April 1864: "If slavery is not wrong, nothing is wrong.... And yet I have never understood that the Presidency conferred upon me an unrestricted right to act officially on this judgment and feeling...." Franklin explains, "Lincoln was troubled by unanswered questions regarding the legality as well as the effect of emancipation on the course of the war and on the peace and well-being of the country. Who could know if the soldiers of Kentucky would lay down their arms if Lincoln set the slaves free?"[19] They might point them at Washington, as Lincoln had feared when he revoked General John C. Frémont's emancipation proclamation. And if they did, would the men of other border states follow?[20] These were the concerns of the commander in chief, though not necessarily of abolitionist activists.

The sentiments expressed at that 1831 convention of black leaders—"this [is] our country"—are indeed laudatory. Hannah-Jones comments, "That the formerly enslaved did not take up Lincoln's offer to abandon these lands is an astounding testament to their belief in this nation's founding ideals." The question is, do Hannah-Jones and the other contributors to The 1619 Project believe in the "nation's founding ideals"? The very purpose of The Project is to *eliminate* the 1776 founding, as the header of Hannah-Jones's Twitter profile so graphically illustrated with the crossed-out "1776."[21] After all, as her essay says, "The United States is a nation founded on both an ideal and a lie."[22]

By confusing issues, cherry-picking quotations, and ignoring the historical and political realities of Lincoln's time, The 1619 Project makes the Great Emancipator out to be a racist who simply wanted to "ship" freed blacks "to another country." Lerone Bennett, the Black Power propagandist and Hannah-Jones's high school hero, whom she still enthuses about, went even further.[23] In *Forced into Glory: Abraham Lincoln's White Dream*, Bennett called Lincoln's colonization policy "racial cleansing," referring to the Holocaust: "[I]t was...the only racial solution he ever had—and under his leadership...racial cleansing became, 72 years before the Third Reich...the official policy of the United States of America." He claimed that the American Revolution "projected a White Utopia in which all White men or, at least, all White men with property were equal" and "defined Blacks and Reds as subhumans...." In Bennett's opinion, the colonization proposal "was based on the wildest idea ever presented to the American people by an American president. What Lincoln proposed...was that the United States government buy the slaves and deport them to Africa or some other hot place."[24]

In fact, as we saw in chapter 9, many advocates for emancipation—both black and white, from across the political spectrum—had turned to colonization in exasperation at the difficulties of the nearly intractable problem of slavery, a problem that was ultimately resolved only at the cost of a bloody Civil War. But that is part of the complicated reality that Hannah-Jones does not want to acknowledge. She ignores not only blacks who were in favor of colonization, but also the very existence of well-off free blacks (some of whom owned slaves) and the sacrifices that so many whites—including Abraham Lincoln—made to achieve the abolition of slavery. In her quasi-Marxist narrative, all blacks are poor and struggle alone for freedom, while all whites are privileged and racist.

Lincoln's True Motives

Lincoln did not just want to "ship black people, once freed, to another country" and abandon them.[25] The reality was, as he told the five men gathered in his office on August 14, 1862, that even once free from slavery, "[Y]ou are yet far removed from being placed on an equality with the white race"—a fact that was unfortunately true at the time. Furthermore, Lincoln acknowledged that blacks had been wronged. He told the men, "I do not know how much attachment you may have toward our race.... It does not strike me that you have the greatest reason to love them."[26] These are hardly the words of a callous man. And he braved serious adverse consequences for his public expressions. Stephen Douglas taunted him throughout the debates for the praise he had received from Frederick Douglass for his anti-slavery position and his "House Divided" speech. Democratic newspapers printed racial slurs,[27] and even before his inauguration, Lincoln was getting death threats.[28] And, we should not forget, Lincoln was ultimately assassinated by a Confederate sympathizer, John Wilkes Booth, who was in the crowd on April 11, 1865, when Abraham Lincoln gave his last public speech. As Lincoln spoke about giving the vote to "very intelligent" African American citizens, John Wilkes Booth turned and told his co-conspirator Lewis Powell, "That is the last speech he will ever make." Three days later, at Ford's Theatre, Booth fatally shot the president.[29]

Lincoln used the political options available to him. As Allen Guelzo explains in *Lincoln's Emancipation Proclamation*, "[C]olonization had another advantage besides putting distance between the oppressor and the 'systematically oppressed.' If free blacks...would pledge themselves now to join a colonization project, it would convince white people who feared any form of emancipation without colonization that the fears were groundless." As James McPherson points out, Lincoln wanted to "defus[e] white fears of an influx into the North of freedpeople." That was why a reporter had been invited to the meeting in 1862.[30] Franklin went so far as to say that "it is almost possible to measure [Lincoln's] approach to emancipation by studying the increasing intensity of his efforts to formulate a feasible program of colonization."[31]

Furthermore, the place of colonization that Lincoln proposed to the men at that White House meeting was not in Africa but much closer, "a great highway from the Atlantic or Caribbean Sea to the Pacific Ocean"—in other words, present-day Panama. He asked for *volunteers* and not a large commitment, saying that even "twenty-five able-bodied men, with a mixture of women and children" would suffice to begin.[32]

The idea of colonization had been debated and re-debated. Lincoln had entertained colonization as early as 1854, when he had "said that his first impulse 'would be to free all the slaves and send them back to Liberia, to their own native land.'"[33] In his speech on the *Dred Scott* decision in 1857, Lincoln had admitted that the "enterprise" was "difficult." Likening the project to the "children of Israel" leaving "Egyptian bondage in a body," he stated, "Let us be brought to believe it is morally right, and, at the same time, favorable to, or, at least, not against, our interest, to transfer the African to his native clime, and we shall find a way to do it...."[34] As Guelzo points out, "Lincoln's lifetime was witness to massive migration of Europeans to North America, India, and Australia...."[35] And in the centuries before then the poor, orphans, single women, and petty criminals left England and other places for indentures in the New World.

In March 1861, Lincoln had directed the American minister to Guatemala to look at places in Central America, and he was approached the following month by the head of the Chiriqui Improvement Company on the eastern shore of the isthmus of Panama. Congress granted his request for appropriations for territorial acquisition and related expenses in the District of Columbia Emancipation Act and Second Confiscation Act.[36] (At his annual message in December 1861, Lincoln, citing the precedent of Jefferson in acquiring the Louisiana territory, had announced his plan to confiscate the "property used for insurrectionary purposes," that is, slaves, and suggested the government declare them free.) Although the contract with the Chiriqui Improvement Company was signed in 1862 and Lincoln's agent, Kansas senator Samuel Pomeroy, had made arrangements for five hundred blacks to emigrate, the neighboring countries of Honduras, Nicaragua, and Costa Rica objected. Lincoln then looked into "Cow Island, off the southern peninsula of Haiti." Going against his advisers, Lincoln agreed to accept the offer of some New York financiers to arrange for the passage of five hundred blacks and provide homes, schools, medical care, and farmland "for a fee of $50 per émigré." The attempt ended in tragedy. In mid-April 1863, the 453 former slaves suffered an outbreak of smallpox on board, and then, on the island, malarial fevers. The financiers failed to pay for the services promised or to assure approval from the Haitian government.[37]

Lincoln, terribly distressed, "ordered a transport to bring them home," according to John Eaton, a chaplain involved in organizing freedmen. Lincoln also asked Eaton questions about the abilities of "the freedmen coming to the Union lines" in handling their new freedom. "A few days earlier he had written Nathaniel Banks, commander of the Union-occupied areas of Louisiana, to express his hopes that the state would 'adopt some practical system by which the two races could gradually live,'" with education "in the plan" as well as job training. Lincoln "was unsure what the new relationship between whites and blacks might look like," says John Stauffer, but "believed that 'negroes, like other people, act upon motives.'" Lincoln asked, "Why should they do any thing for us, if we do nothing for them?"[38]

After the August 14, 1862, White House meeting, Lincoln followed up with an August 22, 1862, letter to Horace Greeley, editor of the *New-York Tribune*, who had accused Lincoln of deferring to "Rebel Slavery." Historian James McPherson calls Lincoln's timing and arrangements in "preparing public opinion" for the Emancipation Proclamation a "stroke of genius": the letter assuaged "conservatives who insisted that preservation of the Union must be the sole purpose of the war" and gave hope to "radicals who wanted him to proclaim emancipation in order to save the Union." "To everyone he made it clear that partial or even total emancipation might become necessary...."[39] The letter, "the colonization 'lecture,'" and the reorganization of the army, as Guelzo writes, "point together toward an expectation that the emancipation moment might be just around the corner."[40]

Black Support

Not all black leaders were rendered speechless and breathless at the mere mention of colonization, as Hannah-Jones implies. John Hope Franklin speculates that some of that group of five may have pledged support, "for in his second annual message [Lincoln] was able to say that many free blacks had asked to be colonized."[41] As we have seen, in the early days colonization was discussed in tandem with gradual emancipation, such as in 1777, when Thomas Jefferson headed a Virginia legislative committee. John Hope Franklin points out that Paul Cuffe's transport of "thirty-eight blacks to Africa in 1815...suggested...that some blacks were indeed interested in leaving the United States." More freed blacks went to Africa under the auspices of the American Colonization Society two years later. After 1827, blacks "were manumitted expressly for this purpose." By 1830, "the society had settled 1,420 blacks in the colony" of Liberia and a total of about 15,000 had migrated. Support for colonization from Southern slaveholders who wanted to strengthen their hold by removing free blacks had much to do with the opposition to colonization. In 1817 Richard Allen and James Forten charged colonizers with "having no other object in view than the benefit of the slaveholding interests of the country."[42]

Some did prefer starting life anew in a foreign land to lifelong enslavement in the United States, or even to living in the same country as their former slave masters. As Stauffer points out, "Many blacks endorsed the idea of emigration and agreed with Lincoln that in America blacks and whites could not live together harmoniously. The black leader Henry Highland Garnet supported Lincoln's vision of colonization as 'the most humane, and merciful movement which this or any other administration has proposed for the benefit of the enslaved.'"[43] Garnet wanted to bring "civilization and Christianity" to Africa and to end the slave trade there.[44] So did other black ministers who went to Liberia, among them Daniel A. Payne, Alexander Crummell, Lott Cary, and Colin Teague.[45] Crummel, a classically educated free black man from a wealthy family, spent almost the entire Civil War period in West Africa, returning twice to recruit blacks to emigrate.[46]

Douglass biographer David Blight admits that "[s]ome blacks, although a diminishing minority, responded favorably to Lincoln's colonization proposals." By October 1862, Pomeroy "claimed he had received

13,700 applications from potential black emigrants, two of whom were [Frederick] Douglass's frustrated sons Lewis [almost 22 years old] and Charles [age 18] who...decided to consider moving to Panama."⁴⁷ In fact, Douglass himself, enraged by Lincoln's conciliatory first inaugural address in March of 1861, planned to leave for Haiti on an exploratory trip on April 25, 1861. But before he could leave, Fort Sumter was bombed on April 12. The conflict had exploded into what Douglass called a "slaveholding rebellion," requiring the force of the U.S. government to suppress it, and he did not go.⁴⁸

Frederick Douglass debated the pro-colonization black leader Garnet about emigration. Douglass said he would rather take his chances with "the slave traders of Maryland and Virginia" than with "the savage chiefs of the western coasts of Africa." Blacks should "stay here"—where their chances for success were greater.⁴⁹ He had no romantic illusions about Africa. And perhaps he understood that despite her flaws, America ultimately represented the best hope for equality and opportunity. Deviating from his white radical abolitionist friends, Douglass argued fiercely for blacks' American identity. In a February 5, 1862, speech, he argued against colonization and revealed that he had rejected an offer of citizenship from another country. He claimed that blacks were American at heart—in contrast to the Indian, who "sees the plowshare of civilization tossing up the bones of his venerated fathers" and "dies of a broken heart." "Not so with the negro," said Douglass. "There is a vitality about him that seems alike invincible to hardship and cruelty. Work him, whip him, sell him, torment him, and he still lives, and clings to American civilization."⁵⁰

Rich Blacks, White Supporters

While Hannah-Jones pretends that only black abolitionists were working against slavery (and were concerned about colonization), Franklin acknowledges the countless numbers of white Americans who worked on behalf of emancipation. Many of these individuals risked death for black freedom. Elijah P. Lovejoy, publisher of the *Alton Observer* in Illinois, was killed by a mob in 1837 after criticizing the "leniency of a judge in the trial of whites accused of burning a black man alive." Abolitionist speakers were routinely attacked, as was a Quaker teacher, Prudence Crandall, for integrating her classroom and then opening a school for black girls in Connecticut. By 1830, Franklin explains, "[w]hen the period of militant abolitionism began, black people were ready to join whites in fighting the hated institution." They had formed fifty black abolitionist societies.[51]

White Americans who have fought for blacks' equal rights include such well-known figures as abolitionists William Lloyd Garrison and John Brown, and later, in the civil rights movement, two young white Jewish men, Michael Schwerner and Andrew Goodman, who were abducted and murdered in Neshoba County, Mississippi, along with a young black man, James Chaney, in June 1964 while working on a campaign to register black voters. The case has been the subject of books, a PBS documentary, and the movie *Mississippi Burning*. The following year, Viola Liuzzo, a housewife from Michigan, traveled to Alabama to march in Selma, but while she was driving black activists from the Montgomery airport, a carful of KKK members shot and killed her.[52] Around the same time, the Reverend James Reeb, a Unitarian minister from Boston, was beaten to death while walking down the streets of Selma.[53]

But there are also countless white Americans whose names are not known to history who sacrificed social acceptance, livelihoods, and their lives. In 1809, white servants in New York testified on behalf of black servants against an abusive couple, Amos and Demis Broad, with two of them giving up their jobs to do so.[54] The famous anti-slavery activist Sojourner Truth, known as Isabella as a slave, was bought— along with her daughter—and then freed by the Van Wagenen family.[55] Anna Shotwell and her niece Mary Murray, after seeing two disheveled black orphans on a stoop on Cherry Street in New York City in the spring of 1834, founded the Association for the Benefit of Colored Orphans, and then, with Hannah Shotwell, the Colored Orphans Asylum.[56] White female reformers who managed and worked at the orphanage were sometimes criticized for neglecting their own families and the needs of poor whites.[57]

Many Southerners opposed slavery. Mary Berkeley Minor Blackford of Fredericksburg, Virginia, hated slavery and tried to convince at least two of her five sons to leave the South instead of serving in the Confederate army. In 1827 she freed her two "house servants" (or slaves), expecting them to leave for Africa, but they refused, preferring to stay with her under employ as free servants. She had tried to intervene on behalf of a slave mother whose son was going to be sold south, even confronting the guard. About a year after the Nat Turner insurrection, while visiting friends in Southampton County, she talked with surviving members of the Whitehead family—most of whom had been killed in the uprising—and emphasized to them that the guilty were "a comparatively small number." Ignoring the law, Blackford ran "a Sunday school for slaves." In March 1866, in her "Notes Illustrative of the Wrongs of Slavery," she described rejoicing in "a new era.... Slavery has been abolished!!!" Upon seeing "a procession of nearly one thousand black children who were attending the local schools," she described her happiness that "the little ones were no longer shut out of the light of God's truth, that the fetters of ignorance were at last broken, and that they might not be forced from their parents and sold at public auction." Blackford gave thanks "to the Great God, not only on their account, but that *we white people* were no longer permitted to go on in such wickedness."[58]

Blacks were terrorized by the Ku Klux Klan—and so were white people who came to their aid. On the eve of the 1868 election, while riding his horse to a campaign event for Ulysses S. Grant in Arkansas, James Hinds, who had moved from Minnesota and been working openly and publicly with blacks for their voting and political rights, was shot and killed by George Clark, a Klansman and a secretary in the Democratic Party—thus becoming the first congressman to be assassinated in office.[59]

Southerners are often vilified as racists, but as this former Georgia resident can testify, many hated segregation. As Harper Lee said when asked in 1963 at the Chicago Press Club about writing *To Kill a Mockingbird*, "I tried to give a sense of proportion to life in the South, that there isn't a lynching before every breakfast. I think Southerners react with the same kind of horror as other people do about injustices in their land."[60]

Harper Lee's hero character, the small-town lawyer Atticus Finch, had real-life counterparts in everyday hero neighbors such as William Lewis Moore, a postman who staged single-person protest marches against segregation and was shot and killed in Attalla, Alabama, in 1963 after planning to deliver a letter to the governor of Mississippi urging him to end segregation.[61] That same year Jonathan Myrick Daniels, a seminary student who had returned home to Hayneville, Alabama, to help with a black voter registration drive, was arrested at a demonstration and then shot by a deputy sheriff after his release while buying soda at a convenience store near the jail.[62] In the North, on April 7, 1964, the Reverend Bruce Klunder, a young minister, was backed over and killed with a bulldozer while lying in the street to protest the building of a segregated school in Cleveland.[63]

"[W]hile the black community in Philadelphia organized the first National Convention of Free Persons of Colour," Frederick Douglass's mentor William Lloyd Garrison sat in a Baltimore jail after being found guilty of libel for accusing a Massachusetts shipper of participating in the domestic slave trade (he was bailed out by a fellow abolitionist after seven weeks). *American Radicals* author Holly Jackson applauds Garrison for his willingness to be "persecuted, imprisoned and bound" and even "to die as one of the white martyrs he believed would be necessary to awake mainstream America to the cause of black suffering." After becoming persuaded by black abolitionists with whom he lived to reject colonization, he began denouncing it in speeches.[64] After the slave insurrectionist Nat Turner was caught in 1831, Garrison received death threats, which he published in his newspaper *The Liberator*—along with a statement declaring "that he was ready to die for the cause."[65] In 1835, "Garrison was mobbed in the streets of Boston, gallows were built in front of his house as a death threat, and he was burned in effigy." Later that year, vigilantes led Garrison down the street "like an animal on a leash," his glasses broken and his pants torn off.[66] On May 22, 1856, after giving a fiery speech against the violence in Kansas over the issue of slavery and naming guilty Southern senators, Massachusetts senator Charles Sumner was beaten in the Senate chamber with a cane to within an inch of his life by South Carolina representative Preston Brooks.[67]

The Kansas-Nebraska Act of 1854, which allowed settlers to decide on the slavery issue, inspired Douglass's friend John Brown to go to Kansas in the fall of 1855 to "make war on slavery," as Blight puts it. In May of the following year, "after proslavery bands attacked and burned Lawrence, Kansas, the Free Soil bastion of the territory," Brown, accompanied by his teenaged son Oliver, a son-in-law, and members of his extended family, conducted "a bloody middle-of-the-night raid" in which five men (supporters of the slave-state cause but non-slaveholders) were "seized from the clutches of their families" and hacked to death with broadswords.[68]

In October 1859, Brown attempted to capture the arsenal at Harpers Ferry, Virginia, to overthrow the government, hoping thousands of slaves and free blacks would rise up and join him. Although Frederick Douglass was sympathetic to the mission, he correctly saw the plan as unfeasible and tried to dissuade Brown. As Stauffer remarks, "Unlike Brown, who was fifty-nine years old and ready to die for the cause of freedom, Douglass preferred to remain alive." The thousands of enslaved blacks who had received word of the plan also remained on their plantations. In fact, Brown may have become confused and waited too long when the "slaves did not rally to his side" as expected. Among the twenty-one men (four of whom were black) who participated and died in the doomed mission were Shields Green, a fugitive slave, and two of Brown's sons. At his trial, Brown gave oratorical performances, "becoming," as Stauffer puts it, "a heroic martyr to countless Northerners" and earning praise from Ralph Waldo Emerson as a "new saint" who made "the gallows glorious like the cross." Among those witnessing Brown's hanging was the actor and future assassin John Wilkes Booth, in disguise as a soldier.[69]

Brown's efforts were financed by the wealthy white abolitionist Gerrit Smith. Smith gave away land and assets worth about $8 million (worth $600 million in 2008), mostly to poor blacks. In 1846 he gave away 120,000 acres in the Adirondacks region of New York State, dividing it up into 40-acre lots for 3,000 poor blacks, thus qualifying them to vote in New York State.[70]

Frederick Douglass, the most influential black abolitionist, was supported every step of the way not only by blacks such as his future first wife Anna Murray, journalist David Ruggles, who was also the head of the New York Underground Railroad, and members of the Zion Methodist Church, but also by whites—from the German blacksmith who recognized him on the train during his daring escape from slavery and did not betray him, to the members of the American Anti-Slavery Society who paid him to speak, to John Collins, with whom he traveled and was attacked, to the most famous abolitionist of the time, William Lloyd Garrison. British abolitionists bought Douglass's freedom so that he would no longer be at risk of being returned to slavery. Wealthy American abolitionists, primarily Gerrit Smith, set up him up in publishing his newspaper. White abolitionists helped him buy a home in Rochester in 1848. The British woman Julia Griffiths tutored him on rules of grammar, edited his articles, and taught him business practices to make his newspaper a success. White women organized anti-slavery societies where he was a celebrated, well-paid speaker. By the 1850s, Douglass, who "commanded almost as much money from lecturing as the most sought-after white orators," had bought a large house that looked like "a European villa" in the Pinnacle Hills area of Rochester.[71]

In fact, the apathy of free blacks was a source of frustration for Douglass, as is revealed by his editorials. Of the half million free blacks in the United States, he wrote, only 2,000 were interested in "self-help," fewer than 1,400 were interested in anti-slavery, and only 100 subscribed to his paper. He charged, "Every colored man should ask himself the question, 'What am I doing to elevate and improve my condition and that of my brethren at large?'" Though only 100 blacks subscribed to Douglass's abolitionist newspaper, "between four and five thousand blacks convened in New York City" in July 1848 for the annual gala "celebration of Odd Fellows, the nation's largest black fraternal order."[72]

Free black men in Charleston and New Orleans divided themselves along lines of complexion and class, with the "mulattoes" of Charleston forming an elite fraternal benevolent organization called the Brown Fellowship Society and those of darker skin forming the Humane Brotherhood. The color caste system in Louisiana, which retained Spanish and French influences, was even more pronounced.[73] And Denmark Vesey, the free black man who was probably from the Gold Coast region of Africa and who had planned a slave uprising in Charleston in 1822, was betrayed by a mixed-race slave, a cook named Peter (who later adopted the name Desverney). Peter told William Penceel, a free member of the exclusive Brown Fellowship Society, who then advised him to confide in his owner, Colonel John Cordes Prioleau.[74]

Desverney saw an opportunity to achieve his own freedom. As Larry Koger put it, he "betrayed the black masses to obtain his own liberty." He then purchased slaves of his own. Similarly, "the reason William Penceel thwarted the slave uprising centered on the simple fact that he," like most of the members of the Brown Fellowship Society, "was a slaveowner for profit" and wanted to protect his "property." For his efforts he was exempted from the capitation tax and awarded $1,000, part of which he used to purchase more slaves. Fellow Brown Fellowship Society members "viewed his role in exposing the slave rebellion as a responsible reaction." And the free colored elite of Charleston "viewed Peter Desverney as a hero."[75]

Free blacks were often given a start by benevolences of property and money from their former owners and "by organizations such as the Society of Friends, the Pennsylvania Society for the Abolition of Slavery, and the North Carolina Manumission Society." As white workers left to go west, free blacks in the South were engaged in dozens of skilled occupations, as they were in the North, where they were also "in the professions of the ministry, teaching, law, and dentistry."[76] These professionals often had white clients, as George Schuyler discovered in traveling through the South in 1925 and 1926.

Like Marxists and similar propagandists who have obscured the diversity and conflicts within groups in order to present a narrative of bad rich whites versus good poor blacks (or kulaks versus proletarians), Hannah-Jones ignores the black upper classes, not only in the antebellum South but also in Northern cities such as Philadelphia and New York. "By the Civil War," wrote one historian, "the Negro community in New York 'had a small social aristocracy which seems to have led a gay life, emphasizing balls, soirées, dancing classes and musicales.'" William B. Gatewood writes, "[A]ristocrats of color in the two cities...not only shared a common social life on occasion but also were often related by blood or marriage." The black emigrants from the South to cities in the Midwest and North included, among the lower-class cotton farmers and laborers, the "upwardly mobile...who acquired wealth and assumed positions of leadership." Many of these families had made their fortunes in the catering business and then started other businesses or entered the professions of medicine, law, and education.[77]

And it was well-off free blacks who financed the efforts of the white abolitionist William Lloyd Garrison, who had grown up poor in a fatherless family in Newburyport, Massachusetts, and started as a printer's apprentice at age thirteen. His newspaper *The Liberator* first appeared on New Year's Day 1831, thanks to major financial backer John Vashon, a Pittsburgh free black man, and the wealthy African American James Forten, who sent him an advance on twenty-seven subscriptions. When Garrison went to England to connect with abolitionists to promote an international movement, Nathaniel Paul of Albany joined with many other African Americans and helped pay Garrison's passage.[78]

Garrison's advocacy went beyond the immediate cause of black emancipation to a radical social justice agenda that included ameliorating the "oppression of the working class and Native Americans." His maiden speech on July 4, 1829, warned his generation to reject the example of the founders. He found "much of their legacy objectionable and their grievances against England 'trifling.'" Rather than rallying his audience around the American flag on the patriotic holiday, he declared, "I am ashamed of my country" and suggested Independence Day be a day of "fasting and prayer" and "great lamentation."[79] Garrison, as Tony Williams explains, "did not merely see slavery as a contradiction or aberration in the American regime," but saw the Constitution as "a pro-slavery document"—in Garrison's words, "a covenant with death and an agreement with hell." He therefore believed in secession—of the North from the South.[80]

In 1845, after Douglass published his first autobiography, he was threatened with re-enslavement by Hugh Auld and fled to Britain on a lecture tour, where donors bought his freedom. On his return to America in 1847, he moved to Rochester, New York. This was when his split with Garrison, who learned of Douglass's activities secondhand and "felt like a spurned lover," began. Other Boston abolitionists considered Douglass an apostate. The purchase of his freedom, they felt, had "compromised abolitionist principles." Many of them also considered it "absurd" for an ex-slave to think he could become an editor, as Douglass planned to do. As Stauffer points out, "A fugitive orator who bared his [whip-scarred] back to shocked audiences was one thing; an editor who enlightened educated readers in the principles of liberty, justice, and humanity was something else entirely."[81] Understandably, Douglass had come to resent "being constrained to only speaking about his experiences as a slave" and being "trotted out as a living exhibit of an escaped enslaved person." As he closely studied the documents of the American founding and considered the arguments of Lysander Spooner, William Goodell, and Liberty Party presidential candidate Gerrit Smith, he came to develop his own political philosophy.[82]

A "Glorious Liberty Document"—
or a Constitution to Protect and Preserve Slavery?

The speech for which Douglass is probably best known was delivered on July 5, 1852 (owing to the Fourth falling on the Sabbath). It was his first address after his shift the previous year to an understanding of the Constitution as a "liberty document." His position was in stark contrast to that of William Lloyd Garrison—and of Nikole Hannah-Jones.

The thirty-four-year-old Douglass spoke to a group of five hundred to six hundred mostly white people at Corinthian Hall, a new "lavish" and "imposing" brick building named for its tall interior Corinthian columns, in Rochester, New York. The meeting was sponsored by the Rochester Ladies' Anti-Slavery Society, whose nineteen members raised money for the immediate abolition of slavery and for fugitive slaves passing through Rochester on their way to Canada.[83]

By this time, Douglass was the most famous black American, an "esteemed abolitionist" speaker and publisher of the *North Star* in Rochester, where he resided. Tall and athletic, with hair swept back but defiantly standing up, he had an imposing presence.[84] Displaying "great dignity and stern countenance," Douglass began his address in the manner common since Aristotle and Cicero, by a display of humility, claiming "limited powers of speech," especially given the "task" before him: delivering a Fourth of July "oration."[85] Douglass's request for "patient and generous indulgence" for a speech that had "no elaborate preparation" or "high sounding exordium" was intended to disarm his audience. Douglass had actually spent two weeks preparing it.

This display also served to underscore the distance between himself and his white audience, whom he addressed in the second person at key points in the speech. The occasion, he said, "is the birthday of your National Independence, and of your political freedom." Recalling his experience as a lay preacher, Douglass reminded them that the holiday "to you" was "what the Passover was to the emancipated people of God." The contrast between his white audience and his own race was highlighted when he told his "fellow-citizens" he was glad "that your nation is so young," and thus more easily reformed. In the manner of Benjamin Banneker, he established common ground by describing his agreement with the founders, whom he called "your fathers." These "brave" and "great" men sided "with the right, against the wrong" and "the oppressed against the oppressor." Douglass would "unite with you to honor their memory."

"Your fathers" who "staked their lives, their fortunes, and their sacred honor, on the cause of their country" provided a contrast to "these degenerate times," he said, unleashing a series of clauses modifying the founding fathers: "Fully appreciating the hardship to be encountered, firmly believing in the right of their cause, honorably inviting the scrutiny of an onlooking world, reverently appealing to heaven…soundly comprehending the solemn responsibility…wisely measuring the terrible odds…your fathers, the fathers of this republic, did, most deliberately, under the inspiration of a glorious patriotism, and with a sublime faith in the great principles of justice and freedom, lay deep the corner-stone of the national superstructure, which has risen and still rises in grandeur around you."

Douglass then characteristically "suddenly revers[ed] course…surprising his audience."[86] The "demonstrations of joyous enthusiasm" on the "nation's jubilee," the "ear-piercing fife and the stirring drum" uniting "with the ascending peal of a thousand church bells" led him to feel "the immeasurable distance between us," for the "rich inheritance…bequeathed by your fathers, is shared by you, not by me. The sunlight that brought life and healing to you, has brought stripes and death to me. This Fourth [of] July is yours, not mine."

"To drag a man in fetters to the grand illuminated temple of liberty, and call upon him to join you in joyous anthems, *were inhuman mockery and sacrilegious irony*." More fitting is "the plaintive lament of a peeled and woe-smitten people!" As with the Jews "[b]y the rivers of Babylon" in Psalm 137, their "chains, heavy and grievous yesterday, are, to-day, rendered more intolerable by the jubilee shouts that reach them."

Seeing "this day, and its popular characteristics, from the slave's point of view," Douglass did "not hesitate to declare, with all my soul, that the character and conduct of this nation never looked blacker to me than on this 4th of July!" Liberty is "fettered." The Constitution and the Bible "are disregarded and trampled upon." And slavery is "the great sin and shame of America!"

After this highly emotional appeal, Douglass made logical arguments, pointing to the self-contradiction of a system that considered a slave a man under the law when it comes to punishment for crime, but not when it comes to rights. Laws forbidding the teaching of reading and writing implicitly acknowledge blacks' intellectual capabilities. Slaves do the work of men—farming, constructing, and mining using mechanical tools. They work as clerks, merchants, ministers, teachers. And they raise families and worship in churches. Yet, "we are called upon to prove that we are men!"

Seeking to rouse the "conscience of the nation," he asked, "What to the American slave is your 4th of July?" It is "a day that reveals...the gross injustice and cruelty to which he is the constant victim"—"your celebration" proven "a sham; your boast liberty, an unholy license; your national greatness, swelling vanity...your shouts of liberty and equality, hollow mockery; your prayers and hymns, your sermons and thanksgivings, with all your religious parade, and solemnity, are, to him, mere bombast, fraud deception, impiety, and hypocrisy—a thin veil to cover up crimes which would disgrace a nation of savages": the "internal slave-trade," "men and women reared like swine for the market," and "human flesh-jobbers, armed with pistol, whip and bowie-knife."

Yet, "a still more inhuman, disgraceful, and scandalous state of things" had come about by an act of Congress, the Fugitive Slave Act of 1850, which effectively "nationalized" slavery by enabling the slave hunter to cross state lines "in tyrant-killing, king-hating, people-loving, democratic, Christian America." Guilty churchmen, like the Pharisees, hypocritically gave "the sanction of religion and the Bible to the whole slave system" and taught "that we ought to obey man's law before the law of God."

But Frederick Douglass, unlike Hannah-Jones, did not conclude that the 1776 founding was "a lie," or that the Declaration and Constitution were racist frauds. Quite the opposite. He appealed to the founding, and to those founding documents, against the evils of slavery.

How far, he complained, the nation had fallen since the founding—away from the principles of the Declaration and Constitution. To claim that the Constitution allows "the right to hold and to hunt slaves" would be to call the founders "the veriest imposters that ever practiced on mankind." It would be a "slander upon their memory." Douglass proclaimed his faith in the Constitution by emphasizing the words he had deliberately capitalized—that there "is neither warrant, license, nor sanction of the hateful thing; but, interpreted as it ought to be interpreted, the Constitution is a GLORIOUS LIBERTY DOCUMENT. Read its preamble, consider its purposes. Is slavery among them? Is it at the gateway? Or is it in the temple? It is neither." In fact, the word *slave* did not appear anywhere in it. The Constitution "in its plain reading," as it was intended to be read, has no single "pro-slavery clause," but contains "principles and purposes, entirely hostile to the existence of slavery." Frederick Douglass's faith in the founders and in the Constitution that they framed makes quite a contrast with Hannah-Jones's assertion that "the framers carefully constructed a document that preserved and protected slavery without ever using the word."[87]

Douglass ended his speech on a hopeful note with an expression of faith. He did not "despair of this country": "'The arm of the Lord is not shortened,' and the doom of slavery is certain." He was encouraged by the Declaration of Independence, "the genius of American Institutions," and "obvious tendencies of the age."[88]

Douglass, like Garrison, wanted immediate emancipation—but based on his interpretation of the Constitution. He "believed that the principles of the Preamble and natural rights basis of the Constitution was sufficient authority for the federal government to end slavery in the states where it existed." Lincoln's own thinking had shifted in this direction after *Dred Scott*, but he saw the authority to emancipate the slaves as residing only in the "constitutional war power" of the executive.[89] Hence, he waited for the opportune moment to issue the Emancipation Proclamation.

Douglass would explicate his position on the Constitution most thoroughly in his 1860 speech in Glasgow, to which he had fled after John Brown's ill-fated raid. Douglass notably began by strongly defending the Constitution against its foreign critics. He addressed some of the very criticisms leveled today, including in The 1619 Project. Frederick Douglass said that it was irrelevant whether the framers were slaveholders, for their *intentions* did not matter. He denied "that the Constitution guarantees the right to hold property in men...." The document, "no vague, indefinite, floating, unsubstantial something," but "plainly written" and "complete in itself," says "We the people," not "we the white people, not we the citizens, not we the privileged class." And it "declares that no person shall be deprived of life, liberty, or property without due process of law." Douglass concluded that slave owners had "trampled" on the Constitution.⁹⁰

Like Lincoln, Douglass insisted that most of the founders, including Jefferson, hated slavery and had struggled to find a way to end it. At a March 19, 1855, speech in Rochester, New York, he acknowledged that "the Anti-Slavery movement in this country is older than the Republic." "The patriots of the American Revolution clearly saw, and with all their inconsistency, they had the grace to confess, the abhorrent character of Slavery, and to hopefully predict its overthrow and complete extirpation. Washington and Jefferson, Patrick Henry, and Luther Martin, Franklin, and Adams, Madison, and Monroe, and a host of earlier Statesmen, Jurists, Scholars, and Divines of the country, were among those who looked forward to this happy consummation."⁹¹

In his May 1857 speech on the *Dred Scott* decision, Douglass claimed that Justice Taney was proven "false" to history and law by "the testimony of the church, and... Washington and Jefferson, and Adams, and Jay, and Franklin, and Rush, and Hamilton," who "held no such degrading views on the subject as are imputed by Judge Taney to the Fathers of the Republic."⁹²

In Poughkeepsie, New York, on August 2, 1858, he again repeated his point that "Franklin, Jefferson, Adams, Madison, Monroe, Patrick

Henry, Roger Sherman, George Mason, Luther Martin, and other distinguished men of the earlier and better days of the Republic, condemned the system of Slavery." The framers of the Constitution "made no provision for the hateful thing.... They nowhere tell us that black men shall be Slaves and white men shall be free. They nowhere make any distinction among men in respect to rights on account of color. They say 'we the people,' never we, the white people. The sentiment of the leading statesmen of that day—the sentiment of leading divines, as well as the position of the church—show that Slavery was regarded as a perishing system...." Douglass called it "wisely said" in Lincoln's "House Divided" speech that "[o]ne system or the other must prevail. Liberty or Slavery must become the law of the land."[93] Lincoln's performance in his debates with Stephen Douglas inspired Frederick Douglass to call him "a man of will and nerve" who "came fully up to the highest marks of Republicanism."[94]

And then in the midst of war, on July 4, 1862, Douglass challenged the claim that the "slaveholding rebels" were continuing the legacy of "Washington, Jefferson, and the long list of worthies who led in the revolution of 1776." In fact, these worthies would hang the rebels "as traitors." Those men, "each and all, considered the system an evil."[95]

The Great Emancipator

Douglass the abolitionist was impatient with Lincoln the president during the war. More than any other abolitionist, he "pressed on President Lincoln the necessity of converting the war into a crusade against slavery," in columns in his paper, including the May 1861 "How to End the War"—by using "Negroes" as soldiers who would "march into the South and raise the banner of Emancipation among the slaves"—and in speeches (in February 1862, criticizing the government's "uncertainty and vacillation and hesitation in grappling with the great question of the war—slavery").[96]

Douglass, who had condemned "our DOCTORS OF DIVINITY" for "consent[ing] that their colored brethren...should leave this country and establish themselves in Africa!" in his July 5, 1852, speech, was among those outraged on hearing about the August 14, 1862, White House meeting. No longer did Lincoln come "up to the highest marks of Republicanism" in his estimation. Douglass's "harshest critique" of the president, according to John Stauffer, was in a "public rebuttal" attacking the claim that the races could not live together and chiding Lincoln for blaming "Negroes" for the war. He accused the president of saying "to the colored people: I don't like you, you must clear out of the country."[97]

John Hope Franklin, author of *The Emancipation Proclamation*, summarizes the situation Lincoln found himself in. He faced competing demands from "the procession of the Charles Sumners, the Orestes Brownsons and the religious deputations," along with Greeley editorials and Douglass speeches, all telling "him what he should do about slavery." Lincoln "needed no convincing that slavery was wrong," as Franklin wrote. "[H]e had been determined for many years to strike a blow for freedom if the opportunity ever came his way."[98] But that clear principle didn't resolve a host of other issues raised by the prospect of freeing the slaves.

So Frederick Douglass, like Nikole Hannah-Jones, was a critic of Lincoln's words at that August 14, 1862, meeting at the White House. But he judged Lincoln's overall character and achievements very differently.

In August 1863, Douglass took his place in the long line waiting to speak to the president. He was going to challenge Lincoln on the unfair treatment of black soldiers. The impression he took away from that meeting was not at all the one that Hannah-Jones impresses on her readers. After meeting Secretary of War Edwin Stanton and being appointed the first black assistant adjutant of the United States Army, Douglass took his place in the stairway to Lincoln's office along with a crowd of "patronage-seekers." Douglass expected to wait at least half a day, considering that some men had to wait a week to see the president, but he was ushered up within two minutes of sending his card, followed by Senator Pomeroy, who was also waiting.[99]

Douglass was treated respectfully and put at ease, as he himself recorded and would recall. Stauffer recreates the scene: "[T]he president was sitting informally in a chair that was much too small for his six-foot-four-inch frame. He was 'taking it easy,' his feet 'in different parts of the room,' as Douglass noted. Lincoln rose to greet him, reached out his hand, and said, 'Mr. Douglass, I know you; I have read about you.... Sit down, I am glad to see you. He put Douglass 'quite at ease at once.'"[100]

Lincoln, on the defensive, referred to a speech in early 1862 in which Douglass had criticized "'the tardy, hesitating, and vacillating policy of the President,' especially Lincoln's policies on freeing and arming blacks." Lincoln admitted that he had sometimes been "slow to act," but he "denied vacillating: 'when I have once taken a position, I have never retreated from it,'" he said. And indeed Douglass could not think of a case where Lincoln had reversed his position. After thanking the president "for issuing the retaliatory order against the rebels who murdered or enslaved captured black soldiers," he "then asked why it took him so long to do it." Lincoln replied that the country had not been ready for it; there would have been an "outcry." He had had to wait "until black soldiers 'distinguished themselves for bravery and general good conduct.'" On the issue of unequal pay, Lincoln said it was a "'necessary concession' for black enlistment"—after all, blacks had "larger motives" for fighting—but assured him "that eventually black soldiers would receive" equal pay and that he would "sign any promotion for blacks that Stanton recommended."[101]

Douglass was not completely satisfied, but as Stauffer says, "[H]e was struck by the president's honesty and sincerity." Douglass wrote in his autobiography, "I was never in any way reminded of my humble origin, or of my unpopular color." Unlike with some of his white abolitionist friends, there were no awkward moments arising from the racial difference between the two men.[102] Two days after the meeting, Douglass told George Stearns he understood "why Lincoln was called 'Honest' Abraham."[103]

Although Lincoln signed Douglass's pass for a commission, the commission never came from Stanton. His pay for recruiting Northern black soldiers would continue to come from private donations. He fondly recalled Lincoln telling him at the meeting, "Mr. Douglass, never come to Washington without calling upon me."[104] Blight claims that Douglass was "awed by Lincoln," and that he would tell audiences about getting quickly past white office-seekers and jokingly warn reporters not to report his story because he had a meeting with the president the next day. (They understood his implication: he would not want to jeopardize his access to the president with such leaks about getting preferential treatment.)[105]

Douglass was "overcome with grief" when he heard about Lincoln's assassination. On the following day, he attended a memorial in Rochester's city hall. He was not on the list of speakers, but he acceded to the audience's demands and gave a short impromptu address. Calling Lincoln "one of the noblest men" who ever "trod God's earth" and his assassination "a personal as well as national calamity," Douglass nevertheless expressed his faith that the nation was "saved and liberty established forever." He recalled shaking the "noble" president's "brave, honest hand" only a few weeks before at the inauguration (the guards were ordered by Lincoln to let him into the reception), and quoted from the inaugural address: "Fondly do we hope, fervently do we pray that this mighty scourge of war may speedily pass away. Yet if God will that it continue until all the wealth piled by the bondman's two hundred and fifty years of unrequited toil shall be sunk, and until every drop of blood drawn by the lash shall be paid by another, drawn with the sword, as was said three thousand years ago, so still must it be said, that the judgments of the Lord are righteous altogether." He warned his audience about the "infernal passions" bequeathed upon the "luckless sons" of the "wretched traitors." Reject the old resentments of region and race, he urged: "[K]now no man…by his complexion, but know every man by his loyalty, and wherever there is a patriot in the North or South, white or black, helping on the good cause, hail him as a citizen, a kinsman…."[106]

Douglass's call for color-blind patriotism and brotherhood is ignored in The 1619 Project. To the contrary, The 1619 Project stokes racial resentment with inflammatory rhetoric and a crude presentation of white America versus black America. Nor will students get a sense of the friendship between Lincoln and Douglass from any curriculum inspired by The Project. Already, even students who are introduced to Frederick Douglass's career and writings rarely read his praise of the founders, the Declaration, and the Constitution. They may read part of his 1852 Fourth of July speech—the one most widely used in the classroom—but not the part where Douglass expresses hope and faith in the national experiment. In textbooks, anthologies, and online curricula, students are given snippets that end before Douglass's critical reversal. They read Douglass's bitter charge: "What to the American slave is your 4th of July?" and his characterization of Independence Day as "a day that reveals...the gross injustice and cruelty, to which he is the constant victim." But that's where it ends. Students do not see the second part of the speech, where Douglass expresses hope and faith in the Constitution and calls it a "GLORIOUS LIBERTY DOCUMENT."

The trend to selectively edit out the good things about Lincoln and America has been exacerbated by the implementation of the Common Core standards, which include recommended readings called "exemplars." The one for eleventh-grade language arts includes a selection from Douglass's Fourth of July speech—that leaves out the second half.[107] Other textbooks that include similarly misleadingly excerpted passages include the widely used *Norton Anthology of African American Literature,* edited by Henry Louis Gates Jr., and the anthology *Let Nobody Turn Us Around,* edited by Manning Marable and Leith Mullings.[108]

Abraham Lincoln is vilified by The 1619 Project. And when it comes to Frederick Douglass, The Project takes only two isolated sentences from his voluminous writings: "I shall never forget that memorable night, when in a distant city I waited and watched at a public meeting, with 3,000 others not less anxious than myself, for the word of deliverance which we have heard read today. Nor should I ever forget the outburst of joy and thanksgiving that rent the air when the lightning brought to us the Emancipation Proclamation"—blown up in large type to take up an entire page in the broadsheet "A Brief History of Slavery" coordinated by the Smithsonian.[109]

Those words are from Douglass's "Oration: In Memory of President Lincoln," delivered at the dedication of the Freedmen's Memorial on April 14, 1876, in Lincoln Park in Washington, D.C. But none of that is stated in The 1619 Project—not even the title of the speech.

Why don't The Project's creators include more of this speech? Why don't they at least give the title of the speech ("In Memory of President Lincoln") if they're going to quote from it? Why not include Douglass's words describing the occasion?

> [I]n the presence and with the approval of members of the American House of Representatives…in the presence of that august body, the American Senate, representing the highest intelligence and the calmest judgment of the country; in the presence of the Supreme Court and Chief Justice of the United States, to whose decisions we all patriotically bow; in the presence and under the steady eye of the honored and trusted President of the United States, we, the colored people, newly emancipated and rejoicing in our blood-bought freedom, near the close of the first century in the life of this Republic, have now and here unveiled, set apart, and dedicated a monument of enduring granite and bronze, in every line, feature, and figure of which the men of this generation may read—and those of after-coming generations may read—something of the exalted character and great works of Abraham Lincoln, the first martyr President of the United States.

The answer is obvious. The 1619 Project creators do not want to celebrate Lincoln, to acknowledge his role in the abolition of slavery, or to draw attention to the fact that Frederick Douglass honored him as "the first martyr President of the United States." As Nikole Hannah-Jones said, discussing The Project at a Harvard event in December of

2019, "We've heard plenty of stories of white heroism, about Abraham Lincoln as the Great Emancipator."[110]

The information about the Emancipation Proclamation in The 1619 Project consists of a short broadsheet article and a creative, genre-defying nine-paragraph piece of prose by novelist Darryl Pinckney under this callout: "Jan. 1, 1863: President Abraham Lincoln issues the Emancipation Proclamation, freeing enslaved African-Americans in rebelling states. The text is read aloud at thousands of gatherings, including at a Union Army encampment in Port Royal, S.C." The body of the piece begins, "Imagine the scene I cannot write" and then veers into a bewildering impressionistic, sometimes surreal, account. Imagine high school students trying to make sense of this "history" as they read sentences like this, the second in the article: "The Colonel steps onto the platform, reciting to himself: I'll tell you how the sun rose, a ribbon at a time." And then, "It is New Year's Day. The president has signed the historic war measure." Identities of individuals at this event merge and fluctuate. But one thing comes out of this nonsense loud and clear: vengeance fantasies. "The Colonel hands the Emancipation Proclamation to a penitent white man who used to be called Master over in Beaufort. The Colonel said Oof when he first got his copy." Somehow the colonel had gleaned that "the orderly" "had read the Proclamation, had felt power naked, actual armed-rebellion naked, suppressing said rebellion naked, shall be free naked, maintain freedom of said persons naked."[111] As someone who has taught the writings of Gertrude Stein and the French surrealists, I can visualize the expressions on the poor high school students' faces as they try to acquire from sentences like these not just some meaning, but lessons about history.

The 1619 Project is about inspiring feelings, notably anger, as another creative work on the same page indicates: "During a constitutional convention called for by abolitionist leaders, in response to the Louisiana Legislature's refusal to give black men the vote, armed white people attack a crowd. More than 35 people die, mostly black men." The body of that article begins, "The bodies all around began to cook and swell...." This is author ZZ Packer's recreation of the disgusting scene of the dead and injured. And she adds to the outrage by putting the N-word into the mouths of Southern whites. (The word is spelled out, following the rule Hannah-Jones declared on Twitter: only black people are allowed to do that.)[112] The juxtaposition of these two creative works conveys the idea that the Emancipation Proclamation had little effect against white racists.

The purported ineffectiveness of the proclamation is reinforced by the broadsheet article titled "Freedom Begins." It notes that the preliminary Emancipation Proclamation of September 22, 1862, freed only the 3.5 million slaves in the rebel states and not the half million in slaveholding states that were not part of the Confederacy or those parts of the Confederacy under Union control. In spite of its shortcomings, the article admits, the Emancipation Proclamation was "deeply meaningful to the...formerly enslaved African-Americans and their allies." The subsequent celebrations in which it was read served as "a reminder that African-Americans, enslaved and free, collectively fought for freedom for all and changed an entire nation." The article states that official freedom did not come until the passage of the Thirteenth Amendment, but does not mention the president, Abraham Lincoln, who pushed for its passage before he was assassinated.[113]

The twelve-foot-tall Freedmen's Memorial monument depicts Lincoln holding the Emancipation Proclamation in his right hand, with his left hand outstretched over a slave rising from his knees, his shackles broken. It was the first representation of a black person in a national monument. The original image proposed by the sculptor Thomas Ball depicted a kneeling slave mimicking the well-known abolitionist image on *The Liberator* masthead of a slave holding up his hands in supplication, but the final approved version portrays a freed slave looking up from a crouch, his muscular torso exposed, his body tensed as if to spring up. In contrast to the active lines of the black man is the image of Lincoln in a suit, his right hand resting on the Emancipation Proclamation lying atop a pedestal and his left arm extended over the black man in a gesture that indicates benevolence, but also appears to hover in an incipient withdrawal to make room. Lincoln also leans back, as if knowing the man is about to leap up. As a pamphlet at the time explained, Ball altered the image from one of the slave as "perfectly passive, receiving the boon of freedom from the hand of the great liberator" to "an agent in his own deliverance," with the slave "exerting his own strength with strained muscles in breaking the chain which had bound him."[114] The statue was modeled on a former fugitive slave named Archer Alexander. Ball, who lived in Italy, worked from photographs of Alexander.[115] In a recently discovered letter, Douglass wrote, "The mere act of breaking the negro's chains was the act of Abraham Lincoln and is beautifully expressed in this monument." But he also wrote that the monument, like all monuments, does not tell the "whole truth." The "act by which the negro was made a citizen of the United States and invested with the elective franchise was pre-eminently the act of President [Ulysses] S Grant...."[116]

The day of the statue's dedication, the eleventh anniversary of Lincoln's assassination, was declared a public holiday in Washington, D.C. The procession to the site of the unveiling included twenty-seven mounted police, three companies of black militia troops headed by the philharmonic band of Georgetown, cornet bands, marching drum corps, youth clubs, fraternal orders, and the Knights of St. Augustine carrying a banner with a painting of Lincoln. John Mercer Langston, dean of Howard University Law School, was master of ceremonies; Bishop John M. Brown of the African Methodist Episcopal Church delivered the invocation; and J. Henri Burch of Louisiana read the Emancipation Proclamation before a largely black audience of 25,000. James E. Yeatman, "a St. Louis banker and head of the Western Sanitary Commission," which had led fundraising for the monument, explained that Charlotte Scott, a former slave, was the first one to donate to the effort. She gave five dollars. The cost of the monument, $17,000, was paid for by former slaves and black Civil War veterans.[117]

After President Ulysses Grant pulled the cord to release the flags covering the monument to the sounds of cannon fire and "Hail to the

Chief," and an original poem by Cordelia Ray was read, Douglass began his oration. He contrasted the United States of 1876 to that of twenty years before, when "no such demonstration would have been tolerated." "The spirit of slavery and barbarism, which still lingers to blight and destroy in some dark and distant parts of our country, would have made our assembling here to-day the signal and excuse for opening upon us all the flood-gates of wrath and violence." Recalling Lincoln's second inaugural address, he stated, "I refer to the past not in malice ... but simply to place more distinctly in front the gratifying and glorious change which has come both to our white fellow-citizens and ourselves," and to express "our grateful sense of the vast, high and preeminent services rendered to ourselves, to our race, to our country, and to the whole world by Abraham Lincoln."[118]

Considering the occasion, Douglass was quite blunt about Lincoln, stating that "truth" "is never more proper and beautiful in any case than when speaking of a great public man whose example is likely to be commended for honor and imitation long after his departure to the solemn shades.... Abraham Lincoln was not, in the fullest sense of the word, either our man or our model. In his interests, in his associations, in his habits of thought, and in his prejudices, he was a white man. He was preeminently the white man's President," and "[w]e are at best only his step-children ... children by force of circumstances and necessity." And yet, President Lincoln deserved honor: "Abraham Lincoln saved for you [white Americans] a country," but "he delivered us from bondage, according to Jefferson, one hour of which was worse than ages of the oppression your fathers rose in rebellion to oppose." Douglass measured the man against the historical circumstances: in his dual task of saving the country and ending slavery, Lincoln needed "the cooperation of his loyal fellow-countrymen. Without this primary and essential condition to success, his efforts must have been vain and utterly fruitless. Had he put the abolition of slavery before the salvation of the Union, he would have inevitably driven from him a powerful class of the American people, and rendered resistance to rebellion impossible. Viewed from the genuine abolition ground, Mr. Lincoln seemed tardy, cold, dull, and indifferent: but measuring him by the sentiment of his country, a sentiment he was bound as a statesman to consult, he was swift, zealous, radical, and determined. Though Mr. Lincoln shared the prejudices of his white fellow-countrymen against the negro…in his heart of hearts he loathed and hated slavery."[119]

Douglass postulated that had Lincoln not been assassinated—"had the solemn curtain of death come down but gradually, we should still have been smitten with a heavy grief and treasured his name lovingly. But dying as he did die, by the red hand of violence; killed, assassinated, taken off without warning, not because of personal hate, for no man who knew Abraham Lincoln could hate him, but because of his fidelity to Union and liberty, he is doubly dear to us, and will be precious forever."[120]

In the summer of 2020, the same place, Freedmen's Memorial in Lincoln Park, was the scene of protesters claiming the monument was racist and demanding it be taken down. White women yelled at black police officers that they were "part of the problem" of racism.[121] The mostly white young activists shouted at "older black men and women defending the memorial," including tour guide Don Folden. A young white woman with her mask slipping down screamed at him as he calmly asked her if she knew who had paid for the memorial (she apparently did not). Marcia Cole, a member of the African American Civil War Museum's Female Re-Enactors of Distinction, dressed as Charlotte Scott, the freed slave who had donated the first five dollars,[122] explained, "That man is not kneeling on two knees with his head bowed. He is in the act of getting up." The movement to remove the statue was organized by Harvard University student Glenn Foster, who bragged about gaming the system by using his race to get into Harvard. He said his group was in sympathy with Black Lives Matter.[123]

Historian David Blight, though deeming the monument a "racist image," argued for maintaining it to respect those who had sacrificed for it. He asked District of Columbia representative Eleanor Holmes Norton, who had introduced legislation to remove the memorial from

Lincoln Park, and her supporters to "consider the people who created it and what it meant for their lives in a century not our own." These were black Americans, most of them former slaves, who had raised the money to build the monument. He recounted how the day of the unveiling had been declared a federal holiday and the parade had "involv[ed] nearly every black organization in the city." Blight also proposed replacing Confederate symbols with another "memorialization of emancipation," perhaps a statue of Douglass giving the address.[124]

It should be noted that in that speech Douglass spotlighted the tribute the monument was to the formerly enslaved, not just to Lincoln: "We have done a good work for our race to-day. In doing honor to the memory of our friend and liberator we have been doing highest honor to ourselves and those who come after us. We have been fastening ourselves to a name and fame imperishable and immortal." The monument symbolized "human brotherhood."[125]

Unlike The 1619 Project writers, Douglass believed that Lincoln and the founders, including those who owned slaves, should be honored. They were not saints or gods, but they set in motion something "glorious," something apart from the bondage of the rest of the world. And it was a monumental undertaking. At a time when few did, "[t]he patriots of the American Revolution clearly saw and...had the grace to confess, the abhorrent character of Slavery."

Sadly, a barrier had to be put up around the Freedmen's Memorial.[126] By the end of the year, a replica of it in Boston was taken down.[127]

In February 2021 Eleanor Holmes Norton reintroduced the bill to take down the statue—in honor of Black History Month.[128]

CHAPTER 11

Choosing Resentment—
or Freedom?

The creators of The 1619 Project, posing as groundbreaking revealers of a hitherto unknown secret history of America, do not acknowledge the many previous commemorations of 1619. But we have seen that as early as the nineteenth century there was discussion of 1619 as an important date in African American history, a year often bookended with 1863, the year of the Emancipation Proclamation.

The tone and import of nineteenth- and early-twentieth-century commemorations of the arrival of the Africans on the *White Lion*, though, was very different from the resentment and radical pessimism of The 1619 Project. In 1893 the *Christian Recorder* described 1619 as the date "when our unfortunate forefathers were first preceded to this country as base, ignoble slaves." But that article put 1619 into the context of 1863, which the same magazine called in an article a few years later "the ending of the most iniquitous system of wrong robbery and oppression that ever prevailed in the world's history."[1] Black poet James Weldon Johnson celebrated, "Far, far the way that we have trod / From heathen kraals and jungle dens / To freedmen, freemen, sons of God, / Americans and Citizens."[2]

The three-hundred-year anniversary of 1619 was commemorated in 1919. But in those tercentenary commemorations, black Americans celebrated the "phenomenal progress" that had been made since,[3] rather than damning every advance in freedom since that date—from the Declaration of Independence through the Civil War, Emancipation, Thirteenth Amendment, and blacks' advances in education and civic life in the twentieth century—as a sham. The "celebration of the 300th anniversary of the landing of Negros in America" that drew over "1,000 colored persons" in Charleston, South Carolina, "set forth Negro American progress and achievement in pageant, pictures, music and speech," reported W. E. B. Du Bois in *The Crisis*, the official publication of the NAACP. Du Bois was not known for accommodating those who were satisfied with the state of race relations in early-twentieth-century America, but he used the magazine to also give encouragement by reporting the positive.

The 1619 Project is a different story. Its creators are clearly making use of the anniversary not for honest reflection on history but as an opportunity to advance political grievances and earn political points, as the *New York Times Magazine* issue filled with hysterical screeds and pseudo-scholarship demonstrates. Unlike the 1919 tercentenary celebrations that optimistically marked progress, the 2019 commemorations a hundred years later marked slavery's dark shadow.

Thus, the inconveniences of modern life, such as the traffic in Atlanta—a black-run city that in 2018, in *Forbes* magazine, tied for first place as a city "Where African-Americans Are Doing the Best Economically," and is commonly referred to as the "black mecca"—are presented as vestiges of slavery. Kevin Kruse's essay "Traffic" is printed under this callout: "A traffic jam in Atlanta would seem to have nothing to do with slavery. But look closer...."[4] And in that same issue, Jeneen Interlandi presents the lack of universal (that is, socialized) health care as particularly hurting blacks and tied to unequal treatment under slavery and segregation: "Why doesn't the United States have universal health care? The answer begins with policies enacted after the Civil War."[5] The callout for the essay "Mass Incarceration" claims, "Slavery gave America a fear of black people and a taste for violent punishment. Both still define our criminal-justice system." Bryan Stevenson, an activist lawyer, ignores the plethora of scholarship produced by criminologists and sociologists that has empirically linked the disproportionately high black rates of crime and imprisonment to the post-1960s breakdown of families. Instead, he attributes them to the "Black Codes" of the post–Civil War South.[6] Every political grievance of the progressive wing of the Democratic Party is cast as emanating from slavery. In his contribution to The 1619 Project, Jamelle Bouie (who as a resident *New York Times* columnist provides a constant drumbeat on the legacy of slavery and resurgent Jim Crow when it comes to criticizing his Republican enemies) asserts that "American democracy has never shed an undemocratic assumption present at its founding: that some people are inherently entitled to more power than others." Bouie speciously connects both Donald Trump and the Tea Party movement of 2009 to the ideas of South Carolina senator John C. Calhoun (who died in 1850) and to a 1957 column by *National Review* founder William F. Buckley on segregation and states' rights, which Buckley repudiated multiple times later in life.[7]

On June 8, 2020, the political moment created by The 1619 Project, "the 1619 riots," and the death of George Floyd was seized dramatically by House Speaker Nancy Pelosi when she led a delegation of Democratic lawmakers, including Senator Kamala Harris, Senate Minority Leader Chuck Schumer, Senator Cory Booker, and Congressman Jerry Nadler, with African kente cloth draped around their necks, to Emancipation Hall, which she recalled was "aptly named for those that built the Capitol, sadly." She also recalled her trip with others the previous summer to Ghana "to observe the 400th anniversary of the first slaves coming across the Atlantic." Pelosi called that a "horror of history," followed by "slavery in our own country, and all the consequences of that." She wanted "to observe that pain" and "to respect the actions of the American people to speak out against that, specifically manifested in police brutality. We are here to honor George Floyd." Calling for "a moment of silence, actually, eight minutes and 46 seconds of silence in honor of George Floyd and so many others who lost their lives and were abused by police brutality," she then read the names of such alleged victims, including Trayvon Martin and Michael Brown. Cameras whirred and clicked as the delegation (except Nadler) knelt.[8]

The kente cloth drew criticism from the Right and the Left; the cloth was actually worn by wealthy African slave traders, but ironically it later came to symbolize black pride.[9] In the *Washington Post*, Nana Efua Mumford, the daughter of a native Ghanaian father, lectured on cultural appropriation and scolded the wearers for wearing a design traditionally used for celebratory, not somber, occasions. Plus, the cloths were too large. But, as Karen Bass told Mumford, "Since [President] Trump, it has become a symbol of protest about his racist depiction of Africa."[10]

Bass, chair of the Congressional Black Caucus and a former and unrepentant member of the Black Panthers, led the trip to Ghana that Pelosi mentioned.[11] As *USA Today* reported, the NAACP had led "pilgrimages to African countries," several members of the Congressional Black Caucus had traveled to Ghana, and a "few traveled to Angola where some of the first slave ships sailed from its shores." *USA Today* also produced, for its own "1619 Project," other reports, including videos, about a woman's emotional trip to Angola in search of her roots. The "legacy of slavery" had become "an issue in the 2020 presidential election," with then candidate New Jersey senator Cory Booker and Texas representative Sheila Lee having introduced legislation to set up a commission to study reparations.[12]

The Last "Black Cargo"

Africa is important in discussions about slavery, but—despite the impression created by The 1619 Project—it was not the case that Africans living in domestic bliss were kidnapped and put in chains by Europeans. As we have seen, the overwhelming majority of slaves shipped from Africa were captured and sold into slavery by other Africans. The chains that bound them together on the long marches to the coast, where they were then purchased from African middlemen by Europeans, were put on them by Africans.

Though she ignored enslavement in Africa in The 1619 Project, Hannah-Jones did tweet about a *60 Minutes* segment that aired on November 29, 2020, about the last known slave ship, the *Clotilda*, which had been sunk in the Mobile River in 1860 and was found in 2018. Captain William Foster had purchased the slaves with Timothy Meaher's "$9,000 in gold and merchandise," but the program was silent about who had made them slaves in the first place. It simply called them "captive Africans from the Kingdom of Dahomey, in West Africa"—not saying who might have captured them. Instead, the segment focused on the suffering of the slaves on the ship and their descendants in Alabama, in Africatown, a place that has seen better days. Among those interviewed were Cassandra and Caprinxia Wallace, descendants of Cudjo Lewis, one of the last survivors of the cargo of slaves that was brought to American shores illegally in 1860.[13]

Cudjo Lewis, who was captured at the age of nineteen, was the subject of *Barracoon: The Story of the Last "Black Cargo,"* a book published in 2018 but written by anthropologist and Harlem Renaissance luminary Zora Neale Hurston for original publication in 1931, based on her interviews in 1927 and 1928 with Lewis, then living in Plateau, Alabama.[14] Alice Walker, who wrote the foreword to the book, admits that "many black people, years ago, especially black intellectuals and political leaders," had a problem with the book, which "resolutely record[ed] the atrocities African peoples inflicted on each other, long before shackled Africans, traumatized, ill, disoriented, starved, arrived on ships as 'black cargo' in the hellish West." She asks, understandably, "Who could face this vision of the violent cruel behavior of the 'brethren' and the 'sistren' who first captured our ancestors?"[15]

Walker does honestly posit, "Who would want to know, via a blow-by-blow account, how African chiefs deliberately set out to capture Africans from neighboring tribes, to provoke wars of conquest in order to capture for the slave trade people—men, women, children—who belonged to Africa?" But she attempts to lay some of the blame even for this on "the hellish West," on the false grounds that those wars were inspired by the European slave trade. She also uses the situation of Cudjo Lewis, "lonely for Africa" and "for his family,"[16] to suggest that blacks are not really at home in America: "[H]ow lonely we are too in this still foreign land."[17]

In the introduction, editor Deborah Plant notes that though "the trans-Atlantic slave trade" had been formally outlawed by the United States in 1808, the ending was resisted by African peoples, "foremost" the Fon of Dahomey. Timothy Meaher, a slaveholder in Mobile, Alabama, happened to read a November 9, 1858, newspaper article about King Ghezo's resumption of slave raiding after renouncing his 1852 treaty to abolish slave traffic. In July 1860, Captain William Foster sailed Meaher's ship, the *Clotilda*, toward the Bight of Benin to pick up a "contraband cargo" of 110 African captives, including nineteen-year-old Kossola, who would later be called Cudjo.[18]

Kossola, the second child of Fondlolu, who was the second of his father's three wives, was born "in the town of Bantè, the home to the Isha subgroup of the Yoruba people of West Africa." Though his father was not of royal heritage, his grandfather was an officer of the king of their town. "By age fourteen, Kossola had trained as a soldier" and was ready for induction into "the secret male society called *oro*," which was "responsible for the dispensation of justice and security of the town." When he was captured in 1860, Kossola was "undergoing initiation for marriage."[19]

Kossola and the others were sold by King Glèlè, who intensified raiding campaigns, including on Kossola's town, to avenge his father's death in battle and "to amass sacrificial bodies for certain imminent traditional ceremonies." It began with the townspeople awakening "to Dahomey's female warriors, who slaughtered them in their daze. Those who tried to escape through the eight gates that surrounded the town were beheaded by the male warriors who were posted there." Kossola tried to avoid seeing the severed heads of his family members and fellow townspeople when they were smoked on the second day of the warriors' march. Like the other survivors, he was "yoked by forked sticks and tied in a chain" and marched for three days to the stockades at Abomey, and then three days later "incarcerated in the barracoons at Ouidah, near the Bight of Benin."[20]

Hurston recorded his painful description in dialect: "De heads of de men of Dahomey got 'gin to smell very bad. Oh, Lor', I wish dey bury dem! I doan lak see my people head in de soldier hands; and de smell make me so sick!" He went on to describe how the heads were smoked all day to prevent them from rotting: "We got to set dere and see de heads of our people smokin' on de stick." In recounting his telling of this traumatic memory, Hurston comments, "Kossula was no longer on the porch with me. He was squatting about that fire in Dahomey. His face was twitching in abysmal pain...."[21]

Kossola's experiences, recorded by Hurston, present an unequaled insight into the slave experience. Thanks to the patronage of a wealthy white woman named Charlotte Mason, Hurston was able to spend years working on this project, first interviewing Cudjo over three months and then writing down his heartrending story. The Depression and Hurston's insistence on maintaining Cudjo's words in dialect were among the reasons the account was not published when completed in 1931. We can be thankful that the account was preserved and published in 2018.[22]

On the *60 Minutes* segment promoted by Hannah-Jones on Twitter, Cudjo Lewis's descendants Cassandra and Caprinxia Wallace claimed to want only an apology from the descendants of Meaher, who declined requests for interviews.[23] There was no mention of any attempt to obtain an apology from the Angolans, including any descendants of the king who had advertised the availability for sale of his fellow Africans.

Mother Africa

The article "When the Slave Traders Were African" by Adaobi Tricia Nwaubani, a Nigerian novelist and journalist and a descendant of slave traders, in the *Wall Street Journal* in September 2019 did not receive much attention. Nwaubani cast the four-hundred-year anniversary of 1619 as "a moment for posing questions of historic guilt and responsibility," noting that "the majority of captives brought to the U.S. came from Senegal, Gambia, Congo and eastern Nigeria," where "local collaborators" in the form of "middlemen and merchants" brought slaves to the Europeans along the coast. Toyin Falola, a Nigerian who teaches African studies at the University of Texas at Austin, told Nwaubani that these middlemen were essential to the slave trade: "The Europeans couldn't have gone into the interior to get the slaves themselves." Yet, as Nwaubani points out, the "anguished debate over slavery in the U.S. is often silent on the role that Africans played."

Africa, too, is largely silent. Nwaubani's education from "nursery school through university in Nigeria" ignored "African involvement in the slave trade." But she heard glowing stories from her father about her great-grandfather, "a chief among our Igbo ethnic group who sold slaves in the 19th century."

Similarly, the great-great-great-grandfather of Yunus Mohammed Rafiq, a professor of anthropology from Tanzania who teaches at New York University's center in Shanghai, "raided villages in Tanzania's hinterland, sold the majority of his captives to the Arab merchants who supplied Europeans and kept the rest as laborers on his own coconut plantations." When Rafiq came to the United States to study at Indiana University, and then Yale and Brown for graduate school, he refrained from mentioning this part of his family history to African American colleagues. He instead highlighted "the beauty of Tanzanian music, architecture and poetry" and worked with the black students' union organizing "events that would build bonds to Africa."

Nwaubani found others who felt no shame, like Donald Duke, a 2019 presidential candidate in Nigeria from the port town of Calabar, where in the eighteenth century about 1.2 million slaves were sold. The Efik, Duke's ethnic group, had collected payments from white traders and their African partners from the hinterlands. When Duke was elected governor of the Cross River state in 1999, his administration built the Slave History Museum.

A pastor from Zambia, Saidi Francis Chishimba, in contrast, felt sorrow and guilt upon visiting the place of his forebears' origin in Zanzibar. At a memorial of "what used to be one of the world's largest slave markets, the photos of limbs amputated from runaway slaves and the airless chambers that once held dozens of slaves at a time shocked him into silence." He finds comfort in "the grace of God."

Others, like Teddy Nwanunobi from Nigeria, seek freedom from the past through fasting and asking God's forgiveness. Nwaubani's own family held an intervention in 2018 with a local Anglican priest, with a service and money offering. Yet her father feels differently. He "does not believe that the descendants of those who took part in the slave trade should now pay for those wrongs"; he points out that "buying and selling human beings had been part of many African cultures...long before the first white people landed on [their] shores." Plus, "though many families still retain the respect and influence accrued by their slave-trading ancestors, the direct material gains have petered out over time." He treats the idea of reparations sarcastically, telling his daughter that he would tell those who demand reparations to pluck them from the tree in his yard.

Professor Rafiq, however, thinks that "Africans owe something to the descendants of slaves in America." What is owed (to recall the title of Hannah-Jones's June 30, 2020, *New York Times Magazine* article endorsing reparations) is not only compensation, but honest history, especially history that includes the facts about the slave trade.[24]

The same recognition of the need for real history has come from surprising places. Back in 2010, Henry Louis Gates Jr., writing in the *New York Times*, charged advocates of reparations (like Hannah-Jones) with ignoring the "untidy problem of the significant role that Africans played in the trade" and instead "choosing to believe the romanticized version that our ancestors were all kidnapped unawares by evil white men...." Or, excuses are made that Africans "didn't know how harsh slavery in America was," that slavery was relatively "humane" in Africa, or, in effect, "the devil made me do it," blaming "greedy European countries" for the Africans' actions. None of this was true. Slavery, in fact, was "a business" for "European buyers and African sellers alike." The "messy history" would make it difficult to sort out who owes what to whom.[25] Given the direction the *New York Times* has since gone, one doubts whether Gates's essay would be published today.[26]

Innumerate Economic Historians

The economic argument for reparations is based on the idea that America's wealth was acquired from slavery, a case made in The 1619 Project primarily by Matthew Desmond, a sociologist, with supporting affirmations from Hannah-Jones and Khalil Gibran Muhammad ("The sugar that saturates the American diet has a barbaric history as the 'white gold' that fueled slavery").[27] Desmond's essay is a rhetorical tour de force which revives the old King Cotton argument advanced by the Confederates—and Karl Marx: American wealth was built on cotton produced by slave labor. Desmond also argues that our current economic inequities are the outcome of an economy that rests on the same kind of exploitation that was used under slavery.

Desmond begins by using the measurements of the Organization for Economic Cooperation and Development to make the case about the backwardness of the United States as compared to other developed nations, evinced by such things as high-priced prescription drugs and low union membership. The "uniquely severe and unbridled" American economy, which is also given to panics such as the one in 1837 and busts like the 2008 recession, traces back to "the gnatty fields of Georgia and Alabama," the "cotton houses and slave auction blocks"—the "birthplace of America's low-road approach to capitalism": "What made the cotton economy boom in the United States...was our nation's unflinching willingness to use violence on nonwhite people and to exert its will on seemingly endless supplies of land and labor. Given the choice between modernity and barbarism, prosperity and poverty, lawfulness and cruelty, democracy and totalitarianism, America chose all of the above."

The "management techniques" and even the bookkeeping methods of nineteenth-century corporations came from those "implemented during the previous century by plantation owners." The cotton plantation was "America's first big business," and the overseer was the "nation's first corporate Big Brother." "And behind every cold calculation, every rational fine-tuning of the system, violence lurked." The violence of the "lash" was "rational, capitalistic." Desmond quotes Cornell history professor Edward Baptist, who claims that the economy's "bottom gear was torture" and that today the American workplace continues in the same torturous vein—with "unremitting workplace supervision" through "surveillance strategies, from drug tests and closed-circuit video monitoring to tracking apps and even devices that sense heat and motion." Thus the plantations, which "sought innermost control over the bodies of their enslaved work force," are recreated. There is no real freedom in America because freedom "became broadly defined as the opposite of bondage. It was...a malnourished and mean kind of freedom that kept you out of chains but did not provide bread or shelter."[28]

The problem with Desmond's analysis arises from the work on which it is based, that of Cornell professor Edward Baptist, a major figure of the New History of Capitalism movement (NHC). For years, Baptist and his colleagues have been the target of criticism from accomplished economic historians, including Peter Coclanis, a professor at the University of North Carolina, Chapel Hill; Phillip Magness, senior research fellow at the American Institute for Economic Research; and Gavin Wright of Stanford University.

Desmond's essay repeats errors from Baptist—from the claim that double-entry bookkeeping was invented by "enslavers" (most historians trace it back to Renaissance Italy)[29] to gross errors of calculation and misrepresentation of the work of economists.

At a National Association of Scholars conference, Peter Coclanis exposed the New History of Capitalism as a rebranding of economic history as "the history of capitalism." The movement was prompted by interest in the issues in vogue at the turn of the twenty-first century, such as "rising inequality, the 1%, the Great Recession," and globalization. Adherents, "mostly Ivy Leaguers," focus "on slavery and on America's financial history." As Coclanis pointed out, many of the terms used by Desmond (and also by Hannah-Jones and other contributors to The 1619 Project), such as "enslavers" and "slave labor camps," are "the preferred coinage of the New Historians of American Capitalism." According to these historians, enslavers and their enablers "built the U.S. economy in the antebellum period, and set the tone for America's low-road capitalism ever since."[30]

Baptist's book *The Half Has Never Been Told*, published in 2014, attracted strong criticism from economists and economic historians. Among these were economists Alan Olmstead (University of California at Davis) and Paul Rhode (University of Michigan), who published a harshly critical paper in 2016. Olmstead even called the book "hocus pocus" at a public event. The controversy was covered in 2016 in the *Chronicle of Higher Education* and the *Washington Post* and then recounted at The College Fix a few days after The 1619 Project issue of the *New York Times Magazine* was published in 2019. Gavin Wright and Peter Coclanis praised the report.[31]

In 2020, Phillip Magness published a book of articles criticizing The 1619 Project. One called for the retraction of Desmond's essay because it had cited Baptist's claim that cotton production accounted for half of the antebellum economy, when in fact it was only 5 percent of the GDP. The error was uncovered by Olmstead and Rhode. Wright noted in his article in the *Economic History Review* that Olmstead and Rhode had demonstrated that the 50 percent "figure is an egregious overstatement, generated by double-counting outputs, inputs, asset sales, and financial transactions." Cotton did dominate "US exports after 1820, but exports never exceeded 7 per cent of GDP during the antebellum period. The chief sources of US growth were domestic."[32]

Magness also notes another major error made by Desmond regarding the claim about the 400 percent increase in cotton picked daily between

1801 and 1862. This figure comes from a 2008 article by Olmstead and Rhode, via Baptist. But Baptist misrepresents Olmstead and Rhode, who attribute the increase to biological innovation, the creation of hybrid strains of cotton. Baptist and other NHC scholars, though *citing* Olmstead and Rhode, claim that "double-entry bookkeeping and systematized beatings of the slaves" are responsible for the increase! In Magness's judgement, Baptist's book is "a mess of misinterpreted data, misrepresented sources, and empirical incompetence." Magness informed Hannah-Jones of the problems via Twitter, but she and others at the *New York Times* simply ignored him, as they have virtually all critics.[33]

Coclanis charged the New Historians with ignoring the protocols of economic history. "With a few exceptions, they are fundamentally innumerate," and they operate from an animus towards capitalism[34]—qualities that are mutually reinforcing. Wright sees a parallel with Karl Marx, who wrote, "Without slavery there would be no cotton, without cotton there would be no modern industry. It is slavery which has given value to the colonies, it is the colonies which have created world trade, and world trade is the necessary condition for large-scale machine industry...to do away with slavery would be to wipe America off the map."[35] (That's not exactly how things worked out.)

According to all three economic historians, slavery actually stymied economic growth in the South. Wright notes that total income for the South "steadily declined as a share of national income, from the Revolution to the eve of the Civil War. Even during the 1850s, the most prosperous decade in southern economic history, the region's share of national income ticked downward from 31.4 per cent to 30.5 per cent, primarily because of slower population growth." Although the "brute fact of history" is that U.S. cotton production did "rise 'on the backs of slaves,'" "the slave South *underperformed* as a world cotton supplier." Slavery discouraged the migration of free labor to the South and stymied foreign investment, which went to the free states. The "fixed-cost character of slavery" resulted in the failure to develop "market specialization." Transportation infrastructure was de-incentivized because of the "mobility of slave property." As Wright points out, "During the canal boom of the 1830s, five times as many miles were constructed in northern than in southern states. Railroad mileage per square mile was three times greater in the North than in the South, where lines were 'generally inferior in construction, rail, motive power and rolling stock.'"[36]

Coclanis notes the "rudimentary conveyor-belt transport system, designed to facilitate exports and imports rather than knit the region together economically, and very low levels of investment in human capital" as contributing to the South's economic lag. In fact, "[f]ew plantation economies anywhere in the world have ever developed into modern high-performance economies, and none based on slave labor have...."[37]

There were wealthy plantation owners, but they were few and did not contribute much to the economic development of the region, much less the nation. Coclanis points out that only about "twenty-five percent of the free families in the antebellum South held slaves," with most of them holding only one slave. And only one out of twelve of the 25 percent could be called planters (having at least twenty slaves). About "three percent of free families in the South would be considered planter families." So, though there was wealth, it was concentrated in a few hands.

Furthermore, the *national* economy "was not based on slavery in the 19th century. Although cotton produced in the South was important early on to the textile industry in New England, in the larger scheme of things the most important economic developments of the century—urbanization and industrialization in the northeastern quadrant of the United States, and the creation of the dynamic agro-industrial complex of the Midwest—owed relatively little to slavery.... Indeed, it is more accurate to say that slavery distorted rather than directed capitalist development in America."[38]

Wright acknowledges that the New Historians "emphasize correctly the extensive financial connections between the slave South and northern lenders, servicing not just cotton but the interstate slave trade." Such financial connections are what Desmond is pointing to when he relates the use of "slave bodies" as collateral. Wright points out, however, that "thriving capital markets in north-eastern cities clearly pre-date the rise of cotton, trading primarily US bonds and shares of state-chartered banks, insurance companies, and turnpike and bridge corporations. In the formative early national period, connections to slavery were remote at best." Furthermore, the Erie Canal (built mostly by Irish laborers) was instrumental in orienting domestic trade along east-west lines and in enabling New York City to beat out Philadelphia as the nation's financial center, "connecting that city's port activity, securities markets, and banks, especially the call loan market." In fact, "[s]lavery was a source of regional impoverishment in nineteenth-century America, not a major contributor to national growth."[39]

After the Civil War, merchants and railroads flooded into the Southeast, and the biggest source of cotton was white farmers in the Piedmont.[40] To be sure, freed slaves, especially after the end of Reconstruction, had to turn to sharecropping, as did the forebears of Hannah-Jones's father. His family continued to sharecrop on a white plantation in Mississippi. By 1900, 85 percent of black Mississippi farmers did not own the land they farmed, but neither did 36 percent of white farmers.[41]

There is also the human element, beyond the statistics about GDP and so forth. Magness therefore rightfully condemns the cynical repurposing of "the horrors of American slavery" into "an ideological attack on free-market capitalism," as the proponents of NHC do, falsely identifying slavery with capitalism and "advocat[ing] a political reordering to remove that stain."[42] One is also reminded of the obscene parallel that Desmond draws between a modern worker required to take drug tests and be monitored on the job to the slave subject to the lash of a plantation overseer. Former slave Frederick Douglass certainly would have been able to tell the difference. Even the manual labor that he did for a while in Massachusetts was a welcome exit from labor under the literal lash. He would be outraged by the claim of Desmond—who enjoys the perquisites and privileges of a tenured position at an Ivy League school—that Americans today are in bondage.

Those Who Remember

Others, who have not experienced slavery but have experienced segregation, are outraged by the claims made in The 1619 Project. One of these is Shelby Steele, who casts Hannah-Jones as a "smirking and smiling" "puppeteer pulling all the strings," sending young blacks into anger and hopelessness. "It breaks my heart," Steele said on *The Ben Shapiro Show*, to go to campuses and see young blacks "huddled off" and talking about black power, Black Lives Matter, and "struggling." Steele says Hannah-Jones's 1619 Project plays into the hands of whites who are seeking to absolve themselves of "white guilt" by buying their "innocence." What the "people who think they are helping blacks" are really doing is "simply recolonizing blacks."[43]

Steele, whose grandfather was born a slave, recalls in his book *White Guilt* experiencing a "segregation flashback" from his boyhood while driving through California in the late 1990s. Cruising into San Luis Obispo, he remembered "cruising into another town, decades earlier, on a trip from Chicago to Kentucky with my father to visit relatives. Just off the highway we did what we always did upon entering a new town— what we had to do before any of our personal needs could be met. We went in search of a black person." The black person would give his father information about "houses where we might spend the night (often run by widows), places to eat, and information about churches, taverns, and barbershops."[44] It is hard for us to imagine an America where the color of one's skin prevented access to such services as bathrooms and hotels.

Amazon, however, refused to carry the film Steele made with his son, *What Killed Michael Brown*, on its platform,[45] while giving millions to various woke organizations.[46] Amazon also dropped *Created Equal*, the documentary about Supreme Court justice Clarence Thomas, which describes his life journey from abject poverty in segregated Georgia in the 1950s and 1960s to the Supreme Court. Amazon did this during Black History Month, February 2021.[47] Thomas received similar treatment from the Smithsonian, which in its new National Museum of African American History and Culture initially mentioned him only in connection with Anita Hill's unsubstantiated accusations of sexual harassment against him in 1992. About a year later, in 2017, it presented Thomas in a joint display with Thurgood Marshall. But while Marshall is respectfully highlighted for his accomplishments, those of Thomas are dwarfed and he is misrepresented.[48] It seems that woke corporations and government employees would rather give a platform to young blacks who suffer from "microaggressions" than to persons who experienced real racial aggressions and discrimination.

Hannah-Jones and the other contributors to The 1619 Project exploit white guilt, which Steele describes as "a vacuum of moral authority visited on the present by the shames of the past." Possibly the worst effect of white guilt, in Steele's opinion, is that it does not allow Americans to appreciate the "moral transformation" the country has undergone. Today, white supremacy is "morally repugnant" to the overwhelming majority of Americans. "This is a fact," Steele wrote in a *Wall Street Journal* op-ed, "that must be integrated into our public life—absorbed as the new history—so that America can once again feel the moral authority to seriously tackle its most profound problems."[49]

Indeed, The 1619 Project ignores this "new history." Instead, it reinscribes the *old* history, grinding out references to slavery and Jim Crow ad nauseam. We've seen the multiple ways in which The 1619 Project pretends that conditions for blacks are even worse than what Carter Woodson observed in 1916. What would Woodson think to hear Hannah-Jones and her collaborators attribute virtually every facet of life in the twenty-first century to the legacy of slavery?

Hannah-Jones, Annette Gordon-Reed, Ibram X. Kendi, and other like-minded writers begin with animus. For whatever reason, they hold a grudge against their country. Gordon-Reed, to recall, begins her books with attacks on whites who would raise doubts about her "evidence," automatically implicating skeptics (a prerequisite for being a scholar!) as racists. Her history focuses not on the weight of the evidence, but on who is presenting that evidence—a tactic of identity politics. Hannah-Jones's bitterness comes through. For whatever reason, she felt conflicted as a biracial child who was bussed to a largely white school and was affirmed by a teacher whose classroom lessons and assigned reading materials promoted a view of the world that attributes all difficulties and injustices to a capitalist white ruling class. This is the world through the distorted lens of Black Power ideology via radical Lerone Bennett. Hannah-Jones has mistaken, or deliberately confuses, such polemic for history. But she is also impervious to criticism, angrily holding on to her belief that this country is a "slavocracy." It would be difficult to find someone more ill-qualified and ill-suited to write a curriculum for schoolchildren. The 1619 Project materials must be removed from schools.

The understanding of history that students get from The 1619 Project is simple and static, whereas actual history is immensely complicated, with actors changing roles and undergoing internal struggles and trans-formations, often due to circumstances beyond their control. The 1619 Project's view of the past is oddly confined to the present, as it applies the impossibly hypersensitive (and ever shifting) standards of today to people of the past, freezing them into categories of "enslaver" or "racist" and "enslaved person." The 1619 Project is not really history. It is pro-paganda that casts white America as statically and uniformly racist through four hundred years of history. All white Americans are stained with the "original sin" of racism; they carry it in their DNA.

What lies behind the evil of white people is Eurocentrism—including a belief in individualism, merit, and private property. The 1619 Project thus follows Marxist theory in tracing every ill in society back to capitalism. White people are evil capitalists, and people of color are their oppressed victims and always virtuous (unless they agree with the capitalists). The 1619 Project is a revival of the Black Power school of Lerone Bennett, which a half century later is still twisting history to align authentic blackness with a vaguely Marxist agenda. African Americans who agree with our founding principles and resist the Black Power agenda are presented as traitors to their race, not only by blacks on board with this program, but also by whites. Some are like the protesters at the Freedmen's Memorial who feel it is their prerogative to shout down older blacks—to literally get in their faces and scream at them about the meaning of their own history. The woke whites, however, are not always unhinged tattooed millennials, but often billionaire heads of corporations.

They see themselves as gatekeepers of virtue. They decide who is without sin: people of color who seek *their* direction. But as this book has tried to show, in reality it is not only white people who are afflicted with sin. The very idea of slavery as a sin, in fact, arose relatively late in history and in the West. It was articulated by abolitionist congressman James Tallmadge in the 1810s during the congressional debate on Missouri's admission to statehood. But while Tallmadge called slavery a "sin," he did not say it originated in America.[50] That such debates were being held, that tensions were rising to such an extent that the country would enter a Civil War a few decades later, gives the lie to The 1619 Project's thesis that America is steeped in "anti-black racism," forever marked by the "original sin" of slavery.[51]

The purpose of The 1619 Project is to get Americans to believe that the stain of racism remains—that it needs to be purged, exorcised from each individual through struggle sessions led by the likes of Robin DiAngelo and Ibram X. Kendi. But the charges of racism do not comport with reality. That is why extensive sessions are needed, first to get the person who is denying his own racism—presumably only because he is under its spell—to admit it, and then to work through elaborate mental and emotional exercises to mitigate it (a complete cure is probably impossible). The 1619 history serves as a tool to alter reality, to get students to disbelieve their lying eyes and "see" that this is a racist nation, one requiring an overhaul, an overhaul that begins within their psyches.

As Robert Woodson, Shelby Steele, John McWhorter, Glenn Loury, Carol Swain, Wilfred Reilly, and so many others affiliated with the Woodson Center and similar institutions point out, such a false and dark view of history harms students and divides us by race. As Robert Woodson wrote shortly after The Project's publication, "The most devastating aspect of the project's narrative is its insinuation that blacks are born inherently damaged by an all-prevailing racism and that their future prospects are determined by the whims of whites." Woodson believes that stories of success need to be told.[52]

Proponents of keeping The 1619 Project and similar materials in classrooms often argue that even young schoolchildren can decide for themselves which presentation of history is correct. They should consider the research of University of London professor Eric Kaufmann, who found that exposure to media representations of racism correlated to a person's perception of actual racism. When Kaufmann asked black respondents to read "a passage from the critical race theory–inspired writer Ta-Nehisi Coates" about how "the police departments of your country have been endowed with the authority to destroy your body," he found that the percentage of respondents who did not believe that they could make their own plans work jumped from 68 percent to 83 percent. Black college graduates were much more likely than those who had not gone to college to see racism in innocuous statements by whites, such as "America is a colorblind society."[53] These Americans have had imbued within them a view of America's past as irredeemable and not worth respecting. College campuses are already hotbeds of radicalism. Imagine the second-grader in a class using The 1619 Project and being inundated with the message that the history of his country is a history of slavery that continues to this day in ways he cannot see, in ways he never dreamed of.

This exploitation, misrepresentation, and misapplication of historic injustices can only tear Americans further apart. How can we live together when we see each other as exploiter and exploited? Already, students on college campuses routinely jump to conclusions about racism. For example, a student at Smith College did irreparable harm to a janitor and cafeteria worker by accusing them of racism when they had simply called campus police because she was in a room that was not to be used.[54] The constant drumbeat about race makes young people see those around them through a distorted lens. An innocent mistake is transformed into an act of racism. More than a half century after the end of legal segregation, college students are demanding separate housing and separate graduations. Young people are screaming at police and anyone who wants to preserve the heritage of his forebears. Accusations about white denial of inherent racism—the charge that racism is in white Americans' DNA—serve only to inflame emotions and breed distrust. The true, and truly dangerous, denial is denying the reality that our history is full of Americans of all races who did good and bad things— and that America and the institutions bequeathed to Americans by the founders of 1776 have been a great force for expanding freedom, both in our own country and around the world.

But that freedom and our constitutional rights and form of government are under threat. The 1619 Project is deliberately aimed to undermine faith in them. And if we lose the United States that was founded in 1776, we will be faced with a new kind of servitude—to the state that will control all Americans, of all races and ethnicities. We are already getting close to it, with censorship of all positions that resist the socialist encroachment.

Thoughts on Freedom from a Former Slave

It is always a good idea to consider the experiences of those who have been denied freedom. The experiences of Frederick Douglass can shed light on a new kind of servitude that threatens all Americans. Consider his February 8, 1855, speech, "An Inside View of Slavery," when, contra everything in The 1619 Project, he said, "Whipping is not what constitutes the cruelty of Slavery. To me the thought that I am a slave is more terrible than any lash, than any chain." Slavery is "manhood denied, ignored, despised." "The mental agony of the slave is never appeased. To feed the body with bread does not satisfy the gnawing hunger for Liberty. Kindness is no substitute for justice. Care for the slave as property is no compensation for a denial of his personality. You may surround the slave with luxuries, place him in a genial climate, and under a smiling and cloudless sky, and these shall only enhance his torment, and deepen his anguish." In this speech Douglass articulated the relationship between master and slave: the slave is "property, and he can have nothing but what must belong to his master.... Property in one man vested in another! Is it not strange that any men, religious or irreligious, divines or not, can be found to argue in defence of a system that makes property in man, and annihilates his personality, breaks down his manhood, scourges him beyond the range of human society?"[55]

I would suggest that students, instead of reading The 1619 Project, read this and other speeches by Douglass. Most certainly they should read "What to the Slave Is the Fourth of July?"—*in its entirety*. They should learn about "the glorious liberty document"—the U.S. Constitution, with its separation of powers, checks and balances, and enumerated powers providing a bulwark against tyranny. The creators of The 1619 Project either don't know or don't want their readers to know the whole story of Frederick Douglass.

Yes, students need to learn about slavery! But they need to learn about it in its historical context—as a global, transracial, transhistorical phenomenon. Slavery continued to exist in other parts of the world after close to three-quarters of a million men died in the Civil War that ended slavery here and inspired the slaveholding nations of Cuba and Brazil to end it.[56] It was not until after World War I that most Muslim states abolished slavery. Yemen and Saudi Arabia did not abolish it until 1962, and Mauritania did so only in 1980.[57] In China today, over a million Muslim Uyghurs and other minority groups are held without charge in actual forced-labor camps.[58] As Daniel Greenfield reported for FrontPage Magazine, multinational companies such as "Apple and Nike lobbied against a slave labor bill," and "Apple and Amazon were caught using slave labor."[59] That's the same Apple whose CEO Tim Cook said, on June 22, 2020, in the wake of George Floyd's death and the ensuing riots, that the previous month's events had made everyone "face longstanding institutional inequalities and social injustices." Parroting 1619 Project talking points, he absurdly stated, "This country was founded on the principles of freedom and equality for all. For too many people, and for too long, we haven't lived up to those ideas." *And* he pledged to spend more of those profits (acquired in good part from cheap foreign labor) on efforts to overcome "longstanding institutional inequalities" in "communities of color" here in the USA.[60]

The social justice warriors should take their focus off the supposed "forced-labor camp" at Monticello and other plantations in a system of slavery that was ended over 150 years ago and direct their efforts to the ones that exist today. And they should learn black history. That would include the stories of black American Communists, such as Lovett Fort-Whiteman, the "First Black Communist," who died in an actual Soviet labor camp.[61] His tragic life and death might help us understand that while the Left has always been ready to use racial inequality as a stick with which to beat America, it has never been so ready to improve the lives of actual black people. These stories need to be told! There is plenty to explore outside the bounds of the neo-Marxist history of The 1619 Project. African Americans' true history is not reducible to a hopeless litany of oppression. An understanding of that true history would begin by learning about the countless black Americans, many forgotten, whose achievements can make us all proud—from the shining examples of Benjamin Banneker and Frederick Douglass to the fascinating and inspiring lives of George Schuyler and Clarence Thomas. They achieved what they did by fighting against the tide of racism, discrimination, and long inequality under the law, yes. But those achievements were also inspired, and made possible, by the true American founding of 1776.

Acknowledgments

Once again, I owe most thanks to The Alexander Hamilton Institute for the Study of Western Civilization for housing me as a resident fellow and providing me with so many resources. Many people worked to make the AHI a reality, including the founders and funders, and I hope my project will advance their mission and make them proud.

As I poked around the bookshelves of the old AHI mansion where much of the library of the late Eugene Genovese found a permanent home, I thought to myself that I could not be in a better place to write this book, my second since arriving here in 2014. As I read his books, respectfully and lightly notated in pencil, I felt the presence of Gene more than at any other time.

Gene's student, the indefatigable AHI president and executive director Robert Paquette, may have felt he was in the classroom again, given all the questions I asked him. Once again, Bob was generous with his time, happily answering these questions and indulging me with impromptu discussions about Jefferson, slavery, the Constitution, and other topics related to this book. I benefited tremendously from his suggestions for sources as I did my research, and from his review of drafts of chapters for historical accuracy and "Germanic sentences." I realize how lucky Hamilton College students have been to have Bob Paquette as a professor.

The AHI can boast of producing outstanding graduates through its many student programs. I was fortunate to be able to employ the research services of Andrew Juchno, former AHI undergraduate fellow, summer research intern, and associate editor for the AHI-sponsored publication Enquiry, as he was completing his master's degree at Yale University. His knowledgeable and quick responses greatly helped me in meeting my deadline and brought additional points to the manuscript.

Christian Goodwillie, director and curator of special collections and archives at the Hamilton College library, cheerfully offered his expertise, research assistance, and additional questions to consider.

Ken and Judy Craft, founders of Georgians for Educational Sovereignty, shared their research on textbooks and obtained pages from textbooks that seem harder to get than gold from the Dahlonega Mountains these days. All Georgians should be grateful to them for their volunteer efforts to keep Georgia schools to their mission of honest education.

For answering questions and sharing resources I want to thank Bruce Gilley, professor of political science, Portland State University; Ann Hartle, professor emeritus of philosophy, Emory University; and Peter Wood, president, and David Randall, research director, National Association of Scholars.

All helped make this book much better than it could otherwise have been, but all errors are my own.

Once again, my agent Alex Hoyt and my editor at Regnery, Elizabeth Kantor, kept me on track with cheerful encouragement.

And finally, I would like to thank my family for all their love and support, including my sister, Regina, and her husband, Eric, and most especially my son, Carson.

Notes

Chapter 1: "The 1619 Riots"

1. Constance Grady, "Do the Soaring Sales of Anti-Racism Books Signal a True Cultural Shift?," Vox, June 11, 2020, https://www.vox.com/culture/2020/6/11/21 288021/anti-racism-books-reading-list-sales-figures.

2. Mary Margaret Olohan, "Men in Chains with Whip Marks Walk through Protests in Slave Demonstration, Video Shows," Daily Caller, June 23, 2020, https://daily caller.com/2020/06/23/charleston-calhoun-protest-white-slave-demonstration/. The article states, "It is unclear whether the lash marks were real or created through makeup."

3. Samantha Chang, "Brain-Washed Whites Convulsing from White Guilt Make Pledge of Allegiance to Black People," Biz Pac Review, June 3, 2020, https://www .bizpacreview.com/2020/06/03/brain-washed-whites-convulsing-from-white-gui lt-make-pledge-of-allegiance-to-black-people-929304/.

4. Toluse Olorunnipa and Griff Witte, "Born with Two Strikes: How Systemic Racism Shaped Floyd's Life and Hobbled His Ambition," *Washington Post*, October 8, 2020, https://www.washingtonpost.com/graphics/2020/national/george-floyd -america/systemic-racism/. This article was part of a six-part "special report" titled "George Floyd's America" that examined "the role systemic racism played throughout Floyd's 46-year life." Floyd was a drug addict who had served several prison terms, one for "aggravated robbery with a deadly weapon" of a woman. Luis Andres Henao, Nomaan Merchant, Juan Lozano, and Adam Geller, "For George Floyd, a Complicated Life and a Notorious Death," Associated Press, June 10, 2020, https://apnews.com/article/virus-outbreak-us-news-ap-top-news-hip -hop-and-rap-houston-a55d2662f200ead0da4fed9e923b60a7.

5. "The 1619 project is a major initiative from The New York Times observing the 400th anniversary of the beginning of American slavery. It aims to reframe the country's history, understanding 1619 as our true founding, and placing the consequences of slavery and the contributions of black Americans at the very center of our national narrative." Jake Silverstein, "Introduction," in "The 1619 Project," *New York Times Magazine*, in the online version originally published on the *New York Times* website. The *Times* silently corrected that version, approximately four months after publication. See Jordan Davidson, "The New York Times Deceptively Edits False Claim at the Center of 1619 Project," The Federalist, September 21, 2020, https://thefederalist.com/2020/09/21/nyt-deceptively-edits-false-claim-at

-the-center-of-1619-project/; Becket Adams, "The 1619 Project Is a Fraud," *Washington Examiner,* September 21, 2020, https://www.washingtonexaminer .com/opinion/the-1619-project-is-a-fraud. Thus the same passage in the current electronic version of that "Introduction," which has been retitled "Why We Published The 1619 Project" and redated December 20, 2019, now says, "The 1619 Project is an ongoing initiative from The New York Times Magazine that began in August 2019, the 400th anniversary of the beginning of American slavery. It aims to reframe the country's history by placing the consequences of slavery and the contributions of black Americans at the very center of our national narrative." That current version also says, "The goal of The 1619 Project is to reframe American history by considering what it would mean to regard 1619 as our nation's birth year." Jake Silverstein, "Why We Published The 1619 Project," *New York Times Magazine,* December 20, 2019, https://www.nytimes.com/interactive/20 19/12/20/magazine/1619-intro.html. Please see note 9 in this chapter, note 3 in chapter 2 below, and also the fuller discussion in chapter 3 below of the significant corrections, both silent and acknowledged, that the *Times* has made to The 1619 Project since its initial publication. A pdf of the entire print edition of the *New York Times Magazine* issue that inaugurated The 1619 Project—which differs from both the original and the current online versions—can be viewed at the Pulitzer Center website, https://pulitzercenter.org/sites/default/files/full_issue_of_the_1619_project.pdf.

6. "It is not incidental that 10 of this nation's first 12 presidents were enslavers, and some might argue that this nation was founded not as a democracy but as a slavocracy." Nikole Hannah-Jones, "The Idea of America," in "The 1619 Project," *New York Times Magazine,* August 14, 2019, https://www.nytimes.com/interac tive/2019/08/14/magazine/black-history-american-democracy.html.

7. "Lee, Jackson Statues in Charlottesville Vandalized with '1619' Graffiti over the Weekend," *Richmond Times-Dispatch,* September 17, 2019, https://richmond.com /news/virginia/lee-jackson-statues-in-charlottesville-vandalized-with-graffiti-over -the/article_1a3b207d-4425-5d6e-8f4b-819617efed64.html.

8. "The 1619 Project," *New York Times Magazine,* August 18, 2019, https://www .nytimes.com/interactive/2019/08/14/magazine/1619-america-slavery.html.

9. In 1619 Virginia was an English colony, not a British one. This erroneous reference has been corrected by the *New York Times Magazine*—in a rare instance of an acknowledged correction. The correction was made on September 4, 2019, according to a current web version of the edition of the *New York Times Magazine* that inaugurated The 1619 Project at this link: https://www.nytimes.com/interac tive/2019/08/14/magazine/1619-america-slavery.html?searchResultPosition=1. However, a different, also current, web version, the one with the editor's introduction retitled as "Why We Published The 1619 Project" and redated

December 20, 2019 (more than three months after the correction), still calls Virginia a "British colony" in 1619. Jake Silverstein, "Why We Published The 1619 Project," *New York Times Magazine*, December 20, 2019, https://www.nytimes .com/interactive/2019/12/20/magazine/1619 intro.html. See note 5 above, note 3 in chapter 2 below, and the fuller discussion of corrections, both acknowledged and unacknowledged, in chapter 3.

10. Silverstein, "Introduction," in the online version originally published on the *New York Times* website. Please see note 5 above and the fuller discussion of significant corrections, both silent and acknowledged, that the *Times* has made to The Project since its initial publication, in chapter 3 below.

11. Charles Kesler, "Call Them the 1619 Riots," *New York Post*, June 19, 2020, https:// nypost.com/2020/06/19/call-them-the-1619-riots/.

12. Silverstein, "Introduction," in "The 1619 Project."

13. James Barrett, "Creator of 1619 Project: 'Honor' If Riots Called '1619 Riots'; Deletes Post on Native Americans Owning Slaves," The Daily Wire, June 22, 2020, https:// www.dailywire.com/news/creator-of-1619-project-an-honor-if-riots-were-called- 1619-riots-deletes-post-on-native-americans-bringing-slaves-on-trail-of-tears.

14. Tonya Mosley, "Bringing the Pulitzer Prize-Winning '1619 Project' to a Wider Audience," WBUR, July 20, 2020, https://www.wbur.org/hereandnow/2020/07 /20/1619-project-nikole-hannah-jones.

15. Jackie Salo, "New York Times Reporter Says Destroying Property Is 'Not Violence," *New York Post*, June 3, 2020, https://nypost.com/2020/06/03/ny-times-reporter-says- destroying-property-is-not-violence/. The deaths of white men in similar holds, such as Tony Timpa's in 2016 (see note 17 below), have aroused no such outrage or protest. Lukas Mikelionis, "Three Dallas Cops Charged in Death of Man Who Called 911 for Help," Fox News, December 8, 2017, https://www.foxnews.com/us/three-dallas- cops-charged-in-death-of-man-who-called-911-for-help.

16. Lois Beckett, "At Least 25 Americans Were Killed during Protests and Political Unrest in 2020," *The Guardian*, October 31, 2020, https://www.theguardian.com /world/2020/oct/31/americans-killed-protests-political-unrest-acled.

17. In 2016 Anthony Timpa, a white man in the Dallas area, died under similar circumstances. The medical examiner found the cause of death to be "sudden cardiac death" from "the toxic effects of cocaine and physiological stress associated with physical restraint," but his death received very little attention. "Dallas DA Dismisses Charges against 3 DPD Officers for 2016 in-Custody Death," CBS DFW, March 18, 2019, https://dfw.cbslocal.com/2019/03/18/da-charges-dismissed-tony -timpa-dpd-officers-in-custody-death/. And while Democrats expressed their support for the protests against the police, they stopped a police reform bill by Senator Tim Scott that addressed such practices, on a procedural vote that prevented it from coming up for debate. Adam Shaw, "Sen. Tim Scott Rips into

Democrats after GOP Police Reform Effort Fails in Senate," Fox News, June 24, 2020, https://www.foxnews.com/politics/tim-scott-democrats-gop-police-reform -senate.

18. Audrey Washington, "Here's How Protests Unfolded Saturday Night," WSB-TV, June 13, 2020, https://www.wsbtv.com/news/local/atlanta/protesters-take-atlanta -streets-3rd-weekend-after-death-black-man-hands-apd/E4AMA3EGXNG75F5 WFZCO5X6SQ4/.

19. Police had responded to a call from Prude's brother, who was worried about Prude, who had been released from Strong Memorial Hospital that evening after having suicidal thoughts. A passing tow truck driver had described Prude as covered in blood (Prude had smashed out storefront windows). Prude died a week later of "complications of asphyxia in the setting of physical restraint due to excited delirium due to acute phencyclidine intoxication." Steve Orr, "Video Released from Arrest of Chicago Man Who Died of Asphyxiation after Being Pinned to Ground by N.Y. Police," *Chicago Sun-Times*, September 2, 2020, https://chicago.suntimes .com/2020/9/2/21419199/daniel-prude-death-rochester-police-chicago; Rachel Treisman et al., "Rochester, N.Y. Mayor Suspends Officers over Asphyxiation Death of Daniel Prude," NPR, September 3, 2020, https://www.npr.org/sections /live-updates-protests-for-racial-justice/2020/09/03/909081869/protesters-in-roc hester-n-y-demand-answers-in-asphyxiation-death-of-black-man.

20. Hannah Bleau, "Black Lives Matter Protesters Riot in Rochester, Harass Restaurant Patrons," Breitbart, September 5, 2020, https://www.breitbart.com/po litics/2020/09/05/black-lives-matter-protesters-riot-in-rochester-harass-restaurant -patrons/.

21. Tristan Justice, "George Floyd Riot Damage Could Cost Companies Upwards of $2 Billion Dollars," The Federalist, September 16, 2020, https://thefederalist.com /2020/09/16/george-floyd-riot-damage-could-cost-insurance-companies-upwards -of-2-billion./.

22. Beckett, "At Least 25 Americans Were Killed."

23. Virginia Allen, "Vandalizing American History: A List of 113 Toppled, Defaced, or Removed Statues," The Daily Signal, July 17, 2020, https://www.dailysignal .com/2020/07/17/vandalizing-american-history-a-list-of-64-toppled-defaced-or -removed-statues/.

24. Zach Goldberg, "America's White Saviors," *Tablet*, June 5, 2019, https://www .tabletmag.com/sections/news/articles/americas-white-saviors.

25. Allen, "Vandalizing American History." One professor, Sarah Parcak, tweeted a drawing and instructions for how to tear down an obelisk, which some took to mean the Washington Monument. Jessica McBride, "Professor Accused of Giving Instructions for Pulling Down Washington Monument," Heavy, June 1, 2020,

https://heavy.com/news/2020/06/sarah-parcak-pulling-down-washington-monu
ment-allegation/.

26. Annie Gowen, "As Statues of Founding Fathers Topple, Debate Rages over Where
Protesters Should Draw the Line," *Washington Post*, July 7, 2020, https://www
.washingtonpost.com/national/as-statues-of-founding-fathers-topple-debate-rages
-over-where-protesters-should-draw-the-line/2020/07/07/5de7c956-bfb7-11ea-b4
f6-cb39cd8940fb_story.html; Visvajit Sriramrajan, "Hofstra Moves Jefferson Statue
amid Outcries," *LI Herald*, July 7, 2020, https://www.liherald.com/stories/hofstra-
moves-jefferson-statue-amid-outcries,126401.

27. Dan Whisenhunt, "Thomas Jefferson Statue Removed from Downtown Decatur,"
Decaturish, June 22, 2020, https://decaturish.com/2020/06/thomas-jefferson-sta
tue-removed-from-downtown-decatur/.

28. Rebecca Shabad and Dartunorro Clark, "D.C. Mayor Bowser Has 'Black Lives
Matter' Painted on Street Leading to White House," NBC News, June 5, 2020,
https://www.nbcnews.com/politics/politics-news/d-c-mayor-bowser-has-black
-lives-matter-painted-street-n1225746; Alex Nester, "Virginia District to Rename
Schools Named after Founding Fathers," Washington Free Beacon, December 10,
2020, https://freebeacon.com/campus/virginia-district-to-rename-schools-named
-after-founding-fathers/. The recommendations in San Francisco came from a task
force appointed in 2018 to study the issue, with the plans bumped up to a priority
level in early 2021. Natalie O'Neill, "San Francisco to Rename Schools Honoring
'Racist' Figures like Washington, Lincoln," *New York Post*, January 27, 2021,
https://nypost.com/2021/01/27/san-francisco-to-rename-44-schools-honoring-ra
cist-founders/.

29. Stella Chan and Amanda Jackson, "San Francisco School Board Votes to Rename
44 Schools, including Abraham Lincoln and George Washington High Schools,"
CNN, January 27, 2021, https://www.cnn.com/2021/01/27/us/san-francisco-sch
ool-name-changes-trnd/index.html.

30. Alex Nester, "San Francisco School Board Reverses Decision to Rename Schools,"
Washington Free Beacon, April 7, 2021, https://freebeacon.com/campus/san-fran
cisco-school-board-reverses-decision-to-rename-schools/.

31. Matt Jones, "Hampton Set to Rename 5 Schools Named for Slave Owners,
Confederates and Segregationists," *Daily Press*, April 28, 2021, https://www.dai
lypress.com/news/education/dp-nw-hampton-school-renaming-20210428-2zqkl
6urzjcstjw52eftkigonq-story.html; "Montgomery Public Schools Seeking Input in
Renaming Three High Schools," Alabama News Network, May 6, 2021, https://
www.alabamanews.net/2021/05/06/montgomery-public-schools-seeking-input-in
-renaming-three-high-schools/.

32. "Montgomery Public Schools Seeking Input," Alabama News Network.

33. Jones, "Hampton Set to Rename 5 Schools."

34. Eugene D. Genovese, *The Southern Front: History and Politics in the Cultural War* (Columbia: University of Missouri Press, 1995), 114–28.

35. Kimberly Ford, "My Great-Grandfather Carved Mount Rushmore on Sacred Land. Now Is the Time to Remove It.," *USA Today*, July 10, 2020, https://www .usatoday.com/story/opinion/voices/2020/07/10/take-down-rushmore-presidents -my-great-grandfather-carved-column/5401088002/; Timothy D. Dwyer, "Op-Ed: Could the Racist Past of Mt. Rushmore's Creator Bring Down the Monument?," *Los Angeles Times*, July 3, 2020, https://www.latimes.com/opinion/story/2020 -07-03/mount-rushmore-sculptor-racist.

36. Kenneth Garger, "Protesters Block Roadway to Mount Rushmore ahead of Trump's Arrival," *New York Post*, July 3, 2020, https://nypost.com/2020/07/03/ protesters-block-roadway-to-mount-rushmore-ahead-of-trumps-arrival/.

37. Ida Bae Wells (nhannahjones), "This more than anything...," Twitter, December 22, 2020. Screenshot in the author's possession.

38. Ashton Pittman, "Trump Taps Ex-Gov. Bryant for '1776' Effort to Keep History Friendly to White 'Heroes,'" Mississippi Free Press, December 21, 2020, https:// www.mississippifreepress.org/7725/trump-taps-ex-gov-bryant-for-1776-effort-to -keep-history-friendly-to-white-heroes/.

39. W. Ralph Eubanks, "'Manufactured Ideas of History': Patriotic Education Fund in the Playbook of Totalitarian Leaders," Mississippi Free Press, December 9, 2020, https://www.mississippifreepress.org/7422/manufactured-ideas-of-history-reeves -patriotic-education-fund-in-the-playbook-of-totalitarian-leaders/.

40. Pittman, "Trump Taps Ex-Gov. Bryant for '1776' Effort."

41. Ibid. Trump in his speech on September 17 invoked Martin Luther King Jr. and referred to the "Garden of American Heroes" that Trump was planning and had said in his July 4 speech would include Frederick Douglass, Harriet Tubman, and Booker T. Washington. Donald J. Trump, "White House History Conference," Rev, transcript of speech given September 17, 2020, https://www.rev.com/blog /transcripts/donald-trump-speech-transcript-september-17-white-house-history -conference; "Read President Trump's Pro-America Independence Day Speech from Mount Rushmore," The Federalist, July 5, 2020, https://thefederalist.com /2020/07/05/read-president-trumps-pro-america-independence-day-speech-from -mount-rushmore/.

42. Nikole Hannah-Jones, "Martin Luther King Jr. Lecture (Featuring Nikole Hannah-Jones)," Georgia Tech, January 14, 2021, https://serve-learn-sustain.ga tech.edu/martin-luther-king-jr-lecture-featuring-nikole-hannah-jones, transcription by the author.

43. Denny McCabe, "Letter: It's Systemic," *The Courier*, September 13, 2020, https:// wcfcourier.com/opinion/letters/letter-its-systemic/article_006f8092-c750-5afa-82 83-7fb69e53ea02.html; Denny McCabe, "Guest Column: Truth, History, and

American Exceptionalism," *The Courier*, October 11, 2020, https://wcfcourier
.com/opinion/columnists/guest_columnists/guest-column-truth-history-and-ame
rican-exceptionalism/article_7679e87d-e4cd-5117-8bc9-f335cf6be879.html;
Denny McCabe, "LETTER: Conservatives Seek to Censor History," *The Courier*,
March 9, 2021, https://wcfcourier.com/opinion/letters/letter-conservatives-seek
-to-censor-history/article_66c665ea-d5dd-5362-bd30-8342373e5b81.html; Jacob
Hall, "Retired Educator Whose Student Developed 1619 Project Says America Is
Exceptional—Exceptionally Fragile, Exceptionally Ignorant of White Privilege,"
Iowa Standard, February 15, 2021, https://theiowastandard.com/retired-educator
-whose-student-developed-1619-project-says-america-is-exceptional-exceptional
ly-fragile-exceptionally-ignorant-of-white-privilege/.

Chapter 2: The Project Is Launched

1. "The 1619 Project," *New York Times Magazine*, August 18, 2019, in the original
    online version of The 1619 Project and in the original print version, a pdf of which
    is available to view at the Pulitzer Center website: https://pulitzercenter.org/sites/de
    fault/files/full_issue_of_the_1619_project.pdf. As we have seen, this erroneous
    reference to Virginia in 1619 as a "British" rather than an "English" colony has
    been corrected in the current online version—in a rare instance of an acknowledged
    correction. See notes 5 and 9 in chapter 1 above, note 3 in this chapter, and the
    fuller discussion in chapter 3 below.

2. In the 2019 production, Atticus Finch was no longer heroic but guilty of complicity
    in white supremacy. Calpurnia was an angry radical. Ironically, the production
    was more like Harper Lee's failed earlier novel than the beloved classic she actually
    published.

3. Jake Silverstein, "Introduction," in "The 1619 Project," *New York Times
    Magazine*, August 18, 2019. This is the version of the editor's words as they
    appeared in the printed magazine, a pdf of which is available on the website of the
    Pulitzer Center at https://pulitzercenter.org/sites/default/files/full_issue_of_the_16
    19_project.pdf. The passage has been altered, with no correction noted, to read
    thus in the current online version at the *Times* website: "What if, however, we were
    to tell you that the moment that the country's defining contradictions first came
    into the world was in late August of 1619?" Jake Silverstein, "Why We Published
    The 1619 Project," in "The 1619 Project," *New York Times Magazine*, https://
    www.nytimes.com/interactive/2019/12/20/magazine/1619-intro.html. The
    original version of the passage, along with editor Silverstein's flimsy defense of the
    silent correction, is preserved in Bret Stephens, "The 1619 Chronicles," *New York
    Times*, October 9, 2020, https://www.nytimes.com/2020/10/09/opinion/nyt-1619
    -project-criticisms.html. For more on these corrections to the original "The 1619

Project," both silent and acknowledged, please see notes 5 and 9 in chapter 1 above and also the fuller discussion in the body of chapter 3 below.

4. Silverstein, "Introduction," in the print edition, pdf available at Pulitzer Center website, https://pulitzercenter.org/sites/default/files/full_issue_of_the_1619_proje ct.pdf.

5. Abraham Lincoln, "Address at Gettysburg, Pennsylvania," in *Abraham Lincoln: Selected Speeches and Writings*, ed. Don E. Fehrenbacher (New York: Library of America, 2009), 405; Silverstein, "Why We Published The 1619 Project."

6. Silverstein, "Introduction," in the print edition, pdf available at Pulitzer Center website, https://pulitzercenter.org/sites/default/files/full_issue_of_the_1619_project.pdf.

7. "Clinton All Red, White and Blue for July 4th Parade," *Rome Sentinel,* July 9, 2019, https://www.romesentinel.com/stories/clinton-fourth-of-july-parade-pics-pa ge-4,79038.

8. Martha Day Zschock, *Hello, Fourth of July!* (Carlisle, Massachusetts: Applewood Books, 2018).

9. Alice Dalgliesh, *The 4th of July Story* (New York: Simon and Schuster, 1956, 1995).

10. Jerry Spinelli, *My Fourth of July* (New York: Neal Porter Books, 2019).

11. Mary Grabar, "Enduring through War and Depression, Independence Day Now Threatened by Blind Hatred of the Past," Just the News, July 3, 2020, https://just thenews.com/nation/culture/enduring-through-war-and-depression-independen ce-day-now-threatened-blind-hatred.

12. Kevin M. Kruse, author of the essay "Traffic," however, appears to be white, and Wikipedia, which customarily identifies nonwhite individuals by race, simply identifies him as "an American historian." "Kevin M. Kruse," Wikipedia, https:// en.wikipedia.org/wiki/Kevin_M._Kruse.

13. Robert Paquette, a leader in the field, names David Eltis, Stanley Engerman, Dan Littlefield, Mark Smith, Philip Morgan, Allan Kulikoff, and Lorena Walsh as experts upon whom the *New York Times* could have called. Robert Paquette, email to the author, May 17, 2021. Paquette recently retired after teaching at Hamilton College for thirty-seven years. Among his many award-winning books are *Sugar Is Made with Blood: The Conspiracy of La Escalera and the Conflict between Empires over Slavery in Cuba* and *The Denmark Vesey Affair: A Documentary History*. See "Robert L. Paquette," Alexander Hamilton Institute for the Study of Western Civilization, https://www.theahi.org/home/people/president-and-execu tive-director/.

14. "Anne C. Bailey," History Faculty page, Binghamton University, n.d., https:// www.binghamton.edu/history/faculty/profile.html?id=abailey; Anne C. Bailey, "Shadow of the Past," in "The 1619 Project," *New York Times Magazine*, August 18, 2019, https://www.nytimes.com/interactive/2019/08/14/magazine/1619-america-slavery.html, 98, pdf of the print version available at the Pulitzer Center website, https://

pulitzercenter.org/sites/default/files/full_issue_of_the_1619_project.pdf; "Tiya Miles," Harvard University Department of History, n.d., https://history.fas.harvard.edu /people/tiya-miles. One contributor, attorney Bryan Stevenson, is director of the Equal Justice Initiative, a nonprofit "committed to ending mass incarceration and excessive punishment, [. . .] to challenging racial and economic injustice, and to protecting basic human rights for the most vulnerable people in American society." "About EJI," Equal Justice Initiative, n.d., https://eji.org/about/.

15. "Nikole Hannah-Jones," The Lavin Agency Speakers Bureau, n.d., https:// www.thelavinagency.com/speakers/nikole-hannah-jones.

16. Mary Grabar, *Indoctrination without Apology: Social Studies Teachers Share Strategies on How to Mold Students* (report on the 2009 meeting of the National Council for the Social Studies), n.d., https://www.marygrabar.com/images/sampledata /pdfs/Indoctrinationwithoutapology.pdf; Mary Grabar, "Terrorist Professor Bill Ayers and Obama's Federal School Curriculum," Accuracy in Media, September 21, 2012, https://www.aim.org/special-report/terrorist-professor-bill-ayers-and -obamas-federal-school-curriculum/; Mary Grabar, "Common Core: Phasing Western Culture Out of Education," FrontPage Magazine, December 16, 2012, https://archives.frontpagemag.com/fpm/common-core-phasing-western-culture -out-education-mary-grabar/.

17. Nikole Hannah-Jones, "The Idea of America," in "The 1619 Project," *New York Times Magazine*, August 18, 2019, pdf of the print version available at Pulitzer Center website, https://pulitzercenter.org/sites/default/files/full_issue_of_the_1619 _project.pdf.

18. Hitler was inspired by the 1915–1917 Armenian genocide, as he said in an August 22, 1939, statement that was used as an exhibit by the Nuremberg Tribunal. "Adolf Hitler, Chancellor of Nazi Germany (1933–45)," Armenian Genocide, August 22, 1939, https://www.armenian-genocide.org/hitler.html. The Nazis were also inspired by a book on eugenics (not limited to blacks) by Madison Grant, a New Yorker, in 1916. Richard Conniff, "How a Notorious Racist Inspired America's National Parks," *Mother Jones*, July/August 2016, https://www.motherjones.com /environment/2016/07/anniversary-national-parks-racist-history-madison-grant/. In 1948 South Africa, apartheid replaced the British system of social segregation with the division of South Africa into ten independent, black-ruled homelands, or nation-states, and one white state. Queensland University professor Eric Louw maintains that the British system of segregation was employed to exploit cheap black labor. Erick Louw, email to the author, January 13, 2021.

19. Hannah-Jones, "The Idea of America."

20. Silverstein, "Introduction."

21. Hannah-Jones, "The Idea of America."

22. Ned Ryun, "Critical Race Theory as a Leftist Hammer," American Greatness, March 5, 2021, https://amgreatness.com/2021/03/05/critical-race-theory-as-a-lef tist-hammer/.

23. Carol Swain, "Black Law Scholar Explains How Critical Race Theory Is a 'Dangerous and Destructive Ideology,'" The College Fix, February 25, 2020, https://www.thecollegefix.com/black-law-scholar-explains-how-critical-race-the ory-is-a-dangerous-and-destructive-ideology/.

24. Hannah-Jones, "The Idea of America."

25. "Philip Reid and the Statue of Freedom," Architect of the Capitol, n.d., https:// www.aoc.gov/explore-capitol-campus/art/statue-freedom/philip-reid; "The Statue of Freedom," Architect of the Capitol, n.d., https://www.aoc.gov/explore-capitol-campus/art/statue-freedom.

26. Hannah-Jones, "The Idea of America."

27. Silverstein, "Introduction."

28. Hannah-Jones, "The Idea of America."

29. Ibid.

30. Wesley Morris, "American Popular Music," in "The 1619 Project," *New York Times Magazine*, August 18, 2019, https://www.nytimes.com/interactive/2019/08 /14/magazine/1619-america-slavery.html.

31. Matthew Desmond, "Capitalism," in "The 1619 Project," *New York Times Magazine*, August 18, 2019, https://www.nytimes.com/interactive/2019/08/14/ma gazine/1619-america-slavery.html.

32. Tonya Mosley, "Bringing the Pulitzer Prize-Winning '1619 Project' to a Wider Audience," WBUR, July 20, 2020, https://www.wbur.org/hereandnow/2020/07 /20/1619-project-nikole-hannah-jones.

33. Nikole Hannah-Jones, "What Is Owed," *New York Times Magazine*, June 30, 2020, https://www.nytimes.com/interactive/2020/06/24/magazine/reparations-sl avery.html; Grace King, "'1619 Project' Creator Nikole Hannah-Jones Says Reparations for Slavery Must Still Be Made," *The Gazette* (Cedar Rapids), April 8, 2021, https://www.thegazette.com/k/1619-project-creator-nikole-hannah-jones -says-reparations-for-slavery-must-still-be-made/.

34. Paulina Enck, "Nikole Hannah-Jones Calls for 'Consequences,' 'Deprogramming' for Republicans," The Federalist, January 12, 2021, https://thefederalist.com/20 21/01/12/nikole-hannah-jones-calls-for-consequences-deprogramming-for-republicans/.

35. "History Experts Link Pro-Trump Capitol Riot and Historical White Supremacist Mobs," Yahoo! News, January 17, 2021, https://news.yahoo.com/history-exper ts-pro-trump-capitol-191759226.html.

36. "Breaking Down White Privilege," Oprah Winfrey Network, n.d., https:// www.oprah.com/own-wheredowegofromhere/breaking-down-white-privilege.

37. Hannah-Jones's speaking fees are listed in contracts obtained by the author from public universities. Also see Ashe Schow, "The Anti-Racism Author Robin DiAngelo Paid More Than Black Woman to Speak at Same Diversity Forum," The Daily Wire, November 23, 2020, https://www.dailywire.com/news/white-anti-ra cism-author-robin-diangelo-paid-more-than-black-woman-to-speak-at-same-diver sity-forum.

38. Lucas Daprile, "The Journalist Who Created the '1619 Project' to Speak at USC in March," The State, February 26, 2021, https://www.thestate.com/news/local /education/article249548318.html.

39. Katie Robertson, "Hannah-Jones Denied Tenure at University of North Carolina," *New York Times*, May 20, 2021, https://www.nytimes.com/2021/05 /19/business/media/nikole-hannah-jones-unc.html.

40. Jonathan Raymond, "Morehouse Commencement to Feature Equal Justice Initiative Founder, 1619 Project Journalist," 11 Alive, May 13, 2021, https://www .11alive.com/article/news/education/morehouse-college-commencement-details /85-efbb54b0-7b67-499d-bf0e-acb1ce240e76; Victoria Yeasky, "Rutgers Board of Governors Announces 2021 Commencement Speakers," *Daily Targum*, April 14, 2021, https://dailytargum.com/article/2021/04/rutgers-board-of-governors-an nounces-2021-commencement-speakers.

41. "New Members Elected in 2021," American Academy of Arts and Sciences, n.d., https://www.amacad.org/new-members-2021.

42. Hillel Italie, "Two Books Based on '1619 Project' Coming Out in November," ABC News, April 13, 2021, https://abcnews.go.com/Entertainment/wireStory/books -based-1619-project-coming-november-77041890.

43. Mychael Schnell, "Prominent Journalists, Athletes and Academics Denounce UNC Decision to Deny Hannah-Jones Tenure," *The Hill*, May 25, 2021, https://thehill .com/homenews/media/555292-prominent-journalists-athletes-and-academics-de nounce-decision-to-deny-hannah.

44. Carole Levine, "Students Urge Public Schools to Develop Anti-Racism Curricula," *Nonprofit Quarterly*, August 3, 2020, https://nonprofitquarterly.org/students-ur ge-public-schools-to-develop-anti-racism-curricula/; Mosley, "Bringing the Pulitzer Prize-Winning '1619 Project'"; "Video: Fringe History, Flawed Scholarship," National Association of Scholars, February 3, 2021, https://www.nas.org/blogs /media/video-fringe-history-flawed-scholarhsip; Peter Wood, email to the author, February 23, 2021. The National Association of Scholars, of which Wood is president, sent Hannah-Jones invitations in September 2019 and October 2019 and in May 2020 and June 2020; Aaron Sibarium, "Nikole Hannah-Jones Scrubs Social Media after Doxxing Free Beacon Reporter," Washington Free Beacon, February 9, 2021, https://freebeacon.com/media/nikole-hannah-jones-scrubs-so cial-media-after-doxxing-free-beacon-reporter/.

45. Ida Bae Wells (@nhannahjones), "This more than anything....," Twitter, December 22, 2020. Screenshot in the author's possession.

46. Liza Mullett, "The 1619 Project's Nikole Hannah-Jones Unpacks Anti-Blackness, History of Slavery in Watson Talk," *Brown Daily Herald*, October 19, 2020, https://www.browndailyherald.com/2020/10/19/1619-projects-nikole-hannah-jo nes-unpacks-anti-blackness-history-slavery-watson-talk/; Peter Wood, email to the author, February 23, 2021. The National Association of Scholars, of which Wood is president, sent Hannah-Jones invitations in September 2019 and October 2019 and in May 2020 and June 2020.

47. Sibarium, "Nikole Hannah-Jones Scrubs Social Media."

48. Ida Bae Wells (@nhannahjones), "The White House Conference on American History has not a single Black historian on it. Strange," Twitter, September 17, 2020. Tweet has since been deleted; screenshot available at "Critics Condemn Trump's Rewrite of Race in America in DC Speech—as It Happened," *The Guardian*, September 17, 2020, https://www.theguardian.com/us-news/live/2020 /sep/17/donald-trump-joe-biden-coronavirus-covid-19-?page=with:block-5f63b8 428f087a1832841a91.

49. In May 2021, Hannah-Jones replaced the crossed-out 1776 with a promotional banner for her forthcoming books. See Ida Bae Wells (@nhannahjones), Twitter, https://twitter.com/nhannahjones. An image of her old banner can be seen at Tyler Durden, "Down the 1619 Project's Memory Hole," Verity Weekly, September 22, 2022, https://www.verityweekly.com/down-the-1619-projects-memory-hole/.

50. Sarah Ellison, "How the 1619 Project Took over 2020," *Washington Post*, October 13, 2020, https://www.washingtonpost.com/lifestyle/style/1619-project-took-over -2020-inside-story/2020/10/13/af537092-00df-11eb-897d-3a6201d6643f_story .html.

51. "The Ida B. Wells Society for Investigative Reporting," Ida B. Wells Society, n.d., https://idabwellssociety.org/.

52. Sam Dorman, "'1619 Project' Founder Loses UNC Tenure Offer amid Criticism: Report," Fox News, May 19, 2021, https://www.foxnews.com/us/1619-project-fo under-hannah-jones-unc-tenure; Ida Bae Wells (@nhannahjones), "I've been staying off of here today, but just know I see you all and I am grateful," Twitter, May 19, 2021, 8:10 p.m., https://twitter.com/nhannahjones/status/13951699107 21073156.

53. Ida Bae Wells (@nhannahjones), "I have been overwhelmed by all the support you all have shown me. It has truly fortified my spirit and my resolve. You all know that I will OK. But this fight is bigger than me, and I will try my best not to let you down," Twitter, May 20, 2021, 5:37 p.m., https://twitter.com/nhannahjones/sta tus/1395493858063048721; Colleen Flaherty, "No Clear Answers," Inside Higher

Ed, May 21, 2021, https://www.insidehighered.com/news/2021/05/21/professors-students-unc-chapel-hill-demand-transparency-about-journalists-tenure-bid.

54. Ellison, "How the 1619 Project Took over 2020."

55. Mattie Kahn, "Nikole Hannah-Jones, Pulitzer Prize Winner, Winds Down with Silk Pillowcases, TJ Maxx PJs, and $10 Candles," *Glamour*, May 11, 2020, https://www.glamour.com/story/nikole-hannah-jones-self-care-skin-care-routine; Ta-Nehisi Coates, "The Case for Reparations," *The Atlantic*, June 2014, https://www.theatlantic.com/magazine/archive/2014/06/the-case-for-reparations/361631/.

56. Nikole Hannah-Jones, "Martin Luther King Jr. Lecture (Featuring Nikole Hannah-Jones)," Georgia Tech, January 14, 2021, https://serve-learn-sustain.gatech.edu/martin-luther-king-jr-lecture-featuring-nikole-hannah-jones, transcription by the author.

57. Natasha Zarinsky, "What the Hell Is Up with 'Bae'?" *Esquire*, July 25, 2014, https://www.esquire.com/lifestyle/news/a29423/where-did-bae-come-from/.

58. Mark Hemingway, "The New York Times Goes All in on Flawed 1619 Project," RealClearPolitics, February 21, 2020, https://www.realclearpolitics.com/articles/2020/02/21/new_york_times_goes_all_in_on_flawed_1619_project_142458.html#; "*1776 Unites* Is a Movement to Liberate Tens of Millions of Americans . . .," 1776 Unites, n.d., https://1776unites.com/.

59. The Lavin Agency did not reply to the author for a confirmation, but she has come across no mention, in the extensive coverage of Hannah-Jones, of any teaching experience.

60. "Reading Guide for *The 1619 Project* Essays," Pulitzer Center and *New York Times Magazine*, n.d., https://pulitzercenter.org/sites/default/files/reading_guide_for_the_1619_project_essays_0.pdf.

61. "Sam Dolnick: Board Member," Pulitzer Center, https://pulitzercenter.org/people/sam-dolnick.

62. "Pierre Omidyar," Influence Watch, n.d., https://www.influencewatch.org/person/pierre-omidyar

63. "Meet Our Global Partners," Facebook Journalism Project, https://www.facebook.com/journalismproject/partnerships.

64. "Get Involved," Pulitzer Center, n.d., https://pulitzercenter.org/get-involved.

65. "We've Got to Tell the Unvarnished Truth," *New York Times Magazine*, August 18, 2019, pdf available at Pulitzer Center website, https://pulitzercenter.org/sites/default/files/18maglabs_1619_issue_shipped_0.pdf.

66. Nikita Stewart, "'We Are Committing Educational Malpractice': Why Slavery Is Mistaught—and Worse—in American Schools," *New York Times*, August 19, 2019, https://www.nytimes.com/interactive/2019/08/19/magazine/slavery-american-schools.html; Kevin Mooney, "Tech Giants Run Silent as Discrimination Charges Shake Up Southern Poverty Law Center," Capital Research Center, April

4, 2019, https://capitalresearch.org/article/tech-giants-run-silent-as-discrimination-charges-shake-up-southern-poverty-law-center/; "New SPLC Polls Finds [*sic*] Overwhelming Support for Anti-Racism Education," Southern Poverty Law Center, September 17, 2020, https://www.splcenter.org/presscenter/new-splc-polls-finds-overwhelming-support-anti-racism-education.

67. Tyler O'Neil, "Cancel Everyone! SPLC Wants to Decimate the Conservative Movement," PJ Media, February 5, 2021, https://pjmedia.com/news-and-politics/tyler-o-neil/2021/02/05/cancel-everyone-splc-wants-to-decimate-the-conservative-movement-n1423501.

68. "Webinar for Educators: How to Get Involved with The 1619 Project Education Network," Pulitzer Center, February 19, 2021, https://pulitzercenter.org/blog/webinar-educators-how-get-involved-1619-project-education-network.

69. Naomi Schaefer Riley, "'The 1619 Project' Enters American Classrooms," Education Next, Fall 2020, https://www.educationnext.org/1619-project-enters-american-classrooms-adding-new-sizzle-slavery-significant-cost/.

70. Ibid.

71. Stanley Kurtz, "The Greatest Education Battle of Our Lifetimes," *National Review*, March 15, 2021, https://www.nationalreview.com/corner/the-greatest-education-battle-of-our-lifetimes/.

72. "Announcing 'The 1619 Project' Education Network," Pulitzer Center, February 1, 2021, https://pulitzercenter.org/blog/announcing-1619-project-education-network; Jay Schalin, *The Politicization of University Schools of Education: The Long March through the Education Schools*, James G. Martin Center for Academic Renewal, February 2019, https://www.jamesgmartin.center/2019/02/schools-of-education/; Riley, "'The 1619 Project' Enters American Classrooms"; Jeff Barrus, "Pulitzer Center Announces Initiative to Bring 'The 1619 Project' to Schools and Universities," Pulitzer Center, February 26, 2021, https://pulitzercenter.org/blog/pulitzer-center-announces-initiative-bring-1619-project-schools-and-universities.

73. Riley, "'The 1619 Project' Enters American Classrooms"; Shannon Garrison, "Why Are 6.1 Million Students Using Newsela?," Thomas B. Fordham Institute, September 28, 2016, https://fordhaminstitute.org/national/commentary/why-are-61-million-students-using-newsela; Chris Weller, "This Education Startup You've Never Heard of Is in 75% of American Classrooms," Business Insider, September 14, 2016, https://www.businessinsider.com/newsela-technology-classroom-literacy-2016-9; "Activities to Extend Student Engagement," Pulitzer Center, May 28, 2020, https://pulitzercenter.org/builder/lesson/activities-extend-student-engagement.

74. "About National Council for the Social Studies," National Council for the Social Studies, n.d., https://www.socialstudies.org/about.

75. "Advancing Social Justice: 2020 Virtual Conference," National Council for the Social Studies, n.d., https://www.socialstudies.org/conference/2020-virtual-conference.

76. "'Saving' American History? Start by Teaching American History," National Council for the Social Studies, February 8, 2021, https://www.socialstudies.org/current-events-response/saving-american-history-start-teaching-american-history; "Teaching about Slavery Using the 1619 Project and Other Resources," National Council for the Social Studies, n.d., https://www.socialstudies.org/current-events-response/teaching-about-slavery-using-1619-project-and-other-resources.

77. "Teaching Black History to Elementary and Middle School Students," Pulitzer Center, February 25, 2021, https://pulitzercenter.org/event/teaching-black-history-elementary-and-middle-school-students.

78. "'The 1619 Project' Law School Initiative Event Series Kicks Off," Pulitzer Center, February 26, 2021, https://pulitzercenter.org/event/1619-project-law-school-initiative-event-series-kicks.

79. "The 1619 Project Law School Initiative," Pulitzer Center, n.d., https://pulitzercenter.org/lesson-plan-grouping/1619-project-law-school-initiative.

80. "Series Event: Focus on Legal and Political Histories," Pulitzer Center, March 10, 2021, https://pulitzercenter.org/event/series-event-focus-legal-and-political-histories.

81. "A Vigil of Hope, a Call to Act against Racism," Hamilton College, June 4, 2020, https://www.hamilton.edu/news/story/george-floyd-police-racism-vigil; "Anti-Racism Resources," Hamilton College, n.d., https://www.hamilton.edu/about/diversity/anti-racism-resources.

82. Skylar Nitzel, "MFJS Department Launches a Racial Justice Book Club," *DU Clarion*, October 19, 2020, https://duclarion.com/2020/10/dus-mfjs-department-launches-a-racial-justice-book-club/.

83. Emily Kokot, "U Oregon's 1619 Project Common Read 'Aims to Reframe' US History," Campus Reform, November 10, 2020, https://www.campusreform.org/article?id=16128; Lela Gallery, "NYT's 1619 Project Will 'Set the Tone' for the School Year at Massachusetts College," Campus Reform, August 14, 2020, https://www.campusreform.org/article?id=15459.

84. Nora McGreevy, "New Project Reimagines the U.S.' First Antislavery Newspaper, the 'Emancipator,'" *Smithsonian*, March 19, 2021, https://www.smithsonianmag.com/smart-news/antislavery-newspaper-boston-university-globe-180977273/.

85. Tom Ciccotta, "Poll: 58% of Young, College-Educated Americans Say Riots Are Justified," Breitbart, June 3, 2020, https://www.breitbart.com/tech/2020/06/03/poll-58-of-young-college-educated-americans-say-riots-are-justified/.

86. Amy Watson, "Leading Daily Newspapers in the United States in September 2017 and January 2019, by Circulation," Statista, November 20, 2020, https://www.st

atista.com/statistics/184682/us-daily-newspapers-by-circulation/; Olivia B. Waxman, "The First Africans in Virginia Landed in 1619. It Was a Turning Point for Slavery in American History—But Not the Beginning," *Time*, August 20, 2019, https://time.com/5653369/august-1619-jamestown-history/; Riley, "'The 1619 Project' Enters American Classrooms"; E. R. Shipp, "1619: 400 Years Ago, a Ship Arrived in Virginia, Bearing Human Cargo," *USA Today*, February 8, 2019, https://www.usatoday.com/story/news/investigations/2019/02/08/1619-african-ar rival-virginia/2740468002/.

87. Blue Telusma, "Janelle Monáe Stars in New NYT Oscars Ad for '1619 Project,'" The Grio, February 6, 2020, https://thegrio.com/2020/02/06/janelle-monae-stars -in-new-nyt-oscars-ad-for-1619-project/.

88. Dave McNary, "Oprah Winfrey, Lionsgate to Bring New York Times' '1619 Project' to Film and TV," *Variety*, July 8, 2020, https://variety.com/2020/tv/news /new-york-times-1619-project-oprah-winfrey-lionsgate-film-tv-1234700720/.

89. Jeroslyn Johnson, "Hulu Set to Release Docuseries on 'The 1619 Project," Black Enterprise, April 5, 2021, https://www.blackenterprise.com/hulu-set-to-release-do cuseries-on-the-1619-project/.

90. "We Respond to the Historians Who Critiqued The 1619 Project" (letter to the editor and the editors' response), *New York Times*, December 20, 2019, updated January 19, 2021, https://www.nytimes.com/2019/12/20/magazine/we-respond -to-the-historians-who-critiqued-the-1619-project.html.

91. Adam Serwer, "The Fight over the 1619 Project Is Not about the Facts," *The Atlantic*, December 23, 2019, https://www.theatlantic.com/ideas/archive/2019/12 /historians-clash-1619-project/604093/.

92. Ibid.

93. "Donald Trump Speech Transcript in Jamestown, Virginia July 30, 2019," Rev, https://www.rev.com/blog/transcripts/donald-trump-speech-transcript-in-jamesto wn-virginia-july-30-2019.

94. Nell Irvin Painter, "How We Think about the Term 'Enslaved' Matters," *The Guardian*, August 14, 2019, https://www.theguardian.com/us-news/2019/aug/14 /slavery-in-america-1619-first-ships-jamestown.

95. Respected historians disagree on what the status in Virginia was of the Africans who were brought on the *White Lion*. Hampden-Sydney College history professor John C. Coombs would agree with President Trump. He argues that the Africans who arrived on the *White Lion* were considered slaves, though he admits, "The surviving record contains frustratingly little direct information regarding the treatment of the first thirty or so captives taken from the Portuguese slaver…who landed at Point Comfort in August of 1619." John C. Coombs, "'Others Not Christians in the Service of the English': Interpreting the Status of Africans and African Americans in Early Virginia," *Virginia Magazine of History & Biography*

127:3 (2019): 212–38. Michael Guasco believes that such questions sidestep more important ones about the agency of the newly arrived Africans. Michael Guasco, "The Misguided Focus on 1619 as the Beginning of Slavery in the U.S. Damages Our Understanding of American History," *Smithsonian*, September 13, 2017, https://www.smithsonianmag.com/history/misguided-focus-1619-beginning-sla very-us-damages-our-understanding-american-history-180964873/. And Linda Heywood and John Thornton claim that, at the time, the word slave "did not have a fixed legal meaning of life-long inheritable servitude." Linda M. Heywood and John K. Thornton, "In Search of the 1619 African Arrivals: Enslavement and Middle Passage," *Virginia Magazine of History & Biography* 127:3 (2019): 200– 211. James Horn notes that the issue has stirred up "a great deal of controversy among historians." Horn explains that historians who argue that they were considered indentured servants point to their placement "in the muster of 1625 alongside white servants." James Horn, *1619: Jamestown and the Forging of American Democracy* (New York: Basic Books, 2018), 103–4. It should be pointed out that the Africans were, in fact, "enslaved" from the time of their capture in Africa and during their first voyage on the Portuguese ship. Once they were on the British ship their status became murky.

96. Serwer, "The Fight over the 1619 Project."

97. Leslie M. Harris, "I Helped Fact-Check the 1619 Project. The Times Ignored Me," *Politico*, March 6, 2020, https://www.politico.com/news/magazine/2020/03/06 /1619-project-new-york-times-mistake-122248.

98. Carole Levine, "Republicans in 5 States Seek to Keep *1619 Project* Curriculum Out of Schools," *Nonprofit Quarterly*, February 15, 2020, https://nonprofitquar terly.org/republicans-in-5-states-seek-to-keep-1619-project-curriculum-out-of-sc hools/.

99. "CRT Legislation Tracker," Christopher Rufo, n.d., https://christopherrufo.com/crt tr acker/; Jeff Reynolds, "Washington Gov. Inslee Signs Bill Requiring Critical Race Training for Public School Teachers," Legal Insurrection, May 9, 2021, https://le galinsurrection.com/2021/05/washington-gov-inslee-signs-bill-requiring-critical -race-training-for-public-school-teachers/; Max Brantley, "Bill Introduced to Ban Howard Zinn Books from Arkansas Public Schools," *Arkansas Times*, March 2, 2017, https://arktimes.com/arkansas-blog/2017/03/02/bill-introduced-to-ban-ho ward-zinn-books-from-arkansas-public-schools; "Mississippi Senate Bill 2538 *(Adjourned Sine Die)*," LegiScan, https://legiscan.com/MS/bill/SB2538/2021.

100. Alex Sundby, "Read the Full Text of Biden's Inaugural Address," CBS News, January 20, 2021, https://www.cbsnews.com/news/president-joe-biden-inaugur ation-address-text/.

101. Austa Somvichian-Clausen, "Biden Rescinds Trump's 1776 Commission, a Report Promoting 'Patriotic Education,'" *The Hill*, January 21, 2021, https://thehill.com

/changing-america/enrichment/education/535323-biden-rescinds-trumps-1776
-commission-a-report; Christopher Hickey et al., "Here Are the Executive Actions
Biden Signed in His First 100 Days," CNN, April 30, 2021, https://
www.cnn.com/interactive/2021/politics/biden-executive-orders/index.html; Kurtz,
"The Greatest Education Battle of Our Lifetimes"; Peter Wood, "Why We Need
a Civics Alliance," National Association of Scholars, March 22, 2021, https://
www.nas.org/blogs/article/nas-announces-the-civics-alliance. Generation Citizen,
an organization pushing the Civics Learning Act, is supported by the Bezos Family
Foundation and other funders of left-wing causes. "Our Supporters," Generation
Citizen, https://generationcitizen.org/our-team/our-supporters/. Stanley Kurtz
points out that Biden has put in place "a veteran supporter of Obama's Common
Core [Carmel Martin] in a high position of authority on the White House Domestic
Policy Council," (email to author, April 9, 2021).

102. Tyler O'Neil, "'A Masterpiece:' Kamala Harris Praises NYT Anti-American
Screed," PJ Media, August 19, 2019, https://pjmedia.com/news-and-politics/tyler
-o-neil/2019/08/19/a-masterpiece-kamala-harris-praises-nyt-anti-american-scre
ed-n68188.

103. David Marcus, "Meet the Rioting Criminals Kamala Harris Helped Bail Out of
Jail," The Federalist, August 31, 2020, https://thefederalist.com/2020/08/31/meet
-the-rioting-criminals-kamala-harris-helped-bail-out-of-jail/.

104. Ben Shapiro, "Why Won't Biden Condemn Antifa or BLM Violence?"
RealClearPolitics, September 2, 2020, https://www.realclearpolitics.com/articles
/2020/09/02/why_wont_biden_condemn_antifa_or_blm_violence_144118.html#.

105. See, for example, O'Neil, "'A Masterpiece'"; Sam Dorman, "Oregon Paid $50K
for '1619' Events Where Founder Criticized Colorblindness, Said US Never Met
Founding Ideals," Fox News, May 20, 2021, https://www.foxnews.com/politics
/oregon-1619-project-founder-nikole-hannah-jones; Len Bestoff, "Follow-Up:
CCSU Professors React to Colleague's Criticism of The 1619 Project," NBC
Connecticut, May 5, 2021, https://www.nbcconnecticut.com/investigations/fol
low-up-ccsu-professors-react-to-colleagues-criticism-of-the-1619-project/2481
546/; Zack Linly, "Mitch McConnell's Own Alma Mater Knows He Doesn't Know
WTF He's Talking about When It Comes to *The 1619 Project*," The Root, May
8, 2021, https://www.theroot.com/mitch-mcconnells-own-alma-mater-knows-he
-doesnt-know-wt-1846852798; Zack Linly, "Students Protest Firing of Arkansas
Teacher Who Called Lawmakers Out for Being Fragile AF Over *1619 Project*
Curriculum," The Root, February 6, 2021, https://www.theroot.com/students-pr
otest-firing-of-arkansas-teacher-who-called-1846213947; Abid Rahman, "'The
1619 Project' Docuseries to Debut on Hulu, Roger Ross Williams to Produce,"
Hollywood Reporter, April 1, 2021, https://www.hollywoodreporter.com/tv/tv
-news/1619-project-docuseries-to-debut-on-hulu-4159516/#!.

Chapter 3: Canceling Thomas Jefferson—and 1776

1. Dumas Malone, *Jefferson the Virginian* (Boston: Little, Brown and Company, 1948), 220–21.

2. Ibid.; Pauline Maier, *American Scripture: Making the Declaration of Independence* (New York: Alfred A. Knopf, 1997), 34–37, 47–48.

3. Merrill D. Peterson, *The Jefferson Image in the American Mind* (New York: Oxford University Press, 1960), 9.

4. Nikole Hannah-Jones, "The Idea of America," in "The 1619 Project," *New York Times Magazine*, August 18, 2019, https://www.nytimes.com/interactive/2019/08/14/magazine/black-history-american-democracy.html.

5. Malone, *Jefferson the Virginian*, 220–21; Maier, *American Scripture*, 55.

6. Robert Paquette, forthcoming manuscript.

7. Malone, *Jefferson the Virginian*, 106–9.

8. Ibid., 223.

9. Ibid.

10. Ibid., 221–22.

11. Ibid., 222–23.

12. Peterson, *The Jefferson Image in the American Mind*, 9.

13. Dumas Malone, "Every Man Was His Own Jeffersonian" (review of Merrill D. Peterson, *The Jefferson Image in the American Mind*, Oxford University Press, 1960), *New York Times*, September 18, 1960, https://www.nytimes.com/1960/09/18/archives/every-man-was-his-own-jeffersonian-the-jefferson-image-in-the.html.

14. Ibid.; Peterson, *The Jefferson Image in the American Mind*, 9.

15. Ibid., 3–4; Thomas Donaldson, *The House in Which Thomas Jefferson Wrote the Declaration of Independence* (Philadelphia: Avil Printing Co., 1898), 49; Gilbert Chinard, *Thomas Jefferson: The Apostle of Americanism*, second edition, revised (Ann Arbor: University of Michigan Press, 1957), 531–32.

16. Peterson, *The Jefferson Image in the American Mind*, 5.

17. Ibid., 3–4.

18. Ibid., 4–5; "Jefferson's Gravestone," Thomas Jefferson Encyclopedia, https://www.monticello.org/site/research-and-collections/jeffersons-gravestone.

19. Peterson, *The Jefferson Image in the American Mind*, viii; Malone, *Jefferson the Virginian*, viii.

20. Robert L. Paquette, "Slave Resistance," in *The Cambridge World History of Slavery, Volume 4, AD 1804–AD 2016*, ed. David Eltis, Stanley L. Engerman, Seymour Drescher, and David Richardson (Cambridge: Cambridge University Press, 2017), 272–95.

21. David Brion Davis, *"Was Thomas Jefferson an Authentic Enemy of Slavery?" An Inaugural Lecture Delivered before the University of Oxford on 18 February 1970* (Oxford: Clarendon Press, 1970), 12–13. There is no citation in the published

speech, and there does not appear to be any reference to Derieux in David Brion Davis, *The Problem of Slavery in the Age of Revolution 1770–1823* (Ithaca, New York: Cornell University Press, 1975). Derieux is mentioned obliquely in a later April 25, 1794, letter from Jefferson to Madame Plumard de Bellanger, from which Robert Paquette surmises that Derieux was living in the West Indies, but the reference is "not entirely clear." Robert Paquette, email to author, March 12, 2021.

22.　Oscar Handlin, "History: A Discipline in Crisis," *American Scholar* XL (Summer 1971), reprinted in Oscar Handlin, *Truth in History* (Cambridge: Harvard University Press, 1979), 3–24.

23.　Oscar Handlin, "A History of American History," in *Truth in History* (Cambridge: Harvard University Press, 1979), 43–84.

24.　Oscar Handlin, "Theories of Historical Interpretation," in *Truth in History* (Cambridge: Harvard University Press, 1979), 85–110.

25.　Oscar Handlin, "Ethnicity and the New History," in *Truth in History* (Cambridge: Harvard University Press, 1979), 383–402.

26.　Theodore Draper, *American Communism and Soviet Russia* (New York: Viking Press, 1960), 320–22.

27.　Mary Grabar, *Debunking Howard Zinn: Exposing the Fake History That Turned a Generation against America* (Washington, D.C.: Regnery History, 2019), 93; Zinn's book remains a top seller in the history category and is used in classrooms, both K–12 and college. Gilbert T. Sewell, "The Howard Zinn Show," *Academic Questions* (May 2012): 209–17; "Best Sellers in United States History," Amazon, May 29, 2021, https://www.amazon.com/Best-Sellers-Books-United-States-History/zgbs/books/4853/ref=zg_bs_pg_2?_encoding=UTF8&pg=2.

28.　Howard Zinn, *A People's History of the United States* (New York: HarperCollins, 1980, 2003), 72, 97; for a full exposition see Grabar, *Debunking Howard Zinn*.

29.　Bruce Weber, "Merrill D. Peterson, Jefferson Scholar, Dies at 88," *New York Times*, October 2, 2009, https://www.nytimes.com/2009/10/02/books/02peter son.html?searchResultPosition=1.

30.　Peterson, *The Jefferson Image in the American Mind* (1998), ix; AP, "Fawn Brodie, Jefferson Biographer," *New York Times*, January 13, 1981, https://www.nytimes .com/1981/01/13/obituaries/fawn-brodie-jefferson-biographer.html; Dumas Malone and Steven H. Hochman, "A Note on Evidence: The Personal History of Madison Hemings," *The Journal of Southern History* XLI, no. 4 (November 1975): 523–28; Robert F. Turner, "The Myth of Thomas Jefferson and Sally Hemings," *Wall Street Journal*, July 11, 2012, https://www.wsj.com/articles/SB1000142405 2702304211804577500870076728362.

31.　Peterson, *The Jefferson Image in the American Mind* (1960), 182, 184–86.

32.　Fawn M. Brodie, "The Great Jefferson Taboo," *American Heritage* 23:4 (June 1972), https://www.americanheritage.com/great-jefferson-taboo.

33. A note on usage: The word "Negro" was used as a term of respect in the past. It became capitalized in standard usage in the early part of the twentieth century. I will be retaining the form that the authors use. See James West, "Power Is 100 Years Old: Lerone Bennett Jr., *Ebony* Magazine and the Roots of Black Power," *The Sixties: A Journal of History, Politics and Culture* 19:2 (2016): 165–88.

34. Herman Belz, "The Legend of Sally Hemings," *Academic Questions* 25 (May 2012): 218–27.

35. Annette Gordon-Reed, *Thomas Jefferson and Sally Hemings: An American Controversy* (Charlottesville: University of Virginia Press, 1997), 7.

36. Belz, "The Legend of Sally Hemings."

37. Annette Gordon-Reed, "Engaging Jefferson: Blacks and the Founding Father," *William and Mary Quarterly* 57:1 (January 2000): 171–82.

38. Annette Gordon-Reed, "Author's Note," in *Thomas Jefferson and Sally Hemings: An American Controversy* (Charlottesville: University Press of Virginia, 1997, 2000), vii; Belz, "The Legend of Sally Hemings," also notes that in 2000 the Hemings descendants refused additional DNA testing.

39. Annette Gordon-Reed, *The Hemingses of Monticello: An American Family* (New York: W. W. Norton, 2008), 290, 301.

40. Annette Gordon-Reed, "Sally Hemings," in *Four Hundred Souls*, ed. Ibram X. Kendi and Keisha N. Blain (New York: Random House, 2021), 158–61; "Titles by All Persons Named: Annette Gordon-Reed," Open Syllabus, n.d., https://opensyllabus.org/result/author?id=Annette+Gordon-Reed.

41. *"Most Blessed of the Patriarchs": Thomas Jefferson and the Empire of the Imagination* is assigned much less often than her solely authored books on Jefferson's alleged relationship with Sally Hemings.

42. Belz, "The Legend of Sally Hemings"; Robert F. Turner, ed., *The Jefferson-Hemings Controversy: Report of the Scholars Commission* (Durham, North Carolina: Carolina Academic Press, 2001, 2011).

43. Robert F. Turner, "The Myth of Thomas Jefferson and Sally Hemings," *Wall Street Journal*, July 11, 2012, https://www.wsj.com/articles/SB1000142405270230421 18045775008700076728362.

44. Belz, "The Legend of Sally Hemings."

45. Paul Finkelman, "The Monster of Monticello," *New York Times*, November 30, 2012, https://www.nytimes.com/2012/12/01/opinion/the-real-thomas-jefferson.html?searchResultPosition=1.

46. Kevin Gutzman, "Making Jefferson Safe for the Historians," *Law & Liberty*, July 13, 2017, https://lawliberty.org/making-jefferson-safe-for-the-historians/.

47. Joseph Moreau, *School Book Nation: Conflicts over American History Textbooks from the Civil War to the Present* (Ann Arbor: University of Michigan Press, 2003), 253.

48. Ibid., 336.
49. Robert Lerner, Althea Nagai, and Stanley Rothman, *Molding the Good Citizen: The Politics of High School History Texts* (Westport, Connecticut: Praeger, 1995), 127–31.
50. Lerner, Nagai, and Rothman, *Molding the Good Citizen*, 127–31.
51. David M. Kennedy and Lizabeth Cohen, *The American Pageant*, 17th edition (Boston: Cengage, 2020), 204. The claim about slaves is misleading. That could have been the total Jefferson had owned over a lifetime, most of them inherited and many of them children of his slaves.
52. Ibid.
53. Ibid., 213. Malone pointed out that Jefferson "denied the story in a personal letter" and directed the reader to pages 212–14 of his *Jefferson the President: First Term, 1801–1805* (Boston: Little, Brown and Company, 1970). Dumas Malone, *The Sage of Monticello* (Boston: Little, Brown and Company, 1981), 513. Belz wrote that Peterson "noted that Jefferson never issued a public denial of the charge." Belz, "The Legend of Sally Hemings."
54. Kennedy and Cohen, *The American Pageant*, 213.
55. James W. Fraser, *By the People: A History of the United States*, 2nd edition (Pearson, 2019), 225.
56. "James Fraser," NYU Steinhardt, https://steinhardt.nyu.edu/people/james-fraser.
57. Fraser, *By the People*, 226.
58. Ibid., 161.
59. Ibid.
60. Kennedy and Cohen, *The American Pageant*, 143.
61. Fraser, *By the People*, 149.
62. Ibid., 225.
63. Joy Pullmann, "Dear Joe Scarborough: More Americans Hate America Than You Think," The Federalist, February 27, 2020, https://thefederalist.com/2020/02/27/dear-joe-scarborough-more-americans-hate-america-than-you-think/.
64. Hannah-Jones, "The Idea of America."
65. Annie Gowan, "As Statues of Founding Fathers Topple, Debate Rages over Where Protesters Should Draw the Line," *Washington Post*, July 7, 2020, https://www.washingtonpost.com/national/as-statues-of-founding-fathers-topple-debate-rages-over-where-protesters-should-draw-the-line/2020/07/07/5de7c956-bfb7-11ea-b4f6-cb39cd8940fb_story.html; Charles Kesler, "Call Them the 1619 riots," *New York Post*, June 19, 2020, https://nypost.com/2020/06/19/call-them-the-1619-riots/; Visvajit Sriramrajan, "Hofstra Removes Jefferson Statue amid Outcries," LI Herald, July 7, 2020, https://www.liherald.com/stories/hofstra-moves-jefferson-statue-amid-outcries,126401; Dan Whisenhunt, "Thomas Jefferson Statue Removed

from Downtown Decatur," Decaturish, June 22, 2020, https://decaturish.com/20 20/06/thomas-jefferson-statue-removed-from-downtown-decatur/.

66. Alex Nester, "Virginia District to Rename Schools Named after Founding Fathers," Washington Free Beacon, December 10, 2020, https://freebeacon.com/campus/vir ginia-district-to-rename-schools-named-after-founding-fathers/; Natalie O'Neill, "San Francisco to Rename Schools Honoring 'Racist' Figures Like Washington, Lincoln," *New York Post*, January 27, 2021, https://nypost.com/2021/01/27/san-francisco-to-rename-44-schools-honoring-racist-founders/; Stella Chan and Amanda Jackson, "San Francisco School Board Votes to Rename 44 schools, including Abraham Lincoln and George Washington High Schools," CNN, January 27, 2021, https:// www.cnn.com/2021/01/27/us/san-francisco-school-name-changes-trnd/index.html; Alex Nester, "San Francisco School Board Reverses Decision to Rename Schools," Washington Free Beacon, April 7, 2021, https://freebeacon.com/campus/san-francisco-school-board-reverses-decision-to-rename-schools/.

67. Kimberly Ford, "My Great-Grandfather Carved Mount Rushmore on Sacred Land. Now Is the Time to Remove It.," *USA Today*, July 10, 2020, https://www .usatoday.com/story/opinion/voices/2020/07/10/take-down-rushmore-presidents -my-great-grandfather-carved-column/5401088002/; Timothy D. Dwyer, "Op-Ed: Could the Racist Past of Mt. Rushmore's Creator Bring Down the Monument?," *Los Angeles Times*, July 3, 2020, https://www.latimes.com/opinion/story/2020 -07-03/mount-rushmore-sculptor-racist.

68. Nikole Hannah-Jones, "Martin Luther King Jr. Lecture (Featuring Nikole Hannah-Jones)," Georgia Tech, January 14, 2021, https://serve-learn-sustain.ga tech.edu/martin-luther-king-jr-lecture-featuring-nikole-hannah-jones, transcription by the author.

69. Hannah-Jones, "The Idea of America."

70. Ibid.

71. Ibid.; David Marcus, "The New York Times' Correction to The 1619 Project Proves It Is Not Fit For Schools," *The Federalist*, March 13, 2020, https://thefederalist .com/2020/03/13/correction-to-the-1619-project-proves-it-is-not-fit-for-schools/.

72. Editor's Note, March 11, 2020, to Nikole Hannah-Jones, "The Idea of America." Besides the softer verb—"adjusted" for "corrected"—note the use of the passive voice "has been adjusted."

73. Jordan Davidson, "The New York Times Deceptively Edits False Claim at the Center of 1619 Project," The Federalist, September 21, 2020, https://thefederalist .com/2020/09/21/nyt-deceptively-edits-false-claim-at-the-center-of-1619-project/.

74. Jake Silverstein, "Why We Published The 1619 Project," *New York Times* Magazine, December 20, 2019, https://www.nytimes.com/interactive/2019/12/20 /magazine/1619-intro.html; Davidson, "The New York Times Deceptively Edits False Claim"; Becket Adams, "The 1619 Project Is a Fraud," *Washington*

Examiner, September 21, 2020, https://www.washingtonexaminer.com/opinion/the-1619-project-is-a-fraud.

75. Silverstein, "Why We Published."

76. See chapter 1, note 9, above.

77. "The 1619 Project," *New York Times Magazine*, August 18, 2019, a pdf of the print edition is available at the Pulitzer Center website, https://pulitzercenter.org/sites/default/files/full_issue_of_the_1619_project.pdf; Davidson, "The New York Times Deceptively Edits False Claim"; Adams, "The 1619 Project Is a Fraud."

78. Adams, "The 1619 Project Is a Fraud."

79. Bret Stephens, "The 1619 Chronicles," *New York Times*, October 9, 2020, https://www.nytimes.com/2020/10/09/opinion/nyt-1619-project-criticisms.html.

80. Silverstein, "Why We Published."

81. Hannah-Jones, "The Idea of America."

Chapter 4: Declaring Independence "to Protect the Institution of Slavery"?

1. David Marcus, "The New York Times' Correction to The 1619 Project Proves It Is Not Fit For Schools," The Federalist, March 13, 2020, https://thefederalist.com/2020/03/13/correction-to-the-1619-project-proves-it-is-not-fit-for-schools/.

2. Sean Wilentz, "A Matter of Facts," *The Atlantic*, January 22, 2020, https://www.theatlantic.com/ideas/archive/2020/01/1619-project-new-york-times-wilentz/605152/; Leslie M. Harris, "I Helped Fact-Check the 1619 Project. The Times Ignored Me," *Politico*, March 6, 2020, https://www.politico.com/news/magazine/2020/03/06/1619-project-new-york-times-mistake-122248.

3. Harris, "I Helped Fact-Check the 1619 Project."

4. Edward Baptist, *The Half Has Never Been Told: Slavery and the Making of American Capitalism* (New York: Basic Books, 2014), xx.

5. Christian Schneider, "Cornell Scholar Cited in NYT '1619' Series Charged with Fabricating Quotes, Evidence," The College Fix, August 23, 2019, https://www.thecollegefix.com/cornell-scholar-cited-in-nyts-1619-series-charged-with-fabricating-quotes-evidence/.

6. Matthew Desmond, "Capitalism," in "The 1619 Project," *New York Times Magazine*, August 18, 2019, pdf available at the Pulitzer Center website, https://pulitzercenter.org/sites/default/files/full_issue_of_the_1619_project.pdf, 30. See chapter 11 below for detailed discussion of the Desmond essay in the issue of the *Magazine* that inaugurated The 1619 Project.

7. David Waldstreicher, *Slavery's Constitution: From Revolution to Ratification* (New York: Farrar, Straus and Giroux, 2009), 46–47.

8. Dumas Malone, *Jefferson the Virginian* (Boston: Little, Brown and Company, 1948), 222.

9. "1776 (1972)," IMDb, n.d., https://www.imdb.com/title/tt0068156/. See SteveBrown2008, "1776 and Slavery," YouTube, September 3, 2008, https://www.youtube.com/watch?v=yk5NAeIRY4k.

10. Richard K. Matthews, *The Radical Politics of Thomas Jefferson: A Revisionist View* (Lawrence, Kansas: University Press of Kansas, 1986), 66.

11. Barry Alan Shain, *The Declaration of Independence in Historical Context* (New Haven: Yale University Press, 2014, reprinted by Liberty Fund), 500.

12. Matthews, *The Radical Politics of Thomas Jefferson*, 66.

13. Ibid.; Thomas Jefferson, *Autobiography* (Thomas Jefferson Society, 2000), 13. "It's" was the form of the possessive that Jefferson and others used at the time.

14. Jefferson, *Autobiography*, 13.

15. Thomas Jefferson, "The Rights of British America," in *Thomas Jefferson: Writings* (New York: Library of America, 1985), 105–22.

16. Benjamin Brawley, *A Social History of the American Negro* (London: Collier Books, 1921; reprint New York: The Macmillan Company, 1970), 9–14.

17. Ibid.

18. A January 1620 (1619, Old Style) letter from John Rolfe to Edwin Sandys also describes the arrival of "20. and Odd Negroes" on "a Dutch man of Warr" "[a]bout the latter end of August." Engel Sluiter, "New Light on the '20. and Odd Negroes' Arriving in Virginia, August 1619," *William and Mary Quarterly* 54:2 (April 1997): 395–98, https://www.jstor.org/stable/2953279?seq=1.

19. Brawley, *A Social History of the American Negro*.

20. Ibid., 9–10; David Brion Davis, *The Problem of Slavery in the Age of Revolution 1770–1823* (Ithaca, New York: Cornell University Press, 1975), 23.

21. Brawley, *A Social History of the American Negro*, 10–14.

22. Martha W. McCartney, with contributions by Lorena S. Walsh, *A Study of the Africans and African Americans on Jamestown Island and at Green Spring, 1619–1803* (Williamsburg, Virginia: Colonial Williamsburg Foundation, 2003), 15.

23. Brawley, *A Social History of the American Negro*, 15.

24. Ibid.

25. Ibid, 14; Robert Paquette, email to the author, May 19, 2021.

26. Edmund S. Morgan, *The Birth of the Republic: 1763–89*, 95–96.

27. Robert Paquette, email to the author, May 28, 2021.

28. Wilentz, "A Matter of Facts."

29. David Brion Davis, "American Slavery and the American Revolution," in *Slavery and Freedom in the Age of American Revolution*, ed. Ira Berlin and Ronald Hoffman (Charlottesville: University Press of Virginia, 1983), 263.

30. Robert L. Paquette, forthcoming manuscript.

31. John P. Kaminski, ed., *A Necessary Evil? Slavery and the Debate over the Constitution* (Madison, Wisconsin: Madison House, 1995), 2–3.

32. Robert Paquette, forthcoming manuscript.

33. Thomas Jefferson, *Notes on the State of Virginia* (New York: Harper & Row, Publishers, 1964), 156.

34. Nikole Hannah-Jones, "The Idea of America," in "The 1619 Project," *New York Times Magazine*, August 18, 2019, https://www.nytimes.com/interactive/2019/08 /14/magazine/black-history-american-democracy.html; Nikole Hannah-Jones, "Martin Luther King Jr. Lecture (Featuring Nikole Hannah-Jones)," Georgia Tech, January 14, 2021, https://serve-learn-sustain.gatech.edu/martin-luther-king-jr-lec ture-featuring-nikole-hannah-jones, transcription by the author.

35. Dumas Malone, *Jefferson the Virginian* (Boston: Little, Brown and Company, 1948), 21.

36. Ibid., 5.

37. Ibid., xvi.

38. Ibid., 32.

39. Ibid., 114.

40. Ibid., 439.

41. Ibid., 440.

42. Ibid., 216.

43. Ibid., 318.

44. Nikole Hannah-Jones, "The Idea of America."

45. "Deed of Manumission for Robert Hemings, 24 December 1794," Founders Online, National Archives, https://founders.archives.gov/documents/Jefferson/01 -28-02-0165; original source: *The Papers of Thomas Jefferson, vol. 28, 1 January 1794 to 29 February 1796*, ed. John Catanzariti (Princeton: Princeton University Press, 2000), 222–23.

46. "Robert Hemings," Google, https://www.google.com/search?client=firefox-b-1 -d&q=%22robert+hemings%22.

Chapter 5: "Unlike Anything That Had Existed in the World Before"?

1. Nikole Hannah-Jones, "The Idea of America," in "The 1619 Project," *New York Times Magazine*, August 18, 2019, https://www.nytimes.com/interactive/2019/08 /14/magazine/1619-america-slavery.html.

2. Ibid.

3. David Brion Davis, "Slavery," in *The Comparative Approach to American History*, ed. C. Vann Woodward (New York: Basic Books, 1968), 125–28.

4. Orlando Patterson, *Slavery and Social Death: A Comparative Study* (Cambridge: Harvard University Press, 1982, 2018), 4–6, 38.

5. Davis, "Slavery," 125–28; Richard Hellie, *Slavery in Russia, 1450–1725* (Chicago: University of Chicago Press, 1982), 86.

6. Joseph C. Miller, "Human Sacrifice: The New World," in *Macmillan Encyclopedia of World Slavery*, vol. 1, ed. Paul Finkelman and Joseph C. Miller (New York: Simon & Schuster Macmillan, 1998), 422.

7. Paul Finkelman, "Human Sacrifice: The New World and Pacific Cultures," in *Macmillan Encyclopedia of World Slavery*, vol. 1, ed. Paul Finkelman and Joseph C. Miller (New York: Simon & Schuster Macmillan, 1998), 421–22.

8. Robin Law, "Sacrifice in Pre-Colonial West Africa," *African Affairs* 84:334 (January 1985): 53–57.

9. Ibid.

10. Ibid.

11. Ibid.

12. Olatunji Ojo, "Slavery and Human Sacrifice in Yorubaland: Ondo, c. 1870–94," *Journal of African History* 46:3 (2005): 379–404.

13. Ibid.

14. Ibid.

15. Robert L. Paquette, "Discipline and Punishment," in *Macmillan Encyclopedia of World Slavery*, vol. 1, ed. Paul Finkelman and Joseph C. Miller (New York: Simon & Schuster Macmillan, 1998), 252–57.

16. Ibid.

17. Ibid.

18. Ibid.

19. Davis, "Slavery," 125–28.

20. Hannah-Jones, "The Idea of America."

21. Davis, "Slavery," 125–28.

22. "Jefferson's *Notes on the State of Virginia*," PBS, https://www.pbs.org/wgbh/aia/part3/3h490t.html.

23. Patrick M. O'Neil, "Christianity: Medieval West," in *Macmillan Encyclopedia of World Slavery*, vol. 1, ed. Paul Finkelman and Joseph C. Miller (New York: Simon & Schuster Macmillan, 1998), 186–88.

24. Douglas Ambrose, "Christianity: An Overview," in *Macmillan Encyclopedia of World Slavery*, vol. 1, ed. Paul Finkelman and Joseph C. Miller (New York: Simon & Schuster Macmillan, 1998), 181–85.

25. Gilbert Chinard, *Thomas Jefferson: The Apostle of Americanism* (Ann Arbor: University of Michigan Press, 1957), 315.

26. Lucia Stanton, "'Those Who Labor for My Happiness': Thomas Jefferson and His Slaves," in Peter S. Onuf, ed., *Jefferson Legacies* (Charlottesville: University Press of Virginia, 1993), 147–80.

27. Jason L. Riley, "Lessons from the Rise of America's Irish," *Wall Street Journal*, March 13, 2018, https://www.wsj.com/articles/lessons-from-the-rise-of-americas-irish-1520982717.

28. Robert William Fogel and Stanley L. Engerman, "Introduction: Changing Views of Slavery in the United States South: The Role of Eugene D. Genovese," in *Slavery, Secession, and Southern History*, ed. Robert Louis Paquette and Louis A. Ferleger (Charlottesville: University Press of Virginia, 2000), 1–13.

29. Eugene D. Genovese, *Roll, Jordan, Roll: The World the Slaves Made* (New York: Random House, 1972, Vintage Books, 1976), 5.

30. Frederick Law Olmsted, "The South," Letters on the Productions, Industry and Resources of the Southern States, Number Forty-Seven, *New-York Daily Times*, January 26, 1854, in *The Papers of Frederick Law Olmsted: Volume II: Slavery in the South, 1852–1857*, ed. Charles E. Beveridge and Charles Capen McLaughlin (Baltimore: Johns Hopkins University Press, 1981), 247–56.

31. Robert Paquette, email to the author, April 6, 2021.

32. Beth Barton Schweiger, "The Literate South: Reading before Emancipation," *Journal of the Civil War Era* 3:3 (September 2013): 331–59.

33. Thomas Sowell, *Race and Culture: A World View* (New York: Basic Books, 1994), 187.

34. "Trans-Atlantic Slave Trade–Estimates," Slave Voyages, n.d., https://slavevoyages.org/assessment/estimates.

35. Shane O'Rourke, "The Emancipation of the Serfs in Europe," in *The Cambridge World History of Slavery, Volume 4, AD 1804–AD 2016*, ed. David Eltis, Stanley L. Engerman, Seymour Drescher, and David Richardson (Cambridge: Cambridge University Press, 2017), 422–40.

36. Ibid.

37. Peter Kolchin, *Unfree Labor: American Slavery and Russian Serfdom* (Cambridge: Harvard University Press, 1987), 41–42.

38. O'Rourke, "The Emancipation of the Serfs in Europe."

39. Bruce Bawer, "Slaves of a Different Color," American Greatness, August 1, 2020, https://amgreatness.com/2020/08/01/slaves-of-a-different-color/.

40. Thomas Sowell, *Ethnic America: A History* (New York: Basic Books, 1981), 18–19.

41. Abbot Emerson Smith, *Colonists in Bondage: White Servitude and Convict Labor in America, 1607–1776* (Chapel Hill: University of North Carolina Press, 1947), 163.

42. Ibid., 165.

43. Sowell, *Ethnic America*, 21–22.

44. Denver Brunsman, *The Evil Necessity: British Naval Impressment in the Eighteenth-Century Atlantic World* (Charlottesville: University of Virginia Press, 2013), 2, 6–7, 9.

45. Ibid., 175.

46. John J. McCusker and Russell R. Menard, "The Origins of Slavery in the Americas," in *The Oxford Handbook of Slavery in the Americas*, ed. Robert L. Paquette and Mark M. Smith (Oxford: Oxford University Press, 2010), 275–92; Aaron S. Fogelman, "Slaves, Convicts, and Servants to Free Passengers: The Transformation of Immigration in the Era of the American Revolution," *The Journal of American History* 85:1 (June 1998): 43–76.

47. Martha W. McCartney, with contributions by Lorena S. Walsh, *A Study of the Africans and African Americans on Jamestown Island and at Green Spring, 1619–1803* (Williamsburg, Virginia: Colonial Williamsburg Foundation, 2003), 16.

48. Gavin Wright, "Slavery and Anglo-American Capitalism Revisited," *Economic History Review* 73:2 (2020): 353–83; McCartney, *A Study of the Africans and African Americans on Jamestown Island*, 54, 10. Around the 1680s slaves began replacing white servants because of a drop in the price of slaves due to an economic depression in the West Indies; after the mid-seventeenth century, New England did not rely on immigration, and "slaves never made up more than 3 percent of the region's population." Food there was produced on family farms, and not for export. David Galenson, *White Servitude in Colonial America: An Economic Analysis* (Cambridge: Cambridge University Press, 1981), 153, 156.

49. Fogelman, "Slaves, Convicts, and Servants to Free Passengers," 43–76.

50. Smith, *Colonists in Bondage*, 89–91.

51. Ibid., 147–49; Galenson, *White Servitude*, 12.

52. Timothy J. Shannon, "A 'Wicked Commerce': Consent, Coercion, and Kidnapping in Aberdeen's Servant Trade," *William and Mary Quarterly* 74:3 (July 2017): 437–66.

53. Smith, *Colonists in Bondage*, 223–24.

54. Sowell, *Ethnic America*, 47–50.

55. Smith, *Colonists in Bondage*, 207.

56. Sowell, *Ethnic America*, 47–50.

57. Smith, *Colonists in Bondage*, 221–23.

58. Fogelman, "Slaves, Convicts, and Servants to Free Passengers."

59. Galenson, *White Servitude*, 171.

60. Smith, *Colonists in Bondage*, 233.

61. Galenson, *White Servitude*, 171.

62. Smith, *Colonists in Bondage*, 278.

63. Silvio A. Bedini, *The Life of Benjamin Banneker* (New York: Charles Scribner's Sons, 1972), 14.

64. McCartney, *A Study of the Africans and African Americans on Jamestown Island*, 33.

65. Smith, *Colonists in Bondage*, 235.

66. Robert Paquette, email to the author, April 6, 2021.

67. Bedini, *The Life of Benjamin Banneker*, 14.

68. Smith, *Colonists in Bondage*, 275.

69. James Curtis Ballagh, *White Servitude in the Colony of Virginia: A Study of the System of Indentured Labor in the American Colonies* (Heritage Books, 2004), 60. Originally published in 1895.

70. Smith, *Colonists in Bondage*, 270.

71. Ibid., 226–27.

72. Ibid., 291.

73. Ibid., 299–300.

74. Ibid., 300–301.

75. Fogelman, "Slaves, Convicts, and Servants to Free Passengers."

76. Nell Irvin Painter, "How We Think about the Term 'Enslaved' Matters," *The Guardian*, August 14, 2019, https://www.theguardian.com/us-news/2019/aug/14/slavery-in-america-1619-first-ships-jamestown.

77. Merrill Jensen, *The Founding of a Nation: A History of the American Revolution, 1763–1776* (New York: Oxford University Press, 1968), 10. Jensen notes that records were not kept on the Scots-Irish because they spoke English.

78. Edmund S. Morgan, *The Birth of the Republic 1763–89*, revised edition (Chicago: University of Chicago Press, 1977), 95.

79. Robert William Fogel, *Without Consent or Contract: The Rise and Fall of American Slavery* (New York: W. W. Norton, 1989), 140.

80. Genovese, *Roll, Jordan, Roll*, 5.

81. Sowell, *Race and Culture*, 200.

82. This analogy is not new. In 1959 the historian Stanley Elkins controversially analogized plantations to Nazi concentration camps, but as Robert William Fogel and Stanley L. Engerman relate, Eugene Genovese pointed out the differences "between the slave plantation, where production was shaped for over a long period, and the concentration camp, which operated to kill people quickly, with only infrequent concern with production." "Introduction: Changing Views of Slavery in the United States South," in *Slavery, Secession, and Southern History* (Charlottesville: University Press of Virginia, 2000), 12.

83. Sue Peabody, "Slavery, Freedom, and the Law in the Atlantic World," *The Cambridge World History of Slavery, Volume 3, AD 1420–AD 1804*, ed. David Eltis and Stanley L. Engerman (Cambridge: Cambridge University Press, 2011),

594–630; David Eltis, *The Rise of African Slavery in the Americas* (New York: Cambridge University Press, 2000), 65. Eltis notes that "as late as the immediate antebellum period, there were ideologues in the southern United States who advocated slavery for poor whites as well as blacks" (66).

84. Sowell, *Race and Culture*, 193.

85. Peabody, "Slavery, Freedom, and the Law in the Atlantic World"; Bawer, "Slaves of a Different Color"; David Eltis, *The Rise of African Slavery in the Americas*, 65.

86. Robert L. Paquette, "Methods of Enslavement," *Macmillan Encyclopedia of World Slavery*, vol. 1, ed. Paul Finkelman and Joseph C. Miller (New York: Simon & Schuster Macmillan, 1998), 303–12.

87. Ibid.

88. Ibid.

89. Ibid.

90. Eltis, *The Rise of African Slavery in the Americas*, 59–60.

91. Robert Paquette, "What Made American Slavery Distinctive?" National Association of Scholars, September 17, 2020, https://www.nas.org/blogs/event/sl avery-or-freedom-the-conception-of-america, presented at the "Slavery or Freedom: The Conception of America," conference sponsored by the Alexander Hamilton Institute, Texas Public Policy Institute, and National Association of Scholars, September 14–18, 2020.

Chapter 6: A History Neither New nor True

1. "The 1619 Project," *New York Times Magazine*, August 18, 2019, https://www .nytimes.com/interactive/2019/08/14/magazine/1619-america-slavery.html.

2. James Weldon Johnson, "Fifty Years," in *Fifty Years & Other Poems* (Boston: The Cornhill Company, 1917), https://www.gutenberg.org/files/17884/17884-h/178 84-h.htm#FIFTY_YEARS_OTHER_POEMS.

3. Mitch Kachun, *First Martyr of Liberty: Crispus Attucks in American Memory* (New York: Oxford University Press, 2017), 70. The seminary was recently acquired by Yale and incorporated into the divinity school.

4. George Washington Williams, *History of the Negro Race from 1619 to 1880*, vol. 1 (New York: Putnam's, 1883, Kindle edition), 158.

5. W. D. Johnson, *Past and Future of the Negro in America* (Boston: C. A. Wastro, 1897), https://www.loc.gov/resource/lcrbmrp.t0c06/?sp=16&st=text .

6. Dudley T. Cornish, "Foreword," in Joseph T. Wilson, *The Black Phalanx: African American Soldiers in the War of Independence, the War of 1812 & the Civil War*, reprint edition (New York: Da Capo Press, 1994), no page numbers.

7. Joseph T. Wilson, *The Black Phalanx: African American Soldiers in the War of Independence, the War of 1812 & the Civil War*, reprint edition (New York: Da Capo Press, 1994), 26.

8. Founded in 1916 with funds from the Julius Rosenwald Foundation and the Phelps-Stokes Fund. "Association for the Study of Negro Life and History," Encyclopedia.com, n.d., https://www.encyclopedia.com/social-sciences/encyclopedias-almanacs-transcripts-and-maps/association-study-negro-life-and-history#F.

9. Carter G. Woodson, *The Negro in Our History*, 3rd edition (Washington, D.C.: Associated Publishers, 1922, 1924), 20–21.

10. Arna Bontemps, *The Story of the Negro*, reprint edition (New York: Alfred Knopf, 1962).

11. J. Saunders Redding, *They Came in Chains: Americans from Africa* (New York: J. B. Lippincott Company, 1950), 11.

12. Ibid., 11–15.

13. Michael Guasco, "The Misguided Focus on 1619 as the Beginning of Slavery in the U.S. Damages Our Understanding of American History," *Smithsonian*, September 13, 2017, https://www.smithsonianmag.com/history/misguided-focus-1619-beginning-slavery-us-damages-our-understanding-american-history-180964873/.

14. "What Has the Negro Done to Develop America?," *Christian Recorder* (Philadelphia), November 16, 1893; "The Dawning of Liberty," *Christian Recorder* (Philadelphia), January 13, 1898.

15. "1913 or 1919, Which?" *The Freeman*, October 30, 1909.

16. "Baptists to Meet. A Big Time in Richmond, Va., Next Week," *Washington Bee*, June 28, 1919; "A Great Celebration," *Kansas City Advocate*, February 7, 1919.

17. Nikole Hannah-Jones, "The Idea of America," in "The 1619 Project," *New York Times Magazine*, August 18, 2019, https://www.nytimes.com/interactive/2019/08/14/magazine/black-history-american-democracy.html.

18. Engel Sluiter, "New Light on the '20. and Odd Negroes' Arriving in Virginia, August 1619," *William and Mary Quarterly* 54:2 (April 1997): 395–98, https://www.jstor.org/stable/2953279?seq=1.

19. Linda M. Heywood and John K. Thornton, "In Search of the 1619 African Arrivals: Enslavement and Middle Passage," *Virginia Magazine of History & Biography* 127:3 (2019): 200–11.

20. Thomas Sowell, *Black Rednecks and White Liberals* (New York: Encounter Books, 2005), 120.

21. Qtd. in Henry Louis Gates Jr., "Ending the Slavery Blame-Game," *New York Times,* April 22, 2010, https://www.nytimes.com/2010/04/23/opinion/23gates.html?ref=opinion&pagewanted=all.

22. Wilson, *The Black Phalanx*, 25.

23. Woodson, *The Negro in Our History*, 15–16.

24. Redding, *They Came in Chains*, 11–15.

25. Hannah-Jones, "The Idea of America."

26. Ibid.

27. Heywood and Thornton, "In Search of the 1619 African Arrivals"; Benjamin Woolley, *Savage Kingdom: The True Story of Jamestown, 1607, and the Settlement of America* (New York: HarperCollins, 2007), 352.

28. John Thornton, *Africa and Africans in the Making of the Atlantic World, 1400–1680* (Cambridge: Cambridge University Press, 1992), 112–16.

29. Ibid., 38–39.

30. Ibid., 125.

31. "Trans-Atlantic Slave Trade–Estimates," Slave Voyages, n.d., https://www.slavevoyages.org/assessment/estimates.

32. Thornton, *Africa and Africans*, 112–16.

33. One of those scholars is Walter Rodney, who has a "neo-Marxist focus." Thornton, *Africa and Africans*, 4, 41.

34. Ibid.

35. Eugene D. Genovese, *The Political Economy of Slavery* (New York: Random House, 1961), 75–76.

36. Ibid., 77–78.

37. Thornton, *Africa and Africans*, 53–55.

38. Sarah Ellison, "How the 1619 Project Took over 2020," *Washington Post*, October 13, 2020, https://www.washingtonpost.com/lifestyle/style/1619-project-took-over-2020-inside-story/2020/10/13/af537092-00df-11eb-897d-3a6201d6643f_story.html.

39. Ida Bae Wells (@nhannahjones), "One, I have to shout out… ," Twitter, December 22, 2020, 9:27 p.m., twitter.com/nhannahjones/status/1341445148253827072?=90. Screenshot in the author's possession.

40. Ida Bae Wells (@nhannahjones), "If you've heard me talk about the genesis…," Twitter, December 22, 2020, 9:25 p.m., twitter.com/nhannahjones/status/1341445148253827072?=90. Screenshot in the author's possession.

41. Mary Lefkowitz, *Not Out of Africa: How Afrocentrism Became an Excuse to Teach Myth As History*, reprint edition (New York: Basic Books, 1997). The criticism of Diop's 1981 book *Civilization or Barbarism* begins on page 16 and continues through Lefkowitz's book.

42. Nikole Hannah-Jones, "Martin Luther King Jr. Lecture (Featuring Nikole Hannah-Jones)," Georgia Tech, January 14, 2021, author transcript, https://serve-learn-sustain.gatech.edu/martin-luther-king-jr-lecture-featuring-nikole-hannah-jones.

43. Lerone Bennett, *Before the Mayflower: A History of Black America*, 4th edition (Chicago: Johnson Publishing Company, 1969), 30–31.

44. Ellison, "How the 1619 Project took over 2020."

45. Neil Genzlinger, "Lerone Bennett Jr., Historian of Black America, Dies at 89," *New York Times*, February 16, 2018, https://www.nytimes.com/2018/02/16/obituaries/lerone-bennett-jr-historian-of-black-america-dies-at-89.html.

46. E. R. Shipp, "1619, 400 Years Ago, a Ship Arrived in Virginia, Bearing Human Cargo," *USA Today*, February 8, 2019, https://www.usatoday.com/story/news/investigations/2019/02/08/1619-african-arrival-virginia/2740468002/.

47. Lorena S. Walsh, *Motives of Pleasure & Profit: Plantation Management in the Colonial Chesapeake, 1607–1763* (Chapel Hill: University of North Carolina Press, 2010), 112–16; Martha W. McCartney, with contributions by Lorena S. Walsh, *A Study of the Africans and African Americans on Jamestown Island and at Green Spring, 1619–1803* (Williamsburg, Virginia: Colonial Williamsburg Foundation, 2003), 27.

48. Walsh, *Motives of Pleasure & Profit*, 112–16.

49. David Brion Davis, "The Problem of Slavery," in *Slavery, Secession, and Southern History*, ed. Robert Louis Paquette and Louis A. Ferleger (Charlottesville, Virginia: University Press of Virginia, 2000), 17–30.

50. David Brion Davis, *Slavery and Human Progress* (New York: Oxford University Press, 1984), 8.

51. Ibid., 42.

52. Abbot Emerson Smith, *Colonists in Bondage: White Servitude and Convict Labor in America, 1607–1776* (Chapel Hill: University of North Carolina Press, 1947), 256.

53. Walsh, *Motives of Pleasure & Profit*, 119.

54. James Horn, *1619: Jamestown and the Forging of American Democracy* (New York: Basic Books, 2018), 104.

55. Ira Berlin, *Many Thousands Gone: The First Two Centuries of Slavery in America* (Cambridge: Harvard University Press, 1998), 29–30; Horn, *1619*, 104.

56. John H. Russell, Samll Goldsmyth, James Radford, David Jones, and Peter Hawkins, "Colored Freemen as Slave Owners in Virginia," *Journal of Negro History* 1:3 (June 1916): 233–42.

57. Ibid.

58. Ibid.

59. Ibid.

60. Ross M. Kimmel, "Free Blacks in Seventeenth-Century Maryland," *Maryland Historical Magazine* 71 (1976): 19–26.

61. J. Douglas Deal, *Race and Class in Colonial Virginia: Indians, Englishmen, and Africans on the Eastern Shore* (New York: Garland Publishing, 1993), 226.

62. Ross M. Kimmel, "Free Blacks in Seventeenth-Century Maryland." The exception was that blacks were excluded from militia duty due to the fear of arming them. Deal, *Race and Class in Colonial Virginia*, 226.

63. Deal, *Race and Class in Colonial Virginia*, 217 n. 1–3, 236.

64. Ibid., 233–34.

65. Nell Irvin Painter, "How We Think about the Term 'Enslaved' Matters," *The Guardian*, August 14, 2019, https://www.theguardian.com/us-news/2019/aug/14 /slavery-in-america-1619-first-ships-jamestown; Adam Serwer, "The Fight over the 1619 Project Is Not about the Facts," *The Atlantic*, December 23, 2019, https:// www.theatlantic.com/ideas/archive/2019/12/historians-clash-1619-project/604 093/. See chapter 2 above for quotation and discussion of these professors' criticism of The 1619 Project.

Chapter 7: A Not So Simple Story

1. Calvin Dill Wilson, "Black Masters: A Side-Light on Slavery," *North American Review* 181:588 (November 1905): 685–98; Calvin Dill Wilson, "Negroes Who Owned Slaves," *Popular Science Monthly* 81 (November 1912): 483–94.

2. Wilson, "Black Masters."

3. W. E. B. Du Bois to Calvin Dill Wilson, April 30, 1907, W. E. B. Du Bois Papers (MS 312) Special Collections and University Archives, University of Massachusetts Amherst Libraries, https://credo.library.umass.edu/view/full/mums312-b006-i204.

4. Wilson, "Negroes Who Owned Slaves."

5. Ibid. See also Michael P. Johnson and James L. Roark, *Black Masters: A Free Family of Color in the Old South* (W. W. Norton & Company, 1984), which refers to Wilson's research.

6. Mary Grabar, "The New A.P. U.S. History Exam: Providing Opportunities for Indoctrination," Heartland Institute, May 5, 2014, https://www.heartland .org/news-opinion/news/the-new-ap-us-history-exam-providing-opportunities-for indoctrination.

7. Deborah Solomon, "Prize Writer," *New York Times*, October 10, 2004, https:// www.nytimes.com/2004/10/10/magazine/prize-writer.html?searchResultPo sition=.8

8. A. O. Scott, "Edward P. Jones's Carefully Quantified Literary World," *New York Times*, August 16, 2020, https://www.nytimes.com/2020/08/11/books/review/ed ward-p-jones-americans-known-world-lost-in-the-city.html?searchResultPo sition=1.

9. Janet Maslin, "Books of the Times; His Brother's Keeper in Antebellum Virginia," *New York Times*, August 14, 2003, https://www.nytimes.com/2003/08/14/boo

ks/books-of-the-times-his-brother-s-keeper-in-antebellum-virginia.html?searchR
esultPosition=7.

10.   The last three examples are from Louisiana. Carter G. Woodson, *The Negro in Our History* (Washington, D.C.: Associated Publishers, 1922, 1924), 127–29.

11.   Carter G. Woodson, *Free Negro Owners of Slaves in the United States in 1830: Together with Absentee Ownership of Slaves in the United States 1830* (CreateSpace Independent Publishing Platform, 2015). Originally published in 1924.

12.   John Hope Franklin, *The Free Negro in North Carolina, 1790–1860* (Chapel Hill: University of North Carolina Press, 1995). Originally published in 1943.

13.   "Paul Heinegg," Archives of Maryland, https://msa.maryland.gov/msa/speccol/sc 3500/sc3520/013100/013118/html/msa13118.html; Paul Heinegg, *Free African Americans of Virginia, North Carolina, South Carolina, Maryland, and Delaware*, Free African Americans, http://freeafricanamericans.com/.

14.   "Document: Colonial Virginia Laws Related to Slavery," Teaching American History, n.d., https://teachingamericanhistory.org/library/document/colonial-virginia-laws-related-to-slavery/.

15.   Ira Berlin, "Foreword," in *Free African Americans of Virginia, North Carolina, South Carolina, Maryland, and Delaware*, Free African Americans, http://freeaf ricanamericans.com/foreword.htm.

16.   See, for example, George S. Schuyler, "Thrusts and Lunges," *Pittsburgh Courier,* March 7, 1925, A8. Schuyler also commented on integrated businesses and neighborhoods in the South. See George S. Schuyler, "The Washingtons of Sparta, Ga.: Whites and Negroes Buy at Their Store," *Pittsburgh Courier,* November 13, 1948, 14. That article was part of a series in the *Courier* exploring "What's Good about the South?" See also George S. Schuyler, "Aframerica Today," *Pittsburgh Courier,* January 9, 1926, in which he reported from Morgantown, West Virginia, about a black dentist. During his interview for his oral history in 1960, Schuyler described integrated neighborhoods in Galveston, Texas, and in Meridian and Jackson, Mississippi, which he had seen during his travels in 1926. George S. Schuyler, interview by William Ingersoll, George Schuyler Papers, Syracuse University Library Special Collections Research Center (1960), 192–93.

17.   George S. Schuyler, "Thrusts and Lunges," *Pittsburgh Courier,* June 6, 1925, 16; George S. Schuyler, "Views and Reviews," *Pittsburgh Courier,* December 5, 1925, 1; George S. Schuyler, "Views and Reviews," *Pittsburgh Courier,* January 15, 1927, A8.

18.   Heinegg, *Free African Americans.*

19.   Ibid.

20.   Berlin, "Foreword."

21.   Heinegg, *Free African Americans.*

22. John H. Russell, Samll Goldsmyth, James Radford, David Jones, and Peter Hawkins, "Colored Freemen as Slave Owners in Virginia," *Journal of Negro History* 1:3 (June 1916): 233–42.

23. Heinegg, *Free African Americans.*

24. Ibid., citing Larry Koger, *Black Slaveowners: Free Black Slave Masters in South Carolina, 1790–1860* (Jefferson, North Carolina: McFarland 1985), 104, 108–10, 112–21.

25. Larry Koger, "Black Masters: The Misunderstood Slaveowners," *Southern Quarterly* 43:2 (Winter 2006): 52–73.

26. Heinegg, *Free African Americans.*

27. Ulrich B. Phillips, *Life and Labor in the Old South* (Boston: Little, Brown and Company, 1929, 1957), 170–71.

28. John W. Blassingame, *Black New Orleans, 1860–1880* (Chicago: University of Chicago Press, 1973), 10–11.

29. Ibid., 10–11, 15.

30. Franklin, *The Free Negro in North Carolina.*

31. Ibid., 155.

32. Ibid.

33. Ibid., 155–56.

34. *State v. Edmund*, Supreme Court of North Carolina, December 1, 1833.

35. Franklin, *The Free Negro in North Carolina*, 156–57, 160–61 n. 159.

36. Ibid., 161.

37. Ibid., 157.

38. Ibid., 144–45, 207–8; William B. Gatewood Jr., "'To Be Truly Free': Louis Sheridan and the Colonization of Liberia," *Civil War History* 29:4, (December 1983): 332–48.

39. Gatewood, "'To Be Truly Free'"; see chapter 9 below for further discussion.

40. Loren Schweninger, *Black Property Owners in the South, 1790–1915* (Champaign, Illinois: University of Illinois Press, 1990); Loren Schweninger, "John Carruthers Stanly and the Anomaly of Black Slaveholding," *North Carolina Historical Review* 67:2 (April 1990): 159–92.

41. Schweninger, "John Carruthers Stanly."

42. Ibid.

43. Ibid.

44. Ibid.

45. David O. Whitten, "Slave Buying in 1835 Virginia as Revealed by Letters of a Louisiana Negro Sugar Planter," *Louisiana History: The Journal of the Louisiana Historical Association* 11:3 (Summer 1970): 231–44.

46. Franklin, *The Free Negro in North Carolina*, 157.

47. Ibid., 141–42, 157–58, 190–91.

48. Woodson, *The Negro in Our History*, 129; Koger, "Black Masters."

49. Phillips, *Life and Labor in the Old South*, 170–71.

50. Heinegg, *Free African Americans*, citing Karen I. Blu, *The Lumbee Problem: The Making of an American Indian People* (Cambridge: Cambridge University Press, 1980), 20, 61, 73.

51. Such class distinctions cut across racial, religious, and ethnic lines—as did other differences among African slaves and Eastern European and other immigrant groups, such as distinctions between long-established groups and recent arrivals.

52. George S. Schuyler, *Black and Conservative* (New Rochelle, New York: Arlington House, 1966), 11–12, 200.

53. David L. Lightner and Alexander M. Ragan, "Were African American Slaveholders Benevolent or Exploitative? A Quantitative Approach," *Journal of Southern History* 71 (2005): 535–58.

54. Schweninger, *Black Property Owners in the South*; Schweninger, "John Carruthers Stanly."

55. David O. Whitten, *Andrew Durnford: A Black Sugar Planter in the Antebellum South*; Whitten, "Slave Buying in 1835 Virginia."

56. Johnson and Roark, *Black Masters*.

57. Edwin Adams Davis and William Ransom Hogan, *The Barber of Natchez: Wherein a Slave Is Freed and Rises to a Very High Status*, illustrated edition (Baton Rouge: Louisiana State University Press, 1973).

58. Lightner and Ragan quote John Hope Franklin to the effect that "[t]here is no doubt that most of the free blacks who owned slaves did so for humanitarian purposes" and that "there are virtually no records similar to those of Andrew Durnford"— despite Franklin's familiarity with documents about Ellison and Johnson, which is clear from Franklin's *The Free Negro in North Carolina* and also from a review Franklin wrote in 1951. John Hope Franklin, review of Edwin Adams Davis and William Ransom Hogan, eds., *William Johnson's Natchez* in the *American Historical Review* 57 (October 1951): 173–74.

59. Lightner and Ragan, "Were African American Slaveholders Benevolent?"; Thomas Sowell estimates in *Ethnic America: A History*, reprint edition (New York: Basic Books, 1981), 195, that in 1790 there were 60,000 free blacks in the United States; in 1830, 300,000+; and in 1860, nearly half a million (compared to 5 million enslaved). A larger proportion of free blacks were mulattoes (37 percent) than of slaves (only 8 percent).

60. Lightner and Ragan, "Were African American Slaveholders Benevolent?"

61. Larry Koger, for example, writes that "black masters believed that punishment was a necessary instrument to control their slaves and preserve a sense of authority. Like white slaveowners, the black masters [of Charleston City] placed disobedient slaves in the city jail or the workhouse," usually for five to thirty days, and then

often gave them a flogging upon their release. Rebellious slaves were put on the auction block. Koger, *Black Slaveowners*, 92–93.

62. J. Carlyle Sitterson, *Sugar Country: The Cane Sugar Industry in the South, 1753–1950* (Lexington, Kentucky: University of Kentucky Press, 1953), 89. Sitterson also quotes the observations of a traveler twenty years later in the lower country reporting better conditions.

63. Lorena Walsh, "Slave Life, Slave Society, and Tobacco Production in the Tidewater Chesapeake, 1620–1820," in *Labor and the Shaping of Slave Life in the Americas*, ed. Ira Berlin and Philip D. Morgan (Charlottesville: University Press of Virginia, 1993): 170–99, 189; original spelling and punctuation retained.

64. Ira Berlin, *The Long Emancipation: The Demise of Slavery in the United States* (Cambridge: Harvard University Press, 2015), 37, 60.

Chapter 8: The Wolf by the Ears

1. Robert Paquette, email to the author, April 16, 2021. Paquette, who is writing a book about Jefferson, notes that there is no mention of an encounter with a black slave owner in Jefferson's "voluminous correspondence." John Hope Franklin, *The Free Negro in North Carolina, 1790–1860* (Chapel Hill: University of North Carolina Press, 1995), originally published in 1943.

2. David Brion Davis, *Was Thomas Jefferson an Authentic Enemy of Slavery? An Inaugural Lecture Delivered before the University of Oxford on 18 February 1970* (Oxford: Clarendon Press, 1970), 12–13.

3. Sean Wilentz, *The Rise of American Democracy: Jefferson to Lincoln* (New York: W. W. Norton, 2005), 220.

4. "Thomas Jefferson: Excerpt from His Letter to Jean Nicolas Demeunier, June 26, 1786," Wake Forest University, https://users.wfu.edu/zulick/340/Jefferson.html.

5. Dumas Malone, *The Sage of Monticello* (Boston: Little, Brown and Company, 1981), 316–17.

6. David Brion Davis, *The Problem of Slavery in the Age of Revolution* (Ithaca: Cornell University Press, 1975), 172.

7. Andrew Levy, *The First Emancipator: The Forgotten Story of Robert Carter the Founding Father Who Freed His Slaves* (New York: Random House, 2005), 29.

8. Davis, *The Problem of Slavery in the Age of Revolution*, 174.

9. "Thomas Jefferson: Excerpt from His Letter to Jean Nicolas Demeunier."

10. Davis, *The Problem of Slavery in the Age of Revolution*, 174; also discussed in Benjamin Brawley, *A Social History of the American Negro* (London: Collier Books, 1921; reprint New York: The Macmillan Company, 1970), 56–57.

11. Davis, *The Problem of Slavery in the Age of Revolution*, 174–75.

12. Winthrop Jordan, *White Over Black: American Attitudes Toward the Negro, 1550–1812* (Chapel Hill: University of North Carolina Press, 1968), 435.

13. Quoted in Silvio A. Bedini, *The Life of Benjamin Banneker* (New York: Charles Scribner's Sons, 1972), 160.

14. Robert Paquette, forthcoming manuscript.

15. Ibid.

16. Ibid.

17. Davis, *The Problem of Slavery in the Age of Revolution*, 166.

18. Thomas Jefferson, *Notes on the State of Virginia*, ed. Thomas Perkins Abernethy (New York: Harper & Row, 1964), 132.

19. Quoted in Joseph T. Wilson, *The Black Phalanx: A History of the Negro Soldiers of the United States in the Wars of 1775–1812, 1861–'65* (New York: Da Capo Press, 1994), 29–30. Originally published in 1871.

20. Jefferson, *Notes on the State of Virginia*, 133–38; Jefferson's insulting observations were bizarrely echoed in an infamous Smithsonian poster published in 2020. The very characteristics that Jefferson saw blacks as lacking—individualism, self-reliance, nuclear family structure, objective scientific thinking (cause and effect), and hard work as the "key to success"—were ascribed to "white culture." Elise Ehrhard, "Smithsonian Debuts Utterly Absurd Whiteness Poster, but It Has Major Problems," Western Journal, July 15, 2020, https://www.westernjournal.com/smithsonian-debuts-utterly-absurd-whiteness-poster-major-problems/.

21. Ibid., 155–56.

22. Ibid., 156.

23. Ibid.

24. Lorena Walsh, "Slave Life, Slave Society, and Tobacco Production in the Tidewater Chesapeake, 1620–1820," in *Labor and the Shaping of Slave Life in the Americas*, ed. Ira Berlin and Philip D. Morgan (Charlottesville: University of Virginia Press, 1993), 170–99, 189.

25. Levy, *The First Emancipator*, 152–54.

26. Thomas Jefferson to James Madison, December 20, 1787, in *Thomas Jefferson: Writings* (New York: Library of America, 1984), 914–18.

27. Nikole Hannah-Jones, "The Idea of America," in "The 1619 Project," *New York Times Magazine*, August 18, 2019, https://www.nytimes.com/interactive/2019/08/14/magazine/black-history-american-democracy.html.

28. Ibid.

29. Robert Paquette, forthcoming manuscript.

30. Thomas Jefferson, "The Rights of British America," in *Thomas Jefferson* (New York: Library of America, 1985), 105–22.

31. Jefferson, *Notes on the State of Virginia*, 156.

32. Robert Paquette, "What Made American Slavery Distinctive?" September 17, 2020, https://www.nas.org/blogs/event/slavery-or-freedom-the-conception-of-ame rica, presented at the "Slavery or Freedom: The Conception of America," conference sponsored by the Alexander Hamilton Institute, Texas Public Policy Institute, and National Association of Scholars, September 14–18, 2020.

33. Dumas Malone, *Jefferson the President: Second Term, 1805–1809* (Boston: Little, Brown and Company, 1974), 544–45.

34. "Statistics on Slavery," Weber State University, n.d., https://faculty.weber.edu/kmackay /statistics_on_slavery.htm.

35. Stewart R. King, "Slavery and the Haitian Revolution," in *The Oxford Handbook of Slavery in the Americas*, ed. Robert L. Paquette and Mark M. Smith (New York: Oxford University Press, 2010), 598–624.

36. Ibid.

37. Robert Paquette, email to the author, April 16, 2021.

38. King, "Slavery and the Haitian Revolution."

39. Dumas Malone, *Jefferson and the Ordeal of Liberty* (Boston: Little, Brown and Company, 1962), 208.

40. Sara Fanning, *Caribbean Crossing: African Americans and Haitian Emigration Movement* (New York: New York University Press, 2015), 3–4.

41. Jordan, *White Over Black*, 385.

42. Ibid., 381–82. "St. Domingo" was often mistakenly used in place of Saint-Domingue, including by Jefferson.

43. Ibid., 384.

44. Ibid., 382.

45. Ibid., 383.

46. Brawley, *A Social History of the American Negro*, 121.

47. Ibid., 121–22; Robert Paquette, email to the author, April 16, 2021.

48. Thomas Jefferson to James Monroe, November 24, 1801, in *Jefferson: Writings* (New York: Library of America, 1984), 1096–99.

49. Thomas Jefferson to John Holmes, April 22, 1820, in *The Portable Thomas Jefferson*, ed. Merrill D. Peterson (New York: Viking Penguin, 1975), 567–69.

50. Peter S. Onuf, *The Mind of Thomas Jefferson* (Charlottesville: University of Virginia Press, 2007), 221–23.

51. Thomas Jefferson to John Holmes.

52. Onuf, *The Mind of Thomas Jefferson*, 221–23.

53. Thomas Jefferson to James Heaton, May 20, 1826, in *Thomas Jefferson: Writings* (New York: Library of America, 1984), 1516.

54. Richard K. Matthews, *The Radical Politics of Thomas Jefferson: A Revisionist View* (Lawrence: University Press of Kansas, 1986), 69–72.

55. Bedini, *The Life of Benjamin Banneker*, 161.

56. Ibid., 68–69 and passim; John P. Kaminski, ed., *A Necessary Evil? Slavery and the Debate Over the Constitution* (Madison, Wisconsin: Madison House, 1995), 252. It has been thought that Banneker's maternal grandmother was a white indentured servant, but that theory has been questioned lately in light of the absence of definitive proof. See Sandra Perot, "Reconstructing Molly Welsh: Race, Memory and the Story of Benjamin Banneker's Grandmother" (master's thesis, University of Massachusetts History Department, 2008).

57. Bedini, *The Life of Benjamin Banneker*, 22–25, 39–40.

58. Ibid., 43–45.

59. Ibid., 70–73.

60. Jordan, *White Over Black*, 446–49.

61. Ibid., 450–51.

62. Bedini, *The Life of Benjamin Banneker*, 148–50.

63. Ibid.

64. Ibid., 150–51.

65. Ibid., 151.

66. Benjamin Banneker to Thomas Jefferson, August 19, 1791, and Thomas Jefferson to Benjamin Banneker, August 30, 1791, in Kaminski, ed., *A Necessary Evil?*, 252–55.

67. Bedini, *The Life of Benjamin Banneker*, 151.

68. Ibid., 280.

69. Thomas Jefferson to Benjamin Banneker, 252–55.

70. Bedini, *The Life of Benjamin Banneker*, 159. Original spelling retained.

71. Ibid. Original spelling retained.

72. Ibid., 160–61.

73. Ibid.

74. Ibid., 281–82; Thomas Jefferson to Henri Grégoire, February 25, 1809, in *The Portable Jefferson*, 517.

75. Bedini, *The Life of Benjamin Banneker*, 282–83.

76. Ibid., 283.

77. It was also published "in at least one popular periodical, the *Universal Asylum and Columbian Magazine*," in 1792. Ibid., 158.

78. Ibid., 187–88.

79. Ibid., 280. Original spelling retained.

80. Ibid.

81. "A Powerful Letter," in "A Brief History of Slavery" (The 1619 Project special section), *New York Times*, August 18, 2019, pdf available at Pulitzer Center website, https://pulitzercenter.org/sites/default/files/18maglabs_1619_issue_shipped_0.pdf.

82. Ibid.

83. "Reading Guide for *The 1619 Project* Essays," Pulitzer Center and *New York Times Magazine*, https://pulitzercenter.org/sites/default/files/reading_guide_for_the_1619_project_essays_0.pdf.

84. See, for example, "To Thomas Jefferson from Benjamin Banneker, 19 August 1791," Founders Online, National Archives, https://founders.archives.gov/documents/Jefferson/01-22-02-0049; "From Thomas Jefferson to Benjamin Banneker, 30 August 1791," Founders Online, National Archives, https://founders.archives.gov/documents/Jefferson/01-22-02-0091.

85. Bedini, *The Life of Benjamin Banneker*, 152–56. Original spelling retained.

86. Ibid., 280.

87. "A Powerful Letter."

88. John Hope Franklin, *From Slavery to Freedom*, 108–9; Sowell, *Ethnic America*, 48–49, citing Abbot Emerson Smith, *Colonists in Bondage: White Servitude and Convict Labor in America, 1607–1776* (Chapel Hill: University of North Carolina Press, 1947), 221–22, and Maldwyn Allen Jones, *American Immigration* (University of Chicago Press, 1960), 67.

89. Malone, *Jefferson and the Ordeal of Liberty*, 208–13.

90. Francis L. Berkeley Jr., Introduction, in *Thomas Jefferson's Farm Book*, ed. Edwin Morris Betts (Charlottesville: University of Virginia Press, 1987), xiii–xxiii.

91. Malone, *Jefferson and the Ordeal of Liberty*, 208–13.

92. Ibid., 207; Monticello historian Lucia Stanton makes similar observations in her essay "'Those Who Labor for My Happiness': Thomas Jefferson and His Slaves," in Peter S. Onuf, ed., *Jefferson Legacies* (Charlottesville: University of Virginia Press, 1993), 147–80.

93. Malone, *Jefferson and the Ordeal of Liberty*, 208–9; "Deed of Manumission for Robert Hemings," *The Papers of Thomas Jefferson: Volume 28, 1 January 1794 to 29 February 1796* (Princeton, New Jersey: Princeton University Press, 2000), 222–23, available online at https://jeffersonpapers.princeton.edu/selected-documents/deed-manumission-robert-hemings.

94. Malone, *The Sage of Monticello*, 321–22.

95. Thomas Jefferson to Edward Coles, August 25, 1814, in *Thomas Jefferson: Writings* (New York: Library of America, 1984), 1343–46.

96. Malone, *The Sage of Monticello*, 325–26.

97. Benjamin Joseph Klebaner, "American Manumission and the Responsibility for Supporting Slaves," *Virginia Magazine of History and Biography* 63:4 (October 1955): 443–53.

98. Matthews, *The Radical Politics of Thomas Jefferson*, 67–68.

99. Malone, *The Sage of Monticello*, 326; Kaminsky, *A Necessary Evil?*, 257.

100. John Stauffer, *Giants: The Parallel Lives of Frederick Douglass and Abraham Lincoln* (New York: Hachette Book Group, 2008), 340 n. 30.

101. Ralph Ketcham, "Coles, Edward," in *Macmillan Encyclopedia of World Slavery*, vol. 1, ed. Paul Finkelman and Joseph C. Miller (New York: Macmillan Reference USA, 1998), 204–5.

102. Malone, *The Sage of Monticello*, 326–27.

103. Ibid., 488–89.

104. Ibid.

105. Kaminsky, *A Necessary Evil?*, 257.

Chapter 9: Colonization and Freedom

1.   Peter S. Onuf, "Jefferson, Thomas," in *Macmillan Encyclopedia of World Slavery*, vol. 1, ed. Paul Finkelman and Joseph C. Miller (New York: Macmillan Reference USA, 1998), 446–48.

2.   Benjamin Brawley, *A Social History of the American Negro* (London: Collier Books, 1921, reprint New York: The Macmillan Company, 1970), 118.

3.   Carter G. Woodson, *The Negro in Our History* (Washington, D.C.: Associated Publishers, 1922, 1924), 154–55.

4.   Brawley, *A Social History of the American Negro*, 123–24.

5.   Woodson, *The Negro in Our History*, 157–59. Woodson's error corrected from "a brother" to "a nephew."

6.   Dumas Malone, *The Sage of Monticello* (Boston: Little, Brown and Company, 1981), 324–25.

7.   Woodson, *The Negro in Our History*, 157–59.

8.   Malone, *The Sage of Monticello*, 41, 325; Thomas Jefferson to John Lynch, January 21, 1811, in *Thomas Jefferson: Writings* (New York: Library of America, 1984).

9.   Woodson, *The Negro in Our History*, 159.

10. Leslie M. Harris, *In the Shadow of Slavery: African Americans in New York City, 1626–1863* (Chicago: University of Chicago Press, 2004), 139–41.

11. Malone, *The Sage of Monticello*, 402–5, 408; Holly Jackson, *American Radicals: How Nineteenth-Century Protest Shaped the Nation* (New York: Crown Publishing, 2019), 11.

12. Thomas Jefferson to Fanny Wright, August 7, 1825, in *Thomas Jefferson: Writings* (New York: Library of America, 1984), 25–27.

13. Jackson, *American Radicals*, 30–31. Jackson claims that Nashoba was typical of the "southern plantation on which black people were held by white enslavers." Not all southern plantations practiced strict segregation or referred to blacks by the term "slaves" (as we have seen with Jefferson).

14. Ibid., 32–33.

15. Ibid., 35, 44.

16. Ibid., 12, 44–47.

17. Ibid., 321–22.
18. Sara Fanning, *Caribbean Crossing: African Americans and the Haitian Emigration Movement* (New York: New York University Press, 2015), 25.
19. Robert Paquette, email to the author, April 16, 2021.
20. Ibid.
21. Ibid.
22. Fanning, *Caribbean Crossing*, 30–31.
23. Ibid., 31–33.
24. Ibid., 37.
25. Ibid., 43–44.
26. Ibid., 53. Fanning accepts Michael P. Johnson's claim that there was no conspiracy by Vesey. But the Johnson theory is debunked in Douglas R. Egerton and Robert L. Paquette, eds., *The Denmark Vesey Affair: A Documentary History* (Gainesville: University Press of Florida, 2017), xxi.
27. Paquette, email to the author, April 16, 2021.
28. Fanning, *Caribbean Crossing*, 61.
29. Ibid., 62.
30. Ibid., 100–1.
31. Ibid., 103.
32. Ibid., 104.
33. Ibid., 105–6.
34. Ibid., 108.
35. Ibid., 110.
36. Ibid., 111.
37. Ibid., 112–13.
38. Ibid., 123.
39. Ibid., 116.
40. Ibid., 122–23.

Chapter 10: Taking Down Abraham Lincoln

1. Abraham Lincoln, *Political Debates Between Lincoln and Douglas* (Cleveland: Burrows Bros. Co., 1897), 431, available online at https://www.bartleby.com/251/pages/page431.html#google_vignette.
2. Nikole Hannah-Jones, "The Idea of America," in "The 1619 Project," *New York Times Magazine*, August 14, 2019, https://www.nytimes.com/interactive/2019/08/14/magazine/black-history-american-democracy.html.
3. Leland B. Ware, Robert J. Cottroll, and Raymond T. Diamond, *Brown v. Board of Education: Caste, Culture, and the Constitution* (Lawrence: University Press of Kansas, 2003), 3.

4. John Stauffer, *Giants: The Parallel Lives of Frederick Douglass and Abraham Lincoln* (New York: Hachette Book Group, 2008), 157; Charles Warren, *The Supreme Court in United States History, Volume 2: 1821–1855* (Boston: Little, Brown, and Company, 1926), 303.

5. Stauffer, *Giants,* 198, 205.

6. Ibid., 157–58, 188, 194–95, 198.

7. Ibid., 265. Here Stauffer relies on Benjamin Quarles, *Lincoln and the Negro* (New York: Oxford University Press, 1962), 115–17.

8. Abraham Lincoln, "From Speech on the Dred Scott Decision at Springfield, Illinois, June 26, 1857," in *Abraham Lincoln: Selected Speeches and Writings*, ed. Don E. Fehrenbacher (New York: Library of America, 2009), 117–22.

9. Ibid.

10. Abraham Lincoln, "From First Lincoln-Douglas Debate, Ottawa, Illinois," *Abraham Lincoln: Selected Speeches and Writings*, ed. Don E. Fehrenbacher (New York: Library of America, 2009), 149–53. The "second Dred Scott decision" was *Lemmon v. People.* Stauffer, *Giants,* 386 n. 323.

11. Abraham Lincoln, "'House Divided' Speech," *Abraham Lincoln: Selected Speeches and Writings*, ed. Don E. Fehrenbacher (New York: Library of America, 2009), 131–39.

12. Lincoln, "From First Lincoln-Douglas Debate, Ottawa, Illinois."

13. See Stauffer, *Giants*; David W. Blight, *Frederick Douglass: Prophet of Freedom* (New York: Simon & Schuster, 2018).

14. Hannah-Jones, "The Idea of America."

15. John Hope Franklin and Alfred A. Moss Jr., *From Slavery to Freedom: A History of African Americans*, 8th edition (New York: Alfred A. Knopf, 2000), 31; John Hope Franklin, *The Emancipation Proclamation* (Garden City, New York: Doubleday, 1963), 136.

16. Franklin, *From Slavery to Freedom,* 229.

17. Franklin, *The Emancipation Proclamation,* 31–32.

18. Franklin, *From Slavery to Freedom,* 229.

19. Franklin, *The Emancipation Proclamation,* 32.

20. Stauffer, *Giants,* 258–59, 264.

21. Tyler Durden, "Down the 1619 Project's Memory Hole," Verity Weekly, September 22, 2020, https://www.verityweekly.com/down-the-1619-projects-memory-hole/. Durden quotes Hannah-Jones's statement that the crossed-out 1776 supports her point that "1619 is our true founding"—from which she flipped.

22. Hannah-Jones, "The Idea of America."

23. Ida Bae Wells (@nhannahjones), "I wrote a call for African-American. . . ," December 22, 2020, 1:25 p.m., twitter.com/hhannahjones/status/131445148253

8270727s=D9. Screenshot in the possession of the author. See chapter 6 for discussion of Hannah-Jones's relationship to Bennett.

24. Lerone Bennett Jr., *Forced into Glory: Abraham Lincoln's White Dream* (Chicago: Johnson Publishing Company, 2000), 150–51, 381–82.

25. Hannah-Jones, "The Idea of America."

26. Quoted in Allen Guelzo, *Lincoln's Emancipation Proclamation* (New York: Simon & Schuster, 2004), 158–59.

27. Stauffer, *Giants*, 201.

28. Allen C. Guelzo and James Hankins, "Of, by & for the Freedmen," *New Criterion*, October 2020, https://newcriterion.com/issues/2020/10/of-by-for-the-freedmen.

29. "Lincoln's Death," National Museum of American History, n.d., https://americanhistory.si.edu/changing-america-emancipation-proclamation-1863-and-march-washington-1963/1863/lincoln%E2%80%99s-death.

30. Guelzo, *Lincoln's Emancipation Proclamation*, 159–60; James M. McPherson, *Tried by War: Abraham Lincoln as Commander in Chief* (New York: Norton, 2013), 127–28.

31. Franklin, *The Emancipation Proclamation*, 33.

32. Guelzo, *Lincoln's Emancipation Proclamation*, 159.

33. Franklin, *The Emancipation Proclamation*, 33; Stauffer, *Giants*, 176. Stauffer discusses this proposal by Lincoln when he was in Congress. The bill included "apprenticeship" for the slaves and delayed freedom until 1870–75. Phillip W. Magness and Sebastian N. Page argue that Lincoln continued to pursue colonization after the Emancipation Proclamation took effect on January 1, 1863, with plans to send freedmen to British Honduras, British Guiana, and the Dutch West Indies, and they impute racist motives to him. Allen Guelzo questions the evidence they use. See Phillip W. Magness and Sebastian N. Page, *Colonization after Emancipation: Lincoln and the Movement for Black Resettlement* (Columbia: University of Missouri Press, 2011) and the review of that book by Allen C. Guelzo, *Journal of the Abraham Lincoln Association* 34:1 (Winter 2013): 78–87. I agree with Guelzo that the charges of "racism" against Lincoln are unjustified. Lincoln was following precedents set by earlier presidents, including Jefferson. He was also working on the basis of an imperfect idea of what blacks wanted and an acknowledgment of the lingering racial tensions on both sides; his concerns on the last score were not entirely unfounded.

34. Lincoln, "From Speech on the Dred Scott Decision," 117–22.

35. Guelzo, *Lincoln's Emancipation Proclamation*, 156–57.

36. Ibid.; Abraham Lincoln, "From Annual Message to Congress," *Abraham Lincoln: Selected Speeches and Writings*, ed. Don E. Fehrenbacher (New York: Library of America, 2009), 320–27.

37. Stauffer, *Giants*, 16–18.

38. Ibid., 18–19.

39. McPherson, *Tried by War,* 129–30.

40. Guelzo, *Lincoln's Emancipation Proclamation,* 161.

41. Franklin, *From Slavery to Freedom,* 230.

42. Ibid., 188–91.

43. Stauffer, *Giants,* 266.

44. Blight, *Frederick Douglass,* 303.

45. Franklin, *From Slavery to Freedom,* 188–91.

46. David W. Blight, *Race and Reunion: The Civil War in American Memory* (Cambridge, Massachusetts: Harvard University Press, 2001), 317.

47. Blight, *Frederick Douglass: Prophet of Freedom,* 373.

48. Stauffer, *Giants,* 215, 221–22.

49. Quoted in Henry Louis Gates Jr., "Ending the Slavery Blame-Game," *New York Times,* April 22, 2010, https://www.nytimes.com/2010/04/23/opinion/23gates.ht ml?ref=opinion&pagewanted=all.

50. Frederick Douglass, "The Black Man's Future in the Southern States: An Address Delivered in Boston, Massachusetts, on February 5, 1862," *The Frederick Douglass Papers, Series One, Speeches, Debates, and Interviews, Volume 3, 1855–63,* ed. John W. Blassingame (New Haven, Connecticut: Yale University Press, 1985), 489–509. The contrast between the black and the Indian with regards to assimilation was a staple of black writers from Joseph T. Wilson to George S. Schuyler.

51. Franklin, *From Slavery to Freedom,* 198, 200.

52. Donna Britt, "A White Mother Went to Alabama to Fight for Civil Rights. The Klan Killed Her for It," *Washington Post,* December 15, 2017.

53. "The Murder of Rev. James Reeb," *White Lies* (podcast), NPR, May 12, 2019.

54. Leslie M. Harris, *In the Shadow of Slavery: African Americans in New York City* (Chicago: University of Chicago Press, 2003), 106–7.

55. Ibid., 96–97.

56. Ibid., 145–47, 168.

57. Ibid., 150.

58. Carl Degler, *The Other South: Southern Dissenters in the Nineteenth Century* (New York: Harper & Row Publishers, 1974), 33–36, quoting L. Minor Blackford, *Mine Eyes Have Seen the Glory* (Cambridge, Massachusetts: Harvard University Press, 1954), 39–40, 42.

59. William B. Darrow, "The Killing of Congressman James Hinds," *Arkansas Historical Quarterly* 74:1 (Spring 2015): 18–55.

60. Quoted in Charles J. Shields, *Mockingbird: A Portrait of Harper Lee* (New York: Henry Holt and Company, 2006), 222.

61. Miles Johnson, "A Postman's 1963 Walk for Social Justice, Cut Short on an Alabama Road," NPR, August 14, 2013, https://www.npr.org/2013/08/14/2117 11898/a-postmans-1963-walk-for-justice-cut-short-on-an-alabama-road.

62. Mary Frances Schjonberg, "Remembering Jonathan Daniels 50 Years after His Martyrdom," Episcopal News Service, August 13, 2015, https://www.episcopalne wsservice.org/2015/08/13/remembering-jonathan-daniels-50-years-after-his-mar tyrdom/.

63. United Press International, "Bulldozer Kills Civil Racial Protester: Cleveland Minister Crushed during Clash at School," *New York Times*, April 8, 1964.

64. Holly Jackson, *American Radicals: How Nineteenth-Century Protest Shaped the Nation* (New York: Crown Publishing, 2019), 56–57.

65. Ibid., 61.

66. Ibid., 71–72.

67. Ibid., 197.

68. Blight, *Frederick Douglass*, 294–95.

69. Stauffer, *Giants*, 158–63; Jackson, *American Radicals*, 213.

70. Jackson, *American Radicals*, 198; Stauffer, *Giants*, 143.

71. Stauffer, *Giants*, 46, 73, 77, 80, 83–87, 139–41, 233.

72. Ibid., 139. Ironically, the case was the opposite for the newspaper of the white abolitionist Garrison; in its first year, 400 of the 450 subscribers were blacks (Franklin, *From Slavery to Freedom*, 200).

73. Robert L. Harris, "Charleston's Free Afro-American Elite: The Brown Fellowship Society and the Humane Brotherhood," *South Carolina Historical Magazine* 82:4 (October 1981): 289–310.

74. Douglas R. Egerton and Robert L. Paquette, eds., *The Denmark Vesey Affair: A Documentary History* (Gainesville: University Press of Florida, 2017), 721.

75. Penceel, however, could not escape the law enacted in 1822 that prohibited entrance into the state by blacks. He had left to go north to visit friends, was trapped, and had to use "his influence to garner the support of white aristocrats of Charleston City," who pressured the state assembly to pass a statute that permitted him to reenter the state. Larry Koger, *Black Slaveowners: Free Black Slave Masters in South Carolina, 1790–1860* (Jefferson, North Carolina: McFarland, 1985), 177–80.

76. Franklin, *From Slavery to Freedom*, 173–75.

77. William B. Gatewood, *Aristocrats of Color: The Black Elite, 1880–1920* (Bloomington, Indiana: Indiana University Press, 1990), 102–3.

78. Jackson, *American Radicals*, 54–58.

79. Ibid., 54–59.

80. Tony Williams, "Frederick Douglass' Constitutional Bedrock," Law and Liberty, March 23, 2021, https://lawliberty.org/book-review/frederick-douglass-constitu tional-bedrock/.

81. Stauffer, *Giants*, 95.

82. Williams, "Frederick Douglass' Constitutional Bedrock."

83. James A. Colaiaco, *Frederick Douglass and the Fourth of July* (New York: Palgrave Macmillan, 2006), 1, 7; Joseph W. Barnes and Robert W. Barnes, "From Books to Multimedia: A History of the Reynolds Library and the Reynolds Audio-Visual Department of the Rochester Public Library," *Rochester History* 36:4 (October 1974), https://www.libraryweb.org/~rochhist/v36_1974/v36i4.pdf.

84. Stauffer, *Giants*, 150.

85. Colaiaco, *Frederick Douglas and the Fourth of July*, 1, 6.

86. Stauffer, *Giants*, 306. This was a technique Douglass learned from reading the *Columbian Orator*.

87. Hannah-Jones, "The Idea of America."

88. Frederick Douglass, "What to the Slave Is the Fourth of July?: An Address Delivered in Rochester, New York, on 5 July 1852," in *The Frederick Douglass Papers, Series One, Volume 2, 1847–54*, ed. John W. Blassingame (New Haven, Connecticut: Yale University Press, 1982), 359–88.

89. Williams, "Frederick Douglass' Constitutional Bedrock."

90. Frederick Douglass, "The American Constitution and the Slave: An Address Delivered in Glasgow, Scotland, on 26 March 1860," in *The Frederick Douglass Papers, Series One, Volume 3, 1855–63*, ed. John Blassingame (New Haven, Connecticut: Yale University Press, 1985), 340–66.

91. Frederick Douglass, "The Anti-Slavery Movement: An Address Delivered in Rochester, New York, on March 19, 1855," in *The Frederick Douglass Papers, Series One: Speeches, Debates, and Interviews, Volume 3: 1855–63*, ed. John W. Blassingame (New Haven, Connecticut: Yale University Press, 1985), 14–51.

92. Frederick Douglass, "The Dred Scott Decision: An Address Delivered, in Part, in New York, New York, in May 1857," in *The Frederick Douglass Papers, Series One: Speeches, Debates, and Interviews, Volume 3: 1855–63*, ed. John W. Blassingame (New Haven, Connecticut: Yale University Press, 1985), 163–83.

93. Frederick Douglass, "Freedom in the West Indies: An Address Delivered in Poughkeepsie, New York, on 2 August 1858," in *The Frederick Douglass Papers, Series One: Speeches, Debates, and Interviews, Volume 3: 1855–63*, ed. John W. Blassingame (New Haven, Connecticut: Yale University Press, 1985), 214–42.

94. Stauffer, *Giants*, 162.

95. Frederick Douglass, "The Slaveholders' Rebellion: An Address Delivered in Himrod's, New York, on 4 July 1862," in *The Frederick Douglass Papers, Series*

One: Speeches, Debates, and Interviews, Volume 3: 1855–63, ed. John W. Blassingame (New Haven, Connecticut: Yale University Press, 1985), 521–43.

96. Franklin, *The Emancipation Proclamation*, 25.

97. Guelzo, *Lincoln's Emancipation Proclamation*, 160–61; Stauffer, *Giants*, 17.

98. Franklin, *The Emancipation Proclamation*, 31–32.

99. Stauffer, *Giants*, 11–12, 19.

100. Ibid., 19.

101. Ibid., 19–20.

102. Ibid., 21–22.

103. Blight, *Frederick Douglass*, 408.

104. Stauffer, *Giants*, 21–24.

105. Blight, *Frederick Douglass*, 408. Of course, advertising such access through humor was a way for Douglass to brag.

106. Stauffer, *Giants*, 300; Frederick Douglass, "Our Martyred President: An Address Delivered in Rochester, New York, on 15 April 1865," in *The Frederick Douglass Papers, Series One, Volume 4, 1864–80*, ed. John Blassingame and John R. McKivigan (New Haven, Connecticut: Yale University Press, 1991), 74–79.

107. "Common Core State Standards for English Language Arts & Literacy in History/ Social Studies, Science, and Technical Subjects, Appendix B: Text Exemplars and Sample Performance Tasks," n.d., http://www.corestandards.org/assets/Appendix _B.pdf.

108. Frederick Douglass, "From 'What to the Slave Is the Fourth of July?'" in *The Norton Anthology of African American Literature*, ed. Henry Louis Gates Jr. and Valerie A. Smith, 3rd edition, vol. 1 (New York: W. W. Norton, 2014), 402–3; Manning Marable and Leith Mullings, eds., *Let Nobody Turn Us Around: Voices of Resistance, Reform, and Renewal* (Lanham, Maryland: Rowman & Littlefield, 2000), 87–91.

109. Mary Elliott and Jazmine Hughes, "A Brief History of Slavery" (The 1619 Project special section), *New York Times Magazine*, August 19, 2019, https://www .nytimes.com/interactive/2019/08/19/magazine/history-slavery-smithsonian.html.

110. Brett Milano, "Twitter and the Birth of the 1619 Project," Harvard Gazette, December 5, 2019, https://news.harvard.edu/gazette/story/2019/12/the-1619-pro ject-started-with-a-tweet-says-nikole-hannah-jones/.

111. Elliott and Hughes, "A Brief History of Slavery."

112. Hannah-Jones had gotten into an extended Twitter fight over the use of the word by fellow *New York Times* reporter Donald McNeil (since ousted), who had repeated it for clarification in discussion with a student. For white people, in her opinion, even such use is evidence of racism. ZZ Packer, however, spells it out, and the *Times* printed it. This may cause a dilemma in the classroom when students are asked to read passages aloud and discuss them. Keith J. Kelly, "War Erupts at

NY Times after Donald McNeil Ousted over N-word Controversy," *New York Post*, February 9, 2021, https://nypost.com/2021/02/09/war-erupts-at-ny-times-after-donald-mcneil-ousted-over-n-word-controversy/.

113. Elliott and Hughes, "A Brief History of Slavery."

114. Stauffer, *Giants*, 414 n. 5.

115. Blight, *Frederick Douglass*, 4, 96; David W. Blight, "Yes, the Freedmen's Memorial Uses Racist Imagery. But Don't Tear It Down," *Washington Post*, June 25, 2020, https://www.washingtonpost.com/opinions/2020/06/25/yes-freedmens-memorial -uses-racist-imagery-dont-tear-it-down/.

116. "DC Congresswoman to Introduce Legislation to Remove Emancipation Memorial from Lincoln Park," Fox 5, June 23, 2020, https://www.fox5dc.com/news/dc-congresswoman-to-introduce-legislation-to-remove-emancipation-memorial-from-lincoln-park; Martin Pengelly, "Discovery of Frederick Douglass Letter Sheds Light on Contested Lincoln Statue," *The Guardian*, July 5, 2020, https://www.theguardian.com/us-news/2020/jul/05/frederick-douglass-letter-lincoln-statue.

117. Blight, *Frederick Douglass*, 1–3; Stauffer, *Giants*, 303. The Western Sanitary Commission raised civilian funds for Union soldiers, much as the USO does today. Guelzo and Hankins, "Of, by & for the Freedmen."

118. Frederick Douglass, "The Freedmen's Monument to Abraham Lincoln: An Address Delivered in Washington, D.C., on 14 April 1876," in *The Frederick Douglass Papers, Series One, Volume 4*, ed. John Blassingame and John R. McKivigan (New Haven, Connecticut: Yale University Press, 1991), 427–40.

119. Douglass, "The Freedmen's Monument to Abraham Lincoln." Douglass was referring to Jefferson's June 26, 1786, letter to Jean Nicolas Démeunier. Douglass's criticism of Lincoln here is often taken as a "rebuke" of the president, but as a former lay preacher Douglass was in the practice of pointing out sinfulness. He was also feuding at the time with the head of the "committee of arrangements" for the ceremony, John Mercer Langston. Guelzo and Hankins, "Of, by & for the freedmen."

120. Douglass, "The Freedmen's Monument to Abraham Lincoln."

121. Emily Jashinsky and Madeline Osburn, "7 Ways White Women Have Used Their Privilege to Fuel Riots and Mayhem," The Federalist, June 25, 2020, https://thefederalist.com/2020/06/25/7-ways-white-women-use-their-privilege-to-fuel-riots -and-mayhem/.

122. Blight, *Frederick Douglass*, 1–3.

123. The $3,000 pedestal was paid for with funds appropriated by Congress. Stauffer, *Giants*, 303; Elise Ehrhard, "Black Man Slams Clueless Protesters Wanting to Destroy Emancipation Memorial," The Western Journal, June 20, 2020, https://

www.westernjournal.com/black-man-slams-clueless-protesters-wanting-destroy-emancipation-memorial/.

124. Blight, "Yes, the Freedmen's Memorial Uses Racist Imagery"
125. Douglass, "The Freedmen's Monument to Abraham Lincoln."
126. Ryan Fahey and Ariel Zilber, "Barriers Are Set Up around the Emancipation Memorial in DC as Protestors Vow to Tear Dow the Statue of Kneeling, Freed Slave 'because It Looks like Black Subservience'—as Trump Deploys National Guard," *Daily Mail*, June 26, 2020, https://www.dailymail.co.uk/news/article-8462613/Barriers-set-Abraham-Lincolns-emancipation-memorial-Washington-DC.html.
127. Morgan Gstalter, "Boston Removes Statue of Slave Kneeling before Lincoln," *The Hill*, December 29, 2020, https://thehill.com/homenews/state-watch/531970-boston-removes-statue-of-slave-kneeling-before-lincoln?fbclid=IwAR2FnFNNhel9sE38Fn4krPnFU_JSDFuPpWlHPdy5vYh2JHVOlkYdEEGv_ZM.
128. Christian Zapata, "D.C. Delegate Reintroduces Bill to Remove Emancipation Memorial from Lincoln Park," NPR, February 19, 2021, https://www.npr.org/local/305/2021/02/19/969419030/d-c-delegate-reintroduces-bill-to-remove-emancipation-memorial-from-lincoln-park.

Chapter 11: Choosing Resentment—or Freedom?

1. "What Has the Negro Done to Develop America?," *Christian Recorder* (Philadelphia), November 16, 1893; "The Dawning of Liberty," *Christian Recorder,* January 13, 1898.
2. James Weldon Johnson, "Fifty Years," in *Fifty Years & Other Poems* (Boston: The Cornhill Company, 1917), https://www.gutenberg.org/files/17884/17884-h/17884-h.htm#FIFTY_YEARS_OTHER_POEMS
3. "1913 or 1919, Which?" *The Freeman*, October 30, 1909.
4. Kevin M. Kruse, "Traffic," in "The 1619 Project," *New York Times Magazine*, August 18, 2019, pdf available at the Pulitzer Center website, https://pulitzercenter.org/sites/default/files/full_issue_of_the_1619_project.pdf, 48; "Where African-Americans Are Doing the Best Economically 2018," *Forbes*, January 14, 2018, https://www.forbes.com/pictures/5a5bfe654bbe6f2652f28b64/no-1-tie-atlanta-ga/?sh=610c9cea4049; "Black Mecca," Wikipedia, n.d., https://en.wikipedia.org/wiki/Black_mecca.
5. Jeneen Interlandi, "A Broken Healthcare System," in "The 1619 Project," *New York Times Magazine*, August 18, 2019, pdf available at the Pulitzer Center website, https://pulitzercenter.org/sites/default/files/full_issue_of_the_1619_project.pdf, 44.

6. Bryan Stevenson, "Mass Incarceration," in "The 1619 Project," *New York Times Magazine*, August 18, 2019, pdf available at the Pulitzer Center website, https:// pulitzercenter.org/sites/default/files/full_issue_of_the_1619_project.pdf, 80; Thomas Sowell, "The Inconvenient Truth about Ghetto Communities' Social Breakdown," *National Review*, May 5, 2015, https://www.nationalreview.com /2015/05/it-isnt-legacy-slavery-caused-social-breakdown-ghetto-communities-th omas-sowell/.

7. Jamelle Bouie, "Undemocratic Democracy," in "The 1619 Project," *New York Times Magazine*, August 18, 2019, pdf available at the Pulitzer Center website, https://pulitzercenter.org/sites/default/files/full_issue_of_the_1619_project.pdf, 50.

8. Nancy Pelosi, "Pelosi Remarks ahead of Moment of Silence to Honor George Floyd," Nancy Pelosi Speaker of the House website, June 8, 2020, https://www.sp eaker.gov/newsroom/6820-1; Hannah Bleau, "Watch: Nancy Pelosi, Democrats Kneel to Protest Police Brutality," Breitbart, June 8, 2020, https://www.breitbart .com/politics/2020/06/08/watch-nancy-pelosi-democrats-kneel-to-protest-police -brutality/.

9. Emma Colton, "*USA Today* Fact Check Finds Kente Cloth Worn by Democrats Has Historical Ties to African Slave Trade," *Washington Examiner*, June 17, 2020, https://www.washingtonexaminer.com/news/usa-today-fact-check-finds-kente-cl oth-worn-by-democrats-has-historical-ties-to-african-slave-trade.

10. Nana Efua Mumford, "Democratic Leaders' Kneeling Was Fine. The Kente Cloth Was Not," *Washington Post*, June 11, 2020, https://www.washingtonpost.com /opinions/2020/06/11/educate-yourself-before-you-wear-kente/.

11. "Karen Bass," Key Wiki, n.d., https://www.keywiki.org/Karen_Bass.

12. Deborah Barfield Berry, "John Lewis, Karen Bass, Nancy Pelosi Remember 1619 Anniversary, Cost of Slavery during Capitol Ceremony," *USA Today*, September 10, 2019, https://www.usatoday.com/story/news/politics/2019/09/10/john-lewis -karen-bass-pelosi-and-cbc-mark-1619-slavery-anniversary/2272806001/; Rick Hampson, "How an Accidental Encounter Brought Slavery to the United States," *USA Today*, August 21, 2019, https://www.usatoday.com/in-depth/news/nation /2019/08/21/american-slavery-began-1619-project-documents-brutal-journey/19 68793001/.

13. "Finding the Last Ship Known to Have Brought Enslaved Africans to America and the Descendants of Its Survivors," *60 Minutes*, CBS News, November 29, 2020, https://www.cbsnews.com/news/clotilda-slave-ship-alabama-60-minutes-2020-11 -29; Sylviane A. Diouf, "The Last Slave Ship Survivor and Her Descendants Identified," *National Geographic*, https://www.nationalgeographic.com/history /article/last-slave-ship-survivor-descendants-identified/.

14. Zora Neale Hurston, *Barracoon: The Story of the Last "Black Cargo,"* ed. Deborah G. Plant (New York: HarperCollins, 2018).

15. Alice Walker, Foreword, in Hurston, *Barracoon*, ix–xi.

16. Ibid. As we have seen, the practice preceded the arrival of the Europeans.

17. Ibid., xi.

18. Deborah Plant, Introduction, in Zora Neale Hurston, *Barracoon*, xvi–xvii.

19. Ibid., xv–xvi.

20. Ibid., xviii–xix.

21. Hurston, *Barracoon*, 48–49. Hurston uses the spelling "Kossula."

22. Plant, Introduction, xiii–xxv.

23. "Finding the Last Ship Known to Have Brought Enslaved Africans to America."

24. Adaobi Tricia Nwaubani, "When the Slave Traders Were African," *Wall Street Journal*, September 20, 2019, https://www.wsj.com/articles/when-the-slave-tra ders-were-african-11568991595.

25. Henry Louis Gates Jr., "Ending the Slavery Blame-Game," *New York Times,* April 22, 2010, https://www.nytimes.com/2010/04/23/opinion/23gates.html?ref=opin ion&pagewanted=all.

26. On August 12, 2019, after the Robert Mueller–led effort to impeach President Trump had failed, *New York Times* executive editor Dean Baquet told staffers at a townhall called to discuss the problem that a front-page headline was not sufficiently anti-Trump that the next line of attack would be to focus on Trump's racism. Byron York, "*New York Times* Chief Outlines Coverage Shift: From Trump-Russia to Trump Racism," *Washington Examiner*, August 15, 2019, https://www.washingtonexaminer.com/opinion/columnists/new-york-times-chief- outlines-coverage-shift-from-trump-russia-to-trump-racism; Ashley Feinberg, "The New York Times Unites vs. Twitter," Slate, August 15, 2019, https:// slate.com/news-and-politics/2019/08/new-york-times-meeting-transcript.html.

27. Matthew Desmond, "Capitalism," in "The 1619 Project," *New York Times Magazine*, August 18, 2019, pdf available at the Pulitzer Center website, https:// pulitzercenter.org/sites/default/files/full_issue_of_the_1619_project.pdf, 30; Nikole Hannah-Jones, "The Idea of America," in "The 1619 Project," *New York Times Magazine*, August 18, 2019, pdf available at the Pulitzer Center website, https:// pulitzercenter.org/sites/default/files/full_issue_of_the_1619_project.pdf, 17; Khalil Gibran Muhammad, "Sugar," in "The 1619 Project," *New York Times Magazine*, August 18, 2019, pdf available at the Pulitzer Center website, https://pulitzercenter .org/sites/default/files/full_issue_of_the_1619_project.pdf, 70.

28. Desmond, "Capitalism."

29. Phillip W. Magness, "The Anti-Capitalist Ideology of Slavery," in *The 1619 Project: A Critique* (American Institute for Economic Research, 2020), 18.

30. Peter Coclanis, "Did Slavery Make America Rich?," National Association of Scholars, September 16, 2020, https://www.nas.org/blogs/event/slavery-or-freedom-the-conception-of-america, presented at the "Slavery or Freedom: The Conception of America" conference, sponsored by the Alexander Hamilton Institute, the Texas Public Policy Institute, and the National Association of Scholars, September 14–18, 2020.

31. Gavin Wright, "Slavery and Anglo-American Capitalism Revisited," *Economic History Review* 73:2 (2020): 353–83; Christian Schneider, "Cornell Scholar Cited in NYT's '1619' Series Charged with Fabricating Quotes, Evidence," The College Fix, August 23, 2019, https://www.thecollegefix.com/cornell-scholar-cited-in-nyts-1619-series-charged-with-fabricating-quotes-evidence/.

32. Wright, "Slavery and Anglo-American Capitalism."

33. Phillip W. Magness, "The Case for Retracting Matthew Desmond's 1619 Project Essay," *The 1619 Project: A Critique* (American Institute for Economic Research, 2020), 52, 61–62.

34. Coclanis, "Did Slavery Make America Rich?"

35. Wright, "Slavery and Anglo-American Capitalism."

36. Ibid. This fact undercuts Hannah-Jones's claims about the contribution of slaves in making the rail lines that formed American wealth.

37. Coclanis, "Did Slavery Make America Rich?"

38. Ibid.

39. Wright, "Slavery and Anglo-American Capitalism."

40. Ibid.

41. Charles C. Bolton, "Farmers without Land: The Plight of White Tenant Farmers and Sharecroppers," Mississippi History Now, March 2004, http://mshistorynow.mdah.state.ms.us/articles/228/farmers-without-land-the-plight-of-white-tenant-farmers-and-sharecroppers.

42. Magness, "The Anti-Capitalist Ideology of Slavery," 13, 17.

43. Ben Shapiro, "Shelby Steele: The Ben Shapiro Sunday Special Ep. 105," YouTube, November 1, 2020, https://www.youtube.com/watch?v=QR6lfDS5SMU.

44. Shelby Steele, *White Guilt: How Blacks and Whites Together Destroyed the Promise of the Civil Rights Era* (New York: HarperCollins, 2006), 7–8; Shapiro, "Shelby Steele."

45. Christopher Arps, "Censorship in America; Amazon Refuses Controversial Documentary on Their Platform," RedState, October 29, 2020, https://redstate.com/christopher-arps/2020/10/29/271154-n271154.

46. "Amazon Donates $10 Million to Organizations Supporting Justice and Equity," Amazon, June 3, 2020, https://www.aboutamazon.com/news/policy-news-views /amazon-donates-10-million-to-organizations-supporting-justice-and-equity.

47. Tristan Justice, "Amazon Strips Clarence Thomas Documentary from Streaming Service During Black History Month," The Federalist, February 26, 2021, https:// thefederalist.com/2021/02/26/amazon-strips-clarence-thomas-documentary-from- streaming-service-during-black-history-month/ .

48. Virginia Allen, "Smithsonian's Clarence Thomas Exhibit Guilty of 'Irresponsible Bias,' Black Conservatives Say," February 11, 2021, The Daily Signal, https://www .dailysignal.com/2021/02/11/smithsonians-clarence-thomas-exhibit-guilty-of-ir responsible-bias-black-conservatives-say/.

49. Shelby Steele, "White Guilt and the Western Past," *Wall Street Journal*, May 2, 2006, reprinted in "About the Book," in Steele, *White Guilt*, 11–13.

50. James Tallmadge Jr., *Speech of the Honorable James Tallmadge Jr. of Duchess County, New York, in the House of Representatives of the United States on Slavery* (New York: E. Contrad, 1819), https://archive.org/details/speechofhonorab l00tall/page/n3/mode/2up; Robert Paquette, email to the author, December 22, 2020.

51. Tallmadge, *Speech*.

52. Robert L. Woodson, "'The 1619 Project' Hurts Blacks," *Wall Street Journal*, August 28, 2019, https://www.wsj.com/articles/the-1619-project-hurts-blacks-11 567033108.

53. Eric Kaufmann, "The Media Is Creating a False Perception of Rising Racism. My New Study Proves It," *Newsweek*, April 13, 2021, https://www.msn.com/en-us /news/opinion/the-media-is-creating-a-false-perception-of-rising-racism-my-new -study-proves-it-opinion/ar-BB1fC4Zz?li=BBnbfcL.

54. Colleen Flaherty, "1 Police Call, Lasting Damage," Inside Higher Ed, April 15, 2021, https://www.insidehighered.com/news/2021/04/15/one-police-call-lasting -damage-smith.

55. Frederick Douglass, "An Inside View of Slavery: An Address Delivered in Boston, Massachusetts, on February 8, 1855," *in The Frederick Douglass Papers, Series One: Speeches, Debates, and Interviews, Volume 3: 1855–63*, ed. John W. Blassingame (New Haven, Connecticut: Yale University Press, 1985), 5–13.

56. Robert L. Paquette and Mark M. Smith, "Introduction: Slavery in the Americas," in *The Oxford Handbook of Slavery in the Americas*, ed. Robert L. Paquette and Mark M. Smith (New York: Oxford University Press, 2010), 3–17.

57. Bernard Lewis, *Race and Slavery in the Middle East: An Historical Enquiry* (New York: Oxford University Press, 1990), 78–79.

58. Isabel Van Brugen, "US House Reintroduces Bill to Ban All Xinjiang Goods Made with Forced Labor," *Epoch Times*, February 19, 2021, https://www.theepocht imes.com/us-house-reintroduces-bill-to-ban-all-xinjiang-goods-made-with-forced -labor_3702951.html.

59. Daniel Greenfield, "The 2021 Project," FrontPage Magazine, January 4, 2021, https://www.frontpagemag.com/fpm/2021/01/2020-project-daniel-greenfield/.

60. Dean Takahashi, "Apple CEO Tim Cook Pledges to Be 'a Force for Change' in Wake of Black Lives Matter Protests," VentureBeat, June 22, 2020, https://ventu rebeat.com/2020/06/22/apple-ceo-tim-cook-pledges-to-be-a-force-for-change-in -wake-of-unrest/.

61. Mary Grabar, "The First African-American Communist," Enquiry, October 29, 2017, http://www.ahienquiry.org/writing-collect/2017/10/29/the-first-african -american-communist.I

Index

1685 Code Noir, 81
1776 Commission, 7–8, 25–26, 37–38, 60
1776 Unites, 28, 37

A

Adams, John, 41, 44–46, 59, 101, 154, 166, 188, 220
Advanced Placement exams, 57, 59, 129
American Colonization Society, the, 139, 141–42, 179, 183–84, 206
American Civil War, the, 92, 106, 110, 126, 141, 151, 159, 179, 195–96, 202, 206, 214, 229, 231, 234–35, 245, 247, 251, 254
American Institute for Economic Research, the, 37, 61–62, 243
American Revolution, the, 36, 59, 60–61, 65–66, 67, 100, 104, 146–47, 149, 165–66, 182, 185, 220, 232
antebellum period, the, 49, 66, 86, 89–90, 99, 123, 136, 137, 142, 144, 214, 244, 246

B

Banneker, Benjamin, 164–75, 217, 255
Baptist, Edward, 67–68, 243–45
Barlow, Joel, 169–70
Bass, Karen, 236
Battle of Derna, 93
Bawer, Bruce, 92–93,
Bedini, Silvio, 166–71, 174
Bennett, Lerone, 51–52, 57, 116–18, 201–2, 250
Berlin, Ira, 120, 122, 131, 147
Biden, Joseph, 8, 37–38
Bill of Rights, the, 157
"Black Codes," 235
Black History Month, 24, 33, 232, 248
Black Lives Matter, 1, 4, 6, 23, 29, 231, 248
Black Panthers, 31, 236
Black Power, 52, 57, 117, 201, 248, 250
Bland, Richard, 151, 177
Blassingame, John W., 136–37
Bodin, Jean, 102
Booker, Cory, 135–36
Boston Massacre, the, 21, 154

Bouie, Jamelle, 235
Bowser, Muriel, 6
Boyer, Jean-Pierre, 186–91
branding, 85–86, 95, 117, 155
Brawley, Benjamin, 70–72,
    181–83
Brooks, George W., 127
Brooks, Rayshard, 4
Brown Fellowship Society, 213
Brown, John, 196, 208, 211–12,
    220
Brown, Michael, 4, 236, 248
Bryant, Phillip (Phil), 8, 25
Buchanan, Thomas, 139
Buckley, William F., 235

C
Calhoun, John C, 235
capitalism, 29, 31, 50, 67–68, 82,
    242–47, 250
Carter, Robert, 156–57
Caritat, Marie Jean Antoine
    Nicholas, 164
Chavers, William, 128
Chavis, Gibeon, 134
Chavis, Phillip, 134
Chavis, William, 134
Christophe, Henri, 188–89
Clay, Henry, 183
Coates, Ta-Nehisi, 28, 252
Coclanis, Peter, 243–46
Code Rural, 190
Coles, Edward, 176–79

colonial period, 36, 66–67, 70,
    84, 97–98, 119, 121, 130–32,
    139, 143
colonists, 11, 19, 36, 59, 61,
    65–67, 70–73, 95, 106, 109,
    118, 182
colonization, 21, 93, 139, 141–42,
    153, 161–63, 179, 181–86, 189,
    191, 196, 200, 202–7, 210, 248,
Columbus, Christopher, 101, 111
Common Core, 16, 31, 38
Communism, 50, 55, 255
Condorcet, 164, 168–70
Confederacy, the, 4, 6, 179, 200,
    203, 209, 228, 232, 242
Congressional Black Caucus, the,
    236
Constitution, the United States,
    56, 67, 74, 157–58, 195, 198,
    200, 215–16, 218–21, 225,
    253–54
Continental Congress, 41, 69,
    73–75, 99
Conventicle Act of 1664, 94
Cornell University, 67, 243
cotton, 19, 59, 128, 214, 242–47
Cuffe, Paul, 182–83, 206

D
Daniel, Joseph, 137–38
Davis, David Brion, 47–48, 73,
    80–81, 87, 119, 151, 153
Davis, Edwin Adams, 145
DiAngelo, Robin, 1, 24, 251

Declaration of Independence, the,
2, 14, 20–21, 39, 41–47, 50,
54–56, 59–61, 67–68, 76, 99,
104, 147, 165, 172–73, 176,
179, 195, 197–98, 218–19, 225
Demeunier, Jean Nicolas, 151
democracy, 18–23, 38, 45, 64, 66,
109, 153, 218, 235, 243
Derham, James, 165
Desmond, Matthew, 22, 31, 68,
242–44, 246–47
Dessalines, Jean-Jaques, 159–60,
188
Douglas, Stephen, 194, 196–98,
203
Douglass, Frederick, 90, 110, 195,
203, 206, 207, 210–26, 229–32,
247, 253–55
Du Bois, W. E. B., 55, 108, 111,
126–27, 234
Duc de La Rochefoucauld, 89,
175
Duke, Donald, 240
Durnford, Andrew, 141–42, 144,
175, 184

E
Eagle, James, 146, 156
Eaton, William, 93, 134
Ellicott, Andrew, 164–65,167
Ellicott, George, 164–67, 170
Ellicott, Joseph, 165, 167
Eltis, David, 101, 103

Emancipation Proclamation, 106,
108, 205, 219, 225, 227–29,
233
Engerman, Stanley L., 89
Enlightenment, the, 75, 88
equality, 12, 17–18, 23, 55, 58,
74, 92, 147, 165, 172, 182,
184, 197, 207, 218, 254

F
Fanning, Sara, 160, 188–90
Finley, Robert, 182–83
First Barbary War, 93
Floyd, George, 3–5, 235–36, 254
Fogelman, Aaron, 99
Fogel, Robert William, 89
Forten, James, 186, 206, 214
Fosset, Joe, 179
Foster, William, 237–38
founders (founding fathers), 5,
12–13, 20–21, 50, 55, 58–60,
66–67, 104, 155–57, 194, 197,
215, 217, 219–20, 225, 232,
253
Franklin, Benjamin, 44, 74–75,
99, 157, 165, 220
Franklin, John Hope, 55, 130,
136–38, 142, 149, 200–3,
205–8, 222
Freedmen's Memorial, 226, 228,
231–32, 250
"Free Negro Code," 135
French Revolution, the, 158, 185
Fuller, Thomas, 166

G

Gabriel's Rebellion, 159, 161, 188
Galenson, David, 97
Gardiner, George, 135
Gardiner, Ruth, 135
Gardiner, Susan Elizabeth, 135
Gates, Henry Louis, Jr., 225,
    241–42
Genovese, Eugene, 6, 90, 114
George III, King, 41, 43, 59,
    67–70, 73, 171
Gibson, Gideon, 133–34
Gordon-Reed, Annette, 52–54,
    56, 58, 249
Greenfield, Daniel, 254
Grégoire, Henri, 169

H

Haiti, 158–60, 186–91, 193,
    204–5, 207
Hall, Jacob, 8, 165
Hamilton, Alexander, 157, 159,
    220, 257
Handlin, Oscar, 48–49
Hannah-Jones, Nikole, 3, 7–9,
    16–18, 20–36, 60–61, 63,
    65–68, 73–74, 76, 79–80, 82,
    85, 87–89, 100, 105, 109–10,
    112, 116–17, 157, 194–202, 205,
    207, 214, 216, 218–19, 222,
    226, 228, 237, 239, 241–42,
    244, 247–50

Harris, Kamala, 38, 235
Harris, Leslie, 36, 66–67, 70, 184
Heaton, James, 163
Heinegg, Paul, 130–33, 135, 143
Hellie, Richard, 81
Hemings, James, 176
Hemings, John, 179
Hemings, Robert (Bob), 76, 176
Hemings, Sally, 6, 51–58
Holland, Edwin, 181
Holmes, John, 162–63
Holton, Lott, 141, 184
human sacrifice, 82–85, 88, 103
Hurston, Zora Neale, 237, 239

I

impressment, 94
indentured servitude, 36, 70,
    94–100, 119–20, 175, 178, 204
independence, 13, 21, 36, 38, 44,
    60–61, 65–67, 73, 93, 109,
    158–60, 189–90, 194

J

Jackson, Holly, 185, 187, 210
Jefferson, Peter, 75
Jefferson, Thomas, 4–7, 13–14, 19,
    39, 41–48, 50–61, 66–70, 73–76,
    79, 85, 88–89, 93, 95, 101, 103,
    127, 147, 149–65, 167–77, 179,

181–83, 185–86, 188, 193–94,
204, 206, 220–21, 230
Jim Crow, 18, 21, 235, 249
Johnson, James Weldon, 106, 233
Johnson, Michael P., 144
Johnson, William, 144
Jones, Edward P., 129, 151
Jordan, Winthrop, 152, 160, 165

K
Kaminski, John P., 74
Kaufman, Eric, 252
Keith, George, 182
Kendi, Ibram X., 1, 33, 53, 249,
251
Kesler, Charles, 3
Ketcham, Ralph, 178
King, Martin Luther, Jr., 8,
23–24, 60
King, Stewart R., 159
Kinloch, Francis, 152
Koger, Larry, 135, 142–43, 145–46,
213
Kolchin, Peter, 92

L
Lafayette, Marquis de, 185–86
Lee, Sheila, 236
L'Enfant, Pierre Charles, 164
Levy, Andrew, 157
Lewis, Cudjo, 237–39

Liberia, 111, 139, 142, 178,
183–84, 204, 206
Lightner, David L., 144–45
Lincoln, Abraham, 4, 6, 12,
20–21, 45, 74–75, 179,
193–207, 219–32
Louisiana Purchase, the, 45,
55–56, 136
Loury, Glenn, 25, 251
Louverture, Toussaint, 259–260,
188

M
Madison, James, 19, 160, 176,
178–79, 185, 220
Magness, Phillip, 61, 63, 243–45,
247
Maier, Pauline, 42, 68
Malone, Dumas, 43–45, 47, 51,
57, 68, 74, 76, 150, 175, 179
manumission, 76, 99, 126, 136,
138, 144, 176–78, 206, 213
Manumission Society, the,
184–85
Marshall, Thurgood, 249
Martin, Trayvon, 236
Marxist theory, 12, 48, 202, 214,
250, 255
Marx, Karl, 242, 245
Maslin, Janet, 129
Mason, George, 6, 157, 221
Matthews, Richard K., 68
McCabe, Denny, 8

McDonogh, John, 141–42, 184
McHenry, James, 166
Meaher, Timothy, 237–39
Middle Ages, the, 102, 119
Middle Passage, the, 22, 96–97
millennials, 5, 60, 251
Mills, Samuel J., 182–83
Mitchell, James, 196, 198
Monroe, James, 160–61, 183, 185, 220
Monticello, 6, 21, 41, 46, 53–54, 56–58, 61, 79–80, 88–89, 100, 175–76, 185, 193, 255
Morgan, Edmund S., 73
Mumford, Nana Efua, 236
Muslims, 82, 86, 92, 101–3, 111, 119, 254

N
NAACP, the, 108, 234, 236
Nadler, Jerry, 235–36
National Museum of African American History and Culture, 29, 171–72, 248
New History of Capitalism movement (NHC), 243–45, 247
Newton, Isaac, 166, 169
New York Times, the, 2–3, 11–12, 16, 23, 26–27, 29, 31, 33–34, 38, 54, 62–63, 65, 105, 117, 129, 171, 234–35, 241–42, 244–45

New World, the, 50, 73, 92, 96, 114, 135, 169, 204

O
Olmstead, Alan, 244–45
Olmsted, Frederick Law, 90, 128
Onuf, Peter, 53, 163, 181
"original sin" of slavery, 2–3, 12, 17, 64, 250–51
O'Rourke, Shane, 91

P
Paine, Thomas, 103
Painter, Nell Irvin, 35, 100, 123
Paquette, Robert, 43, 47, 74, 85, 102–3, 152, 157, 189, 257
Patterson, Orlando, 81
Peabody, Sue, 100–101
Pelosi, Nancy, 235–36
Pétion, Alexandre, 188
Phiquepal d'Arusmont, William S., 187
Prude, Daniel, 4
Pulitzer Center, the, 15, 28–29, 32–33, 172
Pulitzer Prize, the, 23, 25, 27, 29, 129

Q
Quakers, 71, 98, 74, 164, 166, 172, 182, 208

R

racism, 1–3, 12, 17, 21, 23–25,
 30, 32–34, 37, 49–50, 53, 60,
 122–23, 153–54, 184, 188, 195,
 231, 250–53, 255
Rafiq, Yunus Mohammed,
 240–41
Ragan, Alexander M., 144–45
Randolph, John, 158, 183
Raper, William, 135, 145
Reconstruction, 21, 137, 143, 147
redemptioners, 96
Rhinelander case, 131
Rhode, Paul, 244–45
Rittenhouse, David, 166
Roark, James L., 144
Rome, 42, 81, 86, 101–2
Rush, Benjamin, 165–66, 220
Russell, John H., 120–21, 133

S

Saint-Domingue revolution, 159,
 162, 181–82, 188
Sampson, James D., 142
Schuyler, George S., 131, 144,
 214, 255
Schweninger, Loren, 139–41, 144
Second Barbary War, 93
serfdom, 90–92
servitude, 80, 91, 93–95, 97,
 99–100, 104, 108, 119, 121,
 132, 157, 167, 253

Sheridan, Louis, 138–39, 184
Silverstein, Jake, 11, 14, 20,
 63–64
"slavocracy," 2, 5, 35, 39, 42, 66,
 123, 132, 250
"Slave Coast," the, 83
slave trade, the, 20, 35–36, 59, 65,
 67–68, 70–74, 79–81, 84,
 92–93, 101–3, 106–7, 111–17,
 119, 141, 157–58, 161, 171,
 206–7, 210, 218, 236, 238–41,
 246
Smith, Abbot, 95–99
Smith, Adam, 91, 149, 155
Smith, John, 70, 109
Smithsonian, the, 15, 29, 107,
 167, 171–72, 226, 248
social justice, 24, 31–32, 215,
 254–55
Southern Poverty Law Center
 (SPLC), the, 29–30
Sowell, Thomas, 91, 93–94,
 100–101, 110–11
Stanly, John Carruthers, 127,
 139–41, 144, 184
Stanton, Edwin, 222–23
Stanton, Lucia, 89
State vs. Edmund, 137
Steele, Shelby, 248–49, 251
Stevenson, Bryan, 235
Stras, Frederick, 176
Supreme Court, the, 38, 137, 183,
 195, 198, 226, 248

Swain, Carol, 25, 251

T

Tallmadge, James, 251
Taney, Roger, 195, 197, 220
Tappan, Arthur, 139
Taylor, Breonna, 4
Tea Party movement, 235
textbooks, 16, 55–58, 129, 225, 258
Thirteenth Amendment, the, 228, 234
Thomas, Clarence, 248, 255
Thomas Jefferson Foundation, the, 54, 89
Thompson, Draper, 126
Thornton, John, 109, 112, 114–15
Trump, Donald, 7–8, 23–25, 29, 35–37, 235–36
Turner, Nat, 86, 90, 135, 139, 205, 209–10
Tyler, John, 6, 46

U

Union, the, 4, 152, 162–63, 194, 196–97, 199–200, 205, 227–28, 230–31
University of Virginia, 44, 46, 50, 54–55, 185

V

Vesey, Denmark, 140, 181, 189, 213
Virginia Company, 36, 95–96, 118–19
Virginia Constitution, 41, 43, 69, 95, 151, 153
Virginia House of Burgesses, 35, 75, 99, 131, 151

W

Waldstreicher, David, 68
Walker, Alice, 237
Walker, David, 139
Wallace, Caprinxia, 237, 239
Wallace, Cassandra, 237, 239
Walsh, Lorena, 118, 146
Washington, Booker T., 126
Washington, George, 6, 19, 44–45, 55, 106, 166, 183, 221
whipping, 1, 85–86, 98, 129, 146, 207, 215, 218, 253
White House, the, 6, 8, 19, 26, 30, 38, 58, 196–98, 203, 205, 222
Whitten, David O., 141–42, 144
Wilentz, Sean, 34, 66, 149–50
Wilson, Calvin Dill, 125–29, 140
Woodson Center, the, 37, 251
Woodson, Carter G., 107, 111, 129–30, 142, 144–46, 182–83, 249

Woodson, Robert, 37, 251–52
World War II, 21, 47, 48, 89
Wright, Frances (Fanny), 185–87,
    193
Wright, Gavin, 243–47

Z
Zinn, Howard, 8, 37–38, 50

Also by Mary Grabar

Debunking Howard Zinn: Exposing the Fake History That Turned a Generation against America